Survey Analysis for Indigenous Policy in Australia

Policy in Australia

Social Science Perspectives

Survey Analysis for Indigenous Policy in Australia

Social Science Perspectives

Boyd Hunter and Nicholas Biddle (Editors)

Australian
National
University

E PRESS

Centre for Aboriginal Economic Policy Research
College of Arts and Social Sciences
The Australian National University, Canberra

Research Monograph No. 32
2012

ANU
E PRESS

Published by ANU E Press
The Australian National University
Canberra ACT 0200, Australia
Email: anuepress@anu.edu.au
This title is also available online at http://epress.anu.edu.au

National Library of Australia Cataloguing-in-Publication entry

Title: Survey analysis for indigenous policy in Australia : social science perspectives
              / edited by Boyd Hunter and Nicholas Biddle.

ISBN: 9781922144188 (pbk.) 9781922144195 (ebook)

Series: Research monograph (Australian National University. Centre for Aboriginal
              Economic Policy Research) ; no. 32.

Notes: Includes bibliographical references.

Subjects: Aboriginal Australians--Social conditions.
              Torres Strait Islanders--Social conditions.
              Aboriginal Australians--Economic conditions.
              Torres Strait Islanders--Economic conditions.
              Quality of life--Australia.
              Well-being--Australia.
              Social surveys--Australia--Statistics.
              Australia--Government policy.
              Australia--Social policy.

Other Authors/Contributors:
              Hunter, Boyd.
              Biddle, Nicholas.

Dewey Number: 305.89915

Cover design and layout by ANU E Press

Contents

Abbreviations and acronyms

AIATSIS	Australian Institute of Aboriginal and Torres Strait Islander Studies
ABS	Australian Bureau of Statistics
AGPS	Australian Government Publishing Service
AHURI	Australian Housing and Urban Research Institute
AIFS	Australian Institute of Family Studies
AIHW	Australian Institute of Health and Welfare
ANU	The Australian National University
ARIA	Accessibility/Remoteness Index of Australia
ASGC	Australian Standard Geographic Classification
ATSIC	Aboriginal and Torres Strait Islander Commission
CAEPR	Centre for Aboriginal Economic Policy Research
CD	Collection District
CDEP	Community Development Employment Program
CDHSH	Commonwealth Department of Human Services and Health
CNOS	Canadian National Occupancy Standard
COAG	Council of Australian Governments
CURF	confidentialised unit record file (ABS)
DEEWR	Department of Education, Employment and Workplace Relations
FaHCSIA	Department of Families, Housing, Community Services and Indigenous Affairs (Australian Government)
GSS	General Social Survey
HILDA	Household Income and Labour Dynamics in Australia (survey)
IES	Indigenous Employment Strategy
IRR	incidence rate ratio
LSAC	Longitudinal Study of Australian Children
LSAY	Longitudinal Survey of Australian Youth
LSIC	Longitudinal Survey of Indigenous Children
MCATSIA	Ministerial Council for Aboriginal and Torres Strait Islander Affairs
NHRMC	National Health and Medical Research Council
NDSHS	National Drug Strategy Household Survey
NAIDOC	National Aborigines and Islanders Day Observance Committee
NATSIHS	National Aboriginal and Torres Strait Islander Health Survey
NATSIS	National Aboriginal and Torres Strait Islander Survey (1994)

NATSISS	National Aboriginal and Torres Strait Islander Social Survey
NAHA	National Affordable Housing Agreement
NCGS	National Closing the Gap Survey
NIRA	National Indigenous Reform Agreement
NILF	not in the labour force
OECD	Organisation for Economic Co-operation and Development
OLS	ordinary least squares
RADL	Remote Access Data Laboratory
SCRGSP	Steering Committee for the Review of Government Service Provision
SEIFA	Socio-Economic Indexes for Areas
TFR	total fertility rate
VET	Vocational Education and Training (sector)
WHO	World Health Organization

List of tables

List of figures

Acknowledgements

This monograph presents the refereed, and peer-reviewed, edited proceedings of a conference organised by Centre for Aboriginal Economic Policy Research (CAEPR) and the Australian Bureau of Statistics (ABS): 'Social Science Perspectives on the 2008 National Aboriginal and Torres Strait Islander Social Survey'. The conference was held in Haydon Allen Tank at The Australian National University (ANU) in Canberra over two days on Monday 11 and Tuesday 12 April 2011. This conference is generously supported by ANU, ABS, Department of Education, Employment and Workplace Relations, Department of Families, Housing, Community Services and Indigenous Affairs and The Economic Society of Australia. CAEPR is grateful for this support, which has allowed participation by some leading international researchers as well leading national analysts, commentators and researchers in Indigenous policy. While we are extremely grateful to all contributors who were part of a stimulating, enjoyable, and informed debate, I would particularly like to thank Mick Dodson AM who presented a provocative paper on *Indigenous perspectives on national statistical collections* on behalf of his countryman Peter Yu, CEO of Nyamba Buru Yawaru Ltd. Of course we are obliged to Matthew Snipp from Stanford and Harry Patrinos from the World Bank who provided vital international context to understanding of indigenous statistics and disadvantage. Special thanks are also due to the chairs of the respective sessions at the conference who provided rigour, discipline and breadth to the discussion.

The ABS were very supportive of the event as they were keen to facilitate responsible and informed use of their data. The main form of that support was the guidance for authors on the use of their Remote Access Data Laboratory and extra data provided to facilitate our evaluation of the 2008 National Aboriginal and Torres Strait Islander Social Survey (NATSISS).

The final acknowledgement must go to the dedicated and professional CAEPR team who were responsible for the organisation of the conference over several months, especially Hilary Bek, Gillian Cosgrove, John Hughes, Susie Russell and Denise Steele. Without their hard work, the conference would never have been completed successfully. Two anonymous referees and many readers also gave invaluable comments on early drafts of the chapters for this monograph. A final thanks must go to Hilary Bek, and the ANU E Press team, for patient assistance with the copy-editing of a draft of the manuscript for this book.

Contributors

Shafiq Ahmad is currently an Assistant Professor in the School of Business at Al Yamamah University in Saudi Arabia. At the time of writing the paper presented at the conference, he worked in the Performance and Evaluation Branch, Indigenous Coordination Group, in the Australian Government Department of Families, Housing, Community Services and Indigenous Affairs (FaHCSIA).

Jon Altman is a research professor at the Centre for Aboriginal Economic Policy Research (CAEPR), The Australian National University (ANU), where he was foundation Director from 1990 to 2010. His disciplinary background is in economics and anthropology, although in recent years he has veered to political ecology and critical anthropology of development; research interests currently focus on economic hybridity, property rights and appropriate development in remote regions and a long standing interest in the national Indigenous survey instrument extending back over 20 years.

Martin Bell is Professor of Geography and Director of the Queensland Centre for Population Research at University of Queensland. His scholarly interests lie mainly in the fields of population mobility and internal migration, and in developing models to make demographic projections at the regional and local level. Recent contributions include the development and application of new measures to make cross-national comparisons of mobility.

Nicholas Biddle is a Fellow at CAEPR, ANU. He has a Bachelor of Economics (Hons) from University of Sydney and a Master of Education from Monash University. He has a PhD in Public Policy from ANU, where he wrote his thesis on the benefits of and participation in education of Indigenous Australians. Nicholas is currently working on the CAEPR Indigenous population project, funded by the Commonwealth and State/Territory Governments. He is also working on a Research Fellowship for the National Centre for Vocational Education Research and previously worked in the Methodology Division of the Australian Bureau of Statistics (ABS).

Christina Birdsall-Jones' research focus is on issues connected with Indigenous housing, and since joining the John Curtin Institute of Public Policy in 2007 she has conducted several major research projects funded by the Australian Housing and Urban Research Institute. These projects concern Indigenous housing histories, homelessness, home ownership, housing impacts of the mining boom on Indigenous communities and Indigenous mobility. She has published in the fields of anthropology, Indigenous housing, native title and Indigenous tourism. Christina has a BA anthropology from University of Florida Gainesborough, and obtained her MA and PhD at the Department of Anthropology, University of Western Australia. She is currently working on FaHCSIA funded research into Aborginal homelessness and an Indigenous Multi-Year Project on Aboriginal Life Worlds and the Welfare Concept of Conditionality.

Geoff Buchanan is a PhD candidate in anthropology at CAEPR, ANU. He began work as a researcher at CAEPR in 2004 having an undergraduate background in environmental policy and economics as well as Indigenous Australian studies. Geoff has worked on a number of CAEPR research projects relating to the environmental, social and economic significance of the Indigenous estate, caring for country, and customary harvest. His PhD explores the work of Aboriginal rangers in remote Australia.

Timothy Cameron is a Research Officer at CAEPR, ANU. He has a First Class Honours degree in economics and has worked on a number of projects related to the economics of Indigenous education.

Tanya Chikritzhs is Professor and head of the Alcohol Policy Research team at the National Drug Research Institute, Curtin University and NHMRC Fellow. She has academic qualifications in epidemiology, biostatistics and psychology, and some 15 years of experience in alcohol research. Tanya is an expert in the field of alcohol epidemiology and alcohol policy and has received numerous national awards including the 2012 Commonwealth Health Ministers Award for Excellence in Health and Medical Research.

Andrew Clarke is a PhD candidate in Sociology at the School of Social Science at University of Queensland. Prior to his candidature, Andrew worked as a research assistant at the Institute for Social Science Research, where, amongst other things, he worked on projects examining the quantitative determinates of crowding in indigenous households and the spatial variations in indigenous homelessness.

Vanessa Corunna is an Aboriginal researcher based at Curtin University of Technology. She holds a BA from University of Western Australia with a double major in anthropology and archaeology. She also holds a Diploma of Applied Science in Indigenous Community Management from Curtin University of Technology. Prior to gaining work as a researcher in both cultural heritage and housing projects, Vanessa worked in managerial positions in various Aboriginal agencies and services in Western Australia including in an Aboriginal Community School and a Community Centre.

Alfred Michael Dockery is Associate Professor in Economics at Curtin University and Director of the Centre for Labour Market Research. Mike's principal expertise is in the analysis of applied labour market and social issues. His current research focuses upon the effects of labour market experiences on happiness; Indigenous socioeconomic outcomes; the school-to-work transition; and he leads the Population Mobility and Labour Markets project for the CRC for Remote Economic Participation.

Ann Evans is a Fellow in the Australian Demographic and Social Research Institute at ANU. Ann is a family demographer with an interest in comparative research of family dynamics and change. This comparative work explores the impact of social, cultural and welfare settings on family formation behaviours. She is currently conducting research on cohabitation, relationship formation and dissolution, fertility and contraception, young motherhood and transition to adulthood.

Carroll Go-Sam is a researcher and centre manager of the Aboriginal Environments Research Centre in the School of Architecture, at University of Queensland. She is a descendant of the Dyirrbal, Gumbilbarra people of the upper Tully and upper Herbert Rivers in far north Queensland. On completing her Bachelor of Architecture degree in 1997 at University of Queensland, Carroll was one of the few female Indigenous graduates in architecture in Queensland. Her current research interests include Indigenous housing research particularly, modelling crowding and housing procurement in Aboriginal Australia. Other architectural topics in addition to housing include Indigenous Identity constructs in architecture and its role in place-making and nation building

Matthew Gray is Professor of Indigenous Public Policy at CAEPR, Research Director of the College of Arts and Social Sciences and a Public Policy Fellow of ANU. He was previously Deputy Director of the Australian Institute of Family Studies (AIFS) and Executive Project Manager of the Longitudinal Study of Australian Children. Matthew has undertaken research on a wide range of economic and social policy issues.

Kelly Greenop is a lecturer and researcher in the School of Architecture, University of Queensland. Kelly is nearing completion of her PhD at the Aboriginal Environments Research Centre within the School of Architecture at University of Queensland. Her research examines the relationship between Indigenous people and place in urban Brisbane through a case study of Inala, an Indigenous 'centre' in Brisbane. She has undertaken fieldwork with Indigenous people in urban areas of south east Queensland since 2005, and more recently worked on projects examining crowding and homelessness in remote Indigenous communities

William Harvey-Jones graduated from University of Queensland with a Master of Architecture in 2011, and wrote his dissertation on the relationship between mythic landscapes and identities in Australian cultures. He was a Summer Scholar in the Aboriginal Environments Research Centre 2012–11 during which he contributed to the analysis of crowding in this volume.

Boyd Hunter is Senior Fellow at CAEPR, ANU, where he specialises in labour market analysis, social economics and poverty research. He has long term involvement on the Steering Committee for the Longitudinal Study of Indigenous Children (FaHCSIA), the Scientific Reference Group for the National Indigenous (Closing the Gaps) Clearinghouse (Australian Institute of Health and Welfare/ AIFS), and has been the Managing Editor of the *Australian Journal of Labour Economics* since 2008.

Kim Johnstone is Senior Demographer at the New South Wales Department of Planning and Infrastructure. At the time of writing her paper she was completing her PhD at the Australian Demographic and Social Research Institute, ANU. Her research focused on contemporary Indigenous fertility in the Northern Territory. Kim has over 17 years' experience working in Australia and New Zealand, using knowledge of population dynamics to inform evidence-based policy development and implementation

Wenbin Liang is a Research Fellow and Statistician at the National Drug Research Institute, Curtin University, in Western Australia. Wenbin has research expertise in the field of medicine, healthcare, epidemiology and biostatistics.

Paul Memmott is an anthropologist and architect and is Director of the Aboriginal Environments Research Centre at University of Queensland. Paul was the principal of a research consultancy practice in Aboriginal projects during 1980 to 2008, which provided specialised services to Aboriginal organisations and government departments throughout Australia. He is now a full-time professor within the Institute for Social Science Research and the School of Architecture at University of Queensland. Paul's current research addresses social problems of housing design, crowding, homelessness and family violence in both metropolitan and remote parts of Indigenous Australia.

Carrington Shepherd is a senior analyst at the Telethon Institute for Child Health Research in Perth and is undertaking a PhD financially supported by a Sidney Myer Health Scholarship. He is focusing on the wellbeing of Indigenous Australians, and the use of population-level datasets to examine the social determinants of child and youth health. His research interests include Indigenous identification in linked administrative datasets, and the use of these data to investigate intergenerational determinants of health. Carrington was previously the manager of the National Children and Youth Statistics Unit at ABS.

Qasim Shah is a statistician working in the Performance and Evaluation Branch, Indigenous Coordination Group of FaHCSIA. He has previously worked at ABS and AIHW.

Lucy Snowball is a Senior Research Officer at the New South Wales Bureau of Crime Statistics and Research. Her recent work includes research into racial bias in sentencing, bail decisions and juvenile diversion; social and economic factors underpinning Indigenous contact with the justice system; and factors determining the granting of police bail for juveniles. Lucy previously worked in the Methodology Division of ABS. Her current research interests include public confidence in the criminal justice system and screening tools for interventions to reduce juvenile reoffending.

John Taylor is Professor and Director of CAEPR, ANU. For the past 25 years he has conducted research on demographic, social and economic change among Indigenous Australians and has published widely on these issues in Australian and international books and journals. He is a member of the ABS Advisory Group on Aboriginal and Torres Strait Islander Statistics, the Expert Group on Aboriginal and Torres Strait Islander Statistics and a Board member of the Closing the Gap Clearinghouse. He has been prominent in demonstrating the application of demographic analysis to Indigenous policy.

Prem Thapa directs the Indigenous Data Analyses and Research section in the Performance and Evaluation Branch, Indigenous Coordination Group of FaHCSIA. Prem previously worked in the Economic Research Unit in the Australian Government Department of Education, Employment and Workplace Relations and also in the Economics Program of the Research School of Social Sciences at ANU. His research has focused mainly on modelling welfare dependence and transitions using Australian administrative data and on labour market dynamics, analysing employment transitions and wage growth using the Living in Australia (HILDA) panel survey.

Don Weatherburn is Director of the New South Wales Bureau of Crime Statistics and Research in Sydney. He was awarded a Public Service Medal in 1998, appointed an Adjunct Professor in the School of Social Science and Policy at University of New South Wales in 2005, and made a fellow of the Academy of Social Sciences in Australia in 2006. His current research interests include the effectiveness of measures to reduce Indigenous imprisonment, the specific deterrent effect of community-based penalties and the effect of personal and financial stress on violence against women.

Mark Western is Director of the Institute for Social Science Research at University of Queensland. He is a sociologist working on topics including: economic and social mobility and the reproduction of privilege and disadvantage; social networks and labour market outcomes; the life pathways of young people; household and individual preparedness for disasters. Mark is a Fellow of the Academy of Social Sciences in Australia, a Chief Investigator on the ARC Centre of Excellence in Policing and Security, and has led and participated in a number of commissioned studies for the Australian Government in areas such as health and education. In 2012 he is Chair of the Research Evaluation Committee for the Education and Human Society Disciplinary Cluster for the Excellence in Research for Australia (ERA) initiative.

Stephen R. Zubrick is Winthrop Professor of Child Health at University of Western Australia and heads the Division of Population Science at the Telethon Institute for Child Heath Research. He has led studies of children's health, education and wellbeing including the Western Australia Child Health Survey and the Longitudinal Study of Australian Children. He received the Children and Young People Lifetime Achievement Award at the Western Australia Citizen of the Year Awards in June 2011.

1. Towards a broader understanding of Indigenous disadvantage

Boyd Hunter and Nicholas Biddle

Indigenous policy is a diverse and complex domain motivated by a range of social, cultural, political and economic issues. One central component of current Indigenous policy is the Australian Government's stated aim to close the gap between Indigenous and non-Indigenous outcomes. This focus on Indigenous disadvantage is not new and has a considerable pre-history. Under the Hawke government in the 1980s there was considerable concentration on 'statistical equality'. The Howard government placed more emphasis on 'practical reconciliation', which focuses on employment, which he juxtaposed with 'symbolic reconciliation' that was claimed to have been excessively emphasised in the recent past. The 'closing the gaps' agenda is the latest manifestation of the desire to understand Indigenous disadvantage in terms of clear, well defined and measurable outcomes that can inform and, in some sense, is amenable to policy actions.

The language of closing the gap was first used to describe Maori disadvantage in New Zealand in 1999, but it is not entirely clear that gaps have closed substantially in that country (Comer 2008). One issue is that there was a tendency to measure what could be measured rather than what should be measured. That is, rather than understanding and acting where possible, on the processes that lead to the outcomes, the focus has been on small changes in relative outcomes of Maori and other New Zealanders.

The term has a much shorter history in the Australian context. In 2005, Tom Calma called for the governments of Australia to commit to achieving equality for Indigenous people in the areas of health and life expectancy within a generation or 25 years (Aboriginal and Torres Strait Islander Social Justice Commissioner 2005). This call was manifested in the National Indigenous Health Equality Campaign in 2006 with the 'Close the gap' campaign being formally launched in April 2007. Within a year, Council of Australian Governments (COAG) committed to closing the gap in life expectancy between Indigenous and non-Indigenous Australians. However, the agenda has expanded considerably since this initial focus on life expectancy and now includes these six 'Closing the Gap' targets (Steering Committee for the Review of Government Service Provision 2010):

1. Close the life expectancy gap within a generation

2. Halve the gap in mortality rates for Indigenous children under five within a decade

3. Ensure access to early childhood education for all Indigenous four years olds in remote communities within five years

4. Halve the gap in reading, writing and numeracy achievements for children within a decade

5. Halve the gap for Indigenous students in Year 12 attainment or equivalent attainment rates by 2020, and

6. Halve the gap in employment outcomes between Indigenous and non-Indigenous Australians within a decade.

As the name suggests, one of the objectives of the Centre for Aboriginal Economic Policy Research (CAEPR) is to analyse and inform Indigenous policy in Australia and hence the COAG framework is central to its research. CAEPR research informs the debate about the prospects for closing the gaps as well as analysing what policy setting are best able to address the needs of Indigenous Australians (Altman, Biddle and Hunter 2008). On 11–12 April 2011 CAEPR, in conjunction with the Australian Bureau of Statistics (ABS), organised a conference at The Australian National University (ANU) called 'Social Science Perspectives on the 2008 National and Aboriginal Torres Strait Islander Social Survey', or the National and Aboriginal Torres Strait Islander Social Survey (NATSISS) Conference, for short.[1]

We chose the 2008 NATSISS as the basis for the conference as it is the only large quantitative survey in Australia (and indeed the world) that has information on a range of topics designed by and for the Indigenous population for a large nationally representative sample across all ages. In total, there were around 7 800 respondents aged 15 years and over alongside 5 484 respondents aged 0–14 years.

Data for the NATSISS was collected using face-to-face interviews, with enumeration taking place between August 2008 and April 2009. Topics in the survey include language and culture; social networks and support; health; education; labour force status; housing; and financial stress.

There are a number of limitations of the NATSISS which were discussed at the conference. However, as editors and conference organisers, our main aim was to initiate a conversation between stakeholders and academics about data and the research required to enhance the social science evidence base around Indigenous wellbeing and socioeconomic disadvantage. This monograph collates many of the papers presented to that conference.

---

1 The conference was co-sponsored by ANU, Department of Education, Employment and Workplace Relations (DEEWR), Department of Families, Housing, Community Services and Indigenous Affairs (FaHCSIA) and The Economic Society of Australia.

We asked potential contributors to aim to achieve three goals:

- generate new scientific findings (i.e. new understandings)
- demonstrate how the data source utilised advances in social science and informs Indigenous policy making, and
- where possible, offer specific suggestions for how best to implement policy changes based on the findings (i.e. to identify international 'best practice').

Meeting these goals was an essential part of the conference because one of the primary audiences was policy makers with responsibility for the carriage of Indigenous policy. There is a need for a robust debate to understand how meaningful improvement in Indigenous outcomes might be achieved. It is also important to document socioeconomic processes facing non-Indigenous Australians (as several papers do), as well as documenting Indigenous disadvantage, as it is difficult to conceptualise what keeps a gap open if both sides of the gap are not understood.

The conference, which included presentations by some of Australia's leading researchers into Indigenous disadvantage, covered a wide range of topics including: child development, crime and justice, culture, the customary economy, demography, education, employment, fertility, health, housing, income and financial stress, mobility, poverty, social exclusion, substance abuse and, last but not least, wellbeing. The structure of the monograph closely follows the order of proceedings at the conference with some of the more complex multi-disciplinary topics being kept to the end of the conference after outlining key demographic and socioeconomic contexts.

While our preference was for shorter reflective papers that combine a rigorous treatment of the data with a strong narrative, we tolerated considerable diversity in the contributions as not all policy domains can be reasonably described to a concise and simplified terms.

Before providing an integrated discussion of the contents of the monograph, it is necessary to understand some of the history of Indigenous survey evidence. Apart from census data that focuses on broad population issues, the history of evidence with a national scope is relatively short. Some survey data were collected from the 1960s and beyond, but this tended to have a highly specific regional focus. For example, Charles Rowley (1970, 1982) initially collected information on 183 Aboriginal households from New South Wales in 1965 (later a sample from regional South Australia was added). In the 1980s, Russell Ross (1988) collected labour force data on Aboriginals in non-metropolitan New South Wales. The urgent need for a national survey of Indigenous Australians culminated in the Royal Commission into Aboriginal Deaths in Custody recommending a large scale nationally representative survey that could credibly document the complex nature of Indigenous disadvantage identified in the testimony given to the Commission (Commonwealth of Australia 1991). This recommendation was realised in the form of the 1994 National Aboriginal and Torres Strait Islander Survey (NATSIS) conducted by the ABS.

This book is the fourth in a series of monographs that reflects on the national surveys of Indigenous Australians. The first contribution resulted from a Academy of Social Sciences/CAEPR workshop that was held in the design phase of the original NATSIS (Altman 1992). All the contributors to that book identified the key areas of Indigenous disadvantage that needed to be measured and analysed. Even though the urgent data shortfalls were identified, support for a national Indigenous survey was not necessarily unanimous as some thought that alternative approaches may be more cost effective – such as augmenting Indigenous sample in special surveys and creatively using administrative data. Notwithstanding such reservations, the proposal for NATSIS was developed and debated through the pages of that monograph (Sims 1992).

Asking clear and well-defined questions is crucial to any empirical analysis as interpretation depends on the theoretical framework/question that is being addressed. It is one of the great strengths, therefore, of Altman and his fellow contributors that they attempted to focus on policy-relevant questions. Methodological issues tended to dominate in the end though, as the 1994 NATSIS was unique given nothing of that scope had been attempted before (Altman 1992).

After the NATSIS was collected another research monograph was published to explore the findings and future prospects of that survey (Altman and Taylor 1996). Inevitably, the contributors to that volume focused largely on the inadequacies of the 1994 NATSIS data and the methodological issues arising when measuring a small, dispersed population with distinct cultural perspective and unique historical context. The introductory and concluding chapters asked some important questions, mostly revolving around political economy of Indigenous statistics and the ability of the data to improve policy-making. The contributions to that monograph was disseminated to ABS staff and their clients and it is likely to have informed the design of the follow up survey to the NATSIS, the 2002 National Aboriginal and Torres Strait Islander Social Survey (NATSISS).

The immediate successor to the 1996 monograph was Hunter (2006), which self-consciously attempted to get contributors to document the reliability of NATSISS estimates. In particular, an attempt was made to build the capacity of researchers to estimate standard errors so that readers could gain an appreciation of the information contained in the data. The initial release of the 1994 NATSIS only provided approximate estimators of reliability and hence it was difficult to identify which results constituted evidence unless the researcher was conversant with sampling theory. Unfortunately, it was relatively rare in the Indigenous policy field to have the necessary statistical skills so some rudimentary capacity-building exercise was warranted (Biddle and Hunter 2006). Luckily, the recent re-release of reweighted 1994 NATSIS data accessed under the Remote Access Data Laboratory (RADL), allows researchers to relatively easily estimate standard errors accurately using replicate weight methodology (i.e. also enabled in the later releases of the NATSISS under the RADL). While the contributors to Hunter (2006) motivated their research in terms of a similar set of questions to those addressed in Altman (1992) and Altman and Taylor (1996), the main issues identified involved data quality and the intrinsic methodological issues involved when using and interpreting Indigenous data.

Clearly the earlier contributions did ask important questions that could be addressed with national Indigenous data, however the focus almost inevitably strayed towards the data quality and reliability issues. In this present monograph, the authors have been encouraged to ask and, if possible, answer questions that are based on their research experience and knowledge of issues that motivate policy-makers and Indigenous communities. Obviously it is not possible for authors to completely divorce themselves from intractable methodological issues and attendant data quality concerns, but the contributors to this volume have in general attempted to 'structure' their analysis so that it provides evidence for particular propositions. Please note that none of the analysis can really make claims about causality as cross-sectional data such as the 2008 NATSISS have well-known limitations in this regard (i.e. compared to randomised trials or arguably longitudinal data).

The audience for the current monograph is primarily researchers and policy makers. However, we as editors feel that many of the results and much of the discussion is of relevance to the wider national debate and, in particular, Indigenous communities and organisations. With this in mind, the monograph is implicitly divided into three sections. The first section examines both key questions on Indigenous demography and health, while the second section focuses on socioeconomic processes. The final section looks at broader complex social issues and cultural factors such as housing, crime and culture. Clearly this demarcation is arbitrary in that all these more complex outcomes feedback into demography, health and socioeconomic outcomes – a point that is made by most of the authors in parts 1 and 2. For example, Chapter 9 by Altman, Biddle and Buchanan is inextricably linked to culture, but hunting and gathering also clearly have an economic dimension providing goods and services, if not income, to Indigenous family and communities (see Chapter 10 by Hunter on Indigenous poverty). Similarly, Chapter 6 by Carrington and Zubrick acknowledges the likely interactions between cultural identity and child development. Given that the policy implications of the analysis in this monograph are likely to involve complex interactions between Indigenous social/cultural life and the closing the gaps outcomes, it is fitting that Part 3 of the monograph finishes with an integrated policy analysis in Chapter 14 from Matthew Gray.

Questions and answers?

The future direction of Indigenous data collections depends on what research questions can be answered by extant surveys including, but not limited to, the 2008 NATSISS. Many contributors to this monograph triangulate the evidence on Indigenous disadvantage using several sources of information from census or other surveys. Given the policy emphasis on closing the gaps, general Australian surveys are often used to identify what is happening in the Australian community; where those surveys have credible information on Indigenous status, the comparison group is non-Indigenous Australians – unfortunately, all too often such information is not available and the comparator is often the total Australian population.

The first question that needs to be addressed in an Indigenous survey is 'What constitutes an Indigenous households and how should analysts characterise the mobility of Indigenous people over time?' Indigenous people self-identified as Indigenous and Indigenous households are defined in a mechanical sense by the presence of at least one Indigenous adult in a dwelling. As Morphy (2006) points out, the nuclear family structure is not a 'natural' outcome of Australian Aboriginal kinships systems and this has profound implications for the measurement, analysis, and interpretation of Indigenous households. The focus on households defined in terms of dwellings is an operational expedience for most surveys, but it is not something that can be assumed to reflect the social reality of Indigenous families. Indigenous people tend to be relatively mobile among dwellings, but the specific nature of Indigenous social networks, and the renowned connection to country experienced within Indigenous culture, mean that tracking Indigenous people and households will have its own unique issues that will have to be taken into account.

John Taylor and Martin Bell address these questions and more in Chapter 2, which explores household structure and mobility. They argue that population is a complex phenomenon with explicit time and spatial dimensions that are difficult to capture in a ncross-sectional survey such as NATSISS. However, mobility is central to the closing the gaps policy as it conditions opportunities for Indigenous development, not least of which is proximity to existing infrastructure, education, employment and other socioeconomic opportunities.

Fertility and demography are also crucial aspects of the prospects for Indigenous development and the ability to close the gaps. For example, declines in fertility and mortality will lead to ongoing changes in the composition of the Indigenous population – a process sometimes called the 'demographic transition' – that will potentially change the economic opportunities of the Indigenous adult population in the near future, especially in the context of substantial ageing in Australia's overall population (Taylor, Biddle and Hunter 2011). Anne Evans and Kim Johnstone explore what the NATSISS 2008 can tell us about the fertility and demography of Indigenous peoples in Australia (Chapter 3). Unfortunately, the answer is that the 2008 survey was a lost opportunity because it failed to include a question on fertility. The whole thrust of demographic transition theory is that the economic and social opportunities change with the changes in number of children born to Indigenous women. Labour supply will be affected directly as the time out of the workforce is likely to be reduced and hence labour market experience enhanced. Evans and Johnstone were forced to rely on other data, but the omission of fertility from the 2008 NATSISS means that our ability to understand Indigenous development is circumscribed and that researchers will have to rely on other data and take into account demographic factors in a rudimentary fashion (i.e. by controlling for age and sex of respondents).

In contrast to the 2002 NATSISS, the latest NATSISS does not include information on substance abuse. Tanya Chikritzhs from the National Drug Research Institute explores one of the other crucial risk factors for Indigenous development, alcohol abuse (Chapter 4). She triangulates the 2008 NATSISS data on alcohol using sophisticated techniques and other data known to be associated with higher death rates and chronic heavy alcohol use (alcoholic liver cirrhosis and alcohol dependence). The main conclusion is that NATSISS substantially underestimates the actual prevalence of high risk drinking in the Indigenous Australian population.

These first chapters provide crucial background to users of the 2008 NATSISS, but they are of arguably limited interest to policy makers because they necessarily highlight data omissions and data quality issues. While the remaining chapters also address such issues (where relevant), the main focus is on policy issues and questions, especially as they pertain to closing the gaps.

The original closing the gap target focused on life expectancy and the analysis by Nicholas Biddle on health is clearly relevant here (Chapter 5). By definition, health is 'not only the absence of infirmity and disease, but also refers to a state of physical, mental and social wellbeing'. The central question is 'What makes Indigenous health Indigenous?' Are there Indigenous specific determinants of Indigenous health that support a policy focus beyond the standard socioeconomic determinants? Biddle exploits the omnibus nature of the 2008 NATSISS to incorporate social and cultural factors that go well beyond the mainstream determinants of health. Not only is one's own health and wellbeing important, but so too is the wellbeing of the community in which one lives. There is clearly an empirical link between physical health and subjective wellbeing which this contribution develops and explores. This has considerable resonance with a later chapter by Mike Dockery.

Indigenous policy's ability to close the gap between Indigenous and other Australians crucially depends on human capacities and child development. While there are some important data omissions from the 2008 NATSISS, it was the first nationally representative Indigenous survey to include a substantial sample of children under 15 years old, and hence it provides a unique opportunity to address child development and benchmark other important studies – such as the Longitudinal Study of Indigenous Children (LSIC) that has been in the field since 2008. While it is intrinsically difficult to test questions about child development using cross sectional data, Steve Zubrick and Carrington Sheppard from the Telethon Institute for Child Health Research do an admirable job in documenting how stress and discrimination are a relatively common feature of children's lives from an early age with human capital tending to be low in the families with children (Chapter 6). Both of these risk factors pose particular challenges for policy-makers, but it is clear that many Indigenous families with children need considerable support.

Nicholas Biddle and Timothy Cameron ask two important and related questions in Chapter 7: 'What are the benefits of Indigenous education?' and 'Are Indigenous students happy at school?' The answer to the latter question will be crucial in understanding the extent of Indigenous engagement with the education system, and to gain an appreciation of what may be done to optimise participation and maximise the benefits of education. While education is crucial to closing the gap in many of the outcomes nominated in COAG, the benefits clearly go beyond the substantial economic returns and include a range of social benefits often identified for both the individual concerned and the broader community at large. Biddle and Cameron finish with a discussion of a creative proposal to link NATSISS data with other surveys in a way that allows for some longitudinal dimensions to be analysed. Clearly longitudinal analysis is important for definitively identifying the benefits of education, but such analysis is likely to be crucial for almost all of the themes of the following chapters. Policy-makers should seriously consider supporting this proposal.

Education is commonly referred to by economists and policy-makers as human capital (a very utilitarian concept), and in some circles the two terms are almost synonymous. Education is very useful in that it clearly does enhance an individual's employment outcomes in terms of job prospects, wage levels and the types of jobs that are viable, and in enhancing a general sense of control over the working environment (inter alia, by increasing one's market value within the firm). In Chapter 8, Prem Thapa, Qasim Shah and Shafiq Ahmad from FaHCSIA investigate the determinants of Indigenous labour force status and hourly earnings. The creative application of techniques yields insight that previous studies could not provide, largely because of concerns about the veracity of interpreting income data in terms of wages.

Jon Altman, Nicholas Biddle and Geoff Buchanan reflect on the customary sector of the Indigenous economy and speculate about the data, policy and political implications of such data (Chapter 9). The NATSISS is the only official survey instrument that currently provides information about Aboriginal and Torres Strait Islander harvesting and cultural production. The customary sector, that includes hunting gathering and cultural activities, is obviously Indigenous by definition. Furthermore, the intensity and extent of these non-market activities varies significantly between remote and non-remote Australia. This analysis highlights the diversity of styles and content of the customary economy and includes a rather confronting image that illustrates the specific Indigenous skill involved and the visceral nature of some activities. There are less confronting illustrations in many art galleries, including the relatively new permanent Indigenous exhibition at the National Gallery of Australia.

The question of whether Indigenous poverty is different from other poverty is addresssed by Boyd Hunter (Chapter 10). The answer is a resounding 'yes' in that Indigenous poverty differs from other Australian poverty in both the extent of financial stress and the nature of poverty and disadvantage experienced. Measurement error in household income and the equivalence scales that are used to identify poor households, are likely to explain some of this observation. However, another important obeservation is that non-market activities from the customary sector – such as hunting and gathering – allows for some income substitution in terms of goods and services that Indigenous households would otherwise have to buy.

Don Weatherburn and Lucy Snowball from the New South Wales Bureau of Crime Statistics and Research provide an excellent example of what this monograph aspires to achieve: they systematically identify the theories of Indigenous violence and use the 2008 NATSISS to test the propositions identified in those theories (Chapter 11). They found strong support for lifestyle/routine activity theories, moderate support for social disorganisation and social deprivation theories, but little support for cultural theories of Indigenous violence. This chapter attempts to provide a stronger test of cultural theories of Indigenous violence than was possible in Snowball and Weatherburn (2008).

Paul Memmott and Kelly Greenop from the University of Queensland scrutinise the embedded assumptions that underlie extant measures of household utilisation and crowding (Chapter 12). Their chapter does not examine an explicit hypothesis about behaviour, but it does ensure that analysis that is informed by this contribution should not provide misleading conclusions that are inconsistent with the reality of Indigenous lives. Indigenous housing is best understood through a cross-cultural lens that acknowledges that many Indigenous people understand the world in relational, rather than transactional terms. Accordingly, it is important NOT to presume a particular world view (with the associated ontological, epistemological or even cosmological assumptions). The chapter is rather long but takes the reader on a fascinating journey through cultural differences. Housing clearly plays an important role in the gaps identified in the COAG targets – for example, it is hard to be healthy and function in a community unless the dwelling is meeting your basic needs.

The Memmott and Greenop chapter resonates with the other chapters that highlight cultural difference. The need to acknowledge the inter-cultural aspects of the gap being closed is applicable to all COAG targets irrespective of whether policy-makers or researchers explicitly acknowledge the issue.

Mike Dockery from Curtin University explicitly examines inter-cultural issues in the penultimate chapter, interrogating the link between traditional culture and wellbeing. The quantitative methodology applied is clearly Western in origins – and somewhat technical – but it identifies several arguably distinct dimensions of culture (participation in cultural events and activities, cultural identity, language and participation in traditional economic activities) and asks whether these aspects of culture effect Indigenous outcomes in health, education, employment, interaction with the criminal justice system and alcohol abuse. In general, positive effects of cultural attachment on mainstream socioeconomic indicators are confirmed. Indigenous Australians who identify more strongly with their traditional culture are happier and display better mental health, but at the same time experience more psychological stress due to stronger feelings of discrimination. Policy-makers will ignore the role of Indigenous culture at their peril – indeed, they may run the risk of undermining the goal of closing the gaps in the various domains.

Matthew Gray draws together the themes of the monograph in the final chapter. One of the central conclusions is that researchers and policy makers need to work together if the gaps between Indigenous and non-Indigenous Australians are to be closed. Researchers provide intellectual consistency and rigour to the analysis, while policy makers are across the detail of the policy and have a better sense of the political dynamics that may undermine or support any initiative in question. Obviously researchers and policy makers have different comparative advantages and they could work separately; however both skill sets are imperative for establishing a credible policy relevant analysis. The lack of good quality, independent evaluations in Australia relative to the United States, undermine the evidence base on effective policy options. Before and after studies are one underutilised evaluation method in the Indigenous context, although some argue that randomised control trials or experiments are the gold standards of evaluations (Leigh 2009). Such experiments may encounter instrumental difficulties in the Indigenous communities, but at the very least evaluations would benefit from systematic collection of benchmarks from affected groups so that credible claims may be made about what would have happened in the absence of a given program. The analysis of the 2008 NATSISS in this monograph does not focus on individual policies; however it does provide invaluable background that our expectations for such benchmarks can compared against. Moreover the answers to the questions raised throughout this monograph provide useful information on the social and economic processes that policies are designed to address.

References

Aboriginal and Torres Strait Islander Social Justice Commissioner 2005. *Social Justice Report 2005*, Human Rights and Equall Opportunity Commission, Sydney.

Altman, J. C. (ed.) 1992. *A National Survey of Indigenous Australians: Options and Implications*, CAEPR Research Monograph No. 3, CAEPR, ANU, Canberra.

——, Biddle, N. and Hunter, B. H. 2008. 'How realistic are the prospects for 'Closing the gaps' in socioeconomic outcomes for Indigenous Australians?', *CAEPR Discussion Paper No. 287*, CAEPR, ANU, Canberra.

—— and Taylor, J. (eds) 1996. *The 1994 National Aboriginal and Torres Strait Islander Survey: Findings and Future Prospects*, CAEPR Research Monograph No. 11, CAEPR, ANU, Canberra.

Biddle, N. and Hunter, B. H. 2006. 'Selected methodological issues for analysis of the 2002 NATSISS', in B. H. Hunter (ed.), *Assessing Recent Evidence on Indigenous Socioeconomic Outcomes: A Focus on the 2002 NATSISS*, CAEPR Research Monograph No. 26, ANU E Press, Canberra.

Comer, L. 2008. *Closing the Gaps – Lessons from New Zealand*, Presentation to the to the Ministerial Council for Aboriginal and Torres Strait Islander Affairs on 15 July 2008, Wellington.

Commonwealth of Australia 1991. *Recommendations of the Royal Commission into Aboriginal Deaths in Custody*, AGPS, Canberra.

Hunter, B. H. (ed.) 2006. *Assessing Recent Evidence on Indigenous Socioeconomic Outcomes: A focus on the 2002 NATSISS*, CAEPR Research Monograph No. 26, ANU E Press, Canberra.

Leigh, A. 2009. 'What evidence should social policymakers use?', *Australian Treasury Economic Roundup*, 1: 27–43.

Morphy, F. 2006. 'Lost in tranlation? Remote Indigenous households and definitions of the family', *Family Matters*, 73: 12–9.

Ross, R. T. 1988. 'The labour market position of Aboriginal people in non-metropolitan New South Wales', *Australian Bulletin of Labour*, 15 (1): 29–56.

Rowley, C.D. 1970. *Outcasts in White Australia*, ANU Press, Canberra.

——1982. *Equality by Installments: The Aboriginal Householder in Rural New South Wales, 1965 and 1980*, Australian Institute of Aboriginal Studies, Canberra.

Sims, G. 1992. 'A national survey of the Aboriginal and Torres Strait Islander population: The proposal', in J. C. Altman (ed.), *A National Survey of Indigenous Australians: Options and Implications*, CAEPR Research Monograph No. 3, CAEPR, ANU, Canberra.

Snowball, L. and Weatherburn, D. 2008. 'Theories of Indigenous violence: A preliminary empirical assessment', *The Australian and New Zealand Journal of Criminology*, 41: 216–35.

Steering Committee for the Review of Government Service Provision 2010. *National Agreement Performance Information 2009–10: National Indigenous Reform Agreement*, Productivity Commission, Canberra.

Taylor, J., Biddle, N. and Hunter, B. 2011. 'The Indigenous inter-generational report', Plenary address presented to the *Young and Old: Connecting Generations* AIATSIS Conference, 19 September, Canberra.

2. Mobile people, mobile measures: Limitations and opportunities for mobility analysis

John Taylor and Martin Bell

As the third in a (now) regular round of National Aboriginal and Torres Strait Islander Social Surveys (NATSISS), the 2008 survey is an important addition to the ever-growing armoury of statistical information available to governments and others in their analysis of the social, cultural and economic circumstances of Indigenous Australians. This survey activity is important because it provides the basis for determining change in individual and group circumstances since the first survey in 1994 and it lays a foundation for considering this into the future. Current results may also now be added to the volume of information available from the last two census rounds to contribute to what has become an almost constant flow of national and jurisdictional data.

Indeed, such is the accumulating volume of statistical information on Indigenous Australians that a Closing the Gap Clearinghouse has now been established in order to make some systematic sense of the findings from numerous evaluations that make use of these data in attempts to explain progress (or otherwise) in the pursuit of policy goals (Australian Institute of Health and Welfare/Australian Institute of Family Studies n.d.). This practical development is no surprise as it was foreshadowed in discussions leading up to the first National Aboriginal and Torres Strait Islander Survey (NATSIS) in 1994 where the concern was that the NATSIS would go to great lengths to gather data that would turn out to be in excess of the system's available capacity to absorb and utilise it (Altman 1992: 163). Viewed historically, we have therefore shifted over the past three decades from a situation where the main problem was a lack of information – a concern raised by the Miller Report (1985) and then again by the Royal Commission into Aboriginal Deaths in Custody in 1991 (Commonwealth of Australia 1991) and that eventually spawned the first NATSIS (Altman 1992) – to one where there is now almost a surfeit of information. The emphasis has shifted to a consideration of unfolding cross-sectional analyses and what the cumulative evidence from these indicates about patterns and trends in Indigenous outcomes. This chapter takes its cue from this shift by considering the utility of the NATSISS in examining such trends with particular reference to dimensions of population mobility.

The 2002 NATSISS was the first household survey to include a question on Indigenous mobility. With a follow-up mobility module in the 2008 NATSISS we are now in a position to say something about how, and possibly why, mobility and its socioeconomic correlates change over time if, indeed, they do. At least that is the proposition. Some uncertainty exists here because the NATSISS questions that provide for a measure of mobility changed somewhat between 2002 and 2008 raising questions about comparability. As with a number of other questions on the questionnaire, the 2008 survey also asked for the first time about children's mobility. However, this is not considered here as the focus is on adult mobility partly because of the lack of a 2002 comparison for children.

In this chapter we have two main objectives. First, we examine the importance of mobility as a policy issue and test the capacity of the NATSISS to measure change in the intensity and direction of residential movement over time as a contribution to understanding policy impacts. We do this by establishing one-year mobility rates for select characteristics of movers in 2008 and comparing these with equivalent rates for 2002. This reveals a limitation of the NATSISS as a means to establishing underlying trends. The bottom line is, the mobility modules differ between the two surveys to the extent that they produce quite different measures of movement. Second, we focus on the new mobility questions in the 2008 survey and explore the dimensions of mobility analysis that are now accessible. Aside from establishing socioeconomic correlates of movement, we also explore the possibilities for analysis of the tempo of movement that these new data present. Here we draw a distinction between chronic short-term and more stable long-term movers and attempt to estimate probabilities of residential change.

Mobility as a policy issue

Movement of population is a significant concern of Indigenous public policy (Snipp 2004). Of the three demographic components of population change it is the one that is most difficult to conceptualise and measure but also the one that is most likely to impact on regional and local population growth or decline. While the demographic outcome therefore goes directly to the issue of estimating the variable size and composition of identified social policy needs, social scientists have struggled to develop adequate measurement and predictive models of mobility, not least in regard to Indigenous populations where conceptual understanding of change in usual residence can be quite different (Taylor and Bell 2004).

Presently, in policy debate, much is expected and alleged of Indigenous population movement. On the one hand is the proposition that migration to jobs and higher order services is an inevitable requirement for closing the gap and that this invariably involves or requires a shift to an urban centre or growth town (Hughes 2007: 21–23). In previous analysis of NATSISS data, the issue of how to match labour supply and demand in this way was raised with an observation about the likely role of welfare reform in literally 'mobilising' labour (Gregory 2006). There appears no doubt that such a rural-urban redistribution is underway. For some time now, census-based evidence points to a net step-wise movement up the settlement hierarchy from remote areas to regional towns and city areas (Biddle 2010; Gray 1989; Taylor 2006).

In relation to this, the period 2002 to 2008 is ripe for comparative analysis. Since the 2002 NATSISS there have been a number of economic and policy developments that are likely to have encouraged the flows mentioned above and, in the process, might have stimulated an overall rise in residential mobility. Not least has been the substantial and steady rise in non-CDEP (Community Development Employment Program) employment, especially in the private sector (Biddle, Taylor and Yap 2009: 271; Gray and Hunter 2011). Aside from the macroeconomic effects of a buoyant labour market, this increase is also likely to reflect the gradual impact of Indigenous Employment Strategy (IES) programs aimed at raising private sector engagement alongside the removal of remote area exemptions for jobseekers, the scrapping of CDEP in urban areas and its partial transformation elsewhere into a Job Services program, the enhancement of programs to encourage school participation to Year 12 and equivalent further emphasis given to raising levels of tertiary and vocational education and training (VET) qualification enabling more flexibility in the labour market. Indeed, the whole push towards 'closing the gap' and its decade-long precursor of 'practical reconciliation' implies the prospect of significant demographic change including that of enhanced movement for education and employment participation. At the same time, other policies, such as those encouraging home ownership, may have operated to reduce movement propensity as, indeed, would any lowering in levels of unemployment or renting of private dwellings given that these have been found in the past to be strongly associated with mobility (Taylor and Kinfu 2006).

Has the intensity and geography of mobility changed?

So what has happened to the level and composition of mobility against this background of likely influences? On the face of it, this seems to be a simple question to answer, and it is, as long as we have consistent measurement over time. The problem is we don't, at least not from the NATSISS. In the 2002 NATSISS, the focus of attention in measuring mobility was on the multiple locations that an individual may have stayed in over a 12 month period. In particular, the survey asked (in non-remote and remote non-community sample areas), 'In the last 12 months, have you lived in any other dwellings?' and (in remote community sample areas), 'In the last year have you lived in any other houses or places?' In both areas, the survey then went on to elicit how many dwellings, houses/places people had lived in over the course of the designated year.

In deliberating over the content of the 2008 survey, the technical reference group convened by the Australian Bureau of Statistics (ABS) decided to change this question to one that focused on duration of residence in the current and previous dwelling of residence with no limit on time period (although only those who moved in the last five years were coded). The mobility questions became 'how long have you lived in this house?' and 'how long did you live in the house immediately before this one?' These are very different questions to those asked in 2002 and they provide a very different perspective on mobility. According to the ABS the initial proposal for the mobility module was to retain the 2002 questions and even add additional questions to expand the scope of the module. However, following field testing, the extended module was found to be overly long and a decision was made in favour of a shortened module with a revised mobility question that aligned with the question asked in the General Social Survey (GSS) to provide for Indigenous/non-Indigenous comparison. This is an example of where the demands of postcolonial demography for comparative data (Taylor 2011) can override attempts to generate specifically Indigenous survey data and it raises a question about the appropriate degree to which the content of the NATSISS should be driven by the content of the GSS and who should decide (Taylor 2008: 117–120; Yu 2011). This is no trivial matter as, in this instance, we can see that whilst the change in questions opens up new insights, it also closes down the possibility of measuring change over time.

While it is technically possible to construct a group of survey respondents in 2002 and again in 2008 who can be said to have changed their dwelling of residence at least once during the 12 month period prior to the survey, our proposition is that the 2002 survey question on the number of dwellings/houses/places lived in over the past 12 months was designed to capture more movement than the 2008 question on duration lived in a single current dwelling. Because of this we would expect higher movement rates to emerge from the 2002 NATSISS and this is exactly what we find.

Propensities by age

At the 2002 NATSISS, 31 per cent of respondents aged 15 years and over indicated that they had changed residence during the 12 month period prior to the survey. This compares to just 21 per cent of respondents in the 2008 NATSISS. Taken at face value this looks like a dramatic decline in the overall intensity of population movement since 2002 but we would caution against drawing such a conclusion. It is true that one-year movement rates since 1996 derived from census data also point to a decline in the overall intensity of mobility, but the 2002 NATSISS level appears to be an aberration from this time series and we would suggest that it reflects the fact that 2002 data incorporate additional temporary movement. Interestingly, the 2008 NATSISS level is very close to that reported by the 2006 Census.

Fig. 2.1 Census and survey based age-specific Indigenous movement rates, Australia, 1996 to 2008

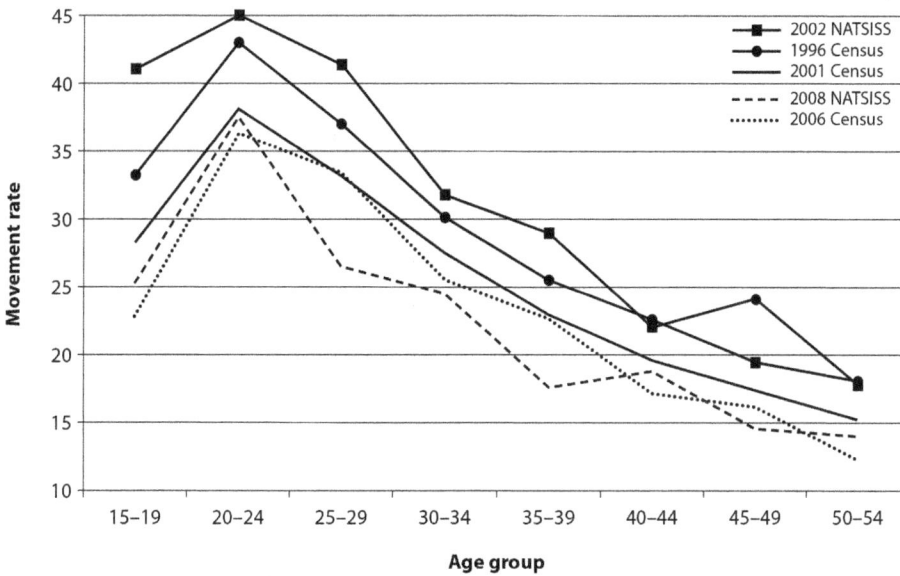

Source: Taylor and Kinfu 2005: 60; 2008 Remote Access Data Laboratory (RADL)

This same variation in the intensity of movement between different collections is evident across the age distribution. In Fig. 2.1 we plot one-year age-specific movement rates using data from the 2002 and 2008 NATSISS alongside one-year rates derived from the 1996, 2001 and 2006 Censuses with due deference to the differences in methodology between the survey questions as outlined above and the fixed-period usual residence questions deployed in the census. In this chart only the three census-based sets of rates are truly comparable over time and they are provided here for triangulation. What this reveals is that the age pattern of movement derived from both NATSISS collections is in broad agreement with census results in so far as movement peaks among young adults aged 20–24 years and steadily declines thereafter. Overall, these patterns conform with more or less universal observations that have long been made by for the United States and Europe (Rogers and Castro 1981), and subsequently in Australia by Bell (1992, 1995). The peak in the age profile of mobility is associated with the combined influence of departure from the parental home, the start of tertiary education, entry into the labour force and the establishment of independent living arrangements; subsequent decline is related to home ownership and prolonged attachment to the labour force.

To the extent that Indigenous people participate in these same lifecourse events the message from Fig. 2.1 is that they are evident regardless of which measure of mobility is used. The other, equally important observation is that movement rates derived using 2002 data are considerably out of step with the other series by being consistently much higher at all ages. If we focus on differentials between the 2002 and 2008 NATSISS rates these are the extremes with substantial gaps of 20 to 30 per cent in rates among 15–19 years and 25–29 year olds and up to as much as 40 per cent in some older age groups.

Spatial pattern

One of the constraints on mobility analysis using NATSISS data to date has been the lack of a spatial dimension describing the direction of population flows – whether up or down the settlement hierarchy. This is useful to know since movement in each direction is known to correlate with key socioeconomic characteristics and, as we have seen, movement up the hierarchy is an implicit goal of much social policy. Tantalisingly, in the 2008 survey, questions were asked about the current and previous location of dwellings therefore opening up the possibility of such analysis. In the processing of data, however, current dwellings were coded by remoteness category whereas previous dwellings were coded by 'same locality/capital city/remainder of state' or by 'section of state' – neither of which concord with remoteness.

This means that the only analysis of spatial change in mobility enabled by the 2008 survey is to compare mobility rates over time at the jurisdictional level but even here this probably only serves to highlight that the 2002 and 2008 surveys produce different measures of mobility. The percentage of Indigenous adults in each jurisdiction who changed residence over the 12 month period prior to each survey in 2002 and 2008 is shown in Fig. 2.2. The results are quite striking – in 2002, movement rates in the Northern Territory and Tasmania/Australian Capital Territory were significantly lower than in all other jurisdictions whereas in 2008 there is no significant difference between reported rates in all jurisdictions due to what appears to be a substantial decline in mobility in all areas except the Northern Territory. On the face of it, it would seem that mobility in the Northern Territory slightly increased while in all other jurisdictions it decreased substantially. Consequently, in 2008 no significant difference in propensity to move was evident between any of the jurisdictions given the spread of the upper and lower bounds of each set of estimates. Consistent with this is the observation that no difference was evident between movement rates in remote and non-remote areas in 2008 (with rates of 22.5 and 20.8 respectively) whereas in 2002 very remote areas displayed significantly lower movement than all other regions and rates elsewhere were generally much higher than in 2008 at 30–35 per cent.

Fig. 2.2 Indigenous movement propensities by State and Territory, 2002 and 2008[a]

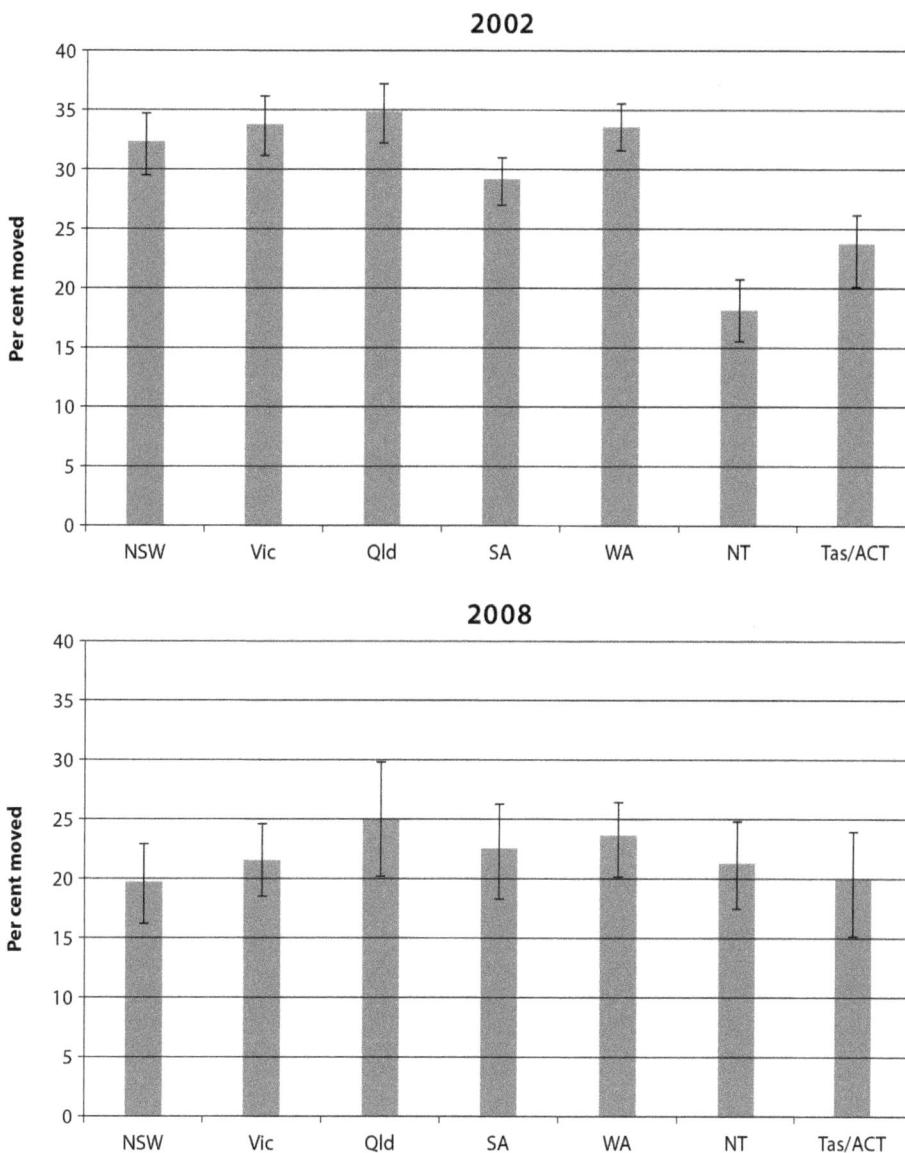

a. The error bars around the point estimates indicate a 95% confiedence interval.

Source: 2002 and 2008 NATSISS

Modelling mobility

From a theoretical perspective and using empirical evidence from around the world, it is argued that the intensity, spatial pattern, and composition of population mobility rises in level, spatial scale, and complexity over time in tandem with transitions in modernisation and economic development that involve shifts in the nature of consumption and production (Zelinksy 1971). While there is variation in the nature of response, the basic relationship nonetheless holds (Skeldon 1990). Ultimately, then, the proposition exists that spatial behaviour tends towards universal norms with urbanisation an inevitable co-requisite of the development process (Skeldon 1997). This general model is confirmed for Australia as a whole (Hugo 1988), and underlying this are the changing locational needs and preferences of individuals and households. These vary according to life cycle stage and correlate with a range of human capital attributes that are ultimately associated with participation in production (labour force status) and consumption (housing, amenity, welfare) (Bell and Maher 1995). If the nature of social and economic participation is reflected in mobility, what then of sub-populations, such as the Indigenous population, who are less engaged with mainstream institutions and who may articulate different priorities?

The situation of Indigenous Australians within this general model has been explored first by Hugo (1988) and then by Taylor and Bell (1996, 2004). They highlight the relative lack of urbanisation among Indigenous people compared to the rest of the population, the contemporary fragmentation of their rural settlement, and the continuity of short-term circular movement for non-economic reasons as distinguishing features that contrast with mainstream mobility. While these findings stem from census analyses and ethnographic studies, the NATSISS now provides a sample survey basis for exploring some of the dimensions of this different mobility by considering the probability of movement according to some of the human capital variables found to be associated with population movement among Indigenous Australians and more generally (Kinfu 2005). It also provides for an examination of the reasons provided by survey respondents to account for their mobility.

Social and economic correlates of movement

We begin by examining the propensity to move across a range of social, economic and cultural characteristics that are selected here for their likely association with movement propensity. As the respondent population differed in age distribution to the overall Indigenous population (in 2008, for example, it was noticeably older) observed results are standardised by age against the total Indigenous population. In some instances this varies the outcome up or down (Table 2.1). Propensity to move was highest among private renters followed by those unemployed. Owner-occupiers had the lowest movement rate. Unfortunately sector of employment was not coded in 2008 even though data to enable this were gathered. This means that the influence on mobility of the substantial rise in Indigenous private sector employment that was observed using 2001 and 2006 Census data (Biddle, Taylor and Yap 2009: 271–73) cannot be tested.

Table 2.1 Movement propensities[a] according to select social, economic and geographic characteristics, 2002 and 2008

	2008 reported	2008 age standardised
Total	21.2	21.2
Sex		
Males	21.6	21.6
Females	21.0	21.0
Marital Status		
Married	19.9	24.8
Not married	22.4	22.4
Labour force		
Unemployed	32.1	28.7
Not in labour force	20.6	21.9
Employed	19.8	19.4
Public	No data	No data
Private	No data	No data
CDEP	21.1	19.9
Education		
Yr 11 and 12	22.9	20.4
Yr 10	22.0	21.4
Yr 9 or below	19.0	21.7
Training		
Attended	22.5	21.4
Not attended	21.8	21.0
Housing tenure		
Owner	8.7	9.0
Private rental	36.2	34.0
Public rental	20.0	19.8
Community rental	20.5	20.6
Place of residence		
In homeland	18.7	18.8
Not in homeland	22.8	23.8

	2008 reported	2008 age standardised
Neighbourhood problems		
Has problems	20.1	20.0
Does not have problems	22.4	22.5
Remoteness		
Non-remote	20.7	20.7
Remote and very remote	22.4	22.5
Health status		
Excellent	22.6	21.1
Very good	21.4	19.8
Good	21.8	21.8
Fair	20.7	25.6
Poor	17.0	22.3

[a] Movers per 100 population

Source: Customised cross-tabulations from the 2008 NATSISS RADL

Net effects of these independent variables can only be assessed using multivariate analysis. For this purpose, we fit a logistic regression with the dependent variable taking the form of 1 if the respondent moved in the 12 months period prior to the survey and 0 otherwise. In this way, the results indicate the effects of all the selected factors simultaneously on the chances of moving or not. Net effects on these chances in relation to a common reference person in 2008 are indicated in Fig. 2.3 which also indicates the characteristics of the reference person.

After removing the effects of other variables, there remains a significant underlying pattern of higher mobility among those unemployed or not in the labour force compared to those in mainstream employment and emphatically among those in private sector rental accommodation compared to other forms of housing tenure. Indeed, home ownership operates as a distinct brake on mobility. The effects of educational attainment and training are evident in the clear gradient from higher mobility among those with qualifications and Year 12 schooling to lower movement among those with Year 9 or below and non attendance in VET courses. Contrary to what might be expected, respondents resident in neighbourhoods with perceived social problems are relatively immobile which may reflect their limited capacity for residential change. It is notable that residence on homelands is negatively associated with mobility compared to remote/very remote residence which is positively associated. This underscores the fact that the former locations are likely to be associated with some form of Indigenous land tenure whereas the latter are simply reflective of ABS taxonomy. Finally, the effect of self-assessed health status appears to operate as might be expected – excellent health leading to higher mobility most likely due to increased opportunity, and poor health leading to reduced mobility most likely due to incapacity.

Fig. 2.3 Net effects of socioeconomic, spatial and household characteristics on Indigenous mobility: Logistic regression results, 2008[a]

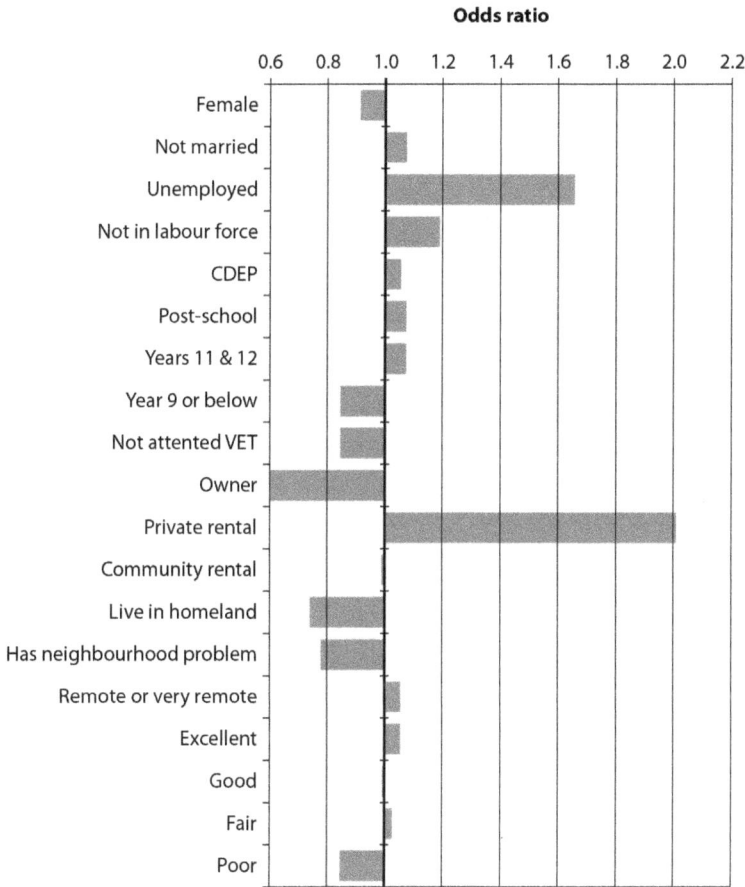

Odds ratio

a. Reference person: male, married, employed in non-CDEP, no post-school qualifications, Year 10, attended vocational training, lives in public rental dwelling, does not live in homeland, does not have neighbourhood problems, does not live in a remote area, reports very good health. The results are not sensitive to the choice of characteristics of the reference person.

Source: 2008 NATSISS RADL

The tempo of mobility

So far, we have discussed mobility in a conventional sense using a mover/stayer framework. This bifurcation is overly simplistic because there is considerable heterogeneity in population movement although data that exposes this is quite rare. For some time now there has been growing recognition of a need for more biographical approaches to the study of population mobility (Halfacree and Boyle 1993). It is argued that these provide a richness of detail that enables the proper interpretation of population movement as culturally situated in social fields and individual and group life courses. While such approaches undoubtedly add texture and meaning to analyses of human mobility a major drawback is the limited capacity for comparison between individuals and groups. More recently, Bell (2004) and Taylor and Bell (2011) have shown how duration and frequency can be combined with information on the sequences of movements to generate a new comparative metric – that of periodicity. In practice, though, exploration of concepts such as periodicity has been restricted by an absence of suitable data on the timing of population movements and the limited development of techniques to derive summary indices. There are compelling reasons for further methodological development in this area, not least in respect of Indigenous populations, and this is where the 2008 NATSISS data are innovative.

Conventional data collections bifurcate the population into two discrete categories – movers and stayers – and this is true whether migration is measured over a one or five year interval, as in the Australian census, or any other period. In practice, however, we know that the vast majority of people change their place of residence at some point in their lives, and many individuals move frequently. Data on duration of residence – captured in the 2008 NATSISS question 'How long have you lived in this house' – go some way to unlocking this detail. Fig. 2.4 graphs median duration of residence in current dwelling for the indigenous population and reveals marked variations by age. As might be expected, median durations are shortest among young adults and (of necessity) among very young children, but reach five years among children of school age, and rise steadily after age 30, climbing to nine years among those aged 55 and over. Fig. 2.4 also reveals some intriguing regional differences in mobility, with Indigenous young adults in remote areas much more likely to move than their counterparts in non-remote areas, as reflected in markedly shorter residence durations. As suggested elsewhere, this might reflect differences in attachment to locationally specific activities and fixed places of employment, as well as variations in the timing and tempo of access to services and customary pursuits in remote communities. Differences in duration of residence emerge again beyond age 40, with people in remote Australia once more recording shorter average durations of residence, probably reflecting the relative constraints of fixed employment and housing in more closely settled areas (Taylor and Bell 2004).

Fig. 2.4 Median duration of residence in current dwelling by age and remoteness, 2008

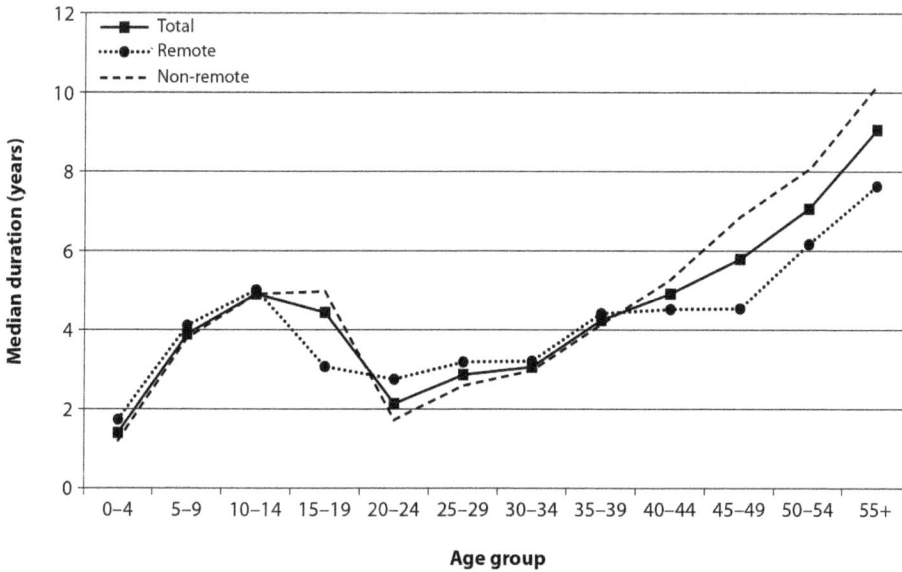

Source: 2008 NATSISS RADL

To some extent, Fig. 2.4 is a mirror image of the conventional age profile of mobility: median durations are low where the propensity to move is high, and vice versa. Thinking about mobility in terms of duration of stay, rather than propensity to go, provides a somewhat different perspective on migration and median duration thus provides an alternative to the conventional statistical indicator, the proportion who moved. However, it is the facility to segment the population by period of residence that represents the real benefit of the data on duration (Fig. 2.5). When this is done, it becomes readily apparent that there is considerable heterogeneity among the population in terms of mobility. Even among young adults, who have the shortest median durations and the highest rates of mobility, there is a significant group who have not moved for more than a decade. This was the case for fully one-quarter of 15–19 years olds and almost one-fifth of those aged 20–24. Conversely, at older ages, half of whom had been in the same dwelling for a decade or more, there was a significant minority of recent movers with more than one in five of those aged 55 and over changing residence in the last three years. While the NATSISS provides little information on distance moved, these variations point to very different sub-groups within individual age cohorts and suggest potentially quite diverse needs profiles based on differing levels of locational knowledge, community attachment, and so on. Classification by period of residence therefore provides a more nuanced framework for survey analysis against which to examine differences in population characteristics, housing and economic circumstances that circumscribe and shape individual and household wellbeing.

Fig. 2.5 Duration of residence in current dwelling by age, 2008

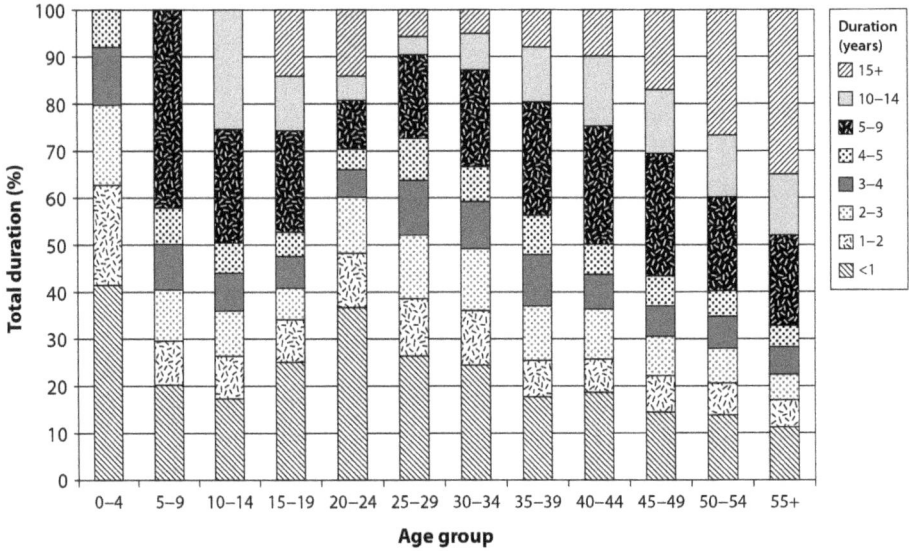

Source: 2008 NATSISS RADL

Other things being equal, mobility is subject to cumulative inertia: the propensity to move declines with increasing duration of stay. However, migration events are variously distributed through time and recent movers may themselves be poised for a lengthy stay while those seemingly more settled may be planning a move. One major drawback of data on current duration of residence is that they are right censored: the current duration of stay is incomplete and Fig. 2.4 and 2.5 therefore represent a somewhat biased picture of the mobility profile of this population. Here, however, the 2008 NATSISS provides an alternative solution through a follow up question which asks respondents to specify their duration of stay in their previous residence. In the literature on migration studies, this is an unusual question normally confined to surveys that trace complete residential histories. Inevitably the information is a little dated because respondents are reporting events that have occurred, in some cases, many years before. Recall errors may also prejudice accuracy. However, the data do have the singular merit of providing a picture of completed residence durations. This, in turn, sets the foundation for analysis that can provide further insights into population mobility.

In Fig. 2.6, the data for two cohorts are arranged in a form of survival analysis to show the progressive increase in proportions moving away from their previous places of residence. As time increases on the x-axis the proportion remaining in their original dwelling drops away, rapidly at first, and then more gradually, so that after around 10 years only 10 per cent of the cohorts remain in their previous dwelling. The decline is significantly faster for those in the 15–19 age group than for 30–49 year olds. After two years, half of young adults had changed residence compared with just two-fifths of the older cohort, and after five years just one in five young adults remained in their original dwelling compared with 27 per cent of 30–49 year olds. While the differences are not stark, they do serve to reveal the way in which mobility processes steadily pervade the entire population. Such analyses cannot be performed reliably with information on duration in current residence because the data are effectively 'censored' since none of the observed durations are complete. But further refinement in analysis of the prior residence data is also possible. As presented in Fig. 2.6 the results depict the combined experience of individuals as aged at the end time of the survey but this conflates moves made a variety of points in time. An alternative would be to transform the data to measure duration of stay by age at the start of the previous move. Although such analysis would require a fine level of data disaggregation, it would deliver a precise measure of movements through the housing stock that has not previously been available from Australian mobility statistics.

Fig. 2.6 Completed durations of stay and proportions remaining, 2008

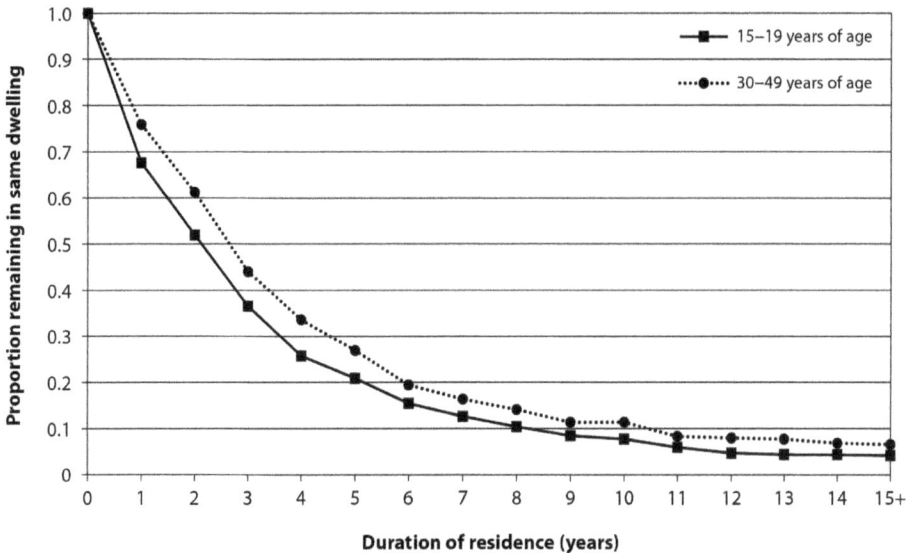

Source: NATSISS 2008 question on duration in previous place of residence; age at time of the survey

Coupling data on current and previous residence has the potential to provide further insights into mobility by segmenting long term stayers from chronic movers. A conceptual framework for this is provided by the matrix of long and short-term duration of stays shown in Fig. 2.7; this should be read in combination with Table 2.2 which sets out a convenient cross-classification of both variables categorised into three broad time intervals and identifies the proportion of respondents in each. Fully two-fifths can be classed as relatively long term residents having lived in their current and previous dwellings for four years or more (cell 9). On the other hand, combining cells 1, 2, 4 and 5, reveals that one-third of respondents had resided in both their current and previous dwellings for three years or less.

Table 2.2 Current duration by previous duration of stay, 2008

Time in previous dwelling	Time in current dwelling	Code	Share of population (%)
< 1 year	< 1 year	1	8.0
< 1 year	1–3 years	2	4.6
< 1 year	> 4 years	3	1.6
1–3 years	< 1 year	4	8.5
1–3 years	1–3 years	5	11.9
1–3 years	> 4 years	6	4.3
> 4 years	< 1 year	7	5.5
> 4 years	1–3 years	8	9.2
> 4 years	> 4 years	9	41.8
Never moved		10	4.5

Source: 2008 NATSISS RADL

Fig. 2.7 Segmenting chronic movers from long term stayers[a]

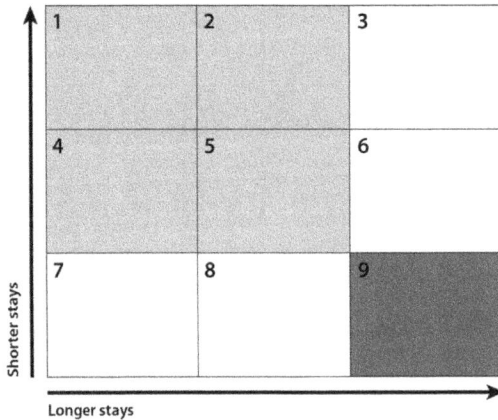

a. Cell numbers correspond with those in Table 2.2.

Source: 2008 NATSISS RADL

The difference in characteristics and composition of these two groups, and in the reasons for their last move is shown in Table 2.3. While the differences are not stark, for chronic movers housing reasons emerge as the strongest motive for migration; employment also features more strongly than among long term stayers. These differences might reflect an earlier life cycle stage among chronic movers with changes of residence triggered by housing transitions and entry to employment. However, Table 2.3 also points to greater vulnerability in this group, with a significantly larger proportion of chronic movers being unemployed and in private rental accommodation and correspondingly fewer in owner occupied housing.

Table 2.3 Percentage distribution of chronic movers and long term stayers by reasons for moving, labour force status and housing tenure, 2008

	Long term	Short term
Reasons for move		
Housing	44.4	47.0
Family	33.8	30.0
Lifestyle	9.0	6.5
Employment	4.5	8.0
Health	3.6	2.1
Education	0.9	0.7
Other	3.8	5.7
Total	100.0	100.0
Labour force status		
Employed	52.1	50.3
Unemployed	6.2	13.2
NILF	41.7	36.5
Total	100.0	100.0
Housing tenure		
Owner	45.0	25.6
Private rental	10.6	33.4
Public rental	26.2	27.1
Community rental	18.2	13.9
Total	**100.0**	**100.0**

Source: 2008 NATSISS RADL

Conclusion

The NATSISS is now an established tool of social analysis in Indigenous affairs. As with any sample survey its chief utility arises from the direction and strength of associations that can be established between characteristics at the individual and group levels. While we have examined some such associations – between movement and select correlates – our primary purpose has been to test the strength of the single variable (residential change) to inform discussion about the relationship between policy and population movement and to provide further insight into the nature of mobility. In respect of the first of these tasks we find the 2008 NATSISS somewhat limited in capacity; with regard to the second it has opened up new possibilities.

While the overall rate of mobility recorded by the 2008 NATSISS was much lower in all jurisdictions compared to 2002 this is not surprising since the methodology used to measure mobility differed in the two surveys in a way that lowered the chances of recording population movement in 2008. Basically, the 2002 questions appear to have picked up excess short term movement across the board, except in the Northern Territory where reported movement is consistently low regardless of the question. It would seem that the more open-ended questions regarding mobility as used in 2002 are more likely to elicit family-related reasons for movement whereas the single-move questions as used in 2008 emphasise housing reasons. Together with the lack of industry sector of employment coding in the 2008 survey output and limited scope for linking current and previous residence, this use of different mobility questions between surveys substantially hampers any attempt to examine the role of population movement in effecting labour force change. This resurrects an important long-standing question about the purpose of the NATSISS as a policy tool and the need to retain identical questions to ensure comparability over time (Altman and Taylor 1996: 198).

While temporal comparisons have been compromised, the new questions in the 2008 survey mobility module do have the benefit of providing novel insights. Questions on duration of residence have rarely been used in Australian migration research, but are comparatively common as part of the standard armoury of statistical agencies in other countries. Of 141 countries collecting migration data in the 2000 round of censuses, fully 82 asked questions on duration of residence while only 56 asked about place of residence one or five years previously (Bell et al. 2011) – the standard questions asked at the Australian census. The key benefit of duration of residence data is in superceding the conventional mover–stayer framework by segmenting the population into more detailed mover categories. Not only does this better recognise the near universality of migration, and the heterogeneous nature of populations, it also allows movement classification to be customised around particular topics of interest: chronic movers, or long term stayers, for example. Set alongside other socioeconomic variables, such as income or level of education, it is the bifurcation of mobility into two discrete categories (moved/did not move) that emerges as unusual, and duration data overcome this limitation. What is additionally unusual in the 2008 NATSISS is the question on duration of residence in the previous dwelling which provides, for the first time, a full picture of completed durations of residence.

Within the confines of this paper, we have been able to explore only a fraction of the potential offered by these data. We have established how the median duration of stay varies across the life course and offers an alternative to the conventional statistic reporting proportions who moved in a given time interval. We have shown how this measure varies across space, with generally shorter durations of residence in remote communities, at young adult ages and among older people. We have also illustrated the considerable heterogeneity which exists in regard to population movement. For example, among young adults (always identified as the most mobile group in the population) we find a substantial group who have not moved for more than a decade, whereas at older ages, conventionally regarded as the most stable, more than 1 in 5 had changed residence within the last three years. Data on previous residence allowed us to chart the rate at which individual cohorts progressively moved from their earlier dwellings, and coupling these data with duration in current residence provided the basis for a crude segmentation of chronic movers and longer-term stayers. One key benefit of surveys is in providing information on reasons for movement and, combining these responses with other housing and labour force statistics, we were able to tease out the differences between these two groups which represent polar opposites on the mobility continuum.

Population mobility is a complex phenomenon. Most people move multiple times during their lives, and these changes of residence occur in response to the interplay of opportunities and constraints in various life domains: family, work, education, health, and so on. Understanding the causes and consequences of these moves, and their underlying dynamics, calls for considerable detail as to their timing, context and fit within the lifecourse. Ultimately, such understanding requires detailed residential life histories which track individual moves through time situated within the family and household context so as to link these with contingent events such as family formation and changes in employment. The 2008 NATSISS falls well short of this aspirational goal, but nevertheless it serves a valuable purpose in providing an alternative perspective on Indigenous population mobility and opening the way for innovative methods of analysis. The challenge for the 2014 survey is to shape a more wide-ranging module on mobility that encompasses the material collected in both 2002 and 2008, and builds a broader framework linking mobility to other lifecourse events.

References

Altman, J. C. (ed.) 1992. *A National Survey of Indigenous Australians: Options and Implications*, CAEPR Research Monograph No. 3, CAEPR, ANU, Canberra.

—— and Taylor, J. 1996. 'Statistical needs in Indigenous affairs: future options and implications', in J. C. Altman and J. Taylor (eds), *The 1994 National Aboriginal and Torres Strait Islander Survey: Findings and Future Prospects*, CAEPR Research Monograph No. 11, CAEPR, ANU, Canberra.

Australian Institute of Health and Welfare/Australian Institute of Family Studies n.d. Closing the Gap Clearinghouse, viewed 2 July 2012, available at <www.aihw.gov.au/closingthegap/>

Bell, M. 1992. *Internal Migration in Australia, 1981–1986*, AGPS, Canberra.

—— 2004. 'Measuring temporary mobility: dimensions and issues', Paper presented at the Council for Australasian University Tourism and Hospitality Education Conference Session on Tourism and Temporary Mobilities, 10–13 February, Brisbane.

—— 1995. *Internal Migration in Australia, 1986–1991: Overview Report*, AGPS, Canberra.

——, Charles-Edwards, E., Kupiszewski, M., Stillwell, J. and Zhu, Y. 2011. 'A global inventory of internal migration', Paper presented to the 6th *International Conference on Population Geographies*, 14–17 June, Umea University, Sweden.

—— and Maher, C. 1995. *Internal Migration in Australia, 1986–1991: The Labour Force*, AGPS, Canberra.

Biddle, N. 2010. 'Indigenous migration and the labour market: A cautionary tale', *Australian Journal of Labour Economics*, 13 (3): 313–30.

——, Taylor, J. and Yap, M. 2009. 'Are the gaps closing? Regional trends and forecasts of Indigenous employment', *Australian Journal of Labour Economics*, 12 (3): 263–81.

Commonwealth of Australia 1991. *Recommendations of the Royal Commission into Aboriginal Deaths in Custody*, AGPS, Canberra.

Gray, A. 1989. 'Aboriginal migration to the cities', *Journal of the Australian Population Association*, 6 (2): 122–44.

Gray, M. and Hunter, B. H. 2011. 'Changes in Indigenous labour force status: Establishing employment as a social norm?', *CAEPR Topical Issue 2011/7*, CAEPR, ANU, Canberra.

Gregory, B. 2006. 'Asking the right questions?', in B. H. Hunter (ed.), *Assessing the Evidence on Indigenous Socioeconomic Outcomes: A Focus on the 2002 NATSISS*, CAEPR Research Monograph No. 26, ANU E Press, Canberra.

Halfacree, K. and Boyle, P. 1993. 'The challenge facing migration research: The case for a biographical approach', *Progress in Human Geography,* 17 (3): 333–48.

Hughes, H. 2007. *Lands of Shame: Aboriginal and Torres Strait Islander 'Homelands' in Transition*, The Centre for Independent Studies, Sydney.

Hugo, G. 1988. 'Population transitions in Australia', in R. L. Heathcote and J. A. Mabbutt (eds), *Land Water and People: Geographical Essays in Australian Resource Management*, Allen and Unwin, Sydney.

Kinfu, Y. 2005. 'Spatial mobility among indigenous Australians', *Working Papers in Demography No. 97*, Department of Demography, ANU, Canberra.

Miller, M. (Chairman) 1985. *Report of the Committee of Review of Aboriginal Employment and Training Programs*, AGPS, Canberra.

Rogers, A. and Castro, L. J. 1981. *Model Migration Schedules*, International Institute for Applied Systems Analysis, Research report RR-81-30, Laxenburg, Austria.

Skeldon, R. 1990. *Population Mobility in Developing Countries: A Reinterpretation*, Bellhaven Press, London.

—— 1997. *Migration and Development: A Global Perspective*, Longman, London.

Snipp, M. 2004. 'American Indians and geographic mobility: Some parameters for public policy', in J. Taylor and M. Bell (eds), *Population Mobility and Indigenous Peoples in Australasia and North America*, Routledge, London.

Taylor, J. 2006. 'Population and diversity: Policy implications of emerging Indigenous demographic trends', *CAEPR Discussion Paper No. 283*, CAEPR, ANU, Canberra.

—— 2008. 'Indigenous peoples and indicators of well-being: Australian perspectives on United Nations global frameworks', *Social Indicators Research*, 87: 111–26.

—— 2011. 'Postcolonial transformation of the Australian Indigenous population', *Geographical Research*, 49 (3): 286–300.

—— and Bell, M. 1996. 'Indigenous peoples and population mobility: the view from Australia', *International Journal of Population Geography*, 2 (2): 153–69.

—— and —— 2004. 'Continuity and change in Indigenous Australian population mobility', in J. Taylor and M. Bell (eds), *Population Mobility and Indigenous Peoples in Australasia and North America*, Routledge, London.

—— and —— 2011. 'Towards comparative measures of circulation: Insights from Indigenous Australia', *Population Space and Place*, available at <DOI: 10.1002/psp.695>

—— and Kinfu, Y. 2006. 'Differentials and determinants of Indigenous population mobility', in B. H. Hunter (ed.), *Assessing the Evidence on Indigenous Socioeconomic Outcomes: A Focus on the 2002 NATSISS*, CAEPR Research Monograph No. 26, ANU E Press, Canberra.

Yu, P. 2011. 'The power of data in Aboriginal hands', Paper presented at the *Social Science Perspectives on the 2008 National Aboriginal and Torres Strait Islander Survey* Conference, 11–12 April, ANU, Canberra.

Zelinsky, W. 1971. 'The hypothesis of the mobility transition', *Geographical Review*, 61: 219–49.

3. Fertility and the demography of Indigenous Australians: What can the NATSISS 2008 tell us?

Kim Johnstone and Ann Evans

The primary concerns of demographers relate to population size, distribution and composition – how big the population is; the rate of population growth; the population's age and gender profiles; and where people are located. There are three components that drive population size and composition changes (or stasis) over time:

- fertility: the number of live births within a population, with a particular interest in the age women have babies and how many they have over their life time

- mortality: not only how many people die, but also what age they die, and

- migration: where are people moving to and from, how long are they moving for, how old are they when they move (Swanson and Siegel 2004).

To understand the demography of Indigenous Australians these are fundamental components that require investigation, and this necessitates counts of people, births and deaths by the Indigenous status of individuals. In Australia our statistical systems remain less than reliable in terms of providing us with population data for the Indigenous population (Johnstone 2009; Taylor 2009). Indeed, Len Smith described Australia's inability to reliably measure Indigenous life expectancy 'a frank failure of the statistical system' (Smith, Barnes and Choi 2008). This paucity of good quality data for Australia's Indigenous population means specialised data systems such as the National Aboriginal and Torres Strait Islander Social Survey (NATSISS) are particularly welcomed. As Taylor (2009: 119) noted in relation to research on Indigenous demography:

The unfolding National Aboriginal and Torres Strait Islander Social Survey program conducted by the Australian Bureau of Statistics (ABS) also now provides an improved basis for establishing proximate determinants (the drivers of fertility change).

This opportunity has not been realised, as the NATSISS 2008 provides very little insight into the demography of Indigenous Australians because the data relating to most demographic processes and events are simply unavailable. This chapter argues that the absence of questions relating to Indigenous demography *per se* from the NATSISS 2008, particularly fertility, represents a lost opportunity.

It outlines what is known about Indigenous demography in Australia, with a particular focus on fertility. Using fertility as a case study, the paper looks at what data are available from other sources and highlights Australia's knowledge gaps based on these data. The chaper closes by exploring what knowledge could have been gained by the inclusion of fertility questions in the NATSISS and discusses the policy implications of properly understanding the fertility drivers of population change.

Demography of Indigenous Australians: What do we know?

Mortality, particularly life expectancy at birth, has been the headline population indicator for Australian Government 'closing the gap' policies with Indigenous populations experiencing higher death rates at all ages compared to non-Indigenous Australians (ABS 2009). The difficulties associated with reporting changes to Indigenous life expectancy at birth has led to a reassessment of the method used to calculate life expectancy (ABS 2008a) and work is underway to improve the counting of Indigenous deaths (for example, through data linkage projects such as SA-NT DataLink). Even with improved counting of Indigenous deaths, however, there remain issues in understanding population mortality measures, particularly over time, because of changing population counts in the census that affect denominator populations (Cunningham 1998).

As Taylor and Bell (Chapter 2, this volume) have shown, analysis of Indigenous population movements is limited by data sources failing to link population movements to contingent events. That said, a higher than average migration rate is apparent – with median duration for residence in a house of less than four years. There is a higher probability of moving house among Indigenous people who are renting or unemployed, although living remotely reduces the propensity to move. There is decidedly more uncertainty around the measurement of short-term, circular mobility (Morphy 2010; Prout 2008) and there is remarkably little known about how population mobility might affect population data collection processes (Johnstone 2011; Zhao et al. 2009).

Fertility levels among Indigenous women in Australia are not high, with total fertility rates (TFRs) of less than three births per woman (ABS 2010). The stand out characteristic of Indigenous fertility is the young age that women have children. Fig. 3.1 shows that over the 10-year period for which fertility data by Indigenous status are available nationally, the number of babies born to Indigenous women (TFR) was relatively stable to 2007 when it started rising. This pattern of rising fertility from 2007 is also seen in the teenage fertility rates, which are exceptionally high (Fig. 3.2).

Fig. 3.1 Total fertility rates, Indigenous and total populations, Australia, 1998–2009

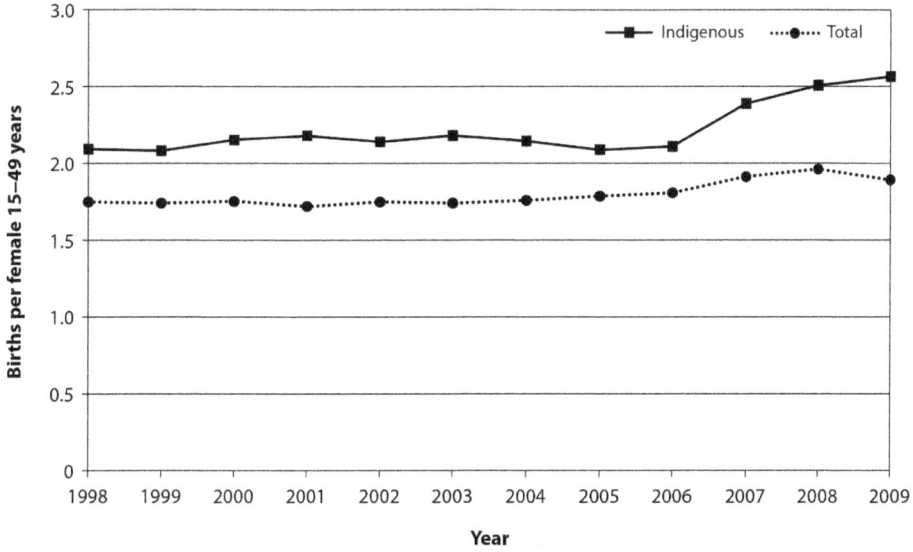

Source: ABS 2010

Fig. 3.2 Teenage fertility rates, Indigenous and total populations, Australia, 1998–2009

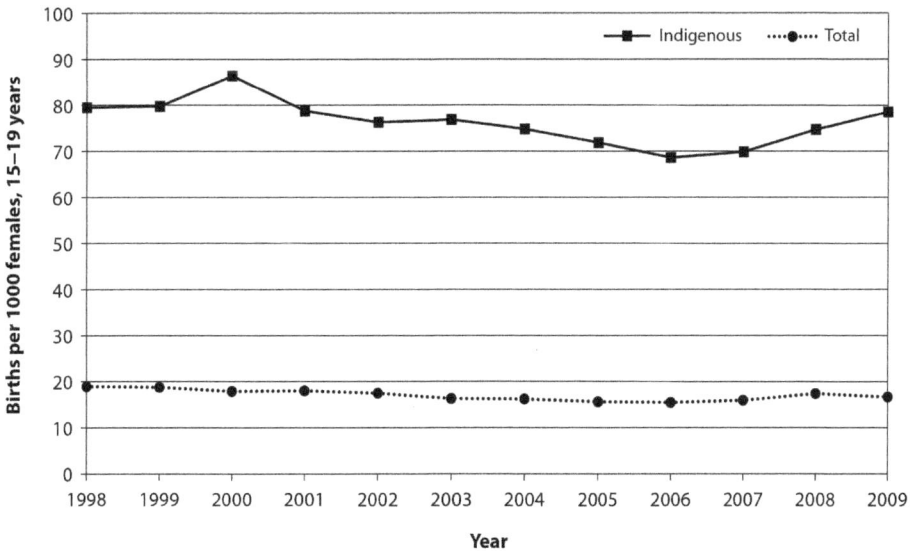

Source: ABS 2010

Despite indications of rising fertility in recent years among Indigenous women in Australia, any apparent trends must be viewed with caution. There are significant caveats on the data because of ever improving collection of birth registration information by Indigenous status. In 2007 it became a requirement that births had to be registered with the Registrar of Births, Deaths and Marriages in the State or Territory where the birth took place in order for mothers to receive the 'baby bonus', an Australian Government payment to mothers following the live birth of a child (Department of Families, Housing, Community Services and Indigenous Affairs (FaHCSIA) 2009). Some States have experienced notable under-registration of Indigenous births in the past (Gerber 2009a, 2009b; Orenstein 2008) and the 'baby bonus' requirement will have obvious flow on effects for fertility rates based on registrations.

Fertility rates based on vital registration data are also affected by the temporal births data reflecting date of birth registration rather than date of birth. Late registrations are thus important in some jurisdictions where there may be significant delays in processing registration and concentrated efforts to clear a backlog for a short period of time. Efforts to ensure all citizens have a birth certificate can also contribute to late registrations, as happened in Dubbo (New South Wales) in 2008 when school-age children needed a birth certificate to participate in sports activities (ABC News 2008). These data caveats are not insignificant, and the issues with registration differ across State and Territory lines.

Fig. 3.3 Indigenous age-specific and total fertility rates, Australian States and Territories, 2009

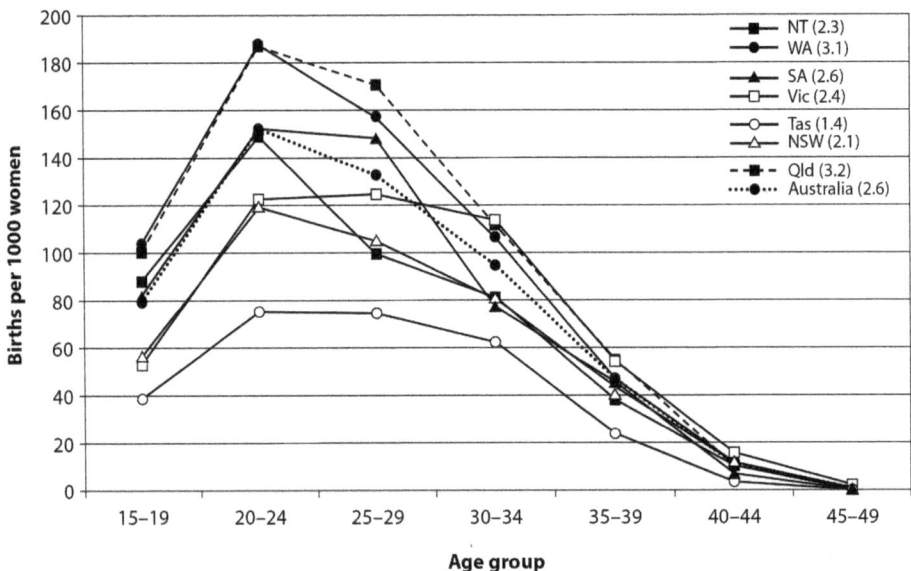

Indigenous age-specific fertility rates across Australia's States and Territories are shown in Fig. 3.3, and in each State and Territory fertility rates are highest among Indigenous women aged 20–24 years. This is notably younger than for Australia as a whole, where fertility is highest in the 30–34 year age group (ABS 2010). There are differences across the States and Territories, with Tasmania having the lowest fertility rates for all age groups. Queensland and Western Australia have the highest fertility, most notably at the youngest ages. This is a recent pattern for these two states, however, as up to 2007 (from the time State/Territory comparisons have been available) the Northern Territory has had the highest fertility among Indigenous women. Northern Territory rates have not risen from 2007 as they have for Queensland and Western Australia and data collection issues are likely influencing trends in these jurisdictions. The Northern Territory rate stands out compared to the other jurisdictions because the peak childbearing at ages 20–24 years is notably higher than at ages 25–29 years, whereas elsewhere the difference is less marked.

These State and Territory differences, and regional investigations of Indigenous fertility patterns (Johnstone 2011; Taylor, Brown and Bell 2006) provide a strong case for looking at fertility by remoteness classifications, particularly across Northern Australia, rather than jurisdictional boundaries. This is where national survey data can be particularly useful because they are not constrained by eight different data collection and processing agencies.

Data sources that help us to understand Indigenous fertility in Australia

While this paper argues that the NATSISS is an appropriate tool for capturing information about Indigenous fertility, an argument for the preclusion of any demography-related questions can be made if the same data are captured elsewhere. This section outlines other sources of data that are available for analysis of Indigenous fertility in Australia.

Vital registration data (on which the figures for this paper are based) are collected by each jurisdiction's Registrar of Births, Deaths and Marriages, and collated by the ABS. They provide information about Indigenous status of the mother, father and child (fertility rates in this paper are based on births to Indigenous mothers only). Other information includes age of parents, place of usual residence, occupation, and country of birth of parents. From 2007, data on parity (or the number of children ever born to the mother) for all previous births has been collected. As already noted, there are issues with completeness of registration for Indigenous births across different jurisdictions and delayed registration. Vital registration data are generally available by year of registration rather than year of the baby's birth, which can affect trend analysis. There are also issues of numerator and denominator mismatch, particularly going back in time with population (denominator) undercounts being greater the further back in time you go (Johnstone 2009).

The other main source of births data is the perinatal data collection, which is collated nationally from State/Territory collections. The perinatal data set records the Indigenous status of the mother, her age, and usual place of residence alongside a range of information about pregnancy and birth by the year the birth took place. Variables available in this data set include number of antenatal visits, type of birth, birthweight, number of post-natal days in hospital, and so forth (Leeds et al. 2007). For the demographer, one of the most important aspects relates to parity information, which enables investigation of the timing and spacing of births, and in particular, changes to these over time. In some States, the perinatal data provide a more accurate count of births than the vital registration data (Parr, Culpin and Wilson 2008) but there are issues with accuracy of identification of Indigenous status in some States (Robertson, Lumley and Berg 1995). It is also important to be mindful that the differences between the perinatal and vital registration data sets can result in different trends if longitudinal analysis is carried out (Johnstone 2010). As ever, there are also issues of numerator and denominator mismatch. Children identified as Indigenous may have a mother who is not Indigenous. Therefore, calculating Indigenous fertility rates results in some children being included in the numerator whose mother is not included in the denominator.

Prior to the inclusion of an Indigenous identifier in the vital registration and perinatal data sets, the quinquennial census was the primary source of information about Indigenous fertility in Australia (Gray 1983). The most important question for fertility analysis asks women aged 15 years of age and older how many children they have ever had born alive. This question was asked prior to 1986 but it only elicited information about number of children ever-born from ever-married women or currently married women, and not asked of Indigenous women for inclusion in the national census counts prior to 1971. A notable advantage of the census for fertility analysis is that the problem of matching numerators and denominators is avoided.

The census data cannot be used uncritically, however, because of undercount and non-response. In 2006, for example, the 2006 post-enumeration survey showed the Indigenous population was undercounted by 11.5 per cent across Australia (ABS 2007). Of women who answered the question about the number of children they have ever born alive, 5 per cent did not provide a response to the Indigenous status question. Of the women older than 15 years of age who did identify as Indigenous, 8 per cent did not answer the question on how many children they had ever had (ABS 2008b). Moreover, observations of census data collection in remote Indigenous communities found that often only currently living children were counted when census forms were filled in (Morphy et al. 2007). These factors combine to make fertility analysis based on the census indicative at best.

National estimates of Indigenous fertility have also been derived from a question included in NATSISS 1994 and NATSISS 2002, asking women for the number of children they have ever had born alive (Kinfu 2005). The utility of these earlier NATSISS data is their inclusion in a questionnaire that captured a range of data that allowed exploration of influences on fertility outcomes, in particular questions relating to cultural participation and cultural identification and health status. One of the shortcomings of the NATSISS data for fertility analysis is that at the sub-national level the numbers are too small in the sample to enable access to data for multi-variate analysis (Johnstone 2011). Another issue has been the lack of use made of the children ever born question from the 1994 or 2002 NATSISS data – there have simply been too few demographers who have been able to prioritise the work.

Indigenous fertility in Australia: Knowledge gaps

While the data sources detailed in the previous section indicate relatively rich sources of data, they are inadequate for answering some key questions about Indigenous fertility in Australia. Primary among these, are questions about future fertility trends for Indigenous women. Following dramatic fertility declines in the 1960s and 1970s among Indigenous Australians it was assumed these fertility declines would continue and that Indigenous women would defer childbearing from young to older ages (Gray 1983, 1990). Quite simply, these expected fertility declines have not eventuated. While there is some evidence of deferred childbearing, it is not of the same magnitude of the patterns seen among the non-Indigenous population (Johnstone 2011). There is not enough information to make an informed estimate of what future trends will look like.

There are significant knowledge gaps surrounding Indigenous fertility differences across rural-remote and urban parts of Australia. International and historical fertility patterns across diverse populations have shown lower fertility in cities compared to rural areas (Carmichael and McDonald 2003; Pool 1991) and it is assumed the same holds true for Indigenous Australians. The work of Taylor, Brown and Bell (2006) point to regional fertility differences for the Indigenous population outside the populous eastern seaboard, with higher fertility in the savanna regions compared to arid zones. Research by Johnstone (2010, 2011) in the Northern Territory points to an emerging trend of higher Indigenous fertility in urban settings compared to rural and remote regions.

The data to ascertain if this trend is an artefact of data collection systems or attributable to other factors such as contraception, health status, or family commitments are unavailable.

Remarkably little is also known about the factors that influence when Indigenous women have children. The timing of childbearing is very important in order to understand population dynamics (e.g. population ageing, dependency ratios). The research that has been done shows that Indigenous women who are employed, who finished high school or who have post-secondary qualifications have less children (albeit not by large margins) and tend to start childbearing later (again, not by long periods) (Gray 1989; Johnstone 2011; Khalidi 1989). Very little is known, however, about the sequence of timing for children, education and employment among Indigenous women. We don't know what will influence Indigenous women's decisions to have children at a particular age. Young childbearing could reflect a high level of family support available to mothers, a lack of other options for young women, lack of access to contraception, a high rate of sexual assault, or deliberate entry to the 'age grades' of adulthood by becoming a mother. All are plausible and supported by small, qualitative studies but none are able to be substantiated at the population level and lead to conclusions about what may happen in the future.

In a similar vein, nothing is known about the factors influencing how many children Indigenous women will have. There is a huge knowledge gap around how many children Indigenous women want to have or how many they will have. It is simply impossible to determine if the relatively low TFR reflects Indigenous women's wanted family size, or whether it is the impact of secondary infertility. The high recorded levels of sexually transmitted infections and health issues that we know affect fertility (e.g. diabetes, smoking) means Indigenous women might be having fewer children than they want.

Understanding these fertility issues is important in order to understand what is happening with the Indigenous population and to establish some reasonable parameters for what will happen into the future. This is essential for planning what services and infrastructure are needed for the birth cohorts being born to Indigenous mothers (see Fig. 3.4). Despite a relatively stable TFR, the number of Indigenous babies being born each year continues to grow (and Fig. 3.4 excludes Indigenous babies born to non-Indigenous mothers). There are implications for housing – among a population for whom overcrowding is well recognised as a problem, for schools, for health services, and so forth. More importantly, there is great uncertainty about what these birth cohorts of babies born to Indigenous mothers will do when they themselves reach childbearing ages.

Fig. 3.4 Total fertility rates and cohort size, births to Indigenous women in Australia, 1998–2010

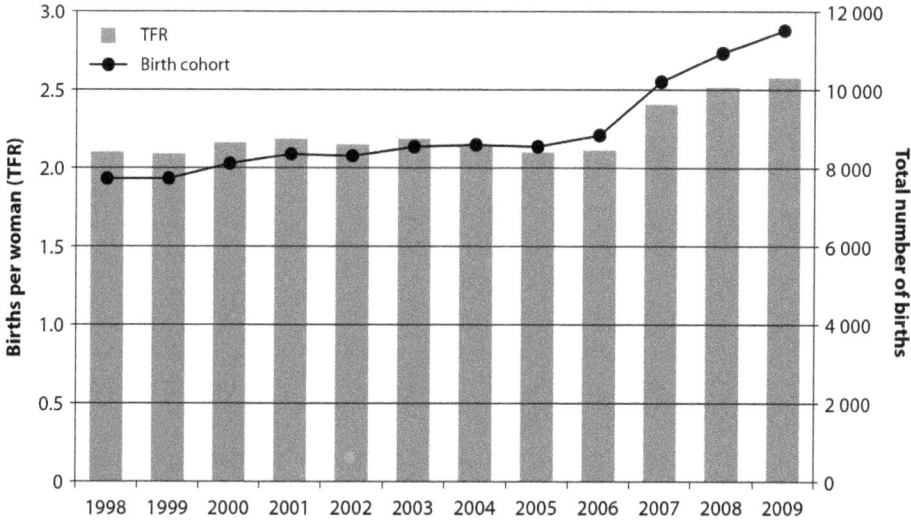

Source: ABS 2010

Understanding the age structure of fertility is critical for the implementation of social policy. In the area of education and employment, for example, any success in 'closing the gap' when women are having babies at a young age will necessitate the provision of child care so women can attend school or go to work. There are health implications for young mothers having babies, and also for the children of those young mothers, as well as socioeconomic impacts (Bradbury 2006; Hendrickson 1998; Jeon, Kalb and Vu 2008; Murphy and Carr 2007).

If the fundamentals of population size and structure are unclear there will always be questions of doubt about the validity of other research that requires a population denominator. It is not just demography, but most social science and epidemiological research that suffer from a less than complete knowledge about Indigenous populations.

Including fertility in the NATSISS

While the NATSISS itself cannot be a catch-all solution to answering these questions about what will happen with Indigenous fertility into the future, its role as a national survey specifically targeting Aboriginal and Torres Strait Islander peoples means it is uniquely placed to help better understand Indigenous population dynamics. In the first instance, including a fertility question in the NATSISS would provide another data source with which to compare the routine data collections. There are important questions about whether all births to Indigenous women are counted in the vital registration and perinatal data sets, and any data source that allows a check and balance is useful. Even for those correlations that are collected in the census such as age, education, employment and income, the NATSISS provides a more reliable source of information because of the way the questions are asked and information elicited from respondents. There are different introductory questions and explanations, and data collection mechanisms that mean the NATSISS results are probably more complete than census data.

The NATSISS 2008 provides its own important clues as to the importance of understanding Indigenous fertility better. Nearly 1 in 10 respondents to the NATSISS 2008 identified pregnancy as a stressor (9%); 2 per cent of the sample found pregnancy a personal stressor. (Unfortunately we can't use these data as a fertility proxy because there would have been people surveyed who experienced pregnancy but were not stressed, or did not view the pregnancy of a friend or family member as a stressor.) That so many respondents found pregnancy to be stressful indicates that it is an area about which more needs to be known.

Because of the NATSISS survey structure, it could provide important information about the timing and spacing of Indigenous childbearing if it included questions about mother's age at the birth of each child. The NATSISS could also include questions about future children, childbearing intentions and ideal family size. In order to understand if education and employment affect family size, and how they might do so, questions about women's education levels and employment status at the time each child was born are important. At the very least, including education and employment status for a woman's first birth provides important clues to the timing of these events.

Ultimately, including a question on parity in future NATSISS would enable investigation of fertility estimates alongside important proximate determinants that are unable to be explored from census data alone. One of the missed opportunities for NATSISS 2008 is an inability to look at the results from a new question on length of time in the workforce alongside number of children ever born. The NATSISS questions on cultural participation and cultural identification, despite their constraints, also provide an opportunity to look at what factors beyond socioeconomic correlates might influence fertility decisions. Other correlates that would have been useful to look at alongside the children ever born question include childcare used, health status, neighbourhood problems, and discrimination.

There is an overwhelming need to better understand Indigenous fertility and the exclusion of the children ever born question from the NATSISS 2008 represents a lost opportunity. If in the future questions about fertility are to be included in the NATSISS, these should focus on timing and spacing of childbearing and try to gather information that might help explain influences on childbearing outcomes.

References

ABC News 2008. 'Birth certificate scheme targets Dubbo indigenous population', viewed 29 September 2011, available at <http://www.abc.net.au/news/stories/2008/03/12/2187060.htm>

Australian Bureau of Statistics (ABS) 2007. *Population Distribution, Aboriginal and Torres Strait Islander Australians,* cat. no. 4705.0, ABS, Canberra.

—— 2008a. *Discussion Paper: Assessment of Methods for Developing Life Tables for Aboriginal and Torres Strait Islander Australians,* cat. no. 3238.0.55.002, ABS, Canberra.

—— 2008b. *Population Characteristics, Aboriginal and Torres Strait Islander Australians, 2006,* cat. no. 4713.0, ABS, Canberra.

—— 2009. *2008 Deaths Australia,* cat. no. 3302.0, ABS, Canberra.

—— 2010. *Births Australia 2009,* cat. no. 3301.0, ABS, Canberra.

Bradbury, B. 2006. 'Disadvantage among Australian young mothers', *Australian Journal of Labour Economics,* 9 (2): 147–71.

Carmichael, G. A. and McDonald, P. 2003. 'Fertility trends and differentials', in S. Khoo and P. McDonald (eds), *The Transformation of Australia's Population 1970-2030,* UNSW Press, Sydney.

Cunningham, J. 1998. 'Implications of changing Indigenous populations estimates for monitoring health trends', *Australasian Epidemiologist,* 5 (1): 6–8.

Department of Families, Housing, Community Services and Indigenous Affairs (FaHCSIA) 2009. 'Baby Bonus – introducing birth registration as a condition, viewed 29 March 2011, available from <http://www.fahcsia.gov.au/about/publicationsarticles/corp/BudgetPAES/budget2007-08/budget2007-07_wnwd/Pages/Budget2007-07_wnwd-07.aspx>

Gerber, P. 2009a. 'Making visible the problem of invisibility', *Law Institute Journal,* 83 (10): 52–5.

—— 2009b. 'Making Indigenous Australians "disappear". Problems arising from our birth registration systems', *Alternative Law Journal,* 34 (3): 158–67.

Gray, A. 1983. Australian Aboriginal Fertility in Decline, PhD Thesis, ANU, Canberra.

—— 1989. 'Aboriginal fertility: Trends and prospects', *NCEPH Working Paper No. 6,* National Centre for Epidemiology and Population Health, ANU, Canberra.

—— 1990. 'Aboriginal fertility: Trends and prospects', *Journal of the Australian Population Association,* 17 (1): 57–77.

Hendrickson, J. 1998. 'The risk of teen mothers having low birth weight babies: Implications of recent medical research for school health personnel', *Journal of School Health,* 68 (7), 271–75.

Jeon, S., Kalb, G. and Vu, H. 2008. 'The dynamics of welfare participation among women who experienced teenage motherhood in Australia', *Working Paper No. 22/08,* Melbourne Institute of Applied Economic and Social Research, University of Melbourne, Melbourne.

Johnstone, K. 2009. 'Indigenous fertility rates – how reliable are they?, *People and Place,* 17 (4): 29–39.

—— 2010. 'Indigenous fertility in the Northern Territory of Australia – what do we know? (what can we know?)', *Journal of Population Research,* 27 (3): 169–92.

—— 2011. Indigenous Fertility in the Northern Territory of Australia: Stalled Demographic Transition?, PhD Thesis, ANU, Canberra, viewed 3 July 2012, available at <http://hdl.handle.net/1885/8742>

Khalidi, N. A. 1989. 'Aboriginal fertility in Central Australia', *NCEPH Working Paper No. 8,* National Centre for Epidemiology and Population Health, ANU, Canberra.

Kinfu, Y. 2005. 'Aboriginal child mortality in Australia: Recent levels and covariates', in B. H. Hunter (ed.), *Assessing The Evidence on Indigenous Socioeconomic Outcomes: A Focus on the 2002 NATSISS,* CAEPR Research Monograph No. 26, ANU E Press, Canberra.

Leeds, K., Gourley, M., Laws, P., Zhang, J., Al-Yaman, F. and Sullivan, E. A. 2007. *Indigenous Mothers and Their Babies, Australia 2001–2004,* AIHW cat. no. PER 38, Periantal Statistics Series no. 19, AIHW, Canberra.

Morphy, F. 2010. '(Im)mobility: Regional population structures in Aboriginal Australia', *Australian Journal of Social Issues*, 45 (3): 363–82.

——, Sanders, W., Taylor, J. and Thorburn, K. 2007. 'Appendix B: Commentary on the 2006 Interviewer Household Form', in F. Morphy (ed.), *Agency, Contingency and Census Process: Observations of the 2006 Indigenous Enumeration Strategy in Remote Aboriginal Australia*, CAEPR Research Monograph No. 28, CAEPR, ANU, Canberra.

Murphy, E. and Carr, D. 2007. *Powerful Partners. Adolescent Girls' Education and Delayed Childbearing*, Population Reference Bureau, Washington, DC.

Orenstein, J. 2008. 'The difficulties faced by Aboriginal Victorians in obtaining identification', *Indigenous Law Bulletin*, 7 (8): 14–17.

Parr, A., Culpin, A. and Wilson, T. 2008. 'Estimating and projecting NSW fertility', Paper presented to the *Australian Population Association 14th Biennial Conference 2008*, Alice Springs.

Pool, I. 1991. *Te Iwi Maori. A New Zealand Population Past, Present & Projected*, Auckland University Press, Auckland.

Prout, S. 2008. 'On the move? Indigenous temporary mobility practices in Australia', *CAEPR Working Paper No. 50*, CAEPR, ANU, Canberra.

Robertson, H., Lumley, J. and Berg, S. 1995. 'How midwives identify women as Aboriginal or Torres Strait Islanders', *Australian College of Midwives Journal*, 8 (3): 26–9.

Smith, L., Barnes, T. and Choi, C. 2008. 'Closing the gap? Monitoring trends in Indigenous Australian's life expectancy', Paper presented to the *Australian Population Association 14th Biennial Conference 2008*, Alice Springs.

Swanson, D. A. and Siegel, J. S. 2004. 'Introduction', in J. S. Siegel and D. A. Swanson (eds), *The Methods and Materials of Demography. Second Edition*, Elsevier Academic Press, San Diego.

Taylor, J. 2009. 'Indigenous demography and public policy in Australia: Population or peoples?', *Journal of Population Research*, 26 (2): 115–30.

——, Brown, D. and Bell, M. 2006. *Population Dynamics and Demographic Accounting in Arid and Savanna Australia: Methods, Issues and Outcomes*, DKCRC Research Report, Desert Knowledge CRC, Alice Springs.

Zhao, Y., Guthridge, S., Li, S. and Connors, C. 2009. 'Patterns of mortality in Indigenous adults in the the Northern Territory, 1998-2003', (Letter to the Editor), *Medical Journal of Australia*, 191: 581–82.

4. Does the 2008 NATSISS underestimate the prevalence of high risk Indigenous drinking?

Tanya Chikritzhs and Wenbin Liang

The 2008 National Aboriginal and Torres Strait Islander Social Survey (NATSISS) estimated that some 9 per cent of Indigenous males and 3.7 per cent of Indigenous females (6.3% for males and females combined) consumed alcohol at levels which placed them at high risk of chronic harm (Australian Bureau of Statistics (ABS) 2010a). This was similar to that estimated by the 2002 NATSISS of 5.6 per cent for males and females combined (ABS 2004).[1] Levels of alcohol use which place the drinker at high risk for chronic harm were defined by the 2001 National Health and Medical Research Council (NHRMC) guidelines as consuming, on average, more than six standard drinks a day for males and more than four for a female. The levels themselves were established based on studies of the relationship between alcohol exposure and alcohol-attributable chronic harms (NHRMC 2001). Chronic alcohol-attributable harms include conditions which result from long term exposure to consistent heavy alcohol use including, in particular, alcoholic liver cirrhosis, alcohol dependence (a chronic condition by definition) and a range of less prevalent conditions (e.g. alcoholic pancreatitis, some cancers for which alcohol is partially attributable).[2]

Chikritzhs and Brady (2006a, 2007) argued that the 2002 NATSISS substantially underestimated actual levels of chronic risky/high risk alcohol use in the Indigenous population. They compared the results from the 2002 NATSISS to other national surveys of Indigenous alcohol use and general population surveys and found the outcomes from the 2002 NATSISS to be implausibly low. The 2002 NATSISS estimated that about 15.2 per cent of Indigenous Australians (aged 15 years and over) drank at levels that placed them either at risk or high-risk[3] for chronic alcohol-related harm (ABS 2004) – the 2008 estimate was similar at 17.2 per cent (ABS 2010a).[4] A particularly stark comparison was drawn with the 1994 National Drug Strategy Household Survey: Urban Aboriginal and Torres Strait

---

1   For comparison purposes, the 2002 and 2008 surveys are methodologically similar (ABS 2010b).
2   It should be noted that the 2001 NHMRC guidelines have been superseded by the 2009 NHMRC guidelines which recommend no more than 2 standard drinks per day on average and 4 standard drinks for a single occasion for both males and females.
3   'Risky use' is defined as more than 4 standard drinks per day for males and more than 2 standard drinks per day for females.
4   The 2002 NATSISS and 2008 NATSISS also estimated similar proportions of Indigenous people as drinking at risk/high risk levels for acute harm in the 2 weeks before the survey (35% and 37% respectively).

Islander Peoples Supplement[5] (Commonwealth Department of Human Services and Health (CDHSH) 1996; referred to below as the 1994 urban Indigenous survey) which estimated that over 50 per cent of regular Indigenous drinkers consumed alcohol at levels which placed them at risk or high risk of harm. The 1994 urban Indigenous survey also compared prevalence estimates of high risk consumption among regular Indigenous drinkers to regular non-Indigenous drinkers (from a 1993 urban general population survey), the ratio for which was about 5.4 (based on all respondents).[6] In other words, for every one high-risk regular drinker among the non-Indigenous population there were at least five Indigenous drinkers consuming alcohol at high risk levels (CDHSH 1996).

One of the main applications for surveys of alcohol and other drug use is the identification of the range and magnitude of use within a population and how it may differ among sub-populations. It is not unreasonable to expect that large national surveys of substance use can be relied upon as fairly accurate indicators of exposure and, by extension, likely levels of harms occurring due to problematic use. The reality, however, is that all alcohol surveys are prone to underestimating actual levels of use. Most surveys typically account for only 40 per cent to 60 per cent of known alcohol sales in a community (Knibbe and Bloomfield 2001), and Stockwell et al. (2008) have demonstrated that on average, respondents to the 2004 National Drug Strategy Household Survey (NDSHS) underestimated their consumption by about 28 per cent – largely due to recall bias. The factors which influence under-reporting in surveys may vary widely depending on the methods used and the population surveyed. Chikritzhs and Brady (2006a) highlighted three potential sources of underestimation in the 2002 NATSISS:

- the use of face-to-face interviews and lack of confidentiality for respondents
- problematic data collection methods, and
- exclusion of residents living in non-private dwellings. In relation to the alcohol component, little has changed for the 2008 NATSISS and these potential sources of error remain salient.

Given the limitations of surveys, triangulation with other data sources on harms and consumption is a useful means of verifying their veracity and highlighting discrepancies. Chikritzhs and Brady (2006a, 2006b) made a preliminary attempt to compare the risky/high risk prevalence estimates from the 2002 NATSISS to independent sources of information on alcohol-related deaths and hospitalisations comparing Indigenous and non-Indigenous people to the

---

5   Urban was defined as a minimum population of 1000.
6   Among all respondents, i.e. not restricted to drinkers. The ratio among only drinkers was about 6.6 (derived from CDHSH 1996: 30, Table 21; note that the relevant Table did not provide sex-specific proportions). This ratio is based on amounts usually consumed, harmful defined as more that 4 standard drinks for females and more than 6 standard drinks for males among current regular drinkers.

general population. They noted for instance that the Steering Committee for the Review of Government Service Provision (2005) cited 2002–03 Indigenous population rates for alcoholic liver disease and alcohol dependence which were 5 and 2.4 times higher respectively than for the non-Indigenous population. From 1990 to 1997, compared to their non-Indigenous counterparts, the Indigenous death rate from all wholly alcohol attributable conditions in Western Australia, South Australia and the Northern Territory combined was about 8 times higher for males and 16 times higher for females (Chikritzhs et al. 2000). Yet, the 2002 NATSISS indicated levels of chronic risky/high risk consumption among Indigenous people which were less than twice that for non-Indigenous people. More recently, despite the known and extreme disparity in alcohol-attributable death rates between Indigenous and non-Indigenous Australians (i.e. up to 800% greater for Indigenous people), a comparison of the 2008 NATSISS to the 2007 NDSHS of the general population (Australian Institute of Health and Welfare (AIHW) 2008) suggests that the discrepancy in the prevalence of high risk drinking between the two groups is only 67 per cent (i.e. 17.2% vs 10.3%).[7] As Chikritzhs and Brady (2006a) point out, the discord between rate of death from disease caused specifically by alcohol and apparent rate of exposure among the Indigenous compared to the general population is not easily reconciled.

In this chaper, we extend the triangulation approach taken by Chikritzhs and Brady (2006a, 2006b) to highlight the implausibility of the 2008 NATSISS. Alcoholic liver cirrhosis and alcohol dependence are two sentinel conditions well established as arising from long term (chronic) exposure to heavy alcohol use (NHMRC 2001; World Health Organization (WHO) 2000). Among death statistics, these two conditions are also relatively common causes of death compared to other wholly alcohol-attributable conditions (e.g. alcoholic cardiomyopathy, alcoholic gastritis, alcoholic pancreatitis). Our approach relies on comparing sex-specific Indigenous and non-Indigenous death rates for alcoholic liver cirrhosis and alcohol dependence while taking into account the magnitude of the populations at high risk indicated by the 2008 NATSISS and the 2007 NDSHS (i.e. the 'exposed' population). We begin this investigation *as if* the veracity of the 2007 NDSHS were not in question (i.e. not underestimated) and assuming that it gives a reasonable approximation of the true prevalence of high risk drinking for chronic harm in the general population. From this, we estimate the potential magnitude of underestimation of the actual proportion of the Indigenous high risk drinking population by the 2008 NATSISS.

---

7   Both the NDSHS and the NATSISS ask respondents to recall usual alcohol use in the past 12 months.

Method

Surveys

The estimated age and sex specific prevalence of high risk alcohol consumption for chronic harms for the Indigenous population was obtained from the 2008 NATSISS (ABS 2010a). The estimated age and sex specific prevalence of high risk alcohol consumption for chronic harms for the general population was obtained from the 2007 NDSHS report on first results (AIHW 2008).

The 2008 NATSISS included 7342 Indigenous respondents aged 15–64 years (ABS 2009) and the 2007 NDSHS included 23 356 respondents from the general population aged 14+ years (AIHW 2008).

Both the 2008 NATSISS and the 2007 NDSHS based their drinking prevalence estimates on levels defined by the 2001 NHMRC drinking guidelines. The 2001 NHMRC guidelines defined alcohol consumption which places the drinker at high risk for chronic harm (long-term harm) for males at seven or more standard drinks per day on average or 43 or more per week, and for females at five or more standard drinks per day on average or 29 or more per week. A standard Australian drink is considered to be 10 grams or 12.5 millilitres (mls) of pure alcohol (NHMRC 2001).

Both surveys asked respondents to recall and report their usual consumption over the past 12 months. In the NDSHS, respondents were asked to complete a graduated quantity frequency table and report their consumption in units of standard drinks with the aid of a show card. The NATSISS did not require respondents to report their consumption as numbers of standard drinks but asked respondents to report their usual consumption in terms of typical container sizes which were later converted into millilitres of pure alcohol by the ABS.

Respondents to the NDSHS self-complete their answers to substance use questions without the overview of an interviewer. Their responses (which do not include name or address details) were sealed in an envelope and returned to the field worker or mailed back to the collection agency. For the 2008 NATSISS, data were collected using face-to-face interviews and respondent answers were verbally related to, and recorded on a computer (for non-remote respondents) by the interviewer. Moreover, although the interviewer was instructed to suggest to respondents that the interview take place in a private, other household members may have been present.

Notably, the NATSISS procedure was somewhat different for questioning related to 'substance use' which included the misuse of prescription drugs and/or the use of illicit drugs such that:

> Due to the potentially sensitive nature of the questions, responses to these questions were voluntary. In non-remote areas, people answered questions through a voluntary self-completion substance use form. In remote areas, people were personally interviewed (ABS 2010b: no page numbers).

The 2007 NDSHS included a small number of Indigenous respondents (less than 2%) who were apparently included in the general population prevalence estimates. Given the likely negligible impact of a small number of Indigenous responses on the overall drinking prevalence of the entire sample it was deemed appropriate for the purposes of this analysis to consider the 2007 NDSHS sample representative of the non-Indigenous national population.

Death data

Unit records of Australian deaths reported from 2000 to 2006 were obtained from the ABS including primary cause of death (ICD-10 coded), age at death, sex, and year of death. Primary cause of death was used to identify deaths from alcoholic liver cirrhosis and alcohol dependence. Cause of death is usually determined by coronial officers. The reliability of Indigenous status flags for death records is high (Chikritzhs et al. 2004).

Estimated residential population

Estimated residential population (ERP) for the national non-Indigenous and Indigenous populations aged by five-year age cohorts (0–4, 5–9, 10–14, 15–19… 65+) and sex were obtained from the 2006 ABS Census (ABS 2007).

Analysis

Random effects panel Poisson regression modelling was used to estimate the sex-specific incidence risk ratio of alcohol caused death by Indigenous status. Poisson regression is preferable where counts of events are modelled and is suitable for small numbers of observations. Counts of deaths from 2000 to 2006 caused by alcoholic liver cirrhosis or alcohol dependence (for ages 15+) formed the dependent variable. Panels were determined by combinations of calendar years and age groups (15–19, 20–24, 25–29…65+).

The exposure variable was the number of people estimated to be at high risk for chronic alcohol-related harm in the Indigenous and non-Indigenous populations based on the population prevalence estimates for high risk chronic drinking derived from the 2008 NATSISS and the 2007 NDSHS. According to the surveys, the age- and gender-specific population supposed to have consumed alcohol at high risk levels was calculated by multiplying the prevalence of high risk drinking and population estimates from the census for each age-gender strata by Indigenous status. For example, the 2008 NATSISS estimated that 7.6 per cent of Indigenous males aged 25–29 years consumed alcohol at a high risk level for chronic harm and in 2006 the Indigenous male population in that age group was estimated to be 14 932, thus, the number of 25–30 year old Indigenous males estimated to be at high risk on the basis of the NATSISS was 1 135 (14 932*0.076). A similar procedure was followed to estimate the exposure variable for the non-Indigenous population, based on the age- and gender-specific population prevalence estimates reported by the 2007 NDSHS.

Results

Drinking prevalence estimates

The 2008 NATSISS and the 2007 NDSHS provided summaries of the prevalence of high risk drinking for chronic harm. Both were based on the 2001 NHMRC drinking guidelines for identifying high risk drinking for chronic harm and both asked respondents to report their usual consumption in the past 12 months. The summaries of the relevant survey results as they appear in AIHW (2008) and ABS (2010a) reports have been compiled in Table 4.1.

Table 4.1 High risk alcohol consumption, estimated Indigenous and non-Indigenous populations, Australia, 2007–08[a]

	Indigenous[b]				Non-Indigenous[c]		
	Male	Female	Total		Male	Female	Total
15–24	7.9	3.6	5.7	14–19	2.6	3.9	3.2
25–34	7.6	5.1	6.3	20–29	6.2	5.4	5.8
35–44	11.2	3.9	7.2	30–39	3.7	3.0	3.3
45–54	12.9	3.0	7.7	40–49	3.5	2.6	3.1
55+	6.9	2.6	4.5	50–59	5.1	2.7	3.9
				60+	2.5	0.8	1.6
Total	9.0	3.7	6.3	Total	3.9	2.8	3.4

a. The age groups provided in the summary reports of the two surveys were not identical.

b. From 2008 NATSISS.

c. From 2007 NDSHS.

As summarised in Table 4.2, the all-ages estimate of male Indigenous high risk drinking for chronic harm from the 2008 NATSISS was more than twice the estimate for non-Indigenous males made by the 2007 NDSHS. The Indigenous and non-Indigenous female estimates were notably similar. Overall, on the basis of the 2008 NATSISS, Indigenous drinkers at risk for chronic harms appear to outnumber non-Indigenous drinkers estimated by the 2007 NDSHS by 1.85 to 1.

Table 4.2 High risk alcohol consumption, all ages, Indigenous and non-Indigenous populations, Australia, 2007–08

	Indigenous[a]	Non-Indigenous[b]	Ratio
Male	9.0	3.9	2.31
Female	3.7	2.8	1.32
Rate ratio	2.4	1.4	
Total	6.3	3.4	1.85

a. From 2008 NATSISS.

b. From 2007 NDSHS.

Death rates and overall high risk drinking prevalence

As shown in Table 4.3, from 2000 to 2006 there were 5 065 non-Indigenous deaths and 425 Indigenous deaths (15+ years) attributed to either alcoholic liver cirrhosis or alcohol dependence. Adjusted for residential population, over the seven year period, this represented a population death rate of about 2.0 per 10 000 for the Indigenous population and 0.44 per 10 000 for the non-Indigenous population. Thus, for every 1 non-Indigenous death about 4.5 Indigenous people died from causes known to be attributable to chronic heavy alcohol use. The rate ratio for Indigenous versus non-Indigenous was particularly high for females. Although death records indicate that Indigenous females suffer a death rate from alcoholic liver cirrhosis and alcohol dependence almost eight times greater than their non-Indigenous counterparts, a comparison indicating the potential populations at risk yields only a marginal ratio of 1.30.

Table 4.3 Death rates from alcoholic liver cirrhosis and alcohol dependence, Indigenous and non-Indigenous population, Australia, 2000–06

	Number of deaths		Death rate per 10 000[a]		Death rate ratio	Prevalence estimate ratio
	Indigenous	Non-Indigenous	Indigenous	Non-Indigenous		
Male	266	3 985	2.58	0.71	3.64	2.31
Female	159	1 080	1.44	0.18	7.86	1.32
Total	425	5 065	2.00	0.44	4.52	1.85

a. This rate based on population aged 15+ not high risk population.

Source: ABS death unit records 2000–06

Regression analysis

Poisson regression modelling indicated that given high risk populations estimated by the NATSISS and the NDSHS, the death rate from either liver cirrhosis or alcohol dependence among high risk drinkers was about 2.2 (95% CI 1.96, 2.53) times higher for Indigenous compared to non-Indigenous males and about 7.2 (95% CI 6.14, 8.57) times higher among Indigenous females compared to non-Indigenous females (see Table 4.4).

For Indigenous deaths only, the incidence rate ratio (IRR) for females to males was 1.54 indicating that, based on exposure indicated by high risk drinking from the 2008 NATSISS, the death rate was greater for females. In the reverse, for the non-Indigenous population, the IRR was 0.50 indicating females were less likely to die from alcoholic liver cirrhosis and alcohol dependence.

Table 4.4 Deaths from alcoholic liver cirrhosis and alcohol dependence, by Indigenous status and gender (Poisson regression modelling), Australia, 2000–06[a]

	IRR	95% Confidence interval		P value
		Lower	Upper	
Indigenous status				
Males: Indigenous (1) vs non Indigenous (0)	2.22	1.96	2.52	0.000
Females: Indigenous (1) vs non Indigenous (0)	7.25	6.14	8.57	0.000
Sex				
Non-Indigenous: females (1) vs males (0)	0.50	0.47	0.54	0.000
Indigenous: females (1) vs males (0)	1.54	1.26	1.88	0.000

Number in sample = 5 490. Death rates for all wholly attributable conditions were also examined and similar outcomes found, see Appendix 4A Table 4A.1.

Source: ABS death unit records 2000–06

Using the Poisson regression results from Table 4.4 it is possible to estimate expected sex-specific ranges for the prevalence of drinking at high risk for chronic harm in the Indigenous population. The estimates below are based on the following assumptions:

- for any population, there is a linear relationship between the number of alcohol attributable deaths from alcoholic liver cirrhosis/alcohol dependence and the size of the population at high risk (i.e. as estimated by prevalence surveys of high risk chronic drinking)
- deaths from alcoholic liver cirrhosis and alcohol dependence arise from, and are representative of, a high risk chronic drinking sub-population
- the reporting of liver cirrhosis/alcohol deaths within sex-groups are not significantly influenced by Indigenous status, and

- the NDSHS consumption estimates approximate actual drinking levels in the non-Indigenous population (i.e. the NDSHS prevalence estimates are not substantial underestimates).

Indigenous males vs non-Indigenous males

Poisson regression on numbers of deaths due to alcohol-caused chronic disease indicated that for Indigenous males, the IRR was 2.2 times non-Indigenous deaths, within a range of 1.96 to 2.52. Since deaths are known, in order to bring the IRR to unity (i.e. the ratio of Indigenous to non-Indigenous = 1), the Indigenous population denominator, which signifies the population exposure to high risk alcohol use (based on prevalence from the 2008 NATSISS would need to increase substantially. This is described in Equation 1 below:

Equation 1

D = number of deaths
HRP = estimated high risk population as a proportion (from surveys)
M = male
i = Indigenous population
g= general population
IRR = incidence rate ratio

If, $(DMi/HRPMi)/(DMg/HRPMg)$ = IRR = 2.22,

Then, to make IRR equal 1, that is, $(DMi/HRPMi*X)/(DMg/HRPMg)$ = 1,

X must = 2.22 (i.e. $2.22*(1/X)$ = 1)

Thus, the actual proportion of Indigenous males drinking at high risk levels for chronic harm would be expected to occur within a range of 1.96 to 2.52 times that of the current estimated prevalence from the 2008 NATSISS (9.0%), which is between 17.6 per cent and 22.8 per cent.

Indigenous females vs non-Indigenous females

For females, Poisson regression results indicated between 6.14 and 8.57 times more deaths among the Indigenous compared to the non-Indigenous population. On this basis, and applying Equation 1 above (substituting the variables relevant to females, we would expect the actual proportion of high risk female drinkers in the Indigenous community to range between 22.7 per cent and 31.7 per cent (i.e. 6.14*3.7 and 8.57*3.7).

Indigenous females vs Indigenous males

Poisson regression results show substantially different risks for females versus males for the Indigenous (1.54) and non-Indigenous populations (0.5). If it is the case that the female to male risk in the Indigenous population is in actuality similar to that for the non-Indigenous population (i.e. less likely for females) then the resultant IRR for Indigenous females to males must be a spurious outcome of underestimation in the 2008 NATSISS. Assuming that the IRR demonstrated for the non-Indigenous population is accurate, it is possible to estimate the approximate true value of the prevalence ratio for Indigenous females to Indigenous males. That is, if the ratio between the Indigenous female to male IRR (1.54 and non-Indigenous female to male IRR (0.50 should equal 1, then:

$$0.50/1.54*(X) = 1, \text{ where X must} = 0.33$$

Thus, for the Indigenous population, in order to achieve a similar female to male risk profile as the non-Indigenous population, the ratio of Indigenous male to Indigenous female high risk populations should be 0.33 times the current NATSISS estimation of 2.4 and about 0.80. To achieve this, the Indigenous male (9.0%) and female (3.7%) prevalence estimates from the 2008 NATSISS would need to converge.

Discussion

The results from this analysis are in keeping with the proposition that the 2008 NATSISS has substantially underestimated the prevalence of high risk alcohol consumption for chronic harms among the national Indigenous population. The current NATSISS prevalence estimates may be underestimated by over 200 per cent for males and 700 per cent for females. Based on alcoholic liver cirrhosis and alcohol dependence deaths from 2000 to 2006, the proportion of the Indigenous population expected to be drinking at high risk levels for chronic harm was estimated to range from 17.6 per cent to 22.8 per cent for males and 22.7 per cent and 31.7 per cent for females.[8] On this basis, the overall ratio of Indigenous to non-Indigenous high risk drinking prevalence for chronic harm in the population is expected to be about 4.7 to 1. This is substantially larger than the ratio of 1.85 to 1 indicated by a straight comparison of the high risk drinking prevalence estimates for Indigenous people in the 2008 NATSISS (6.3%) to the general population estimates from the 2007 NDSHS (3.4%). Moreover, the Indigenous to non-Indigenous high risk drinking ratio derived from the analyses

---

8 It should be noted that the NHMRC guidelines give a lower cut-off for females (>4) compared to males (>6).

performed in this study (4.7 to 1) is in relatively close alignment with the ratio of about 5.4 to 1 produced by the 1994 urban Indigenous survey compared to a 1993 urban general population survey.

The original proposition put forward by Chikritzhs and Brady (2006a) – that the 2002 NATSISS substantially underestimated Indigenous alcohol consumption – was based on a range of observations. It is difficult to imagine a credible scenario which would cause high risk levels of alcohol use for chronic harm among the national Indigenous population to fall so substantially from the mid 1990s that the actual ratio of Indigenous to non-Indigenous high risk drinking would currently be less than 2 to 1. It is hypothetically possible that the 1994 Indigenous urban survey overestimated Indigenous consumption (by a large factor) but given that the major sources of error in substance use surveys tend almost exclusively toward under-reporting of actual consumption, the possibility is remote. In addition, national surveys of the general population do not indicate any exceptionally large increases in high risk consumption for chronic harm since the mid 1990s (Clement et al. 2007) which could account for convergence of the Indigenous and non-Indigenous prevalence estimates. It is far more plausible that the NATSISS underestimates Indigenous alcohol consumption substantially.

Why then, might the NATSISS be so prone to underestimating alcohol consumption? Chikritzhs and Brady (2006a, 2006b) identified several potential sources of error including the use of face-to-face interviews and lack of confidentiality for respondents, problematic data collection methods, and exclusion of residents living in non-private dwellings. An important characteristic which was common to both the 1994 urban Indigenous survey and the 2007 NDSHS, but distinctly absent from the NATSISS, was a clear recognition that participants should be afforded a minimum level of privacy when asked to report their personal alcohol use. As Chikritzhs and Brady (2006b: 231) indicated:

> It is important at the outset to acknowledge with candour that questioning Aboriginal or Torres Strait Islander people about their use of alcohol and other drugs is always fraught with difficulty, whatever the circumstance.

For instance, throughout the 1994 urban Indigenous survey, although an interviewer was present and initial questioning was conducted face-to-face, sensitive questions about any type of substance use were contained in a confidential sealed section for the respondent's self-completion, and there was no direct questioning from the interviewer (although the interviewer was able to provide assistance when asked). The general population NDSHS also use a self-complete questionnaire which is sealed by the respondent after completion (without any personal identifying information) and returned to the survey field worker or via mail in a reply paid envelope. The 2008 NATSISS (and 2002), however, takes an approach which requires the respondent to verbally relate their alcohol use to the interviewer. This differs to the questions relating to prescription drugs and/or the use of illicit drugs which are voluntary and able to be privately self-completed (at least by non-remote respondents).

It is a remarkable contrast that all the national drug strategy surveys, including the 1994 urban Indigenous survey recognise the personal nature of all alcohol and other drug use questions asked, while repeatedly and explicitly making clear its strict protocol for maintaining privacy. Yet, the ABS takes this view only for drugs other than alcohol (and tobacco). It is even more striking a discord when it is considered that for Indigenous people, alcohol use imparts a social burden well beyond that experienced by the general population and 'carries with it a complex political, legislative and racialised past and is the cause of polarised views among Aboriginal practitioners and commentators' (Chikritzhs and Brady 2006a: 278). In this context, it would be naïve to assume that because alcohol is a legally available drug, that its consumption is not a highly loaded and sensitive issue for individuals, families, and communities. It is not certain that lack of privacy is a major cause of underestimation in the NATSISS, but it is certainly worth investigating further, as are the other potential sources of error.

Limitations

On the basis of the regression results, it was possible to estimate a more probable range for actual high risk alcohol exposure in the Indigenous population. It should be kept in mind, however, that the intention of this study was not to re-estimate the prevalence of Indigenous alcohol consumption, but to highlight, via triangulation with death records, the implausibility of the current estimates of chronic levels of consumption derived from the 2008 NATSISS. The ranges given depend heavily on the assumption that the 2007 NDSHS (which forms the basis for comparison) is a reliable and accurate indicator of high risk consumption in the non-Indigenous population. In fact, the 2007 NDSHS, like most other surveys, almost certainly underestimates the proportion of people in the general population who drink at high risk levels for chronic harm (e.g. Stockwell et al. 2007). In which case, the Indigenous prevalence ranges estimated from the regression analyses would also be underestimated.

It is also possible that Indigenous deaths from alcoholic liver cirrhosis and alcohol dependence are over-reported compared to the non-Indigenous population. For instance, it is possible that coroners tend to focus on alcohol-related causes of death more often for Indigenous people and under-report for non-Indigenous people. Alternatively, the detection and treatment of alcoholic liver cirrhosis and alcohol dependence among Indigenous people may be inferior compared to their non-Indigenous counterparts, leading to a greater likelihood of death in the former. However, while this may explain a portion of the difference between Indigenous and non-Indigenous death rates, it is unlikely to fully explain the extremely large discrepancies found. In particular, it does not explain why the discrepancy should be so very much larger for females than for males, nor why the Indigenous female to male risk ratio should be 1.5 (based on Indigenous deaths and the 2008 NATSISS Indigenous prevalence estimates), while the reverse relationship is demonstrated for the non-Indigenous population (0.5).

It is also worth noting that the estimates of drinking prevalence examined here relate to high risk levels of alcohol use only. We have not considered levels of use which would be considered risky use for chronic alcohol related harm (that is, 5–6 standard drinks per day on average for males and 3–4 per day on average for females), which presumably are also likely to be underestimated.

Conclusion

To the extent possible, triangulation with deaths attributable to chronic heavy alcohol use has supported the proposition that the prevalence of high risk drinking detected by the 2008 NATSISS (and the 2002 NATSISS) is underestimated to a substantial extent. The ABS acknowledges that its surveys underestimate actual consumption levels for alcohol and other substances (e.g. ABS 2009). In this, the ABS surveys are not unique: most surveys of alcohol and drug use underestimate consumption, most of the time. Regarding the NATSISS, the concerns which require further consideration are whether the magnitude of the underestimate is so large that it is beyond reasonable and acceptable bounds of error for national population surveys and whether it should be relied upon as in any way an accurate source of information on Indigenous alcohol consumption.

Appendix 4A: Tables

Table 4A.1 Deaths from wholly alcohol attributable conditions (Poisson regression modelling), Australia, 2000–06[a]

	IRR	95% Confidence interval		P value
		Lower	Upper	
Indigenous status				
Males: Indigenous (1) vs non Indigenous (0)	2.53	2.28	2.80	0.000
Females: Indigenous (1) vs non Indigenous (0)	6.54	5.64	7.57	0.000
Sex				
Non-Indigenous: females (1) vs males (0)	0.52	0.49	0.55	0.000
Indigenous: females (1) vs males (0)	1.24	1.04	1.47	0.014

a. Number in sample = 5 955 males, 1 738 females. Includes the following conditions: alcoholic psychosis, alcohol abuse, alcohol dependence, alcoholic cardiomyopathy, alcoholic gastritis, alcoholic liver cirrhosis, alcoholic pancreatitis, alcoholic polyneuropathy, alcoholic poisoning, aspiration (vomitus).

Source: ABS death unit records 2000–06

Acknowledgements

The authors would like to thank Professor Dennis Gray, Dr Steven Skov and Dr Maggie Brady for their helpful comments on earlier drafts.

References

Australian Bureau of Statistics (ABS) 2004. *National Aboriginal and Torres Strait Islander Social Survey 2002*, cat. no. 4714.0.55.001, ABS, Canberra.

—— 2007. *2006 Census of Population and Housing Australia,* cat. no. 2068.0, ABS, Canberra.

—— 2009. *National Aboriginal and Torres Strait Islander Social Survey 2008: Summary*, cat. no. 4714.0, ABS, Canberra.

—— 2010a. *National Aboriginal and Torres Strait Islander Social Survey (NATSISS 2008*, cat. no. 4714.0, ABS, Canberra.

—— 2010b. *National Aboriginal and Torres Strait Islander Social Survey: Users' Guide, 2008*, cat. no. 4720.0, ABS, Canberra.

Australian Institute of Health and Welfare (AIHW) 2008. *2007 National Drug Strategy Household Survey: First Results*, Drug Statistics Series No. 20, cat. no. PHE 98, AIHW, Canberra.

Chikritzhs, T. and Brady 2006a. 'Fact or fiction? A critique of the National Aboriginal and Torres Strait Islander Social Survey, 2002', *Drug and Alcohol Review*, 25: 277–87.

—— and —— 2006b. 'Substance use in the 2002 NATSISS', in B. Hunter (ed.), *Assessing the Evidence on Indigenous Socioeconomic Outcomes: A Focus on the 2002 NATSISS*, CAEPR Research Monograph No. 26, ANU E Press, Canberra.

—— and —— 2007. 'Postscript to: Fact or fiction? A critique of the National Aboriginal and Torres Strait Islander Social Survey, 2002', *Drug and Alcohol Review*, 26: 221–22.

——, Gray, D., Stockwell, T., Stearne, A., Pascal, R. and Saggers, S. 2004. *Applying National Indicators of Alcohol-Related Harms to Indigenous Australians: A Discussion Paper*, National Drug Research Institute, Curtin University of Technology, Perth.

——, et al. 2000. *Alcohol-caused Deaths and Hospitalisations in Australia 1990–1997*, National Alcohol Indicators Technical Report no. 1, National Drug Research Institute, Curtin University of Technology, Perth.

Clement, S., Donath, S., Stockwell, T. and Chikritzhs, T. 2007. *Alcohol Consumption in Australia: National Surveys from 1989 to 2004*, Technical Report, National Drug Research Institute, Curtin University of Technology, Perth.

Commonwealth Department of Human Services and Health (CDHSH) 1996. *National Drug Strategy Household Survey Urban Aboriginal and Torres Strait Islander Peoples Supplement1994*, AGPS, Canberra.

Knibbe, R. and Bloomfield, K. 2001. 'Alcohol consumption estimates in surveys in Europe: Comparability and sensitivity for gender differences', *Journal of Subtance Abuse*, 22: 23–38.

National Health and Medical Research Council (NHMRC) 2001. *Australian Alcohol Guidelines: Health Risks and Benefits*, NHMRC, Canberra.

—— 2009. *Australian Guidelines to Reduce Health Risks from Drinking Alcohol*, NHMRC, Canberra.

Steering Committee for the Review of Government Service Provision 2005. *Overcoming Indigenous Disadvantage: Key Indicators 2005, Overview*, Productivity Commission, Canberra.

Stockwell, T., Jinhui, Z., Chikritzhs, T. and Greenfield, T. 2008. 'What did you drink yesterday? Public health relevance of a recent recall method used in the 2004 Australian National Drug Strategy Household Survey', *Addiction*, 103: 919–28.

World Health Organization (WHO) 2000. *International Guide for Monitoring Alcohol Consumption and Alcohol Related Harm*, T. Stockwell and T. Chikritzhs (eds), WHO, Geneva, viewed 27 September 2011, available at <http://whqlibdoc.who.int/hq/2000/who_msd_msb_00.4.pdf>

5. Improving Indigenous health: Are mainstream determinants sufficient?

Nicholas Biddle

The headline target of the Council of Australian Governments 'closing the gap' agenda is the elimination of the difference between Indigenous and non-Indigenous life expectancy in Australia. While this in and of itself is a worthwhile (if difficult to achieve) aim, life expectancy represents just one aspect of physical and mental health. Instead, the World Health Organization (WHO 2006) defines health as 'not only the absence of infirmity and disease but also a state of physical, mental and social wellbeing'.

This definition of health makes it clear that individuals can be completely free of disease and appear in a physical sense to be healthy but, because of low mental or social wellbeing, be quite unhealthy. Similarly, a person may have one or a number of chronic conditions but, because of a supportive family or community, consider themselves to be quite healthy.

Indigenous Australians extend the definition of health even further and also use a much broader definition of health than the absence of disease. In 1990, the National Aboriginal Health Strategy defined health as follows: 'Health does not just mean the physical wellbeing of the individual but refers to the social, emotional, spiritual and cultural wellbeing of the whole community' (National Health and Medical Research Council (NHMRC) 1996, cited in Jackson and Ward 1999). That is, not only is one's own wellbeing important, but so too is the wellbeing of the community in which one lives and has ongoing attachment. This definition is not without problems and may, according to Boddington and Raisanen (2009) be 'so broad in compass it may with some justification be said not to be a definition of health at all, but of something far more encompassing'.

Notwithstanding this complicated relationship between physical health and wellbeing, previous research has demonstrated a clear empirical link between physical health and subjective wellbeing. For example, in Kahneman and Deaton (2010), having a health condition was found to be negatively associated with emotional wellbeing and life satisfaction. What's more, the size of the association was quite large – similar in magnitude to marital status and income. Unlike changes in income (Shields, Wheatley Price and Wooden 2009), however, individuals only tend to experience partial adaptation to disability (Oswald and Powdthavee 2008). That is, even after a number of years, individuals who become disabled reported lower levels of life satisfaction than previously.

Analysis has also shown that reporting relatively low levels of subjective wellbeing was associated with worse self-assessed health into the future (Siahpush, Spittal and Singh 2008). That is, not only does physical health determine emotional wellbeing and life satisfaction, but it is also determined by it. The link between mental health and subjective wellbeing (and emotional wellbeing in particular) is even clearer. Operationally, the question often used to identify negative affect (or periods of intense feelings of sadness) often comes from the module on psychological distress and either the Kessler-5 (K5) or Kessler-10 (K10) scale (Australian Bureau of Statistics (ABS) 2010). Scores on these scales are used as predictors of mental health-related conditions and are, empirically, negatively correlated with positive measures of emotional wellbeing (like happiness) and life satisfaction. Nonetheless, mental health and wellbeing are distinct concepts, as noted by the Social Health Reference Group (2004), with those with mental health conditions often able to obtain high levels of wellbeing (provided they receive sufficient support in doing so).

Indigenous Australians report lower levels of physical health than the non-Indigenous population. At around 22 per cent, Indigenous Australians were around twice as likely to report that their health was either fair or poor compared to non-Indigenous Australians (ABS/Australian Institute of Health and Welfare (AIHW) 2010). Although Indigenous adults were found to be only slightly less likely to have a long-term condition than non-Indigenous adults (based on analysis of the 2004–05 National Aboriginal and Torres Strait Islander Health Survey (NATSIHS)), the difference was much greater when the relatively young Indigenous age profile is taken into account. When age-standardised, Indigenous Australians in 2004–05 were 1.6 times as likely to report that they had asthma, 3.4 times as likely to report diabetes/high sugar levels and 10.0 times as likely to report a kidney disease.

There is a large literature on the determinants of Indigenous health. However, most of the empirical analysis has tended to focus on reasonably narrow definitions of health and narrowly defined determinants. This is not surprising, because the focus of much of the analysis is on explaining the difference between Indigenous and non-Indigenous Australians. Explaining differences between the two populations necessitates using data that contains both populations and measures that are applicable to both. The aim of this paper is to summarise new research on the determinants of Indigenous health using data from the 2008 National Aboriginal and Torres Strait Islander Social Survey (NATSISS). Before then, I summarise some of the available literature on the determinants of Indigenous health.

The determinants of Indigenous health

There is a considerable amount of research on the physical health of Indigenous Australians in general, and the determinants of the gap between Indigenous and non-Indigenous Australians in particular. Firstly, Indigenous Australians are more likely to live in remote and very remote Australia than the non-Indigenous population – areas where access to health services can be difficult. Indigenous Australians need to travel greater distances to access primary health services and, even more so, hospitals and other expensive health procedures (ABS/AIHW 2010).

Secondly, Indigenous Australians start off with worse health outcomes than the non-Indigenous population. They are more likely to be born prematurely and to have low birth weight (ABS/AIHW 2010), due in part to the fact that Indigenous mothers are much more likely to be relatively young and to smoke and/or drink alcohol during pregnancy. Indigenous Australians also experience worse physical health outcomes through childhood and into adolescence. They are less likely to have been breastfed up until 12 months, have a worse diet, were less likely to be vaccinated at a young age, more likely to be exposed to passive smoking, more likely to have a long term health condition, and more likely to have been hospitalised due to illness and/or injury (ABS/AIHW 2010).

Research in other contexts clearly demonstrates a link between childhood physical and mental health and later health outcomes. For example, Blackwell, Hayward and Crimmins (2001: 1280) conclude that:

> ...respondents who experienced childhood health problems were more likely to experience a variety of chronic illnesses and conditions such as cancer, lung illnesses, cardiovascular conditions, and arthritis/rheumatism.

Results from the Aboriginal Birth Cohort study are beginning to show this link for a cohort of Aboriginal children born between January 1987 and March 1990 in Darwin (Sayers et al. 2011). One of the explanations for poor adult physical health amongst Indigenous Australians is likely to be poor child and adolescent health.

The socioeconomic status of Indigenous children is one of the main determinants of their poor physical health status. However, socioeconomic status also has an effect on health throughout the lifecourse. The association between an individual's social and economic status and their health has long been established (Matthews, Jagger and Hancock 2006; Wilkinson and Marmot 2003). In the Indigenous context, Biddle (2006) showed that not only were there high returns to education for Indigenous health, but that the difference between Indigenous and non-Indigenous Australians in terms of education outcomes explained a large component of the gap in self-assessed and physical health. Using a greater range of socioeconomic variables, Booth and Carroll (2008) found that economic factors explained around half of the gap in self-assessed health between Indigenous and non-Indigenous Australians.

The link between socioeconomic status and health is not unique to the Indigenous population. However, there are other factors that in the Australian context at least are unique to the Indigenous population. First is a history of dispossession of land and exclusion from citizenship rights. Much of the social determinants of health literature focuses on the negative health effects of having a lack of control of one's life (Wilkinson and Marmot 2003). Given the importance of land to Indigenous culture and the historic removal of Indigenous Australians from many parts of the Australian continent (Broome 2010), it is quite likely that this has had long-lasting effects on physical and mental health.

Related to the dispossession of Indigenous land is the denigration of Indigenous culture within Australia through much of its history since European colonisation. Since at least the mid 1800s, Indigenous Australians were seen as part of a 'dying race' that would either be incorporated into the non-Indigenous population through intermarriage or die out through excess mortality or low fertility (Smith 1980). The clearest expression of this is the 'stolen generations' or Indigenous children who were forcibly removed from their natural families due to their indigeneity (Broome 2010). As will be seen later in this chapter, this is still having ongoing health effects on those who were removed and on their families.

A final potentially negative effect on health is ongoing discrimination in Australia towards Indigenous Australians and racism in everyday life. Discrimination refers to:

> ...a situation in which persons ... who are equally productive in a physical or material sense are treated unequally in a way that is related to an observable characteristic such as race, ethnicity or gender (Altonji and Blank 1999: 3168).

According to Dunn et al. (2004: 411), this includes 'a belief in a racial hierarchy, in racial separation and in "race" itself' as well as new forms of racism like intolerance towards specific cultural groups.

Discrimination is very difficult to detect using standard data sources, however there is evidence that an Indigenous Australian with the same level of education and experience as a non-Indigenous Australian has a lower probability of employment and a lower income (Hunter 2004). While it is not possible to control for unobservable characteristics in the data used in Hunter (2004), experimental data would suggest that a person with a recognisably Indigenous name is less likely to be treated favourably in the labour market than someone with a name not identifiable as being Indigenous (Booth, Leigh and Varganova 2010).

Regardless of whether a person is actually discriminated against, in terms of health effects it is perhaps equally important whether they themselves perceive that they experienced discrimination. Biddle (2011a) showed that Indigenous Australians were significantly and substantially more likely to report that they were discriminated against compared to non-Indigenous Australians both when applying for a job and also in their current job (in terms of seeking promotion and other employment conditions).

Despite the potential negative effects on Indigenous health just discussed, there are also a number of positive aspects identified in the literature. While the pressures on Indigenous culture have been cited as a potential determinant of ill health, it should always be kept in mind that the converse of this is that those who are able to maintain key aspects of Indigenous culture and heritage are likely to benefit from the protective health benefits that cultural participation can bring. Related to this, Rowley et al. (2008) found relatively low morbidity and mortality in a remote Northern Territory Indigenous community (compared to the rest of the Territory). The authors speculated that the ability to maintain a healthy lifestyle and the ability to maintain control over their own culture was a key explanation for this positive health effect.

Relationship between self-assessed health and other measures of wellbeing

Previous analysis (Biddle 2006; Booth and Carroll 2008) has shown that even after controlling for a wide range of socioeconomic variables, Indigenous Australians are more likely to report their health as being fair or poor than the non-Indigenous population. Although this analysis gives some indication as to what the determinants of self-assessed health are in general, they did not give any indication as to whether these determinants held, and what the size of the association is for the Indigenous population in isolation. Furthermore, it is not possible with datasets like the NATSIHS to look at Indigenous-specific determinants of health like cultural/language maintenance or discrimination.

In order to test for Indigenous-specific determinants of health, Table 5.1 presents summary statistics and Table 5.2 results from econometric analysis of the 2008 NATSISS. The dependent variable is the probability of reporting one's health as being fair or poor.[1]

---

1   The main conclusions from the analysis hold when using all five self-assessed health categories and estimating using the ordered probit model. However, it is more difficult to interpret the size of the association using ordered probit so the simpler binary probit model is used.

Table 5.1 Explanatory variables assumed to be associated with self-assessed health, Indigenous Australians, 2008

Explanatory variables	Proportion
Female	0.568
Aged 15–24	0.250
Aged 25–34	0.231
Aged 55 plus	0.162
Aged 15–24, female	0.138
Aged 25–34, female	0.139
Aged 55 plus, female	0.093
Lives in remote Australia	0.337
Not married	0.540
Lives in a couple family with children	0.332
Lives in a couple family with no children but dependents	0.077
Lives in a single parent family with children	0.194
Lives in a single parent family with no children but dependents	0.079
Lives in an 'other' family type	0.161
Has a non-Indigenous person living in the household	0.363
Main language spoken at home is not English	0.147
Changed usual residents in the previous five years	0.607
Not in the labour force	0.398
Unemployed	0.093
Works part-time	0.195
Occupation is neither a manager or a professional	0.407
Main job is in the CDEP scheme	0.062
Completed Year 10 or 11 only	0.445
Completed Year 9 or less	0.364
Has a degree or higher as highest qualification	0.052
Has a diploma as highest qualifications	0.047
Has a certificate as highest qualification	0.222
Victim of physical or threatened violence in previous 12 months	0.254
Arrested in previous five years	0.152
Lives in a house that does not meet the occupancy standard	0.204
Speaks, understands or is learning an Indigenous language	0.295
Involved in cultural events, ceremonies or organisations in the previous 12 months	0.647
Able to have a say on important issues within the community all or most of the time	0.272
Strongly agrees or agrees that in general people can be trusted	0.357
Did not run out of money for basic living expenses in the last 12 months	0.717
Feels very safe or safe at home after dark	0.788
Did not report any neighbourhood or community problems	0.233
Felt discriminated against in the previous 12 months due to Indigenous status	0.276
Was removed from natural family	0.097
A relative was removed from their natural family	0.416

Source: Customised calculations using the 2008 NATSISS

One of the limitations of the 2008 NATSISS for analysing the determinants of health is the focus on self-reported health measures. However, the subjective nature of self-assessed health is also one of its strengths. By focusing on how an individual actually feels (rather than how one might expect them to feel based on objective characteristics) it is possible to obtain more accurate predictions of future behaviour. According to Clark, Frijters and Shields (2008: 119; referring to Kahneman et al. 1993):

> ...[m]any panel studies have found that subjective wellbeing at time t predicts future behaviour, in that individuals clearly choose to discontinue activities associated with low levels of wellbeing.

Results in Table 5.2 are presented across two models. Model 1 is very similar to previous analysis with the explanatory variables being standard demographic and socioeconomic measures. In Model 2, on the other hand, a range of Indigenous-specific variables are used, representing different aspects of Indigenous language and cultural maintenance, financial stress, feelings of safety, neighbour or community problems, discrimination and forcible removal from one's natural family.

Table 5.2 Factors associated with self-assessed health, Indigenous Australians, 2008

Explanatory variables	Model 1		Model 2	
Female	−0.022		−0.047	**
Aged 15–24	−0.168	***	−0.324	***
Aged 25–34	−0.101	***	−0.172	***
Aged 55 plus	0.037		0.079	***
Aged 15–24, female	0.069	**	0.089	**
Aged 25–34, female	−0.012		−0.005	
Aged 55 plus, female	−0.022		−0.010	
Lives in remote Australia	−0.053	***	−0.057	***
Not married	−0.042	**	−0.058	*
Lives in a couple family with children	−0.045	***	−0.057	**
Lives in a couple family with no children but dependents	−0.020		−0.002	
Lives in a single parent family with children	0.006		−0.011	
Lives in a single parent family with no children but dependents	0.069	**	0.070	*
Lives in an 'other' family type	0.071	**	0.071	*
Has a non-Indigenous person living in the household	−0.003		0.007	
Main language spoken at home is not English	−0.041	**	−0.039	
Changed usual residents in the previous five years	0.010		−0.009	
Not in the labour force	0.248	***	0.223	***

Explanatory variables	Model 1		Model 2	
Unemployed	0.146	***	0.104	***
Works part-time	0.066	***	0.067	***
Occupation is neither a manager or a professional	−0.008		−0.017	
Main job is in the CDEP scheme	0.027		0.050	
Completed Year 10 or 11 only	0.007		−0.005	
Completed Year 9 or less	0.079	***	0.078	***
Has a degree or higher as highest qualification	0.001		−0.017	
Has a diploma as highest qualifications	−0.007		−0.030	
Has a certificate as highest qualification	0.016		0.012	
Victim of physical or threatened violence in previous 12 months			0.025	
Arrested in previous five years			0.042	**
Lives in a house that does not meet the occupancy standard			−0.012	
Speaks, understands or is learning an Indigenous language			0.003	
Involved in cultural events, ceremonies or organisations in the previous 12 months			−0.028	*
Able to have a say on important issues within the community all or most of the time			−0.030	*
Strongly agrees or agrees that in general people can be trusted			−0.052	***
Did not run out of money for basic living expenses in the last 12 months			−0.101	***
Feels very safe or safe at home after dark			−0.081	***
Did not report any neighbourhood or community problems			−0.068	***
Felt discriminated against in the previous 12 months due to Indigenous status			0.030	*
Was removed from natural family			0.063	***
A relative was removed from their natural family			0.044	***
Probability of the base case	0.216		0.537	
Pseudo R-Squared	0.1287		0.1468	
Number of observations	7 536		7 240	

Notes: The base case individual for all estimations is: male; aged 35–54; lives in non-remote Australia; is married; lives in a couple family without children with Indigenous Australians only in the household; speaks English at home and did not change usual residence in the previous 5 years; employed full-time as a manager or professional outside of the CDEP scheme; has completed Year 12; and does not have a qualification.

*** Marginal effect for which the coefficient is statistically significant at the 1% level of significance.

** Marginal effect for which the coefficient is statistically significant at the 5% level of significance.

* Marginal effect for which the coefficient is statistically significant at the 10% level of significance.

Source: Customised calculations using the 2008 NATSISS

There are a number of policy-relevant results contained in Model 1. Indigenous Australians in remote Australia are less likely to report their health as being fair or poor compared to those in non-remote Australia. This may reflect language differences in interpreting the question with Sibthorpe, Anderson and Cunningham (2001) noting the limitations of a global self-assessed health measure when applied to all Indigenous populations regardless of language background. However, it is important to note that the results hold after controlling for whether or not the person speaks a language other than English at home or when estimating on those who speak English only. Taking the results at face value, however, analysis of the 2008 NATSISS would tend to support the findings in Rowley et al. (2008) that living in a remote area has a protective effect on health.

Being out of the labour force was associated with poorer health on average. There is, however, a strong potential that having poor health leads to opting out of the labour force rather than the other way around. At the very least, the causal influence is likely to run in both directions. However, those who are unemployed are, by definition, actively seeking work and willing to commence work if the opportunity arises. The fact that they are also significantly and substantially more likely to report that they had fair or poor health suggests that for Indigenous Australians, employment status does impact on health.

It is important to note that those whose main job was in the Community Development Employment Program (CDEP) scheme did not have a significantly different probability of reporting fair or poor health than those in mainstream employment. Furthermore, using a separate (but unreported) test, those in the CDEP scheme were less likely to report fair or poor health than those who were unemployed, the other natural comparison group. To the extent that the CDEP scheme provided an alternative to unemployment benefits in certain communities in 2008, the analysis in Table 5.2 gives circumstantial evidence of a positive effect on health. This supports the finding in Biddle (2011b) that Indigenous Australians in the CDEP scheme reported higher subjective wellbeing (happiness and sadness) than those who were unemployed.

There was a non-linear association between education and health. Those who had completed Year 9 or less had a significantly and substantially higher probability of reporting fair or poor health than the base case (those who had completed Year 12) and, based on a separate test, those who had completed Year 10 or 11. However, there was no difference between those who had completed Year 10 or 11 and those who had completed Year 12, nor was there any association with post-school qualifications. This supports the finding in Biddle (2011b) that, in terms of wellbeing, lower levels of education are of greatest importance for Indigenous Australians.

The results in Model 1 generally represent mainstream determinants of health. Estimating the associations for the Indigenous population separately shows how these determinants manifest for the Indigenous population, although there is nothing particularly Indigenous-specific about them. The additional variables included in Model 2, however, show that Indigenous-specific variables are important in explaining variation within the Indigenous population in terms of self-assessed health. While there was no association with Indigenous language maintenance, results presented in Table 5.2 showed a small association between involvement in Indigenous culture. Furthermore, those who felt they were able to have a say on important issues and those with high levels of generalised trust were less likely to have fair or poor health, as were those who did not experience financial stress (through running out of money) and those who felt safe at home.

One cannot be too confident about the direction of causality in the above Indigenous-specific variables. It is quite possible that one's health affects these variables as much as being affected by them. However, they do give an indication that cultural maintenance and broader notions of community wellbeing have a strong interaction with health. It would really only be with an Indigenous-specific longitudinal dataset that the causal direction could be established (a point returned to in the concluding section).

Given the way the variables are defined, it is much more likely that the last three variables are affecting health rather than being affected by it. Specifically, those who were discriminated against were more likely to report fair or poor health as were those who were removed from their natural family and those who had relatives removed. While this is likely to represent a causal influence, it is a little difficult to identify specific policies that stem from these results. On the one hand, most forms of discrimination based on Indigenous status are illegal in Australia. However, more than one-quarter of the population reported that they felt discriminated against, so clearly policies alone are not sufficient in this area. Furthermore, the policy of forcibly removing children from their family is a historical rather than a current one. This notwithstanding, the results do demonstrate the potentially long-term effects of such policies, and do support to a certain extent calls for compensation by those who were affected.

Concluding comments

The determinants of Indigenous health are likely to interact in complex ways, with no single factor completely dominating. Those Indigenous Australians who start off with poor health are likely to find it relatively difficult to complete education, achieve stable employment and receive a decent income. Furthermore, mainstream education completion has been shown to enhance rather than act as a barrier to Indigenous cultural participation – a further determinant of broad notions of health. Despite this complexity, there exists a rich range of data sets that can be used to show the size and strength of the association between potential health risk factors and physical or self-assessed health, including the 2008 NATSISS. While it is not possible to conclusively test for the effect of particular policies, nor is it possible to establish causal relationships, the analysis of associations at least hints at policy priorities.

Ultimately, what the results presented in this paper show is that focusing on mainstream determinants of health (like those in the Closing the Gap agenda) will quite possibly lead to improvements in health. Increasing Indigenous education is likely to extend Indigenous life expectancy, as will improving access to employment opportunities. However, it will not be enough to close the gap entirely. Until Indigenous Australians no longer feel they are discriminated against and until a complete rapprochement with the stolen generations takes place, gaps between Indigenous and non-Indigenous Australians in health outcomes are likely to remain.

Furthermore, results presented in this paper would suggest that it does matter how policies on Closing the Gap are pursued. Indigenous Australians living in remote Australia have better self-assessed health (on average) than those in non-remote parts of the country, after controlling for other characteristics. If Indigenous Australians in remote areas are forced or even encouraged to move to other parts of the country in an attempt to improve employment and education, then there may be countervailing effects on health. Furthermore, removal of the CDEP scheme is a current aim of government policy. I have not seen any evidence that convincingly links having a CDEP scheme available in an area to Indigenous Australians opting out of mainstream employment. It is doubtful, therefore, that removing the scheme will in and of itself improve access to mainstream employment. It would appear from results in this paper though that the scheme (as it was structured in 2008) may have a protective effect on health. Removing the CDEP scheme and moving Indigenous Australians onto unemployment benefits will quite likely worsen Indigenous health with debatable effects on non-CDEP employment.

The results presented in this paper were all based on cross-sectional data. While this analysis provides useful insights, the strength of the policy conclusions are seriously constrained. However, there are no specific datasets with a large enough Indigenous sample and enough Indigenous-specific questions to be able to accurately identify the factors that influence Indigenous health. For example, it is not possible to test whether moving into or out of employment in general – or the CDEP scheme in particular – changes one's health. It may well be that those who are currently employed have other unobserved characteristics that influence their health. Alternatively, it is not possible to show whether changes in cultural participation influence health. Perhaps more importantly, it is not possible to analyse or even control for the effect of child health on later physical or mental health.

The Closing the Gap agenda on life expectancy is generational. There is still time in 2011 to develop the evidence base that will enable governments to achieve this aim. A part of this evidence base is analysis of the NATSISS (or the NATSIHS). However, this alone will not be enough. Proper randomised controlled trials that test for the causal effect of specific policies is a part of this process. So too is a longitudinal survey specifically designed for the Indigenous population that contains data across the lifecourse. With this in mind, I renew the call for a National Closing the Gap Survey (first raised in Biddle and Yap 2010) that would provide an annual tracking of progress in achieving the Closing the Gap targets, and allow the development of a more robust evidence base to support Indigenous policy in Australia by allowing researchers to ask 'what influences Indigenous health', rather than 'what is associated with Indigenous health'.

References

Altonji, J. G. and Blank, R. M. 1999. 'Race and gender in the labor market', in O. Ashenfelter and D. Card (eds), *Handbook of Labor Economics*, Elsevier, North Holland.

Australian Bureau of Statistics (ABS) 2010. *National Aboriginal and Torres Strait Islander Social Survey: Users' Guide, 2008*, cat. no. 4720.0, ABS, Canberra.

——/Australian Institute of Health and Welfare (ABS/AIHW) 2010. *The Health and Welfare of Australia's Aboriginal and Torres StraitIslander Peoples 2008*, cat. no. 4704.0, ABS, Canberra.

Biddle, N. 2006. 'The association between health and education in Australia: Indigenous/non-Indigenous comparisons', *The Economic and Labour Relations Review*, 17 (1): 107–42.

—— 2011a. 'Income, work and Indigenous livelihoods', Lecture 5, Measures of Indigenous Wellbeing and Their Determinants Across the Lifecourse, 2011 CAEPR Lecture Series, CAEPR, ANU, Canberra.

—— 2011b. 'Measuring and analysing wellbeing', Lecture 2, Measures of Indigenous Wellbeing and Their Determinants Across the Lifecourse, 2011 CAEPR Lecture Series, CAEPR, ANU, Canberra.

———— and Yap, M. 2010. *Demographic and Socioeconomic Outcomes Across the Indigenous Australian Lifecourse: Evidence from the 2006 Census*, CAEPR Research Monograph No. 31, ANU E Press, Canberra.

Blackwell, D. L., Hayward, M. D. and Crimmins, E. M. 2001. 'Does childhood health affect chronic morbidity in later life?', *Social Science and Medicine*, 52: 1269–84.

Boddington P, and Räisänen U. 2009. 'Theoretical and practical issues in the definition of health: Insights from Aboriginal Australia', *Journal of Medicine and Philosophy*, 34: 49–67

Booth, A. and Carroll, N. 2008. 'Economic status and the Indigenous/non-Indigenous health gap', *Economics Letters*, 99 (3): 604–6.

————, Leigh, A. and Varganova, E. 2010. 'Does racial and ethnic discrimination vary across minority groups? Evidence from a field experiment', *CEPR Discussion Paper No. DP7913*, Centre for Economic Policy Research, London.

Broome, R. 2010. *Aboriginal Australians: A History Since 1788*, Allen and Unwin, Sydney.

Clark, A. E., Frijters, P. and Shields, M. 2008. 'Relative income, happiness and utility: An explanation for the Easterlin paradox and other puzzles', *Journal of Economic Literature*, 46: 95–144.

Dunn, K. M., Forrest, J., Burnley, I. and McDonald, A. 2004. 'Constructing racism in Australia', *Australian Journal of Social Issues*, 39 (4): 409–30.

Hunter, B. H. 2004. *Indigenous Australians in the Contemporary Labour Market*, cat. no. 2052.0, ABS, Canberra.

Jackson, L. R. and Ward, J. E. 1999. 'Aboriginal health: Why is reconciliation necessary?', *Medical Journal of Australia*, 170: 437–40.

Kahneman, D. and Deaton, A. 2010. 'High income improves evaluation of life but not emotional well-being', *Proceedings of the National Academy of Science*, 107 (38): 16489–93.

————, Frerickson, B. L., Schreiber, C. A. and Redelmeier, D. A. 1993. 'When more pain is preferred to less: Adding a better end', *Psychological Science*, 4 (6): 401–5.

Matthews, R., Jagger, C. and Hancock, R. 2006. 'Does socio-economic advantage lead to a longer, healthier old age?', *Social Science and Medicine*, 62 (10): 2489–99.

National Health and Medical Research Council (NHMRC) 1996. 'Promoting the health of Indigenous Australians. A review of infrastructure support for Aboriginal and Torres Strait Islander health advancement. Final report and recommendations', NHMRC, Canberra.

Oswald, A. J. and Poddthavee, N. 2008. 'Does happiness adapt? A longitudinal study of disability with implications for economists and judges', *Journal of Public Economics*, 92 (5–6): 1061–77.

Rowley, K. G., O'Dea, I., Anderson, R., McDermott, K., Saraswati, K., Tilmouth, R., Roberts, I. F. J., Zaiman, W., Jenkins, A., Best, J. D., Wang, Z. and Brown, A. 2008. 'Lower than expected morbidity and mortality for an Australian Aboriginal population: 10-year follow-up in a decentralised community', *The Medical Journal of Australia*, 188 (5): 283–87.

Sayers, S., Davison, B., Fitz, J. and Singh, G. 2011. 'Aboriginal Birth Cohort Study-Wave 3: Selected results: The good news and the bad news', *Aboriginal and Islander Health Worker Journal*, 35 (5): 23–4.

Shields, M. A., Wheatley Price, S. and Wooden, M. 2009. 'Life satisfaction and the economic and social characteristics of neighbourhoods', *Journal of Population Economics*, 22 (2): 421–43.

Siahpush, M., Spittal, M. and Singh, G. K. 2008. 'Happiness and life satisfaction prospectively predict self-rated health, physical health, and the presence of limiting, long-term health conditions', *American Journal of Health Promotion*, 23 (1): 18–26.

Sibthorpe, B., Anderson, I. and Cunningham, J. 2001. 'Self-assessed health among indigenous Australians: How valid is a global question?', *American Journal of PublicHealth* , 91 (10): 1660–3.

Smith, L. R. 1980. *The Aboriginal Population of Australia*, ANU Press, Canberra.

Social Health Reference Group 2004. 'Social and emotional well being framework: a national strategic framework for Aboriginal and Torres Strait Islander mental health and social and emotional well being 2004–2009', Australian Government, Canberra, viewed 4 July 2012, available at <http://www.atns. net.au/agreement.asp?EntityID=4388>

Wilkinson, R. and Marmot, M. 2003. *Social Determinants of Health: The Solid Facts*, 2nd edition, World Health Organization, Copenhagen.

World Health Organization (WHO) 2006. Constitution of the World Health Organization 2006, viewed 31 January 2011, available at <www.who.int/ governance/eb/who_constitution_en.pdf>

6. What shapes the development of Indigenous children?

Carrington Shepherd and Stephen R. Zubrick

Descriptions of the Australian Indigenous circumstance have been dramatically enriched through improvements in, and delivery of, high quality quantitative survey findings over the past 20 years. Since 1901 – when Indigenous Australians were effectively excluded from even being counted in the populations of the States of the Commonwealth (Briscoe 2003) – Australia has made significant improvements in its capacity to detail the demographic and developmental status of its Indigenous peoples. Amid this progress though, it still remains the case that good quality descriptions of the developmental circumstances of Indigenous children, as distinct from Indigenous adults, are surprisingly few and far between. The 2008 National Aboriginal and Torres Strait Islander Social Survey (NATSISS) provides an opportunity to specifically describe the health and development of Indigenous children using an important and high quality data source.

To make sense of the findings about the health and development of Australian Indigenous children, it is important to place their development in the context of the healthy development of *all* children. This is not to discount the vital and obvious importance of Indigenous culture. Rather, by starting with some principles of healthy development that apply universally to all children, some of the underpinnings of the current Australian Indigenous circumstance and its apparent intractability are brought into perspective. We believe this opening perspective offers opportunities for better policies, services and practices to improve the life prospects of Australian Indigenous people.

Early development in the course of human development

Healthy development in early life is important for all children. The empirical literature now provides abundant evidence confirming that a child's developmental pathway shapes the subsequent course of their life. Child development is influenced not just by what occurs in infancy and beyond, but by processes that take place in-utero and prior to conception. Exposures in the earliest stages of life – such as the effects of maternal drug use, for example – can affect early brain development and play a critical role in shaping health prospects into adulthood (Keating and Hertzman 1999).

The evidence-base supporting healthy child development has been built-up over the course of decades, from research fields as diverse as neurobiology, psychology and social sciences, and confirms that children and their development have many spheres of influence – as depicted in Fig. 6.1. A child's immediate family and the household environment have the most direct impact on their development, although extended family networks, schools, formal services, neighbourhood characteristics and elements of the broader social, economic and political society, can all impact on a family's ability to provide the necessary support to a child's development (Bronfenbrenner 1979; Jessor 1993).

Fig. 6.1 Children within contexts of influence

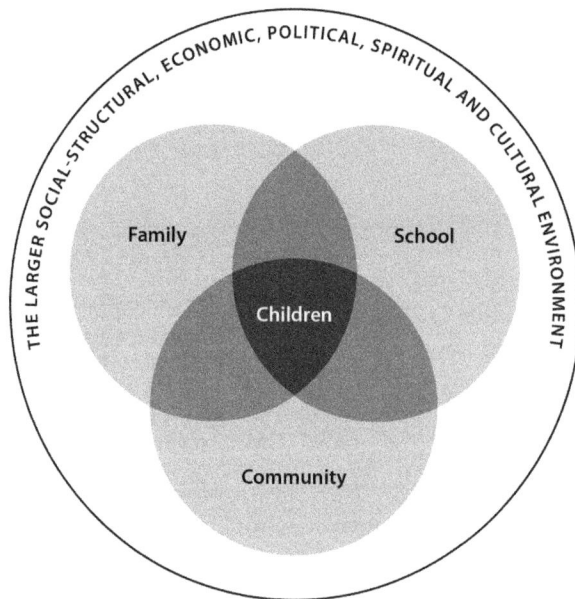

Source: Jessor 1993

The experiences of children at home and in daycare from birth to age of entry into kindergarten play a substantial role in their development, particularly in early cognitive and language development and in emotional and behavioural regulation. Young children who are well nurtured do better in school and develop the skills needed to take their place as productive and responsible adults (Zubrick et al. 2006).

Understanding the relationships between the factors that influence child development and their timing is important if communities and governments are to take appropriate action to ensure a fair start for all children. Nurturing children in their early years is vital for attacking the worst effects of disadvantage. Governments around the world are now seeking better ways to re-invest in their human service infrastructure to better meet the needs of children in order to bring about population-level improvements in health and human capability. The emerging consensus is that the greatest gains in overcoming disadvantage are likely to be achieved through universal preventions which give all children a better start in life. This is the preferred policy approach to reducing poverty being advocated by international agencies such as UNICEF and the World Bank and has been termed 'human development though early child development' (Young 2002).

Human development is broadly about expanding human capabilities, so that individuals can participate economically, socially and civically and choose lives that they value. Childhood is centrally located in models of human development, as it represents a critical period where skills are acquired and accumulated for benefit throughout the lifecourse. In the progression from childhood onwards there is a general consensus of evidence that human capability is optimised when individuals:

- are able to regulate their emotions
- are able to engage in exploratory behaviour
- are able to communicate effectively
- are self-directed
- have intellectual flexibility
- possess some degree of introspection, and
- possess self-efficacy in meeting life's challenges.

How these seven 'strengths' develop in childhood are critical in enabling onward capability – in essence, those that start at a low 'threshold' are likely to lose opportunities for further development at later stages in life (Zubrick 2010).

Quite importantly, the evidence in the child development literature supports a relatively *small* set of mechanisms that change developmental strengths. These mechanisms work in one of three ways – they either prompt, facilitate or constrain the development and maintenance of strengths. While these mechanisms will be elaborated on later in the paper, it should be noted that they operate similarly among Indigenous and non-Indigenous children, albeit in vastly different population contexts. They also operate across the lifecourse. Fig. 6.2 offers a lifecourse perspective on child development in the context of a selection of global and national events from 1945 to present, and highlights the variation in a hypothetical outcome of interest from birth to late life. The outcome could take many forms including specific health conditions, general health status, mental health, and any of the developmental strengths cited above. The variation in the outcome of interest can be thought of as the variation in the lifecourse of an individual life or as a time series of the population estimate over the relevant period. The occurrence of parental divorce, the onset of smoking and alcohol abuse, the sudden closure of an industry and unemployment are included as examples of exposures of interest. All of these exposures (and the outcome) can be influenced by broader, macrosocial factors – these include global and national events that occur over time, such as the introduction of free higher education in the 1970s or the emergence of the World Wide Web in the 1990s (Zubrick et al. 2009).

This paper uses a human development framework to explore the developmental status of Indigenous children in Australia, using data from the 2008 NATSISS. We examine how Indigenous children are faring in terms of some traditional markers of child development and the mechanisms that prompt, facilitate and constrain Indigenous child development. We also explore what the NATSISS can tell us about the relative importance of factors that influence key child development outcomes.

Child development and the 2008 NATSISS

The NATSISS is a vital source of data for addressing the human capability story in an Australian Indigenous context. The 2008 NATSISS is significant in that it enables, for the first time, an examination of the development of children. As such, it is one of the few reliable quantitative resources that have detailed information on both developmental outcomes and their risk factors for Indigenous persons aged 0–14 years.

In terms of child developmental outcomes, the 2008 NATSISS asked about birthweight and gestational age (for 0–3 year olds only), a global question on health status, and questions regarding specific problems with ears/hearing, eyes/sight and teeth/gums. In addition, some information can be gleaned on educational attendance. All responses for 0–14 year olds were provided by parents/guardians in most instances, or a member of the household with responsibility for the child. In addition, the NATSISS included a rich set of variables that can be described as either prompts, facilitators or constraints of child development. These include aspects of diet and nutrition, connection with culture, carer education, informal learning, stress and supports.

Fig. 6.2 Child development in the context of the lifecourse

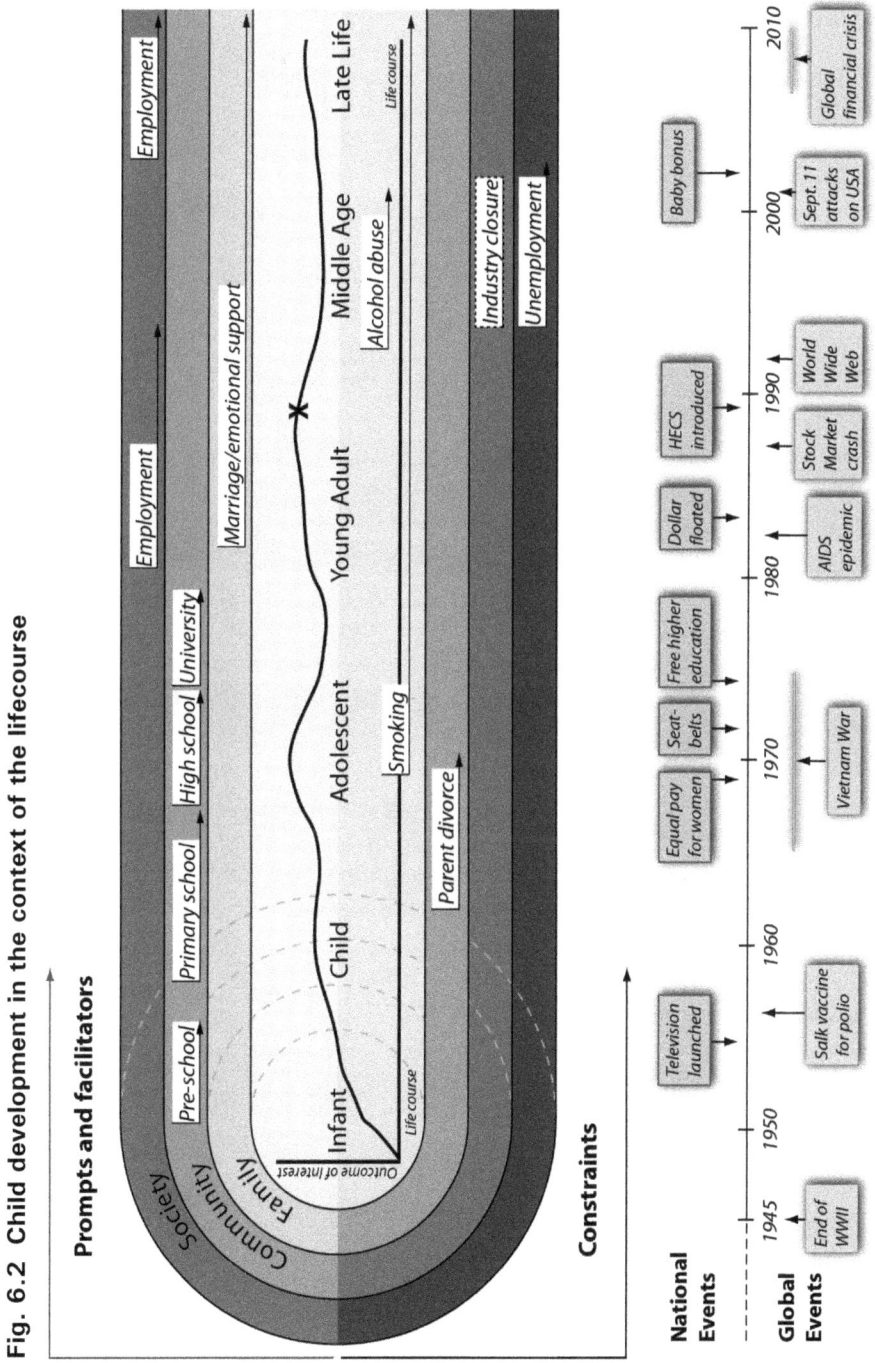

Source: Zubrick et al. 2009

The large scale of the 2008 NATSISS (almost 5500 children were sampled) enables a robust analysis of child developmental outcomes and their antecedents, with potential for regional comparisons (by State/Territory or geographic remoteness). All analyses in this paper were conducted on the *State/Territory by ASGC Remoteness Structure Confidentialised Unit Record File* (CURF), accessed via the Australian Bureau of Statistics (ABS) Remote Access Data Laboratory (RADL). This CURF provided a dichotomous national remoteness data item (remote/non-remote) and a 13-part derived item that cross-classifies State/Territory by remoteness.

The depth (in terms of sample size) and breadth (in terms of data items) of the 2008 NATSISS offer considerable strength for the purposes of examining aspects of Indigenous child development. However, there are, as with any study, a range of limitations to the NATSISS data which restrict what can be achieved in this paper. First, the NATSISS uses a cross-sectional design which reduces any discussion of causal inference to a discussion about associations. Second, there is a lack of information on academic performance and social and emotional wellbeing, and a narrow range of educational attendance variables in the survey. This limits our ability to examine some of the key domains of child development. Third, all of the questions relating to 0–14 year olds rely on the perceptions and recall of parents and caregivers, which are inherently open to issues of bias (e.g. problems with interpretation, willingness to answer openly) and inaccuracy (Sen 2002). In relation to the 2008 NATSISS, the difficulties with interpreting a child's health are two-fold – a carer's views may not accord with that of a medical expert or with the view of the child themselves. Fourth, the available CURFs do not allow a full examination of the effects of geographic location. This is particularly limiting in Indigenous contexts because of the heterogeneity of Australian Indigenous population groups (Bell 1995) and the relative importance that a sense of place and connection to land has on the health of Indigenous peoples (Boddington and Raisanen 2009; Saggers and Gray 2007). Lastly, the CURF does not include stratum or Collection District (CD) information which precludes a multi-level analysis of the data, and therefore we are not able to fully examine the relationships between factors at the individual, family and neighbourhood level and child health outcomes.

Developmental outcomes for Indigenous children

Before we begin to describe the developmental status of Indigenous children we must ask the question, 'what constitutes an outcome?' In this paper, the overarching outcome is the capability to participate – economically, socially and civically. These outcomes are largely at the core of what public policy and its funding effort seeks to achieve. Public policy and expenditure on human services is deliberately organised to influence human capability with the express aim of enabling more people to choose lives that they value. There has been a heavy emphasis historically on economic participation and only in recent times have developed countries begun to listen to citizen demands that there is more to life than participating in the labour market – social participation and civic participation form part of the mix of what human development is all about (Fukuda-Parr and Kumar 2004).

Focusing on a human capability framework enables us to examine specific types of outcomes, i.e. diseases, good health, literacy, as well as those that may be considered as developmental 'means'. For example, the achievement of good health or the occurrence of specific diseases, are typically studied as 'outcomes' in their own right. These outcomes may also be thought of as the means through which the capability to participate economically, socially and civically is achieved or diminished. Using this as a guiding framework, we have selected seven outcomes for children from the 2008 NATSISS:

- birthweight
- gestational age
- overall (global) health status
- eye/sight problems
- ear/hearing problems
- teeth and gum problems, and
- educational attendance.

Birthweight

High rates of low birthweight in developing countries are primarily due to intrauterine growth restriction, which is associated with a range of poor outcomes that commence at birth (death, disability and poor health) and can lead to complications in childhood and the development of chronic illnesses in adult life (Australian Institute of Health and Welfare et al. 1999; Ford et al. 2003; Zubrick et al. 2008). Low birthweight babies are generally more prevalent in Indigenous populations, where population rates correspond more closely with those observed in developing nations (Steering Committee for the Review of Government Service Provision (SCRGSP) 2009).

Low birthweight is typically defined as less than 2500 grams, while those born less than 1500 grams are of very low birthweight. The NATSISS found that 11.2 per cent of Indigenous children aged 0–3 years in Australia were of low birthweight and 1.9 per cent were born at very low birthweight (Table 6.1).

Gestational age

Babies born prior to 37 weeks gestation are considered to be 'preterm' or to have 'low' gestational age. This cut-off point aligns with the development of several organ systems, and evidence suggests that low gestation is associated with a greater risk of neonatal mortality and a range of morbidities into childhood and beyond (Kuh and Ben-Shlomo 2004). Close to one-quarter (24.1%) of Indigenous children aged 0–3 years were considered preterm at birth. A higher proportion of females than males were preterm (26.9% compared with 21.4%).

Global health

Global health status was assessed on a five-point ordinal scale: excellent; very good; good; fair; or poor. Less than 4 per cent of children aged 0–14 years had fair or poor health. The majority were in either excellent (46%) or very good health (32%). There was some variation by age, with older children generally less likely to be in excellent or very good health than younger age groups. This pattern can be observed in both non-remote and remote areas (see Fig. 6.3).

Fig. 6.3 Proportion of Indigenous children in excellent or very good health, by age, Australia, 2008[a]

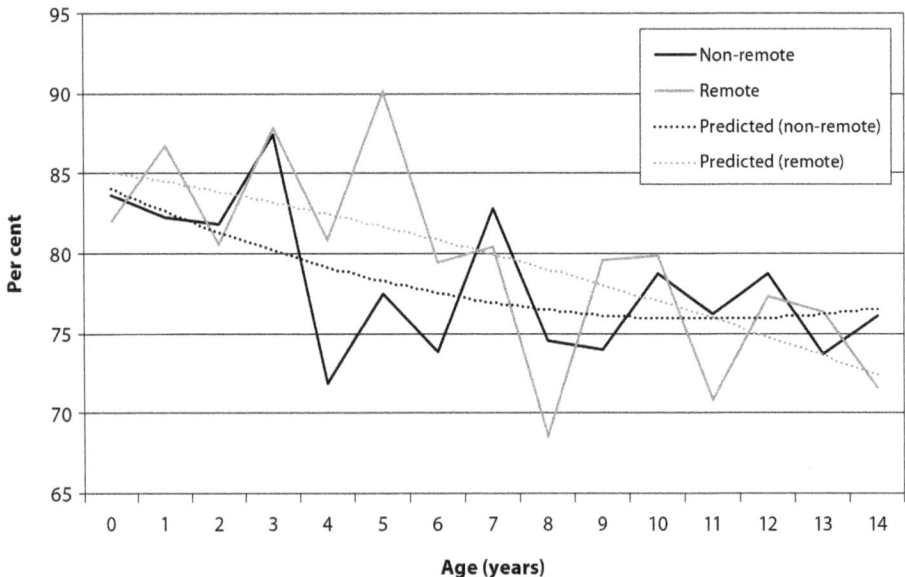

a. The broken lines represent a 'best fit' line, based on the coefficients of a second order polynomial regression.

Source: Authors' customised calculations using the 2008 NATSISS (accessed using the RADL)

When aggregated together, global health levels were broadly similar in remote and non-remote areas of Australia – however, this masks differences that were evident at finer geographic levels. For example, only 72 per cent of Indigenous children in 'outer regional' areas of New South Wales were in excellent/very good health, whereas the same was true of 90 per cent of children in Queensland 'inner regional' areas.

Hearing and vision

Hearing impediments can delay speech and language development in children, with undesirable consequences for both social development and a child's ability to engage in educational opportunities. Previous studies have highlighted that hearing loss and impediments are more prevalent among Indigenous children (ABS 2006), particularly in more remote communities with poor environmental health conditions (Coates et al. 2002; Zubrick et al. 2004). Middle ear infection, or otitis media, is a persistent problem in many Indigenous communities and is regarded as the most common cause of hearing impediments among Indigenous children (Morris et al. 2005).

From the NATSISS, 9 per cent of children aged 0–14 years had an ear or hearing problem, which includes partial or full hearing loss and conditions such as tinnitus, runny/glue ear and tropical ear. The trend by age is roughly a reverse U-shape, peaking at age six (see Fig. 6.4). While we may have expected ear/hearing problems to be more prevalent in remote areas, we found similar proportions in remote (10%) and non-remote areas (8%).

Only a small proportion (7%) of children had an eye or sight problem. These problems were mainly of a less severe nature (long or short sightedness), with relatively few cases of blindness, trachoma, glaucoma, and cataracts. Similar to the findings of the Western Australian Aboriginal Child Health Survey, there were fewer cases of eye or sight problems in remote (4%) than non-remote (8%) areas (Zubrick et al. 2004). This is likely to reflect differences between remote and non-remote areas in the factors that are associated with short sightedness (for example, type of school work undertaken and lifestyle factors).

Fig. 6.4 Proportion of Indigenous children with ear or hearing problems, by age, Australia, 2008[a]

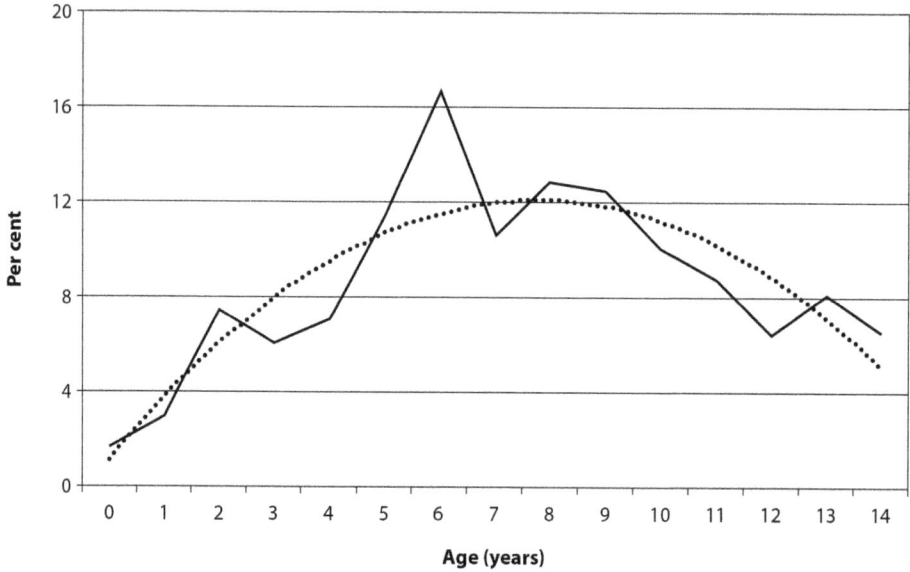

a. The broken lines represent a 'best fit' line, based on the coefficients of a second order polynomial regression.

Source: Authors' customised calculations using the 2008 NATSISS (accessed using the RADL)

Fig. 6.5 Proportion of Indigenous children with eye or sight problems, by age, Australia, 2008[a]

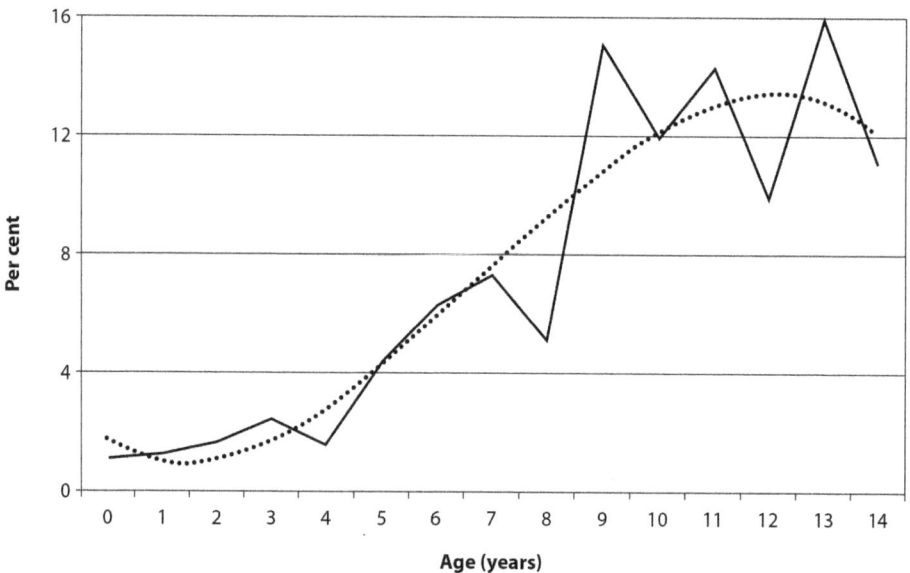

a. The broken lines represent a 'best fit' line, based on the coefficients of a third order polynomial regression.

Source: Authors' customised calculations using the 2008 NATSISS (accessed using the RADL)

Oral health

About 36 per cent of children aged 2–14 years had at least one problem with their teeth or gums – this includes cavities, decay, fillings, breakage, having no teeth, and bleeding or sore gums. The NATSISS highlights that dental problems were less prevalent among children in remote settings (26%) than non-remote areas (37%), which may reflect a greater reliance on bush tucker in the most remote regions of Australia and a correspondingly smaller reliance on diets high in energy derived from refined carbohydrates and saturated fats (National Health and Medical Research Council 2000). This is consistent with the findings for Indigenous children in Western Australia (Zubrick et al. 2004) but contrasts the evidence of Jamieson Armfield and Roberts-Thomson (2007) in a study of Indigenous children in New South Wales, South Australia and the Northern Territory. The discrepancy between studies is likely to be attributable to differences in sample characteristics, collection methods, or the measurement of oral health between studies. The binary, carer-reported measure of dental problems used here may be a greater reflection of dental services use than dental problems *per se*. If so, then our findings would suggest that dental services are more accessible (and affordable) to Indigenous children living in less remote areas.

Educational attendance

The NATSISS design did not allow the collection of a robust range of variables on child education, and this naturally limits what can be examined in this important domain of child development. The survey questions mainly focus on issues of attendance, although the included items could only be considered proxy indicators of attendance patterns. Encouragingly, the vast majority of 'eligible' Indigenous children were going to school (97.5%) and only a relatively small proportion of school children (7%) were seen to have a problem with attendance (not attending without permission).

The carers of 27 per cent of school children stated that they had missed at least one day of school in the previous week, with the modal response for this group being five days (all days) missed. About 30 per cent of absence was due to sickness/injury, although many reported that the absence was because the school was not available or not open. These results are difficult to interpret but almost certainly support the observation that Indigenous students have poorer rates of attendance than their non-Indigenous counterparts (SCRGSP 2009).

Despite no data in the NATSISS on child academic performance, this outcome merits a short comment here. Other studies demonstrate clearly that there are considerable gaps in the performance of Indigenous and other children at school (SCRGSP 2009; Zubrick et al. 2006). Importantly, disparities are evident at Year

1 and widen further in subsequent school years. These gaps are arguably the most important in terms of predicting onward disparities in human capabilities between Indigenous and other Australians.

Table 6.1 Proportion of Indigenous children with selected health/ development problems, Australia, 2008

Health/development factor	Non-remote (%)	Remote (%)	Total (%)
Birthweight[a]			
Less than 2 500 grams	11.9	8.8	11.2
Less than 1 500 grams	2.1*	1.4**	1.9*
Low gestation (less than 37 weeks)[a]	23.8	25.2	24.1
Global health			
Excellent	48.0†	41.4†	46.4
Very good	30.4†	38.3†	32.2
Good	17.8	17.0	17.6
Fair	3.0	2.6	2.9
Poor	0.8*	0.8*	0.8
Eye or sight problem	8.2†	3.9†	7.2
Ear or hearing problem	8.0	10.2	8.5
Teeth or gum problems[b]	37.1†	25.8†	34.4
Educational attendance			
'Eligible' children not going to school[c]	4.3	5.0	4.5
Problem with attendance[d]	5.4†	12.8†	7.0

a. 0–3 year olds only.

b. 2–14 year olds only.

c. Excludes those who are too young, too old or ineligible for school.

d. Of those attending school.

† Denotes a statistically significant difference (at 95% level of confidence) in the proportions in remote and non-remote areas.

* Relative standard error between 25% and 50%.

** Relative standard error greater than or equal to 50%.

Source: Authors' customised calculations using the 2008 NATSISS (accessed using the RADL)

Prompts, facilitators and constraints of child development

As we outlined earlier, developmental strengths are influenced by a small set of mechanisms that either prompt, facilitate or constrain their development.

- Developmental 'prompts' are particularly critical in the initiation of the acquisition and accumulation of skills. The developmental prompts of these skills include biology (including genes), expectations, and opportunities.

- Developmental 'facilitators' increase leverage from developmental prompts. These facilitators include: at least average intelligence; an easygoing temperament; emotional support in the face of challenge; and good language development.

- Developmental 'constraints' are those influences that impede or diminish the effects of the prompts or interact with the facilitators. These constraints include multiple accumulative stress, 'chaos' (i.e. war, social upheaval) that prevents the establishment of developmental stability, social inequality, and social exclusion.

Many of the factors that prompt or facilitate child development are either missing in the lives of Indigenous children or are too limited to produce sustainable benefits and opportunities in life. When skills and abilities are sufficiently acquired their benefits are, too often, constrained or overwhelmed by the influences of the living environment. Some of these constraints are characteristics of individuals or families, and have a direct influence on Indigenous children. Others are population-wide characteristics that impact on children in indirect ways, and reflect the fact that Indigenous populations have a diminished capability base relative to other Australians.

From a policy perspective, these prompts, facilitators and constraints offer avenues for deliberate investment at a variety of levels, from those that focus on individuals to those that affect national and global policy. There is plenty of flexibility to address them through one or more settings (e.g. family, school, care environments, work) using different instruments (legislation, remuneration, transfers and benefits, goods and services) to effect change.

Population-wide constraints

Population-wide constraints include lower life expectancy and higher fertility rates. These two factors conspire to produce a very young population (median age is 20 years) with a relatively low adult-to-child ratio. The NATSISS data highlight that there was 1.3 Indigenous adults (18+) for every Indigenous person aged 0–17 years, which compares with an approximate 3:1 ratio in the total population (ABS 2010). This indicates that Indigenous children have less access to older, experienced people available for care, protection, cultural guidance and general life-skills education (Silburn et al. 2006). This is compounded by high rates of imprisonment, father absence and family breakdown and consequent sole parent status. Over one-third (37%) of Indigenous children less than one year of age were in one parent families; this proportion rose to 46 per cent among those aged 14 years.

Furthermore, the socioeconomic disadvantage experienced by Indigenous peoples in the form of low levels of education, employment and income, can generate stress. These circumstances change the capacity of populations to participate in, and benefit from, mainstream services (Zubrick et al. 2008). Indigenous children are vastly overrepresented in the lower levels of all socioeconomic constructs included in the NATSISS, including the area-based Socio-Economic Indexes for Areas (SEIFA) measure (see Fig. 6.6).

Fig. 6.6 Distribution of Indigenous children aged 0–14 years by SEIFA deciles, Australia, 2008[a]

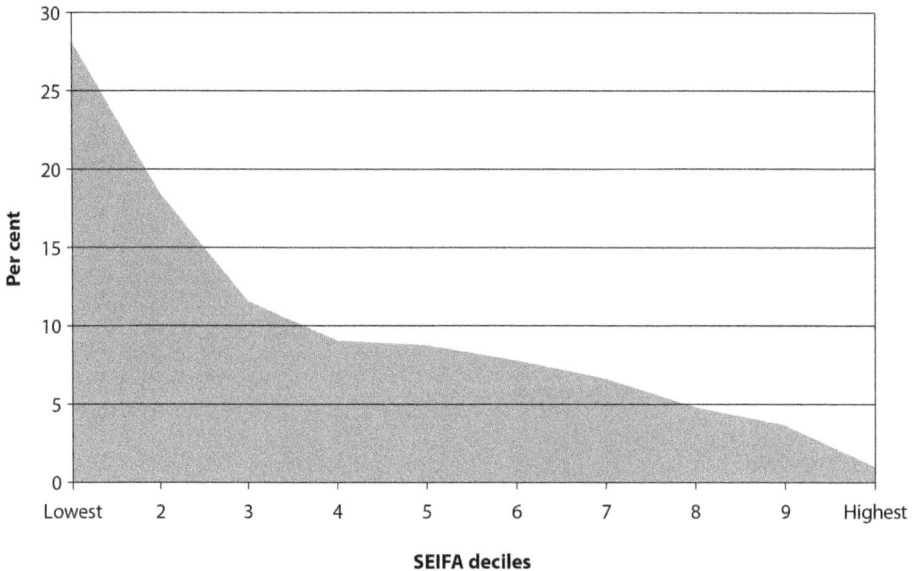

a. SEIFA deciles were determined based on the distribution of values for all Australian CDs.

Source: Authors' customised calculations using the 2008 NATSISS (accessed using the RADL)

A profile of prompts, facilitators and constraints

Here we attempt to categorise 2008 NATSISS items as either prompts, facilitators or constraints of child development (see Table 6.2). The NATSISS cannot fully inform the breadth of these constructs nor are they necessarily the most salient measures. In some instances the selected items are proxy indicators of the constructs discussed earlier – for example, we use carer involvement in informal activities as an indicator of early language development. Despite these shortcomings, the NATSISS items, collectively, provide insight into the capability profile of Indigenous children in Australia.

The most prominent feature of the data presented in Table 6.2 is the high prevalence of development constraints. They document a profile of stress and discrimination that are experienced at levels unique to Indigenous children. For example, 44 per cent of 0–3 year olds and 65 per cent of 4–14 year olds experienced at least one of the stressors that were asked about in the NATSISS. These stressors commonly included serious events such as the death of a close family member/friend, having a really bad illness/accident, and being physically hurt by someone. When these types of stressors occur frequently in early life they can have serious longer-term effects on the development of the brain, endocrine and immune systems, and are a key mechanism in the biological embedding of disadvantage (McEwen 1998). Carers also reported that 15 per cent of school children aged 6–14 years were bullied or treated unfairly at school because they were Indigenous, 9 per cent needed to stayed overnight somewhere else due to a family crisis in the six months prior to the survey, and 62 per cent of 5–14 year olds had moved house in the last five years.

Table 6.2 Summary of selected developmental prompts, facilitators and constraints of Indigenous child development, by remoteness, Australia, 2008

	Non-remote (%)	Remote (%)	Total (%)
Developmental prompts			
Birthweight[a]			
Less than 2,500 grams	11.9	8.8	11.2
Less than 1,500 grams	2.1*	1.4**	1.9*
Breastfeeding[a]			
Never been breastfed	24.6†	13.7†	22.2
Breastfed but less than 3 months	23.2†	10.0†	20.3
Does not usually eat fruit[b]	4.8†	2.3†	4.2
Does not usually eat vegetables[b]	3.5	2.4	3.3
Identified with a clan, tribe or language group[c]	40.6†	69.2†	47.4
Some involvement in cultural events, ceremonies or organisations in last 12 months[c]	66.5†	80.9†	70.0
Participation in cultural activities[c]	60.4†	79.4†	64.9
Developmental facilitators			
Education of main carer			
Completed Year 12	22.8	19.4	22.0
Non-school qualification	38.2†	23.6†	34.8

	Non-remote (%)	Remote (%)	Total (%)
Time spent by main carer doing informal learning activities with child in last week[d]			
None	3.3	4.1*	3.5
1–6 days	26.3	26.5	26.3
7 days	70.2	69.1	69.9
Type of informal learning activities main carer did with child in last week			
Read a book (0–6 year olds)	74.7†	54.6†	69.8
Told a story (0–6 year olds)	60.1	60.7	60.3
Listened to child read (7–10 year olds)	71.6†	53.3†	67.2
Developmental constraints			
Experienced a stressor in last 12 months			
0–3 year olds	46.6†	35.1†	44.0
4–14 year olds	66.3	59.8	64.8
Bullied or treated unfairly at school[e]	16.1†	10.8†	14.9
Stayed overnight somewhere else due to family crisis in the last 6 months	9.1	9.6	9.2
Affected by friends/family members with alcohol problem	11.6	13.2	12.0
Affected by friends/family members with drug problem	9.1	8.2	8.9
Moved house in the last 5 years[f]	63.3	57.6	62.0
Needed more formal child care[g]	12.8	17.3	13.8

a. 0–3 year olds.

b. 1–14 year olds.

c. 3–14 year olds.

d. 1–6 year olds.

e. 2–14 year olds that were attending school.

f. 5–14 year olds.

g. 0–12 year olds.

† Denotes a statistically significant difference (at 95% level of confidence) in the proportions in remote and non-remote areas.

* Relative standard error between 25% and 50%.

** Relative standard error greater than or equal to 50%.

Source: Authors' customised calculations using the 2008 NATSISS (accessed using the RADL)

Associations with child developmental outcomes: An example using socioeconomic constructs

To this point we have presented some indicators of Indigenous child development, described the mechanisms that prompt, facilitate and constrain development and outlined some general principles for improving human capabilities in Indigenous contexts. Here we provide an insight into the relative importance of factors that influence Indigenous child development.

There is a relatively circumscribed literature on the nature of the associations between Indigenous child developmental outcomes and their antecedents. The empirical evidence suggests that there is a fairly weak relationship between income, education and employment of Indigenous adults and the developmental outcomes of their children (Zubrick et al. 2005). We test this observation with 2008 NATSISS data and focus on three constructs of socioeconomic status and their association with the overall (global) health of children: the educational attainment of the main carer of the child, household income (equivalised), and area-level relative disadvantage (SEIFA). We chose these for this analysis as they represent three different dimensions of socioeconomic status at multiple levels (parent, family and neighbourhood). The result of greatest interest is children who are reported to have excellent or very good health at the time of the survey. The shape and magnitude of the associations between socioeconomic status and child health is highlighted by Fig. 6.7, which shows the odds ratios from logistic regression analyses. There appears to be no association between the parent-rated measure of child health status and carer education and no statistically significant trend by the SEIFA measure, although those children in the third quintile of SEIFA were 1.4 times more likely (95% CI: 1.31–1.46) to be in excellent or very good health than those in the lowest quintile. Household income is positively associated with child health, although the relationship is non-linear in nature and only features an elevated odds of having excellent or very good health for children in the top two quintiles (OR = 1.8; 95% CI: 1.64–1.95) and second quintile (OR = 1.5; 95% CI: 1.39–1.54), relative to those in the lowest quintile. Household income continues to have a statistically significant independent effect on child health when analysed collectively with carer education and SEIFA (p=0.0024).

Fig. 6.7 Relative odds of excellent or very good health in Indigenous children, by constructs of socioeconomic status, Australia, 2008[a]

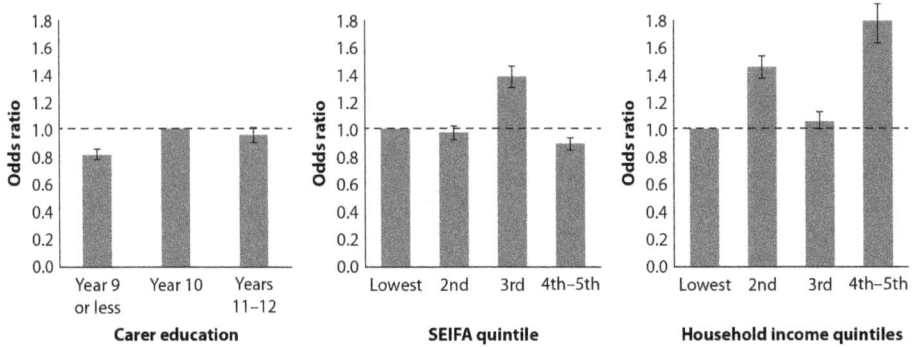

Carer education   **SEIFA quintile**   **Household income quintiles**

a. All logistic regression models include age and sex as covariates. Household income is derived using equivalence scales; quintiles have been derived based on the distribution of total household income for Indigenous and non-Indigenous households. SEIFA quintiles were determined based on the distribution of values for all Australian CDs.

Source: Authors' customised calculations using the 2008 NATSISS (accessed using the RADL)

Fig. 6.8 Relative odds of excellent or very good health in Indigenous children, by household income, Australia, 2008: Simple and full models[a]

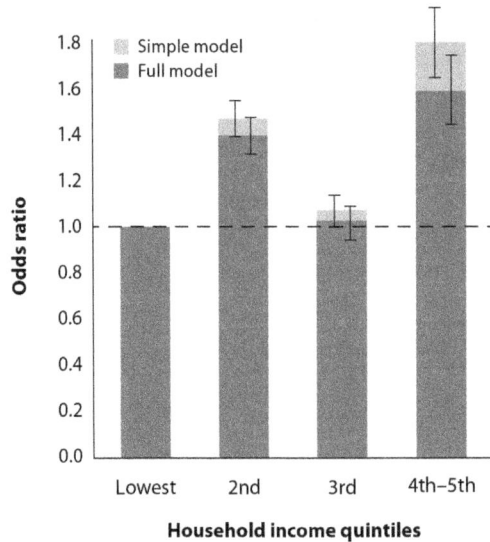

Household income quintiles

a. 'Simple' logistic regression model includes age and sex as covariates. The 'full' model also includes the following covariates: remoteness, SEIFA quintiles, carer education, experience of stressors, carer engagement in informal activities with the child, whether bullied or treated unfairly, whether child stayed overnight somewhere else because of family crises, whether child was involved in cultural events, ceremonies or organisations or participated in cultural activities in last 12 months, and whether child eats fruit and vegetables. Household income is derived using equivalence scales; quintiles have been derived based on the distribution of total household income for Indigenous and non-Indigenous households.

Source: Authors' customised calculations using the 2008 NATSISS (accessed using the RADL)

The association between household income and child health is only slightly attenuated by the inclusion of other factors in the model that are known to influence health in early life (see Fig. 6.8). We found that stress, carer engagement in informal activities with the child, and bullying and discrimination were all factors significantly associated with a child being in excellent or very good health, and that household income has an effect on child health over and above the influence of these factors.

Implications

Our findings suggest that the strong associations characteristically seen in mainstream populations between child health and development outcomes and socioeconomic status do not necessarily hold in Indigenous populations. This does not imply that these factors are unrelated to the development of Indigenous children or that improving education, for example, is unwarranted. Instead it is likely to reflect that there are other circumstances in the social and physical environment that disrupt these associations for large segments of the Indigenous population (Zubrick et al. 2008).

Weak health gradients are particularly problematic for populations with low levels of health because they imply that there are greater barriers to improving health. If traditional levers do not produce improvements in health then these populations are in danger of being 'trapped' in poor health (Buttenheim et al. 2010). It is difficult to underestimate the implications of this for Indigenous Australia. The current policy imperative is one that aims to 'close the (developmental) gap' between the mainstream and Indigenous population within a generation (Department of Families, Housing, Community Services and Indigenous Affairs 2009). These findings of weak associations between determinants of human development and human capital formation would suggest that either the policy expectation is overly ambitious or that greater effort will be needed to compensate for the reduced effect size.

The findings here confront policy and practice settings with competing demands: the urgency to be seen to be 'doing something' to address the acute needs and demands of families overwhelmed by crises while at the same time diverting government resources and energies to the longer and slower process of enabling demographic restitution of capability. As noted above, this process is commencing from a very low base and it is unlikely that there is any generational short-cut in the time that it will take to effect true change. We have highlighted that Indigenous children have less access to older, experienced people available for their care, protection, cultural guidance and general life-skills education. The 'treatment' for this is primarily a demographic treatment: delay the onset of age of first pregnancy while concurrently increasing the proportion of Indigenous children that receive high quality early childhood educational daycare and support into primary school. The goal here is to prolong enrolment, attendance and retention into the upper secondary school to increase the proportion of the Indigenous population that has vocational and tertiary experiences – this will build greater human capital. It will have the ultimate effect of expanding choices for Indigenous adults and, concomitantly, improve the wellbeing and life opportunities of Indigenous populations.

While this is slowly transforming the capability profile of the Indigenous population, there is a need to specifically enrol Indigenous people in understanding how to reduce the developmental chaos which is the major constraint affecting Indigenous children. This will take different forms depending on where the child and family are living – the major areas here are demarked by the metropolitan setting (urban), transition zone (rural and remote regional centres) and extremely remote areas. The short-term strategies require establishing effective buffering around the child and stabilising the level of chaos the child is exposed to: reducing the effects of direct and indirect violence, improving the quality of the material environment particularly for children aged 2–4 years, establishing emotional support for the adult carer, and providing regularity in routine and setting realistic expectations for the child. The treatment for the population is a focus on slow, progressive, upstream and distal changes in human capital formation; the treatment for children living today is a proximal approach with an explicit engagement of Indigenous adults in enhancing life prospects.

Conclusion

We have been able to utilise the 2008 NATSISS to explore the developmental status of Indigenous children in Australia. We have demonstrated three significant results from the 2008 NATSISS data. First, the majority of Indigenous children are in excellent or very good overall health, although there are some developmental danger signs – that are evident from birth – for a significant number of children. Second, the profile of developmental constraints in Indigenous Australia is likely to overwhelm the critical acquisition of skills and abilities for many children. This analysis confirms that stress and discrimination are part of many Indigenous children's lives, and from an early age. Third, the associations between child development outcomes and determinants of human development may be weaker in Indigenous populations relative to mainstream Australia. This suggests that policy responses that are suitable for the general population need to be modified in order to significantly benefit the health of Indigenous peoples.

There are a number of limitations to what we have presented here. The cross-sectional nature of the NATSISS, the limited information on aspects of education, social and emotional wellbeing and geography, and the use of questions that rely on carer perception and recall, has curbed the breadth of potential analyses and what can be inferred from our results.

Acknowledgement

Carrington Shepherd is financially supported by a Sidney Myer Health Scholarship.

References

Australian Bureau of Statistics (ABS) 2006. *National Aboriginal and Torres Strait Islander Health Survey, 2004–05*, cat. no. 4715.0, ABS, Canberra.

—— 2010. *Population by Age and Sex, Australian States and Territories, Jun 2010*, cat. no. 3201.0, ABS, Canberra.

Australian Institute of Health and Welfare (AIHW), Mathers, C., Vos, T. and Stevenson, C. E. 1999. *The Burden of Disease and Injury In Australia*, cat. no. PHE 17, AIHW, Canberra.

Bell, S. 1995. 'Building Aboriginal health from the ground upwards', Paper presented at the *Aboriginal Health: Social and Cultural Transitions* Conference, viewed 7 May 2010, available at <www.caac.org.au/pr/index.php?dl=28>

Boddington, P. and Raisanen, U. 2009. 'Theoretical and practical issues in the definition of health: Insights from Aboriginal Australia', *Journal of Medicine and Philosophy*, 34 (1): 49–67.

Briscoe, G. 2003. *Counting, Health and Identity: A History of Aboriginal Health and Demography in Western Australia and Queensland*, Aboriginal Studies Press, Canberra.

Bronfenbrenner, U. 1979. *The Ecology of Human Development: Experiments by Nature and Design*, Harvard University Press, Cambridge, Massachusetts.

Buttenheim, A., Goldman, N., Pebley, A. R., Wong, R. and Chung, C. 2010. 'Do Mexican immigrants "import" social gradients in health to the US?', *Social Science and Medicine*, 71 (7): 1268–76.

Coates, H., Morris, P., Leach, A. and Couzos, S. 2002. 'Otitis media in Aboriginal children: Tackling a major health problem', *Medical Journal of Australia*, 177 (4): 177–78.

Department of Families, Housing, Community Services and Indigenous Affairs 2009. *Closing the Gap on Indigenous Disadvantage: The Challenge for Australia*, Australian Government, Canberra.

Ford, J., Nassar, N., Sullivan, E. A., Chambers, G. and Lancaster, P. 2003. *Reproductive Health Indicators, Australia 2002*, cat. no. PER 20, AIHW National Perinatal Statistics Unit, Canberra.

Fukuda-Parr, S. and Kumar, A. K. S. 2004. *Readings in Human Development: Concepts, Measures and Policies for a Development Paradigm*, Second ed., Oxford University Press, New Delhi.

Jamieson, L. M., Armfield, J. M. and Roberts-Thomson, K. F. 2007. 'Indigenous and non-indigenous child oral health in three Australian states and territories', *Ethnicity and Health*, 12 (1): 89–107.

Jessor, R. 1993. 'Successful adolescent development among youth in high-risk settings', *American Psychologist*, 48 (2): 117–26.

Keating, D. P. and Hertzman, C. 1999. *Developmental Health and the Wealth of Nations: Social, Biological, and Educational Dynamics*, Guilford Press, New York.

Kuh, D. and Ben-Shlomo, Y. 2004. *A Life Course Approach to Chronic Disease Epidemiology*, Second edn, Oxford University Press, New York.

McEwen, B. S. 1998. 'Protective and damaging effects of stress mediators', *New England Journal of Medicine*, 338 (3): 171–79.

Morris, P., Leach, A., Silberberg, P., Mellon, G., Wilson, C., Hamilton, E., et al. 2005. 'Otitis media in young Aboriginal children from remote communities in Northern and Central Australia: A cross-sectional survey', *BMC pediatrics*, 5 (1): 27.

National Health and Medical Research Council 2000. *Nutrition in Aboriginal and Torres Strait Islander Peoples: An Information Paper*, National Health and Medical Research Council, Canberra.

Saggers, S. and Gray, D. 2007. 'Defining what we mean', in B. Carson, T. Dunbar, R. D. Chenhall and R. Bailie (eds), *Social Determinants of Indigenous Health*, Allen & Unwin, Sydney.

Sen, A. 2002. 'Health: Perception versus observation', *BMJ*, 324 (7342): 860–61.

Silburn, S. R., Zubrick, S. R., De Maio, J. A., Shepherd, C., Griffin, J. A., Mitrou, F. G., et al. 2006. *The Western Australian Aboriginal Child Health Survey: Strengthening the Capacity of Aboriginal Children, Families and Communities*, Telethon Institute for Child Health Research, Perth.

Steering Committee for the Review of Government Service Provision (SCRGSP) 2009. *Overcoming Indigenous Disadvantage: Key Indicators 2009*, Productivity Commission, Canberra.

Young, M. E. 2002. *Early Child Development:Investing in the Future*, World Bank, Washington DC, viewed 29 September 2011, <http://siteresources.worldbank. org/EDUCATION/Resources/278200-1099079877269/547664-1099079922573/ ECD_investing_in_the_future.pdf>

Zubrick, S. R. 2010. 'Where do strengths come from? The contribution of childhood in the course of human development', Paper presented at the 6th National Family and Community Strengths Conference, November– December 2010, University of Newcastle, Newcastle.

——, Lawrence, D. M., Silburn, S. R., Blair, E., Milroy, H., Wilkes, T., et al. 2004. *Western Australian Aboriginal Child Health Survey: The Health of Aboriginal Children and Young People*, Telethon Institute for Child Health Research, Perth.

——, Silburn, S. R., De Maio, J. A., Shepherd, C., Griffin, J. A., Dalby, R. B., et al. 2006. *The Western Australian Aboriginal Child Health Survey: Improving the Educational Experiences of Aboriginal Children and Young People*, Telethon Institute for Child Health Research, Perth.

——, Silburn, S. R., De Maio, J., Shepherd, C., Griffin, J. A., Dalby, R. B., et al. 2008. 'The Western Australian Aboriginal Child Health Survey: Are there any policy implications?', in G. Robinson, U. Eickelkamp, J. Goodnow and I. Katz (eds), *Contexts of Child Development – Culture, Policy and Intervention.*, Charles Darwin University, Darwin.

——, Silburn, S. R., Lawrence, D. M., Mitrou, F. G., Dalby, R. B., Blair, E. M., et al. 2005. *The Western Australian Aboriginal Child Health Survey: The Social and Emotional Wellbeing of Aboriginal Children and Young People*, Telethon Institute for Child Health Research, Perth.

——, Taylor, C. L., Lawrence, D., Mitrou, F., Christensen, D. and Dalby, R. 2009. 'The development of human capability across the lifecourse: Perspectives from childhood', *Australasian Epidemiologist,* 16 (3): 6–10.

7. The benefits of Indigenous education: Data findings and data gaps

Nicholas Biddle and Timothy Cameron

Although the headline target for the Council of Australian Governments (COAG) Closing the Gap agenda is the elimination of the life expectancy gap between Indigenous and non-Indigenous Australians, in numerical terms, education dominates with three of the six targets related to it. This includes targets related to preschool access (Target 3), literacy and numeracy (Target 4) and Year 12 completion (Target 5). The setting of these targets clearly recognises that not only is education important in and of itself, but without reducing disparities between Indigenous and non-Indigenous Australians in education, other targets on health and employment are unlikely to be met.

Closing the gap between Indigenous and non-Indigenous Australians in education outcomes will not be easy. To indicate the scale of the challenge, consider findings from the most recent (2006) Census. First, 47.8 per cent of Indigenous 3–5 year olds (who had not started school) were attending preschool compared to 57.5 per cent of non-Indigenous children. Across the Indigenous lifecourse, this gap only widens. By age 20–24, 36.0 per cent of Indigenous Australians (who were not still at school) had completed Year 12 compared to 74.5 per cent of non-Indigenous Australians. For all education types, 34.5 per cent of Indigenous 15–24 year olds were undertaking education compared to 55.3 per cent of non-Indigenous young adults.

One potential reason for this education disparity is physical and financial access. Biddle (2010) showed that Indigenous youth were more likely to live in remote areas than their non-Indigenous counterparts and that within the Indigenous population there were substantial disparities by region in terms of education participation and attainment. Furthermore, on average Indigenous Australians grow up in families with fewer material resources meaning that financially it is more difficult to attend relatively expensive private schools (Biddle and Yap 2010).

While important, the above financial and geographic disparities alone do not explain the gap in education attendance and attainment between Indigenous and non-Indigenous Australians. In all regions, including Australia's largest capital cities, Indigenous Australians had lower levels of education than their non-Indigenous counterparts (Biddle 2010). Biddle (2007) also showed that the gap between the two populations in terms of participation also remained after controlling for family income, employment and education. Access is not the only issue driving the disparity in education between the two populations. For most Indigenous youth there is usually one high school or a tertiary institution available relatively close by that is free or, in the case of universities, may be paid for later in life. For many Indigenous youth, it would appear that the benefits of engaging with these educational opportunities do not outweigh the costs.

To a certain extent, the choice being made by some Indigenous youth to not participate in formal education should be respected. There are many activities outside the non-Indigenous mainstream that do not require extended formal education. If an Indigenous youth or their family does not see later secondary school or post-school education as being worthwhile, then compelling them to attend is likely to be counterproductive. Not only will the negative effects outweigh the positive, but students who do not want to be at school can have a detrimental effect on those who do. However, if these students are opting out of school or post-school options without full information, then this is potential grounds for government intervention. Furthermore, it is also of concern if childhood and early school experiences are having an undue influence on the choices available to Indigenous Australians when they are considering their education options.

Ultimately, the policy response to low education participation by Indigenous Australians will be determined by the reasons why Indigenous Australians make alternative education decisions and the constraints that they face in making these decisions. Unfortunately, the data available to analyse these decisions is far from perfect. There is no longitudinal data that allows analysis of the effect of early childhood experiences on later school choice. However, we know from other contexts that the early years are crucial in determining future educational options and constraints (Cunha et al. 2006). We also do not have information for estimating accurate returns to education for Indigenous Australians, information which is crucial when trying to gauge whether economic incentives are driving the education decision.

In situations such as these where data is lacking, it is important to have a solid theoretical model, based on empirical research in other contexts but also informed by the unique circumstances of the Indigenous population. Such a model will help to identify the likely impacts on the education decision, the key research questions that need to be answered, and the data required to answer the questions. In the next section of the paper, we outline the beginnings of such a model and pose two research questions that will guide the analysis in this paper.

A model of Indigenous education

In developing a model of Indigenous education, we begin with the well known human capital model. At the heart of the human capital model outlined by Becker (1964) is the assumption that when deciding whether or not to undertake a certain type of education, potential students are rational (in the economic sense) utility maximisers who, above all, see education as an investment. An investment in education will improve one's performance in the workplace and an individual will invest until the returns to an additional unit of education (measured by increases in discounted future income) just equal the cost. That is, until marginal returns equal marginal cost.

Although the human capital model has been quite influential in education research and policy making, it has also been recognised that it has a number of limitations, under the basic specification presented above. The first of these is whether education enhances productivity directly (as assumed in the model), or instead acts as a signalling or screening device whereby already productive workers are identified (e.g. Arrow 1973; Spence 1973).

Under the alternative specification, employers assume that those with a higher innate ability find education easier (or less costly) and are therefore more likely to invest heavily in education than those who find education a struggle. An employer is therefore more likely to hire a person with relatively high levels of education, not just because the education they have undergone has made them more productive, but also because it has demonstrated that they were more productive in the first place.

Whether or not it is human capital or screening/signalling that is driving the differences in earnings has important implications for some aspects of policy development. If governments are trying to decide on the level of investment they make in education or the type of education to focus on, then under the human capital model across-the-board increases in education lead to higher economy-wide productivity: therefore there is a much stronger argument for government provision of education. Under a signalling/screening model, however, education only affects relative earnings, and therefore economy-wide increases in education have little or no effect on economic growth. However, this distinction matters less when considering participation in education from the individual's point of view as they are arguably more concerned with whether they will have a higher income if they study, rather than the source of that higher income.

The basic human capital model also assumes that a person's utility is determined mainly by their income, and if discounted future additional income is higher than the cost of education, then people will invest in education. It is likely, though, that a student's current social situation is also important in influencing their behaviour. Specifically, children who have positive attitudes to school when they are in the middle secondary years are more inclined to further school participation. They are more likely to intend completing Year 12 and consequently are also more likely to actually do so (Khoo and Ainley 2005; Marks 1998). Students who do not like school are more likely to leave without completing their secondary education (Wehlage and Rutter 1986) and children who are happy in the later years of secondary school are more likely to complete university (Dockery 2010).

Despite the above research, there is a lack of literature relating happiness at school to school completion rates both on the whole, and especially with respect to Indigenous Australians. Most literature linking education and happiness tells the other side of the story: how education affects future happiness. Higher levels of education lead to, on average, higher future incomes but it has been shown that education correlates weakly with happiness scores in rich countries (Hartog and Oosterbeek 1998). A recent study shows that Australian university graduates, despite their improved labour market outcomes, have lower levels of happiness compared to those that have only completed Year 12 (Dockery 2010).

In addition to income and school-level wellbeing, there are also a number of other outcomes that are likely to be associated with higher education levels that people may take into account when deciding whether or not to invest in education. Although there are indirect effects that operate via income, education may also have direct effects on things like health, the schooling of one's children, the efficiency of consumer choices and the ability to plan fertility decisions (Wolfe and Haveman 2001).

Finally, the human capital model assumes that potential students make decisions based on a comparison between their future income streams with and without education. However, potential students cannot know their precise future income and must therefore form expectations based on what they do know. Different students have access to different information, so it is possible that expectations are also formed differently (Dominitz and Manski 1996).

Pulling this discussion together, an economic model of Indigenous education participation would take into account the factor that Indigenous Australians start school with lower levels of cognitive and non-cognitive ability (as valued in formal education) with the gap widening throughout the early school years. When making the decision to continue on at school beyond the post-compulsory years, Indigenous students may have different potential benefits of education due to the types of labour markets they have access to. However, these returns may be estimated with uncertainty as they have relatively few role models to provide information. There are also other non-economic returns to education that may be important, but these must be traded off against different non-economic costs of schooling.

In this paper, we focus on two aspects of the education decision. The first relates to the potential benefits of studying and the second the potential social costs of studying. Specifically, we consider the following two research questions:

- What are the apparent benefits – economic and non-economic – of education and do they vary by gender or remoteness?

- Are Indigenous Australians happier or less happy at school than non-Indigenous Australians and do any differences change after controlling for other characteristics?

The relationship between education attainment and wellbeing

The first step is to consider the relationship between an Indigenous Australian's level of education and a number of outcome measures. Ideally, we would like to be able to measure a return to education across a number of domains. Returns are usually calculated by comparing the benefit of education – the average difference in a particular outcome measure for a person with a given level of education and another person with a lower level of education but otherwise identical characteristics – with the cost. If this return was lower for the Indigenous population across a range of measures, then this might explain why Indigenous Australians are less likely to participate in education.

Unfortunately, it is not possible to measure such returns to education with the data available. This is because although we know what a particular outcome is for a person with a given level of education (on average) we do not observe what their outcome would be if they had a different level of education (the counterfactual). What we can and do measure is the average difference within the Indigenous population between those with a given level of education and a separate set of individuals with a different level of education. This would be roughly equivalent to a return to education (after taking into account costs) if the level of education was the only thing that differed between the two groups. However, we know from the literature used to develop the model in the previous section, as well as analysis presented later in this chapter, that those with different levels of education also differ in important ways.

Specifically, we know from other contexts that having higher levels of cognitive and non-cognitive ability makes education easier or less costly (Card 2001). Similarly, those who are more intrinsically motivated and who value the future relatively highly are also more likely to undertake and complete education. This would not be an issue if education was the only thing that these characteristics affected. However, they are also potentially associated with a number of the outcome measures that are considered to be measures of wellbeing or that influence wellbeing directly. For example, being highly numerate makes education easier, but it also makes it easier to obtain a job whatever a person's education levels.

If these other factors were observable, then we could control for them in the model and still estimate a return to education. However, while they are often observable to the individual making the decision, they are rarely observable to the researcher attempting to estimate a return to education. This is particularly the case with cross-sectional data. Longitudinal databases with a much greater age range than is currently available, or evaluations of policies that add a degree of randomness to the education decision, would be allow us to shed some light on this issue.

While it is not possible to calculate a return to education with currently available data, it can still be instructive to compare the average difference in outcomes by education across a number of domains of interest. This is useful for three reasons. First, although there are undoubtedly omitted variable biases when trying to estimate returns to education with cross-sectional data, they are not always large (Leigh and Ryan 2008). A simple comparison by education level can therefore identify those outcomes where returns to education are potentially high – areas for further study with better data if/when it becomes available. Secondly, it is not clear whether individuals use such a sophisticated analysis when deciding to undertake education. It is entirely possible that they make a simple comparison between those with and without a particular qualification when making their decision.

The final reason for calculating average differences by education is that, even if returns to education are necessary for studying the education decision, when targeting policy towards adults one might still be interested in the extent to which one particular group in the population has better outcomes than another. That is, in certain contexts, policy makers are less concerned with what is causing the difference in outcomes as opposed to what types of people have relatively poor outcomes on average.

With that in mind, we calculate differences by education across eight measures/determinants of wellbeing:

- employment
- income for those employed
- happiness: feeling happy in the past four weeks all or most of the time

- sadness: feeling so sad that nothing could cheer one up at least a little bit of the time in the past four weeks
- health fair/poor: reporting one's own health as being fair or poor (as opposed to good, very good or excellent
- cultural: being involved in cultural events, ceremonies or organisations in the previous 12 months
- have a say: feeling that one is able to have a say within the community on important issues all or most of the time, and
- raise $2 000: feeling that household members could raise $2 000 in an emergency within a week.

Differences are calculated separately by high school education and post-school qualifications. For the former, those who have completed Year 9 or less and those who have completed Year 10 or 11 are compared separately with those who have completed Year 12. In terms of post-school qualifications, individuals are compared by their highest qualification, with those with no qualifications treated as the base case and four other qualification types compared: those with a degree or higher; those with a diploma; those with a Certificate I/II; and those with a Certificate III/IV.

Comparisons are made using a modelling framework controlling for h a limited set of variables. Other explanatory variables in the model include: age; remoteness; marital status; family type; Indigenous status of others in the household; language spoken at home and mobility. We are interested in the net relationship between education and the measures of wellbeing and hence other variables that are likely to be strongly influenced by education or which could potentially be influenced by the dependent variables are not included in the model. Separate estimates are undertaken for males and females (in Table 7.1 and Table 7.2 respectively).

For seven of the eight variables, the dependent variable is constructed as the probability of that particular event occurring (e.g. being employed as opposed to not employed). For income, on the other hand, the dependent variable is the natural log of personal income (with results converted back to linear personal income).

Table 7.1 Association between education and measures of wellbeing, Indigenous males, Australia, 2008

Explanatory variables	Employed	Income if employed	Happiness	Sadness	Health	Cultural	Have a say	Raise $2 000
Aged 15–24	-0.028	-315 ***	0.052 **	-0.090 ***	-0.222 ***	0.008	-0.128 ***	-0.017
Aged 25–34	0.010	-114 ***	0.041 *	-0.071 ***	-0.135 ***	0.001	-0.071 ***	-0.048 *
Aged 55 plus	-0.262 ***	-67	0.052 **	-0.096 ***	0.110 ***	-0.008	0.051 *	0.069 ***
Lives in remote Australia	0.099 ***	-60	0.096 ***	-0.022	-0.094 ***	0.160 ***	0.022	-0.056 **
Not married	-0.236 ***	-384 ***	0.013	-0.005	-0.046	-0.045	-0.052	0.012
Lives in a couple family with children	0.003	13	0.004	-0.030	-0.063 **	0.071 ***	0.031	-0.073 **
Lives in a couple family with no children but dependents	0.053 *	109	0.003	-0.025	-0.072 *	-0.063	0.151 ***	-0.030
Lives in a single parent family with children	0.059 *	311 ***	-0.041	-0.013	0.017	0.031	0.042	-0.154 ***
Lives in a single parent family with no children but dependents	0.075 **	250 **	-0.039	0.032	0.097 *	-0.010	0.067	-0.101 **
Lives in an 'other' family type	0.109 ***	404 ***	-0.103 **	0.062	0.053	-0.006	0.049	-0.113 **
Has a non-Indigenous person living in the household	0.085 ***	66 *	-0.011	-0.054 **	-0.025	-0.206 ***	0.028	0.171 ***
Main language spoken at home is not English	-0.020	-346 ***	0.025	0.085 ***	-0.052 *	0.156 ***	0.164 ***	-0.170 ***

Explanatory variables	Employed	Income if employed	Happiness	Sadness	Health	Cultural	Have a say	Raise $2 000
Changed usual residents in the previous five years	-0.031 *	13	-0.015	0.021	0.031	0.000	-0.061 ***	-0.049 **
Completed Year 10 or 11 only	-0.111 ***	-178 ***	-0.012	0.023	0.010	-0.063 **	-0.037	-0.079 ***
Completed Year 9 or less	-0.294 ***	-278 ***	-0.068 **	0.091 ***	0.151 ***	-0.076 ***	-0.057 **	-0.199 ***
Has a degree or higher as highest qualification	0.152 ***	373 ***	0.060	-0.026	-0.061	0.180 ***	0.058	0.147 ***
Has a diploma as highest qualifications	0.136 ***	294 ***	-0.053	0.053	-0.077	0.177 ***	0.060	0.142 ***
Has a Certificate I or II as highest qualification	0.056 **	139 **	0.040	-0.016	-0.003	0.098 ***	0.048	0.023
Has a Certificate III or IV as highest qualification	0.142 ***	218 ***	0.009	-0.029	-0.058 **	0.070 ***	0.046 *	0.091 ***
Probability of base case	0.768	959	0.729	0.362	0.314	0.630	0.320	0.674
Pseudo/Adjusted R-Squared	0.1582	0.2681	0.0256	0.0245	0.1219	0.1103	0.0485	0.1315
Number of observations	3 259	1 839	3 202	3 199	3 259	3 259	3,259	3,094

Note: The base case individual is: aged 35–54; lives in non-remote Australia; is married; lives in a couple family without children with Indigenous Australians only in the household; speaks English at home; and did not change usual residence in the previous 5 years.
*** Marginal effect for which the coefficient is statistically significant at the 1% level of significance.
** Marginal effect for which the coefficient is statistically significant at the 5% level of significance.
* Marginal effect for which the coefficient is statistically significant at the 10% level of significance.
Source: Customised calculations using the 2008 NATSISS

111

Table 7.2 Association between education and measures of wellbeing, Indigenous females, Australia, 2008

Explanatory variables	Employed		Income if employed		Happiness		Sadness		Health		Cultural		Have a say		Raise $2 000	
Aged 15–24	-0.169	***	-270	***	0.050	**	-0.032		-0.155	***	-0.042	*	-0.101	***	-0.027	
Aged 25–34	-0.086	***	-25		0.017		-0.035	*	-0.111	***	-0.041	**	-0.066	***	-0.025	
Aged 55 plus	-0.315	***	-77	**	0.080	***	-0.101	***	0.071	***	-0.031		0.056	**	0.117	***
Lives in remote Australia	0.099	***	38		0.078	***	0.000		-0.065	***	0.138	***	-0.005		-0.018	
Not married	0.096	***	-209	***	0.006		0.025		-0.022		0.035		-0.013		0.018	
Lives in a couple family with children	-0.103	***	-72	**	0.033		-0.038		-0.027		0.045	*	-0.017		-0.072	***
Lives in a couple family with no children but dependents	-0.018		9		0.036		0.004		0.010		-0.044		0.012		0.073	*
Lives in a single parent family with children	-0.272	***	333	***	-0.039		0.008		0.029		-0.052		0.055		-0.207	***
Lives in a single parent family with no children but dependents	-0.118	**	233	***	-0.007		0.004		0.055		-0.055		0.046		-0.191	***
Lives in an 'other' family type	-0.135	***	323	***	-0.025		-0.004		0.093	**	-0.082	*	0.032		-0.128	***
Has a non-Indigenous person living in the household	0.125	***	-59	**	0.024		-0.056	***	-0.016		-0.186	***	0.047	**	0.178	***
Main language spoken at home is not English	-0.020		-189	***	0.063	***	0.028		-0.023		0.092	***	0.100	***	-0.186	***

Explanatory variables	Employed	Income if employed	Happiness	Sadness	Health	Cultural	Have a say	Raise $2 000
Changed usual residents in the previous five years	-0.049 ***	26	-0.043 ***	0.058 ***	0.009	0.023	-0.024	-0.079 ***
Completed Year 10 or 11 only	-0.136 ***	-106 ***	-0.039 *	0.067 ***	0.043 *	-0.025	-0.024	-0.119 ***
Completed Year 9 or less	-0.317 ***	-188 ***	-0.122 ***	0.120 ***	0.147 ***	-0.074 ***	-0.085 ***	-0.260 ***
Has a degree or higher as highest qualification	0.259 ***	382 ***	-0.039	-0.028	-0.058 *	0.173 ***	0.119 ***	0.183 ***
Has a diploma as highest qualifications	0.225 ***	357 ***	0.033	-0.084 **	-0.052 *	0.150 ***	0.137 ***	0.093 ***
Has a Certificate I or II as highest qualification	0.110 ***	57	0.013	0.050 *	0.030	-0.002	0.066 **	-0.006
Has a Certificate III or IV as highest qualification	0.236 ***	180 ***	0.040 *	-0.030	-0.048 **	0.109 ***	0.071 ***	0.114 ***
Probability of base case	0.649	717	0.710	0.391	0.263	0.689	0.283	0.664
Pseudo/Adjusted R-Squared	0.1814	0.2866	0.0257	0.0212	0.0855	0.0813	0.0337	0.1614
Number of observations	4 303	1 751	4 256	4 249	4 303	4 303	4,303	4,051

Note: The base case individual is: aged 35–54; lives in non-remote Australia; is married; lives in a couple family without children with Indigenous Australians only in the household; speaks English at home; and did not change usual residence in the previous 5 years.

*** Marginal effect for which the coefficient is statistically significant at the 1% level of significance.

** Marginal effect for which the coefficient is statistically significant at the 5% level of significance.

* Marginal effect for which the coefficient is statistically significant at the 10% level of significance.

Source: Customised calculations using the 2008 NATSISS

Beginning in the first column of Table 7.1 and Table 7.2, Indigenous males and females are both more likely to be employed if they have relatively high levels of education. This is not necessarily a causal effect as those who would otherwise be more likely to be employed are more likely to undertake education. However, it does show that if COAG is to meet its target on halving the gap in employment outcomes between Indigenous and non-Indigenous Australians, then the employment rate of the relatively low skilled will probably need to be raised by the largest proportion.

There appears to be greater variation in employment by education for females, particularly by post-school qualifications. This is a consistent finding across the literature and probably reflects the fact that females still tend to take on a greater childcare role, care within the community, and unpaid work in general (Biddle and Yap 2010). As shown in the second column of results, in deciding whether or not to work in addition or instead of providing care, the opportunity cost of not working is higher for females with relatively high levels of education.

For those who were working, there was a greater difference by education in terms of personal income for males rather than females, particularly at the lower end of the education distribution. This is explained once again by higher levels of caring responsibilities and unpaid work for females, with those females with low skills and low income having lower opportunity costs if they opt out of employment.

There is a somewhat different association between education and the two measures of emotional wellbeing for males and females. For both sexes, higher levels of education are associated with higher levels of emotional wellbeing. However, not all levels of education have an association. For males, the only differences are between those who have completed Year 9 or less and the rest of the population. For females on the other hand, those who have completed Year 10 or 11 also have lower levels of emotional wellbeing than those who have completed Year 12. Furthermore, having a diploma was associated with a lower level of sadness than having no qualification at all, whereas having a Certificate I/II was actually associated with a higher level of sadness (albeit at the 10% level of significance only). In addition to emotional wellbeing, there is also a greater health gradient for Indigenous females with regards to reporting one's health as fair or poor (in terms of statistical significance in particular).

Ultimately, all three of these measures of wellbeing are lower for those with relatively low levels of education, as is the probability of participating in cultural events, ceremonies and organisations. Undertaking formal education may impose significant social and emotional costs on Indigenous Australians (though as discussed later in this chapter, the empirical evidence for this is mixed). However, it would appear from these results that those Indigenous adults who have completed formal education are on average happier, less sad, have better health and are more likely to engage in Indigenous cultural activities.

Perhaps the biggest difference by gender in terms of the association between the measures of wellbeing and education is with regard to the ability with which individuals feel they are able to have a say within the community on important issues. For males, those who have completed Year 9 or less have lower levels of this measure of efficacy than those who have completed Year 12. There are small differences by qualifications but these tend to not be significant or only significant at the 10% level of significance. For females on the other hand, the differences by qualification are large and consistently significant. It is possible that those who would otherwise have a high sense of efficacy are more likely to undertake education in the first place. Nonetheless, the results presented in this section give qualified support to the view that prestige or stature within one's community is one of the motivating factors in undertaking education for the Indigenous population.

The final outcome included in Table 7.1 and Table 7.2 is whether or not a person feels that their household could raise $2 000 within a week in an emergency. This measure of financial security is much higher for those with relatively high levels of education, with differences slightly larger for females compared to males. There are three potential causal explanations for this. Firstly, those with higher levels of education have greater income and wealth. Secondly, those with higher levels of education are more likely to be married to someone who also has relatively high levels of education (so called assortative mating, see Mare 1991), compounding the income effect at the household level. Finally, those with higher levels of education may be more likely to plan their finances and seek alternative forms of credit beyond household income. However, there is also a possible reverse causal effect associated with this variable – with those with greater financial security growing up within their household and within their wider social networks better able to undertake education. Whatever the explanation, those with lower levels of education are much less likely to feel financially secure than those who have completed Year 12 or have qualifications.

In general, the results presented in Table 7.1 and Table 7.2 show a large association between education and a number of outcome measures. It is unfortunate that we cannot be more definitive with regards to the causal direction of these associations. However, one of the more consistent findings from the analysis here is that there is a much greater education gradient for females for many of the wellbeing measures analysed. Putting this another way, Indigenous females may need to have a higher level of education than an Indigenous male to have the same level of wellbeing. If this is causal and Indigenous females take this into account when making education decisions, then this may be a reason for the generally higher levels of education participation amongst Indigenous females outlined in Biddle (2010) and demonstrated in later sections of this paper.

Factors associated with school happiness and expectations

Results presented in the previous section suggested one potential explanation for variation within the Indigenous population in terms of education participation. Differences by education in terms of social outcomes were higher for females than males, as is education participation. However, this does not explain why Indigenous Australians are less likely to undertake education compared to the non-Indigenous population. For this, we need to consider school and family background characteristics.

We now look at one aspect of school participation results by analysing the factors associated with an index of school happiness. This index is calculated based on a factor analysis of seven variables in the Longitudinal Survey of Australian Youth (LSAY) and scaled to have a mean of zero and a standard deviation of one. However, it should be noted that results do not change qualitatively if any of the single variables that are used to construct the index are used instead.

The main aim of the analysis in this section is to test whether Indigenous Australians have a higher or lower index value than non-Indigenous Australians indicating that, at the age of 15 at least, they are more or less happy at school. To test for this, the first model includes basic demographic information only. The discussion in the second section of this paper outlined how in previous research socioeconomic status is associated with happiness at school. In addition to testing whether this holds in the LSAY, the analysis presented in Model 2 allows us to test whether any differences between Indigenous and non-Indigenous Australians remain after controlling for language spoken at home, parental education and parental occupation.

The final model includes a number of school specific variables. This includes an assessment of one's own ability, other information on school satisfaction, an index of the individual's test scores across maths, English and science (administered as part of the international component of the LSAY), and the average test scores of individuals in one's school. In essence, Model 3 allows us to test whether there are differences between Indigenous and non-Indigenous Australians in terms of happiness after controlling for other components of the human capital model.

As the dependent variable in the analysis is continuous, we use the linear model estimated via Ordinary Least Squares (OLS). Marginal effects and statistical significance are to be interpreted in comparison to the base case, given underneath Table 7.3.

Table 7.3 Factors associated with an index of student happiness, by Indigenous status, Australia, 2006

	Model 1		Model 2		Model 3	
Age	0.025	*	0.026	*	0.024	*
Female	0.039	***	0.041	***	0.026	***
Indigenous	0.058	**	0.053	**	0.089	***
Born overseas	0.093	***	0.052	***	0.045	***
Mother born overseas	0.032	**	0.021		0.008	
Father born overseas	0.020		0.011		0.007	
Lives in provincial Australia	−0.019	*	−0.003		−0.005	
Lives in remote Australia	−0.034		−0.015		0.023	
Speaks a language other than English at home			0.097	***	0.080	***
Number of years of education for parent with highest level			0.014	***	0.005	**
Mother works as a manager or professional			0.027	***	−0.003	
Father works as a manager or professional			0.063	***	0.016	*
Assessed own ability as 'very well'					0.276	***
Assessed own ability as 'above average'					0.119	***
Assessed own ability as 'below average'					−0.142	***
Agree or strongly agree that 'Teachers are fair and just to me' at school					0.176	***
Agree or strongly agree that 'The work I do is good preparation for the future' at school					0.316	***
Agree or strongly agree that 'I feel safe and secure' at school					0.298	***
Index of test scores					−0.018	***
Index of test scores for school					0.019	*
Predicted index value for base case	0.140		0.094		−0.610	
Adjusted R-Squared	0.0126		0.0288		0.2964	
Number of observations	12 846		12 846		12 324	

Note: The base case individual for all estimations is: aged 15; male; non-Indigenous, born in Australia; and living in a major city. For Model 2, the base case is further defined to speak English at home; have a parent with 13 years of education (but no more); and have a mother and father not employed as a manager or professional. For Model 3, the base case is further defined to assess one's own ability at school as average; disagree or strongly disagree with the statements on their school; have an index value of zero for their test scores (the mean); and attend a school where that is the mean value.

*** Marginal effect for which the coefficient is statistically significant at the 1% level of significance.

** Marginal effect for which the coefficient is statistically significant at the 5% level of significance.

* Marginal effect for which the coefficient is statistically significant at the 10% level of significance.

Source: Customised calculations using Wave 1 of the LSAY (enumerated in 2006)

Beginning with Model 1, we can see an Indigenous Australian is on average happier at school than a non-Indigenous Australian (born in Australia) of the same age, gender and broad region of usual residence. Looking across the models, this difference not only holds once other characteristics are controlled for, but actually widens between Model 2 and Model 3. In other words, Indigenous Australians are on average happier at school than their non-Indigenous counterparts.

This is an important finding because other research (e.g. Munns and McFadden 2000) has shown that Indigenous Australians in certain contexts resist aspects of formal education. The results presented in Table 7.3 do not contradict that research. However, the results do nonetheless suggest that there are other aspects of education that counterbalance this resistance.

A student's happiness is important in its own right. Simply for the fact that school makes up a large proportion of most people's lives, the greater one's happiness whilst at school the higher one's emotional wellbeing across the lifecourse. However, happiness is also important because of its potential impact on school completion. The standard human capital model assumes that individuals focus on the economic costs and benefits of schooling only. While students probably do take this into account, most extensions to the model recognise that a student's happiness is also important.

Summary and data gaps

In discussing previous models of education participation and attempting to tie them to the development of a model of Indigenous education, we identified two research questions related to the costs and benefits of education. In any applied empirical analysis, the number of research questions that cannot be answered is always frustrating. However, this would appear to be particularly the case when it comes to analysing Indigenous education. Nonetheless, by combining information from a few datasets (the LSAY (Waves 1–4), and the 2008 NATSISS), we were able to partially answer some of the questions and be a little more definitive with others.

Research question 1: What are the apparent benefits of education and do they vary by gender or remoteness?

For the most part, those with relatively high levels of education tend to have better outcomes than those without qualifications or who drop out of school at a young age. Differences tend to be greatest for the economic variables (employment, income, financial security), but are also present for a number of broader measures of wellbeing. Differences also tend to be greatest for females and those who live in non-remote Australia – two groups within the Indigenous population with relatively high levels of participation.

Research question 2: Are Indigenous Australians happier or less happy at school than non-Indigenous Australians and do any differences change once other characteristics are controlled for?

Using an index of student happiness, Indigenous Australians are on average happier at school at the age of 15 than non-Indigenous Australians. This difference widens after controlling for other characteristics. There is more to student utility than happiness and analysis of data on life satisfaction and other related concepts (were it available) would provide a more rounded picture of student wellbeing. Nonetheless, the results presented in this paper would tend to suggest that happiness at school is not the reason for low Indigenous completion rates.

The analysis presented in this paper utilised two data sets, the 2008 NATSISS and the 2006 cohort of the LSAY. It may seem strange to have presented analysis using a separate set of data at a conference on the NATSISS. However, this was done for two main reasons. First, because analysis of the LSAY produced interesting, policy-relevant findings that were expected to be of interest to the audience. The second reason though is that it highlighted the benefit of longitudinal data for answering policy relevant research questions. For example, by combining information across waves, it was shown that this difference in completion was explained by socioeconomic background and academic ability at age 15.

Much analysis presented of Indigenous employment, income, mobility or health would also benefit from longitudinal data. However, at present, there is no dataset that tracks individuals across the entire lifecourse. There is some information at key points (for example youth in the LSAY or children in the Longitudinal Study of Indigenous Children (LSIC)), but no information on adults. With this data gap in mind, we renew the call made in Biddle and Yap (2010) for a National Closing the Gap Survey (NCGS).

The NATSISS (and other ABS collections) provide important national level estimates that would be compromised through data attrition if they were replaced by a single longitudinal survey. However, the Indigenous population already experiences a reasonably large survey burden. One alternative would be to implement a rolling-panel approach to the collection of national statistical

datasets. A hypothetical structure of a six-year collection cycle beginning with
a NATSISS in 2012 (2 years ahead of schedule) and 2018 as well as a National
Aboriginal and Torres Strait Islander Health Survey (NATSIHS) in 2015 (5 years
after the current survey) and 2021 is given in Table 7.4. In the intervening years,
Biddle and Yap (2010) propose that a reduced module of questions be asked that
would allow key lifecourse events to be tracked and the COAG Closing the Gap
targets to be analysed. Depending on costs, this survey could be carried out on
a subset of the original cohort only.

Table 7.4 Proposed National Closing the Gap Survey

Year	Cohort 1	Cohort 2	Cohort 3	Cohort 4
2012	NATSISS			
2013	NCGS			
2014	NCGS			
2015	NATSIHS	NATSIHS		
2016		NCGS		
2017		NCGS		
2018		NATSISS	NATSISS	
2019			NCGS	
2020			NCGS	
2021			NATSIHS	NATSIHS
...				...

Note: NCGS = National Closing the Gap Survey

NATSISS = National Aboriginal and Torres Strait Islander Social Survey

NATSIHS = National Aboriginal and Torres Strait Islander Health Survey

Source: Author's extrapolation

Biddle and Yap (2010) outline three benefits of the above structure. Firstly, it will
be possible for the first time to undertake robust longitudinal analysis of a core
set of Indigenous outcomes across the lifecourse. This would be restricted those
questions that are available on the NATSISS, the NATSIHS and the new National
Closing the Gap Survey. However, this would include the major aspects of the
Closing the Gap agenda covered at this conference. The second benefit of the
above structure (as opposed to a single longitudinal study) would be that the
sample for the major surveys would still be nationally representative. That is,
Cohort 1 for the 2012 NATSISS, Cohort 2 for the 2015 NATSIHS and so on. The
third major benefit is that, by overlapping the cohorts, the representativeness of
the longitudinal aspects of the cohorts could be tested against the new cohorts
that replace them. For example, the characteristics of Cohort 1 in 2015 could
be tested against the characteristics of Cohort 2 in the same year. It may not
be possible to maintain a sufficient sample to undertake robust-through-time
analysis for all jurisdictions. However, the Closing the Gap targets are set at the
national level, and hence it is vital that they be evaluated in these broad terms.

The above structure would clearly require a significant investment from all levels of government. It would not be possible for the ABS to follow such an approach within their existing budget. However, the investment in adequate data collection is inconsequential compared to the investment governments have made, and will need to make in order to substantially reduce Indigenous disadvantage.

References

Akerlof, G. A. and Kranton, R. E. 2002. 'Identity and schooling: Some lessons for the economics of education', *Journal of Economic Literature*, 40 (4): 1167–1201.

Arrow, K. J. 1973. 'Higher education as a filter', *Journal of Public Economics*, 2 (3): 193–216.

Becker, G. S. 1964. *Human Capital*, National Bureau of Economic Research, New York.

Biddle, N. 2007. Does it Pay to Go to School? The Benefits of and Participation in Education of Indigenous Australians, PhD Thesis, ANU, Canberra, available at <http://thesis.anu.edu.au/public/adt-ANU20071008.152249/index.html>

—— 2010. 'A human capital approach to the educational marginalisation of Indigenous Australians', *CAEPR Working Paper No. 67*, CAEPR, ANU, Canberra.

—— 2011. 'Income, work and Indigenous livelihoods', Lecture 5, *Measures of Indigenous Wellbeing and Their Determinants Across the Lifecourse*, 2011 CAEPR Lecture Series, CAEPR, ANU, Canberra.

—— and Yap, M. 2010. *Demographic and Socioeconomic Outcomes across the Indigenous Australian Lifecourse: Evidence from the 2006 Census*, CAEPR Research Monograph No. 31, ANU E Press, Canberra.

Borland, J. and Hunter, B. H. 2000. 'Does crime affect employment status? The case of Indigenous Australians', *Economica*, 67 (265): 123–44.

Card, D. 2001. 'Estimating the return to schooling: Progress on some persistent econometric problems', *Econometrica*, 69 (5): 1127–60.

Clark, A. E., Frijters, P. and Shields, M. 2008. 'Relative income, happiness and utility: An explanation for the Easterlin paradox and other puzzles', *Journal of Economic Literature*, 46: 95–144.

Cunha, F., Heckman, J. J., Lochner, L. and Masterov, D. V. 2006. 'Interpreting the evidence on life cycle skill formation', in E. Hanushek and F. Welch (eds), *The Handbook of the Economics of Education*, Elsevier Science, Amsterdam.

Dockery, A. M. 2010. 'Education and happiness in the school-to-work transition', National Centre for Vocational Education Research, Research Report Item 2239, viewed 10 July 2012, available at <http://www.ncver.edu.au/publications/2239.html>

Dominitz, J. and Manski, C. F. 1996. 'Eliciting student expectations of the returns to schooling', *Journal of Human Resources*, 31 (1): 1–26.

Frey, B. S. and Stutzer, A. 2002. 'What can economists learn from happiness research?', *Journal of Economic Literature*, 40 (2): 402–35.

Hartog, J. and Oosterbeek, H. 1998. 'Health, wealth and happiness: Why pursue a higher education?', *Economics of Education Review*, 17: 245–56.

Khoo, S. T. and Ainley, J. 2005. 'Attitudes, intentions and participation', *LSAY Research Reports*, Longitudinal Surveys of Australian Youth Research Report Number 41, viewed 10 July 2012, available at <http://research.acer.edu.au/lsay_research/45>

Leigh, A. and Ryan, C. 2008. 'Estimating returns to education using different natural experiment techniques', *Economics of Education Review*, 27: 149–60.

Marks, G. 1998. 'Attitudes to school life: Their influences and their effects on achievement and leaving school', *LSAY Research Reports*, Longitudinal Surveys of Australian Youth Research Report Number 5, viewed 10 July 2012, available at <http://research.acer.edu.au/lsay_research/62>

Mare, R. D. 1991. 'Five decades of educational assortative mating', *American Sociological Review*, 56 (1): 15–32.

Munns, G. and McFadden, M. 2000. 'First chance, second chance or last chance? Resistance and response to education', *British Journal of Sociology of Education*, 21 (1): 59–75.

Spence, M. 1973. 'Job market signaling', *The Quarterly Journal of Economics*, 87 (3): 355–74.

Wehlage, G. G. and Rutter, R. A. 1986. 'Dropping out: How much do schools contribute to the problem?', *Teachers College Record*, 87: 374–92.

Wolfe, B. and Haveman, R. 2001. 'Accounting for the social and non-market benefits of education', in J. Helliwell (ed.), *The Contribution of Human and Social Capital to Sustained Economic Growth and Well-being*, University of British Columbia Press, Vancouver.

Yap, M. 2011. 'Gender and Indigenous wellbeing', Lecture 7, *Measures of Indigenous Wellbeing and Their Determinants Across the Lifecourse*, 2011 CAEPR Lecture Series, CAEPR, ANU, Canberra.

8. What are the factors determining Indigenous labour market outcomes?

Prem Thapa, Qasim Shah and Shafiq Ahmad

The aggregate gaps in employment rates and other labour market outcomes between the non-Indigenous and Indigenous sub-populations in Australia are well documented and form a key plank in the Closing the Gap agenda adopted by the Council of Australian Governments (COAG). Successful employment outcomes with well-paying jobs are critical components of Indigenous wellbeing.

Behind these aggregate gaps however lies a wide variation in the labour market engagement and outcomes for Indigenous Australians. What is less well understood are the various drivers of successful labour market outcomes within the Indigenous sub-population that lead to the aggregate gaps. This occurs because the national surveys on employment and earnings conducted regularly by the Australian Bureau of Statistics (ABS) do not have a sufficiently large sample of Indigenous persons to reliably analyse the underlying determinants of Indigenous employment.

While there is a large literature that looks at labour market outcomes for Indigenous persons, this has focused mainly on analyses of the census data (i.e. Biddle and Yap 2010; Daly 1995; Hunter 2004). While providing valuable insights, the range of explanatory variables available in the census is limited, and also the full extent of different employment status is not regularly recorded.[1] In this context the periodic National Aboriginal and Torres Strait Islander Social Survey (NATSISS) carried out with a large representative sample of Indigenous households fills a vital gap. It provides the scope for taking a much broader approach to understanding the complex inter-linkages between Indigenous labour market engagement and the other wider dimensions of Indigenous disadvantage.

In this chapter we utilise the full extent of the 2008 NATSISS data to model in detail the determinants of the various components of the labour market status of Indigenous working-age men and women. A specific interest is to analyse how educational attainments affect the employment of Indigenous Australians and whether this relationship is any different from what is found for the general Australian population.

A key related research question is to identify the factors that have driven the changes in Indigenous employment between 2002 and 2008, and to assess the

---

1   For instance, participants in the Community Development Employment Program (CDEP) are not reliably identified in all censuses because some of the census forms used in specific areas of Australia do not include CDEP employment as a separate category (Gray and Chapman 2006).

contribution of increasing educational attainment. Unfortunately, because of the rules about how the NATSISS data can be accessed via the Remote Access Data Laboratory (RADL) of the ABS, estimations cannot be done combining the sample data for 2002 and 2008 to directly test changes in the effects of variables such as education over time. We analyse the effects of increasing educational status of Indigenous Australians on their employment status in a simpler way by comparing our estimation results from the 2008 NATSISS with previous results based on analyses of the 2002 NATSISS.

We had a related interest to model the returns to education for Indigenous workers in terms of its effects on increased hourly wages, and to assess whether the returns to education vary according other factors, such as remote location and gender. But this aspect has been left for further research given the difficulty encountered in deriving reliable measures of hourly wages for a large enough sample of Indigenous workers with the variables available in the 2008 NATSISS via RADL.[2]

In analysing the determinants of Indigenous labour force status we specify a categorical model that distinguishes four different labour market outcomes: (a) not in the labour force (NILF), (b) unemployed, (c) participating in the Community Development Employment Program (CDEP) and (d) regular employment.[3] Given the unique features of the CDEP program, its heavy concentration in remote areas, and the potential differences in motivations for persons wanting to participate in CDEP instead of regular employment, it is necessary to distinguish between CDEP and regular employment. Also, it is important to distinguish the not in labour force category from the unemployed because a distinctive feature of Indigenous labour force status is that a high proportion of Indigenous men are classified as being NILF compared to the general Australian population of working-age men.

In what follows in this chapter, the next section briefly summarises the data from the 2008 NATSISS on labour force status for working-age Indigenous persons by selected characteristics, and compares it with results from the previous NATSISS for 2002, highlighting what have been the major changes that have occurred in this period. We then present the estimation results for the multinomial logit regressions for the determinants of employment status in the 2008 NATSISS, using a standard model specification with conventional personal characteristics and locational indicators as the set of explanatory variables. Our results are compared with a previous study carried out by Stephens (2010a) that estimated a similar model for the 2002 NATSISS. We specifically look at the effects of education, represented with five different categorical educational level variables, on the probability of being in the various labour market status categories separately for men and women.

---

2   The data reported for both earnings and hours of work (necessary to compute hourly wages) are categorical, and earnings data are not clearly distinguished from other sources of income.

3   Note that in this chapter we use the term 'regular employment' to mean non-CDEP employment. It should not be taken as a description of the permanence or regularity of a job.

The following section presents additional results for the standard model which is now estimated separately for working-age men and women in remote and non-remote locations. The expanded confidentialised unit record file (CURF) data from the 2008 NATSISS unfortunately has a limited regional classification structure that only distinguishes either State/Territory of residence or remote and non-remote locations, without these two classifications being overlayed.[4] We chose to work with the remote and non-remote dimension because there are only a few studies (i.e. Stephens 2010a) that have looked at the determinants of Indigenous employment status specifically in remote Australia, and compared how this may differ from other regions. Estimation of separate models for remote and non-remote locations allows us to test whether the explanatory variables can have different effects in these locations, compared to an aggregated model that usually only has a level effect of remote location specified as dummy variable without a full set of interaction terms.[5] The final section concludes and draws some implications for further research.

Summarising the 2008 and 2002 labour force status outcomes

Table 8.1 summarises the proportion of the Indigenous population of working age (15–64) by labour force status in both the 2008 and 2002 NATSISS data. The results are tabulated separately for men and women by selected characteristics (age, education and location) and represents weighted estimates. The aggregate results for men and women are quite different in 2008 compared to 2002, with large increases in the proportion employed in regular jobs and corresponding large falls in the proportion participating in CDEP. In the total Indigenous population of working-age men and women, the CDEP participation rate has fallen from 12.7 per cent in 2002 to 5.6 per cent in 2008. The estimated total number of working-age Indigenous persons engaged in CDEP in 2008, based on the NATSISS sampling framework, reduced by more than one-half from 38 800 in 2002 to 17 600 in 2008. These NATSISS based estimates of the total number of CDEP participants are consistent with the administrative data on CDEP participants that show a decline from around 35 000 individuals in 2002–03 to 18 800 in June 2008.[6]

---

4 The regional dimensions available on the RADL version of the 2008 NATSISS are even more limited than what was available for the 2002 NATSISS. Several commentators (i.e. Biddle and Hunter 2006) have pointed out the weakness with the 2002 classifications with a plea for *more* rather than *less* regional disaggregation to get the most value out of the infrequently collected NATSISS data.

5 This is one key difference between our analyses and a recent contribution from the Productivity Commission that analysed factors influencing Indigenous labour market outcomes with the 2008 NATSISS, using an aggregate model with a remote area dummy variable as one of the explanatory factors (Savvas, Boulton and Jepsen 2011).

6 Refer to the Steering Committee for the Review of Government Service Provision (SCRGSP) 2011: p. 4.86, for the irregular time series administrative data on the total number of CDEP participants.

Table 8.1 Labour force status of Indigenous working-age men and women in 2002 and 2008 by selected characteristics (proportions in each category)

All persons	2008				2002			
	NILF	Uemp	CDEP	Emp	NILF	Uemp	CDEP	Emp
Estimated population numbers (in '000)	110.3	33.4	17.6	149.8	100.8	38.8	34.1	95.6
Proportions in each category (%)	35.5	10.7	5.6	48.2	37.4	14.4	12.7	35.5
Male sample only								
(% in each labour force category)	25.1	12.2	7.2	55.5	26.8	17.2	16.5	39.4
Age								
15–24	29.4	17.8	6.7	46.2	30.6	24.3	18.9	26.2
25 –34	13.2	15.2	9.6	62.0	17.3	17.9	18.3	46.5
35–44	19.3	7.9	8.3	64.5	19.8	15.7	15.7	48.8
45–54	27.6	5.9	6.4	60.0	29.9	8.8	13.2	48.1
55–64	48.3	2.2	2.0	47.5	60.5	4.1	7.9	27.5
Education								
Year 9 & below	47.9	11.3	8.2	32.6	42.4	18.1	17.6	21.9
Year 10	23.2	14.9	9.2	52.7	23.1	21.1	17.8	38.0
Year 11	18.4	15.8	9.6	56.2	20.5	18.2	23.1	38.3
Year 12	12.8	11.7	7.0	68.6	12.6	16	19.1	52.3
Certificate	11.2	9.8	4.7	74.3	16	10.3	9.8	63.9
Degree/Diploma	6.5	6.8	0.8	85.9	15.3	11.6	2.8	70.4
Location: Remote	27.2	10.1	25.3	37.4	29.3	7.9	42.1	20.7
Non-remote	24.4	12.9	1.3	61.4	25.9	20.8	6.7	46.6
1. NSW & QLD Major Cities	20.8	13.7	0.0	65.5	19.6	18.3	4.3	57.7
2. NSW & QLD Inner Regional	22.6	15.3	0.9	61.2	25.5	24.1	9.4	41.0
3. NSW & QLD Outer Regional	32.9	9.8	4.1	53.2	28.7	26.3	7.1	38.0

	2008				2002			
4. Victoria Total	24.7	12.3	0.9	62.1	28.5	12.5	4.2	54.9
5. Balance of Australia	23.7	12.6	1.0	62.7	29.4	19.0	7.4	44.2
Female sample only								
(% in each labour force category)	45.0	9.4	3.9	41.7	47.2	11.8	9.1	31.9
Age								
15–24	48.9	13.2	3.8	34.2	47.2	19.9	8.4	24.5
25–34	45.0	9.8	4.1	41.2	46.4	11.1	11.2	31.3
35–44	34.7	9.4	5.4	50.5	40.3	9.4	10.3	40.0
45–54	36.9	5.7	2.8	54.6	49.8	5.7	6.3	38.2
55–64	70.1	1.1	2.1	26.8	65.2	0.1	7.1	27.6
Education								
Year 9 and below	68.3	9.6	3.9	18.2	64.9	10.6	9.3	15.2
Year 10	50.4	9.0	5.0	35.6	45.1	13.9	11.1	30.0
Year 11	50.5	13.3	5.5	30.7	48	12.6	10.3	29.1
Year 12	31.7	8.8	4.3	55.2	35.8	8.7	8.4	47.1
Certificate	23.9	10.0	2.8	63.3	38.2	15.9	7.3	38.5
Degree/Diploma	18.6	4.6	1.1	75.8	14.7	6.8	3.7	74.8
Location: Remote	49.1	8.3	13.0	29.7	49.2	4.5	26.6	19.7
Non-remote	43.7	9.7	1.0	45.6	46.5	14.4	2.8	36.3
1. NSW & QLD Major Cities	35.8	11.1	0.0	53.1	36.8	16.1	2.4	44.7
2. NSW & QLD Inner Regional	52.5	8.9	1.1	37.5	50.9	17.2	1.9	30.0
3. NSW & QLD Outer Regional	50.6	8.3	3.2	37.9	56.8	12.9	3.2	27.1
4. Victoria Total	41.9	9.4	0.3	48.4	49.7	11.9	2.8	35.6
5. Balance of Australia	40.5	10.2	0.5	48.8	45.5	12.6	3.7	38.2

Source: Authors' customised calculations using the 2002 and 2008 NATSSIS (accessed via RADL)

One should note that the decline in the proportion of working-age Indigenous persons participating in CDEP noted in the 2008 NATSISS estimates pre-dates the major changes made to the CDEP program from 1 July 2009. This included the termination of CDEP program in many locations with established economies where Job Services Australia became the main provider of employment services for Indigenous people.[7] Thus, the increase in non-CDEP employment and corresponding decline in CDEP employment observed in the 2008 NATSISS (which conducted survey interviews between August 2008 and April 2009) is quite independent of the subsequent changes to the CDEP program that took effect from 1 July 2009.[8] In the absence of panel data, it is not feasible to verify what proportion of those who were previously employed in CDEP in 2002 were employed in non-CDEP jobs by 2008. But given the large increase in non-CDEP employment observed in 2008, this is a likely pathway (in addition to the unemployed and NILF persons also moving into regular employment).

The estimated total number of working-age Indigenous persons with a regular job increased to almost 150 000 in 2008, compared to 95 600 in 2002.

Excluding CDEP, about 55 per cent of working-age men reported regular employment in 2008 compared to 39 per cent in 2002. Including CDEP, the increase in the employment ratio is more subdued, from about 56 per cent in 2002 to 63 per cent in 2008. The proportion of working-age males who are classified as unemployed also declined to 12.2 per cent in 2008 from 17.2 per cent in 2002.[9]

The increase in the proportion of working-age women who are employed in a regular job was more modest between 2002 (31.9%) and 2008 (41.7%). Almost 55 per cent of working-age women are either unemployed or NILF.

The further disaggregation of the employment status in 2008 of working-age Indigenous men and women by age, education and location reveal expected patterns. The age profile of being in regular employment is particularly strong for

---

7   Also new CDEP participants from 1 July 2009 in all locations had to apply for regular income support payments from Centrelink. CDEP participants who were receiving CDEP wages at 30 June 2009 can continue receiving CDEP wages until June 2017, as long as they remain eligible. The continuation of CDEP wages to June 2017 is a part of the new Remote Jobs and Communities Program that will come into operaton from July 2013.

8   There were ongoing changes to the CDEP program even before the major reforms that became effective from 1 July 2009. The July 2009 changes had also been foreshadowed early in a government discussion paper released in May 2008. So some of the changes in CDEP employment observed in the 2008 NATSISS could be partially policy induced, in response to the anticipation of the changes that took effect from 1 July 2009.

9   These unemployed percentages are not to be confused with the working-age male *unemployment rate* for which the number of unemployed persons is represented as a proportion of the labour force, and not the total population, as we have reported in Table 8.1. It is a straightforward adjustment to obtain the unemployment rate from the unemployed proportion in Table 8.1, by dividing by the proportion by the labour force to population ratio for each category.

males where around 62 per cent of men aged 35–44 report regular employment, compared to 38 per cent in the youngest (15–24) age group, and 34 per cent in the oldest (55–64) working-age group.

The gain in regular employment between 2002 and 2008 has occurred across all age groups for men, and for all but one age group for women (the 55–64 year olds being the exception), as shown in Fig. 8.1. Some of these gains for specific age groups are quite large, with the proportion employed in a regular job for young males in the 15–24 age group and older males in the 55–64 age group both increasing by 20 percentage points from 2002 to 2008.

Fig. 8.1 Proportion employed (excluding CDEP) by age group, Australia, 2002 and 2008

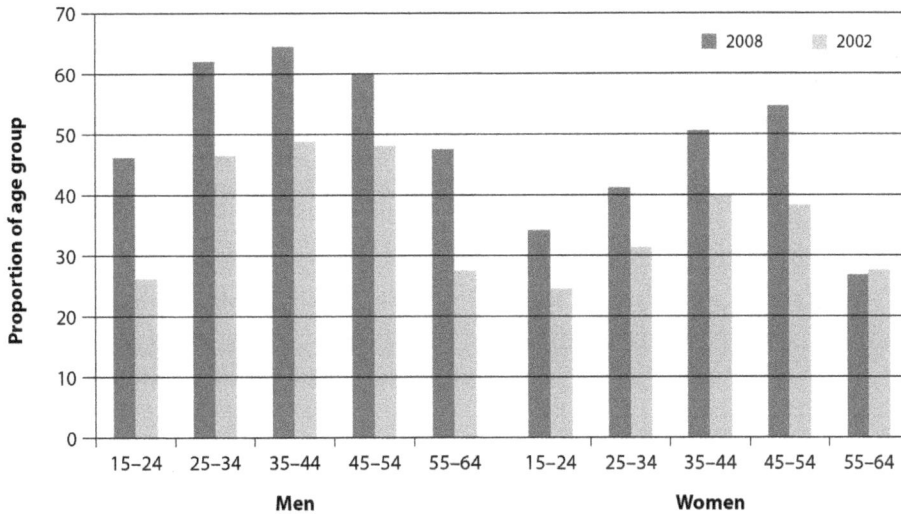

Source: Table 8.1, this chapter

Higher levels of education lead to a continuous increase in the employment ratio for men, which doubles from 36 per cent for those with a Year 9 or lower level of schooling to 73 per cent for those with a degree or diploma. The NILF category also falls consistently for men with higher levels of education. The age profile differences for working-age women are more muted, with the highest employment ratio (of 48%) observed for 35–45 year olds. Education has an even stronger effect for women with the proportion in regular employment increasing dramatically from a low of 23 per cent for those with Year 9 or lower schooling to 78 per cent for those with a degree or diploma.

Fig. 8.2 Proportion employed (excluding CDEP) by education, Australia, 2002 and 2008

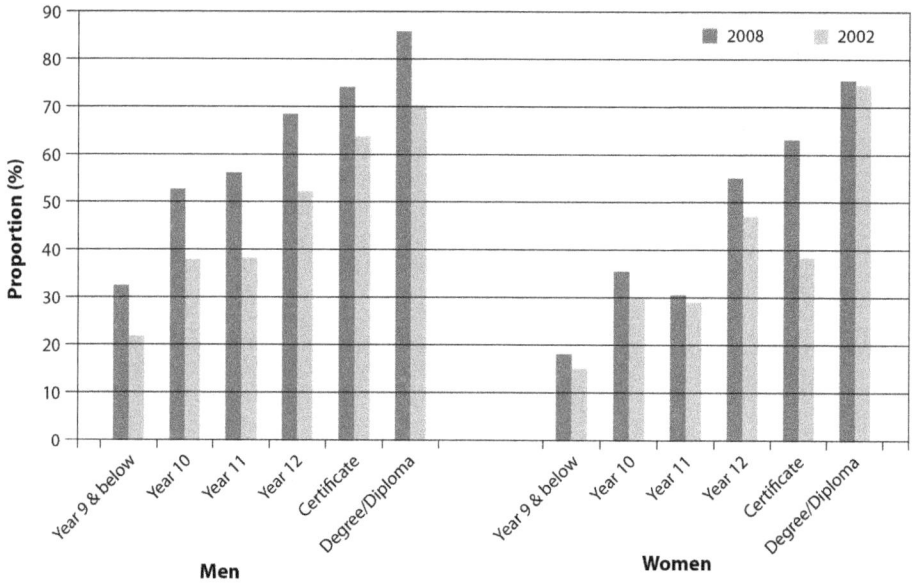

Source: Table 8.1

The consistent increases in the proportion of men employed for each education category between 2002 and 2008 is again shown in Fig. 8.2. There have been some strong gains even at the lowest levels of education – Year 9 or below, and Year 10. The pattern in changes between 2002 and 2008 is slightly different for women. There are only modest increases in the proportion employed (excluding CDEP) at low levels of education. Surprisingly, there is also no increase in employment at the highest level of education for women (with a Degree/ Diploma). This result could possibly be due to the fact that the proportion of women employed in this category is already high (over 70% in 2002) and near universal employment is uncommon for all women. But it can also indicate a differential impact of education on employment status for men and women over time, perhaps reflecting differences in the mix of degrees and diplomas between men and women.

The increase between 2002 and 2008 in the proportion of working-age Indigenous men and women who have a regular job has occurred more or less evenly between remote and non-remote locations. For men this proportion increased by about 15–16 percentage points in both locations between 2002 and 2008. For women the increase in the proportion with regular jobs was about 10 percentage points in both remote and non-remote locations. This however means that the large gaps in the proportions who are regularly employed between remote and non-remote locations still persist. For instance, only 37.4 per cent of Indigenous working-age men in remote locations were in regular employment in 2008, compared to 61.4 per cent in non-remote locations.

Including CDEP participation in employment, the gap between remote and non-remote employment proportions disappears for men, but still persists at around 4 percentage points lower employment for women in remote areas.

Fig. 8.3 shows the change in employment patterns in remote locations only, but including changes in CDEP participation. This presents a more sobering perspective – that the large gains in the proportion with regular jobs have been more or less counter-balanced by the fall in CDEP participation. For men, the combined proportion with a regular or CDEP job is more or less unchanged between 2002 and 2008 (though of course it will usually be more advantageous to have a regular job than be a CDEP participant). But women in remote locations have gone backwards on this combined indicator, which has fallen from 46.3 per cent in 2002 to 42.7 per cent in 2008. For women in remote Australia, although there has been a large gain in the proportion with regular jobs, the fall in CDEP participation has been even larger than the increase in regular employment.

When the non-remote locations are further broken down into major cities and inner and outer regional areas, as specified in Table 8.1, the employment ratio is highest in the major cities of New South Wales and Queensland for both men and women. For men there is a small dip in the employment ratio for the outer regional areas of New South Wales and Queensland, but in all other non-remote locations the employment rate for working-age Indigenous men is more than 60 per cent. Also more than 53 per cent of working-age women in the major cities of New South Wales and Queensland are in regular employment. This is an indication that even by 2008 (before the termination of CDEP in non-remote locations) non-CDEP employment was being established as a social norm for Indigenous working-age persons in the main urban and inner regional population centres. This developing social norm of being in regular employment is even stronger when comparing Indigenous employment outcomes between 1994 and 2008, as Gray and Hunter (2011) have noted.

Fig. 8.3 Remote locations: Proportion employed and in CDEP, Australia, 2002 and 2008

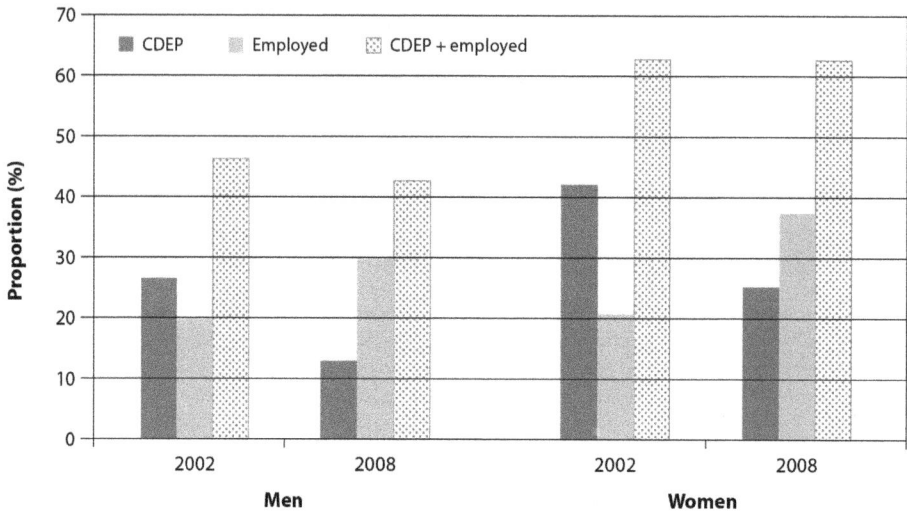

Source: Table 8.1

Factors affecting Indigenous labour market status

In this section we report the results for the multinomial logit regressions for employment status where four status categories are distinguished:

1. not in the labour force (NILF)

2. unemployed (using standard ABS definitions)

3. CDEP employment participation

4. regular employment (non-CDEP).

The multinomial logit regression model is a standard approach to estimating labour force status when there are more than two categorical outcomes identified that are not ranked or ordered. In our model specification we follow closely the model and variable definitions used by Stephens (2010a) to estimate labour force status from the previous 2002 NATSISS in order to assess changes over time. Like Stephens we specify the NILF category as the base category and estimate logit coefficients for the other three labour force categories, relative to the base category. We differ slightly in our model specification because we ignore the 'Housing' subset of variables used by Stephens because these variables, such as having structural problems or not being able to carry out repairs, are not likely to be independent determinants of labour force status. The choice of housing tenure and the quality of housing stock that Indigenous persons live in are more likely to be the consequences of their employment status and income levels.

In this section we report on the multinomial logit regressions results which are estimated separately for men and women but have a combined sample of the remote and non-remote locations, with only a dummy variable indicator used to identify the effect of remote locations. We present two different sets of results for each model: the estimated odds ratios are reported in Tables 8.2 and 8.3, for men and women, respectively; and Appendix 8A Tables A8.2 and A8.3 present the corresponding marginal effects on the probability of being in each labour force category.

Table 8.2 Multinomial logit regression estimates on the determinants of labour force status for Indigenous working-age men[a] (odds ratios)

NILF is the base outcome	Uemp odds ratio		Uemp std. error	CDEP odds ratio		CDEP std. error	Emp odds ratio		Emp std. error
Remote	0.75		0.20	9.39	**	3.70	0.86		0.19
Age									
25–34	0.92		0.27	0.74		0.25	1.30		0.34
35–44	0.36	**	0.12	0.65		0.25	1.03		0.30
45–54	0.25	**	0.11	0.53		0.22	0.98		0.29
55–64	0.06	**	0.03	0.11	**	0.06	0.50	*	0.16
Married	1.42		0.34	1.72	*	0.46	2.69	**	0.52
Number of dependents									
1	0.66		0.20	1.09		0.42	0.85		0.18
2–3	0.68		0.20	0.95		0.29	0.67		0.17
4 & above	0.95		0.39	0.52		0.22	0.53		0.18
Education									
Year 9 or below	0.55	*	0.16	0.55		0.17	0.52	**	0.12
Year 11	1.70		0.67	1.73		0.75	2.17	*	0.74
Year 12	1.29		0.51	1.24		0.47	2.31	**	0.69
Certificate	2.27	*	0.85	1.73		0.68	3.55	**	1.01
Degree/Diploma	3.01		1.76	0.62		0.47	5.77	**	2.44
Difficulty in English speaking	0.22	**	0.12	0.63		0.25	0.60		0.27
Self-assessed health status									
Good	0.85		0.22	0.65		0.18	0.65	*	0.13
Fair	0.64		0.19	0.26	**	0.10	0.28	**	0.07
Poor	0.37	*	0.17	0.28	**	0.13	0.06	**	0.02

NILF is the base outcome	Uemp odds ratio		Uemp std. error	CDEP odds ratio		CDEP std. error	Emp odds ratio		Emp std. error
Has disability	0.41	**	0.10	0.55	*	0.14	0.48	**	0.09
Live in homelands	0.84		0.21	1.05		0.25	0.69		0.14
Mixed household	0.77		0.20	0.24	**	0.12	1.36		0.28
Attends cultural events	1.04		0.25	1.99	*	0.65	1.20		0.23
Indigenous language at home	0.96		0.36	1.11		0.34	0.37	**	0.11
Removed from natural family	1.09		0.33	0.71		0.29	0.48	*	0.14
Queensland only: Torres Strait Islanders	1.31		0.89	1.51		0.79	2.74		1.47
Arrested in last 5 years	1.87	**	0.43	1.44		0.37	0.65	*	0.13

Sample N for regression = 2 722, Psuedo $R^2 = 0.27$

a. These estimated odds ratios are relative to being NILF.

* and ** indicate statistical significance at 5% and 1% respectively.

Source: Authors' customised calculations using the 2008 NATSSIS (accessed via RADL)

Table 8.3 Multinomial logit regression estimates on the determinants of labour force status for Indigenous working-age women[a] (odds ratios)

NILF is the base outcome	Uemp odds ratio		Uemp std. error	CDEP odds ratio		CDEP std. error	Emp odds ratio		Emp std. error
Remote	0.83		0.16	7.27	**	2.44	1.17		0.16
Age									
25–34	1.00		0.23	0.75		0.23	1.78		0.37
35–44	0.92		0.23	1.76		0.57	2.35	**	0.49
45–54	0.59		0.21	0.96		0.34	2.59	**	0.59
55–64	0.05	**	0.02	0.39	*	0.16	0.57	*	0.15
Married	0.64	*	0.13	1.11		0.26	0.90		0.13
Number of dependents									
1	0.63		0.17	0.71		0.26	0.49	**	0.09
2–3	0.42	**	0.11	0.58		0.18	0.37	**	0.06
4 & above	0.34	**	0.10	0.43	*	0.15	0.15	**	0.03
Education									
Year 9 or below	0.64		0.16	0.56	*	0.16	0.36	**	0.07
Year 11	1.36		0.38	1.09		0.44	0.89		0.17
Year 12	1.07		0.34	1.19		0.43	1.93	**	0.42
Certificate	2.15	**	0.62	2.16	*	0.80	3.59	**	0.71
Degree/Diploma	1.47		0.62	0.62		0.32	4.20	**	1.07

NILF is the base outcome	Uemp		CDEP		Emp	
	odds ratio	std. error	odds ratio	std. error	odds ratio	std. error
Difficulty in English speaking	1.70	0.82	0.80	0.32	0.84	0.35
Self-assessed health status						
Good	0.87	0.18	0.93	0.23	0.68 **	0.10
Fair	0.95	0.29	0.80	0.28	0.56 **	0.11
Poor	0.96	0.34	0.64	0.44	0.24 **	0.08
Has disability	1.27	0.26	0.93	0.24	0.82	0.11
Live in homelands	1.14	0.23	1.66 *	0.37	0.76 *	0.11
Mixed household	0.76	0.17	0.55	0.26	1.68 **	0.28
Attends cultural events	1.17	0.24	1.38	0.41	1.37 *	0.20
Indigenous language at home	1.07	0.32	1.76 *	0.44	0.84	0.20
Removed from natural family	1.43	0.43	0.07 **	0.05	0.85	0.23
Queensland only: Torres State Islanders	0.76	0.43	1.43	0.81	1.07	0.38
Arrested in last 5 years	1.08	0.25	1.50	0.47	0.37 **	0.10

Sample N for regression = 3 573, Psuedo R^2 = 0.21

a. These estimated odds ratios are relative to being NILF.

* and ** indicate statistical significance at 5% and 1% respectively.

Source: Authors' customised calculations using the 2008 NATSISS (accessed via RADL)

The underlying estimated model is the same in both of these results, but their interpretations are quite different. The odds ratios compare outcomes across the different categories of labour force status, indicating how the probability of being in a particular category – such as being unemployed, or in CDEP or in regular employment – are determined by the explanatory variables, relative to being in the base category of being NILF. On the other hand, the marginal effects measure how a particular variable increases or decreases the probability of being in a specific labour force category, relative to the average probability of being in that particular category. So we can determine the marginal effects of a specific variable for each of the four labour force status categories defined, whereas the odds ratios make sense only for the remaining three categories relative to the nominated base category of being in NILF.

Summary statistics on the entire explanatory variables used in these regressions are presented in Appendix 8A Table A8.1 for men and women separately and in aggregate. The sample consists of 3 058 working-age men and 4 027 working-age women. The actual estimation sample used for the multinominal logit regressions is slightly smaller because full time students have been excluded and there are some missing values on several variables.

When the odds ratio estimate for a specific combination of a particular labour force status category and explanatory variable is close to 1, this means that variable does not have any effect on changing the probability of being in that labour force category, in comparison to being in the base category of NILF. Variables that increase the relative probability (or odds) of being in a specific labour force category (compared to being NILF) will have odds ratios significantly greater than 1. Variables that lower the relative probability of being in that labour force category will have an odds ratio less than 1.

Looking at the results for men in Table 8.2, and focusing on the last column of the odds ratio coefficient estimated for being in regular employment, the odds of being employed are not affected much by age group. Only the highest age group of 45–54 has a significantly lower odds of being employed compared to the reference age group of 15–24.[10]

The educational category effects on being in regular employment are very strong. Compared to the reference case of persons with only Year 10 schooling, the odds of regular employment improves considerably and progressively with higher levels of education. With a Year 12 qualification, men have a 2.3 times higher chance of being employed compared to only Year 10 qualification. With a degree or graduate diploma, this relative advantage increases to 5.8 times higher odds of being employed. Similarly for those with only a Year 9 or lower schooling, the odds of regular employment are about one-half of those who have completed Year 10.

Another variable that increases the odds of regular employment for men is being married.

Variables that significantly reduce the odds of being employed for men are having a disability, having low levels of self-assessed health (compared to being in excellent health), living in their traditional homeland area, speaking an Indigenous language at home, having been removed from their natural family, and also for having been arrested in the past five years. The effect of having been removed is quite strong – the negative effect on the odds of being in regular employment for removed men is equivalent to the effect of having a disability (both have estimated odds ratios of 0.48).[11]

---

10   The estimation sample excludes all full time students. Many full-time students in the 15–24 age group are likely to be in regular employment. So excluding this category may reduce the age profile on the odds of being employed, compared to a model specification where all persons aged 15–64 are used in the estimation sample irrespective of their student status.

11   The NATSISS asks a very simple question of survey respondents on whether they have ever been removed from their natural family. It does not provide any additional context on why and when the removal happened; but the inference is that this response provides an approximate way to identify the surviving members of the Stolen Generations. Our results show the additional disadvantage they suffer in terms of employment outcomes.

After having controls for the above variables, being in a remote location by itself does not affect the odds of regular employment relative to being NILF. Unfortunately the RADL version of the 2008 NATSISS data does not permit a further disaggregation into remote and very remote locations. Our results show that the average effect of being in a remote or very remote location is not a statistically significant determinant of the probability of being in regular (non-CDEP) employment. This result does not preclude there being a very different effect of living in very remote locations compared to being in just a remote location.[12] The fact that some of the other variables which are closely correlated with very remote locations – such as living in a traditional homeland or speaking an Indigenous language – have significant negative effects indicate that they could be acting as proxy variables for living in very remote locations, and having an adverse effect on the probability of regular employment.[13]

No significant effect is also found for living in a mixed Indigenous and non-Indigenous household.

Looking at the results for CDEP participation of Indigenous men (in the second column of Table 8.2) there are clear contrasts with the results for regular employment. Remote location, as expected, is highly correlated with participation in CDEP, with increased odds of more than nine times. Secondly, higher levels of education do not significantly affect the odds of CDEP participation in a consistent manner. Disability, poor health and living in a mixed household significantly reduce the odds of CDEP participation.

The logistic regression results for the determinants of employment status for women, as reported in Table 8.3, in general follows the pattern for men, but with some key differences on specific variables. Considering firstly the column of results for regular employment, being of prime working age and having higher levels of education significantly improve the odds of being in regular

---

12   ABS unpublished data from the 2008 NATSISS cited in SCRGSP (2011) shows there is a 10 percentage points difference between remote and very remote locations in the regular employment rate of all working age Indigenous persons (men and women). The proportion of the working-age population in regular employment in each of the five detailed Accessibility/Remoteness Index of Australia (ARIA) categories are: 58.6 % in major cities, 49.6% in inner regional, 48.4% in outer regional, 39.6% in remote and 29.3% in very remote areas (see SCRGSP 2011: Attachment Table 4A.6.15).

13   For instance, there is a clear correlation between living in very remote locations and living in a traditional homeland. In other tabulations of the 2008 NATSISS data reported with the full set of ARIA categories, of the total population that recognises a traditional homeland in very remote locations, more than half (51%) of this sub-group actually lives in their homelands. The corresponding proportion is much lower in remote areas at 33% only (see Table 2.17.3b in AIHW 2011). Given that there is also a higher proportion of persons who recognise a traditional homeland among residents of very remote locations, the relative distribution of persons who live in traditional homelands (excluding non-remote Australia) is heavily skewed towards very remote locations compared to remote locations. Among persons who live in traditional homelands in either remote or very remote locations, almost 72% are in very remote locations compared to only 18% in remote locations (derived from AIHW 2011: Table 2.17.3a). Hence it is likely that the significant negative effect of living in a homeland that are reported in Table 8.2 is picking up the extra employment disadvantage of being in very remote locations compared to just a remote location.

employment. Poor self-assessed health reduces the odds of regular employment, as does having been arrested. Living in a mixed Indigenous and non-Indigenous household increases the likelihood of being in regular employment for women — which was not found to be the case for men.

Women also don't get an employment boost from being married, compared to the significantly higher odds for married men being in regular employment. Having a higher number of dependents also significantly reduces the odds of being in regular employment for women.

The logit regression results for the CDEP category of female employment status also differ qualitatively from the corresponding results for men. While remote location has a consistent positive effect on CDEP participation in both cases, several education categories have a significant effect for women only. Having a Certificate qualification more than doubles the odds of CDEP participation for women; and having only Year 9 schooling or less almost halves the odds of CDEP participation. The effect of living in a homeland and speaking an Indigenous language at home both significantly increase the odds for female CDEP participation, while having been removed from family significantly reduces the probability of CDEP participation, which was not the case for men.

The marginal effects of the regression variables on the probability of being in each of the four labour market status categories are presented in Appendix 8A Tables 8A.2 and 8A.3 for men and women, respectively. The marginal effects are computed at the mean of the data. The base case probability noted in the first row under the labour force status column headings of Tables 8A.2 and 8A.3 (and other similar tables) for each labour force category gives the estimated probability of being in that particular category for a specific reference person.[14] For such a reference male person, the probability of being in regular employment is estimated at 68 per cent (Table 8A.2).

The marginal effects reported for specific variables then measure the additional change (either an increase or decrease) in this base probability when there is a change in a specific characteristic of that reference person. For instance, our reference person is unmarried. If he were to be married (but has all other characteristics unchanged) the estimated marginal effects coefficient for the 'married' variable shows that the probability of regular employment is now increased by 17 percentage points. Similarly, having a degree or diploma

---

14   The estimated base case probability of employment is for a reference person who lives in a non-remote location, age 15–24, not married, no dependents, Year 10 education, no English difficulty, non-smoker, excellent self-assessed health status, no disability, does not live on homelands, household composition all Indigenous, does not attach importance to attending selected cultural events, no Australian Indigenous languages spoken at home, not removed from natural family, and not arrested in last 5 years.

compared to Year 9 or below increases the probability of regular employment by 21 percentage points. This is a large effect given that the base probability of being in regular employment is already a very high 68 per cent.

The statistical significance of the estimated marginal effects can differ from the statistical significance of the odds ratios. The former are evaluated for a specific reference person and these changes in probability are non-linear at different data points when there is a change in a specific characteristic for the reference person. But in general we expect consistency in the statistical significance of the results based on the odds ratio and the marginal effects, as is mostly the case in comparing Tables 8A.2 and 8A.3 (marginal effects) with Tables 8.2 and 8.3 (odds ratios).

One divergent result is that for men living in a mixed household there is a significant positive marginal effect but the odds ratio is not significantly higher than 1 in Table 8.2.

The marginal effects coefficients can also be compared across variables since each effect is relative to the base probability. So it is of interest to note from Appendix 8A Table 8A.2 that having been arrested has the same magnitude negative effect on the probability of regular employment for men as having been removed (17 percentage points reduction in both cases).

Looking at the marginal effects for women in Appendix 8A Table 8A.3, there is even more consistency with the odds ratio results of Table 8.3. The only divergent result is that living in a homeland has a significantly negative marginal effect (at the 5% significance level) while this effect was not significant when measured as an odds ratio in Table 8.3.

The marginal effect of higher education levels on the probability of being in regular employment is even higher for women. A degree or diploma increases this probability by 33 percentage points. For women, the effect of having been arrested is also larger (minus 22 percentage points off a lower base probability than the minus 16 percentage points off a higher base probability for men).

Factors affecting Indigenous labour market status in remote and non-remote locations

This section presents the results for the multinominal logit models when estimated separately for the remote and non-remote locations. In the previous section the effect of remoteness was restricted to a level effect on the change in the odds ratio or the base probability of being in a specific labour force category, independent of the other variables in the model. For both men and women the only consistently significant effect of remote location was found to be an increased probability of being a CDEP participant, with a higher marginal effect observed for men.

Estimation of separate models allows us to test if the effects of other variables in the model are different between remote and non-remote locations. We are particularly interested in the role of education on the probability of being in regular employment.

For brevity only the marginal effects results of the estimated models in this section are presented in Appendix 8A. Appendix 8A Tables 8A.4 and 8A.5 present the marginal effects of the regression variables estimated for non-remote locations, for men and women respectively. Appendix 8A Tables 8A.6 and 8A.7 present the corresponding results for remote locations.

Comparing the non-remote and remote locations results for men (Tables 8A.4 and 8A.6) there are several divergent estimates. Employment is increasing with age in remote locations but is either not significant or decreasing at the highest age group in non-remote locations. The effects of higher levels of education are much stronger in remote locations, with a degree or diploma increasing the probability of regular employment by almost 43 percentage points in remote areas compared to only 15 percentage points in non-remote location (although the underlying base probabilities also differ considerably).

Living in a homeland and speaking an Indigenous language have significant negative effects only in remote locations. As noted in the previous section III, this may again be a proxy for distinguishing the lower levels of regular employment in very remote locations where persons living in a traditional homeland or speaking an Indigenous language are concentrated within our broader definition of remote Australia. Being removed from natural family has no effect in remote locations but has a significant negative effect in non-remote locations. The negative effect of having been arrested is similar in both locations.

For women (comparing Tables 8A.5 and 8A.7) there is more similarity in the significance of results by location than for men. But the magnitudes do vary greatly, particularly for the education variables. While the base probabilities of being in regular employment are similar for women between the two locations, the boost provided by higher levels of education (Certificate and Degree/Diploma) are quite large in remote locations: 34 and 54 percentage points, respectively, compared to 26 and 29 percentage points in non-remote locations. The effects of age groups are similar with a higher probability of regular employment in the 35–44 and 45–54 age groups. Being married has no effect on this probability in both locations. There also are consistent positive marginal effects for living in a mixed household and a consistent negative effect of having been arrested in both locations.

Finally in Table 8.4 in the main text we present a comparison of our key results on the marginal effects of higher levels of education by location with the corresponding results obtained by Stephens (2010a) with the 2002 NATSISS data for remote and non-remote locations. The top panel of Table 8.4 summarises the 2008 computations of the marginal effects of education which are the same as the detailed results in Appendix 8A Tables 8A.4 to 8A.7. The bottom panel of Table 8.4 presents the marginal effects of education estimated by Stephens with the 2002 NATSISS data.

Though there is a degree of similarity in the magnitude of these marginal effects, looking at the effects on the probability of regular employment in the last set of columns by location, the difference between remote and non-remote locations appear to be narrower in 2002 than in our 2008 results.

For instance, in 2002 the estimated marginal effect of a degree or diploma for men was about 12 percentage points in non-remote and 9 percentage points in remote locations. But in 2008 the corresponding ratios are wider apart – 15 percentage points in non-remote and a much bigger 43 percentage points in remote locations. There is a similar widening of gaps in the marginal effects of a degree or diploma on a women's probability of being in regular employment. In our 2008 computations, the estimated marginal effect in remote locations is almost double that in non-remote areas (0.54 versus 0.29); while in 2002 the relativity was much smaller (0.59 and 0.45).

Unfortunately the way the NATSISS survey data is made available by ABS on RADL does not permit a direct test of the possibly widening gaps in the marginal effects of higher education between remote and non-remote locations between 2002 and 2008. These two data sets cannot be combined to estimate a joint model with the combined data set with varying coefficients for 2002 and 2008 that can be tested for statistically significant differences. But our simple comparisons in Table 8.4 do point to such a widening gap and this merits further investigation.

This issue can be analysed in a broader context of why and how the returns to Indigenous education, and particularly the highest levels of education, can differ across regions and what might be the mechanisms that lead to this difference. This needs more structured analyses, allowing for persons to be mobile across regions in response to better employment and earning opportunities, and distinguishing the effects of differing personal characteristics across regions from the pure regional effects. Unfortunately, despite the many strengths of the NATSISS, it is not the panel data on Indigenous employment choices that is best suited for the detailed analyses required to unpack these different effects.

Table 8.4 Marginal effects of education in non-remote and remote areas: Comparing 2002 and 2008 estimates[a]

NATSISS 2008 computations

	Non-Remote				Remote			
	NILF	Ue	CDEP	Empd	NILF	Ue	CDEP	Empd
Men								
≤year 9	0.12 *	-0.03	0.00	-0.10	0.06	0.04	-0.03	-0.06
Year 11 (n.s.)	-0.05	-0.04	0.00	0.08	-0.17 **	0.06	0.04	0.07
Year 12	-0.05	-0.05	0.00	0.10 *	-0.14 **	0.01	-0.03	0.16 *
Certificate	-0.10 **	-0.03	0.00	0.13 **	-0.15 **	0.00	-0.09	0.23 **
Degree or diploma	-0.12 **	-0.03	0.00	0.15 **	-0.13 *	-0.07 **	-0.22 **	0.43 **
Women								
≤Year 9	0.23 **	0.00	0.00	-0.23 **	0.18 **	-0.01	-0.02	-0.14 **
Year 11 (n.s.)	0.02	0.02	0.00	-0.04	0.01	0.06	-0.06 *	-0.01
Year 12	-0.15 *	-0.02	0.00	0.17 **	-0.09	0.00	-0.02	0.11
Certificate	-0.27 **	0.00	0.00	0.26 **	-0.33 **	-0.02	0.01	0.34 **
Degree or diplomat	-0.26 **	-0.03	0.00	0.29 **	-0.42 **	-0.05 *	-0.07 *	0.54 **

NATSISS 2002 computations[b]

	Non-Remote				Remote			
	NILF	Ue	CDEP	Empd	NILF	Ue	CDEP	Empd
Men								
≤Year 9	0.25	-0.05	0.01	-0.20	0.07	0.01	0.00	-0.08
Year 11 (n.s.)	-0.01	-0.06	0.05	0.01	-0.09	0.01	0.07	0.00
Year 12	-0.14	-0.06	0.24	-0.04	-0.08	0.21	-0.17	0.04
Certificate	0.02	-0.11	-0.01	0.10	-0.14	0.01	-0.10	0.23
Degree or diploma	-0.04	-0.03	-0.04	0.12	0.03	0.06	-0.17	0.09
Women								
≤Year 9	0.19	-0.05	-0.01	-0.13	0.23	-0.02	-0.10	-0.11
Year 11 (n.s.)	0.00	0.00	0.01	0.00	0.01	-0.02	-0.04	0.06
Year 12	-0.22	0.10	0.06	0.07	-0.13	0.17	-0.05	0.01
Certificate	-0.07	0.01	0.00	0.06	-0.13	-0.03	-0.06	0.22
Degree or diplomat	-0.33	-0.09	-0.03	0.45	-0.39	-0.03	-0.17	0.59

a. These marginal effects of education are computed for a reference person aged 15–24, not married, no dependants, Year 10 education, no English difficulty, non-smoker, excellent self-assessed health status, no disability, does not live on homelands, household composition, all Indigenous, does not attach importance to attending selected cultural events, no Australian Indigenous languages spoken at home, not removed from natural family, not arrested in last 5 years.

b. The standard errors and statistical significance of the marginal effects of education from the 2002 NATSISS estimations are not available because they were not reported in either Stephens (2010a or 2010b).

Source: For 2008 NATSISS computations: authors' customised calculations using the 2008 NATSISS; for 2002 NATSISS computations: Benjamin (2010) using NATSISS 2002

Summary and conclusions

This paper has summarised and modelled the factors behind the changes in Indigenous labour market status observed between the 2002 and 2008 NATSISS. Many of these changes were quite substantial with large numbers of working-age Indigenous men and women moving to regular employment, and dependence on CDEP schemes declining even in remote locations. Slightly more than 55 per cent of Indigenous working-age men have regular jobs while the corresponding ratio is about 42 per cent for working-age women.

The technical analyses in this chapter investigated the determinants of labour force status for working-age adults, using a multinomial logit regression approach that defined four labour force status categories – NILF, unemployed, CDEP participant and regular employment.

The estimated models utilised the wide range of demographic and socioeconomic variables collected in the 2008 NATSISS (i.e. education, health, culture, contact with the criminal justice system, etc.) to explain their effects on labour market status. The 'fit' of the estimated models is limited in that the proportion of the correct predictions made by the model is in the middle range of such models.[15] But the results nevertheless highlight several key factors determining Indigenous employment and show that they are broadly similar to what has been reported for the general population, such as the age profile, health and education (Cai 2010; Laplagne, Glover and Shomos 2007).

The discussion of the results in the chapter, however, focused on the role of education and remote geographic location in explaining the differences in labour market status. Our overall estimation results were similar to what Stephens (2010a) had reported from the 2002 NATSISS, as well as with a recent contribution from the Productivity Commission (Savvas, Boulton and Jepsen 2011) using the 2008 NATSISS data.

Our results show that increasing educational attainment has been one of the key drivers of increasing Indigenous employment. There is a strong and near universal effect of higher levels of education in boosting the prospects for regular (non-CDEP) employment for working-age Indigenous men and women. Even small increases in educational achievements increase employment prospects by significant amounts. Completing Year 12 relative to only Year 10 increases the prospects of being employed by more than two times for Indigenous men and by about two times for Indigenous women. At higher levels of education, such as a degree or diploma, the boost to female employment prospects was usually stronger than for men.

Given these large effects of higher levels of educational attainment on the probability of being in regular employment, the overall increase in the education levels of Indigenous Australians account for some of large increase in the employment to

---

15   The pseudo R^2 for our estimated models range from 0.18 to 0.27; but given we have run a logistics regression these *psuedo* R^2 values are not clear measures of the proportion of the variance explained by the model.

working-age population ratio observed between 2002 and 2008. In the Stephen (2010a) estimation sample from the 2002 NATSISS, about 35 per cent of all Indigenous working-age men and women had only a Year 9 (or below) qualification, and only 4.7 per cent had a degree or diploma. In our sample from the 2008 NATSISS, the proportion with Year 9 (or below) education has dropped to 27.6 per cent and the proportion with a degree or diploma has increased to 8.8 per cent (comparing our Appendix 8A Table 8A.1 with Table A.2 in Stephens 2010b).

Being in a remote location consistently increased the probability of being a CDEP participant, as expected, for both men and women. But living in a remote location by itself did not detract from the prospects for regular non-CDEP employment, controlling for other factors. We were not able to test separately for the effects of living in very remote locations compared to non-remote and just remote locations.

This chapter also estimated a more specific model with different impacts of the explanatory variables in remote and non-remote locations. There were substantial differences both in the set of variables that had significant effects and also in the magnitude of the marginal effects of these variables. One general result was that the marginal effects associated with higher levels of education were considerably higher in remote than in non-remote locations. Also the payoffs to higher levels of education in terms of increased probability of regular employment were higher for better educated women than for men.

The mechanisms driving these differential impacts of education in remote locations were not explored in this chapter; but if this result proves to be a robust finding it can have important implications for the design of regional specific labour market interventions and supporting educational policies.

In conclusion, it is worth noting that despite the unique nature of the design and coverage of the NATSISS and the detailed data it collects on a wide range of socioeconomic variables, it remains a cross-sectional survey. Hence identification of clear causal relationships between the explanatory variable used and the labour market states modelled will always be weak, given the many unobserved factors and differences in individual ability and circumstances of the selected sample. In addition our analyses did not control for any differences in labour market conditions arising from the labour demand side of the labour market. The geographic level of detail in the State by Remoteness version of the 2008 NATSISS data available on RADL is very limited, so that proxy variables to measure demand conditions at small regional levels cannot be implemented.

Increasing the level of regional disaggregation in future rounds of NATSISS and facilitating an easier concordance with other ABS geographic classifications, for which regional unemployment rates and other labour market data can be computed and linked, would be helpful for future analyses. This would not only facilitate developing proxy variables to control for changing labour demand considerations but also make it feasible to introduce smaller neighbourhood effects that may arise in determining the labour market outcomes of Indigenous working-age men and women.

Appendix 8A: Tables

Table 8A.1 Summary statistics on regression variables for labour force status (means/proportions and standard deviations)

Variables	All persons Mean (%)	Std Dev (%)	Men Mean (%)	Std Dev (%)	Women Mean (%)	Std Dev (%)
Male	43.0		1		0	
Remote location	24.8	0.45	24.9	0.48	24.6	0.43
Age						
15–24	33.6	0.49	35.3	0.53	32.0	0.47
25–34	22.5	0.44	22.3	0.46	22.7	0.42
35–44	20.6	0.42	19.7	0.44	21.4	0.41
45–54	14.8	0.37	14.6	0.39	15.0	0.36
55–64	8.5	0.29	8.1	0.30	8.9	0.28
Married	44.8	0.52	46.5	0.55	43.2	0.50
Number of dependents						
0 dependants	39.9	0.51	46.1	0.55	34.3	0.47
1	21.0	0.43	18.9	0.43	22.8	0.42
2–3	28.2	0.47	25.6	0.48	30.6	0.46
4 & above	10.9	0.33	9.3	0.32	12.4	0.33
Education						
Year 9 or below	27.6	0.47	28.7	0.50	26.6	0.44
Year 10	23.4	0.44	24.1	0.47	22.7	0.42
Year 11	10.7	0.32	9.6	0.32	11.7	0.32
Year 12	12.4	0.35	12.6	0.36	12.3	0.33
Certificate	17.1	0.39	18.2	0.42	16.2	0.37
Degree/Diploma	8.8	0.30	6.8	0.28	10.6	0.31
Difficulty in English speaking	3.1	0.18	3.5	0.20	2.8	0.16
Current smoker	47.9	0.52	50.0	0.55	46.1	0.50
Self-assessed health status						
Very good	44.7	0.52	47.3	0.55	42.3	0.49
Good	34.5	0.50	32.7	0.52	36.3	0.48
Fair	14.5	0.37	13.6	0.38	15.3	0.36
Poor	6.3	0.25	6.4	0.27	6.1	0.24
Has disability	48.3	0.52	47.4	0.55	49.2	0.50
Alcohol consumption						
High risk	58.1	0.52	63.1	0.53	53.6	0.50
Low/medium risk	6.5	0.26	9.4	0.32	3.9	0.19
Not consumed	35.3	0.50	27.5	0.49	42.5	0.49
Live in homelands	25.4	0.46	26.4	0.49	24.6	0.43
Mixed household	39.1	0.51	42.3	0.54	36.1	0.48
Attends cultural events	67.6	0.49	65.6	0.52	69.4	0.46
Indigenous language at home	11.4	0.33	11.8	0.35	11.2	0.32
Removed from natural family	7.8	0.28	7.5	0.29	8.1	0.27
Queensland only: Torres Strait Islander	5.9	0.25	6.3	0.27	5.4	0.23
Arrested in last 5 years	15.6	0.38	22.8	0.46	9.1	0.29
Sample N	7 085		3 058		4 027	

Source: Authors' customised calculations using the 2008 NATSISS (accessed via RADL)

Table 8A.2 Multinomial logit regression estimates on the determinants of labour force status for Indigenous working-age men (marginal effects)

Base case probability	NILF 0.17		Uemp 0.11		CDEP 0.03		Emp 0.68	
	marginal effects	std. error	marginal effects	std. error	marginal effects	std. error	marginal effects	std. error
Remote location	0.00	0.03	-0.03	0.02	0.11 **	0.02	-0.09 *	0.04
Age								
25–34	-0.03	0.03	-0.03	0.02	-0.01	0.01	0.06	0.04
35–44	0.01	0.04	-0.09 **	0.02	-0.01	0.01	0.08	0.05
45–54	0.02	0.04	-0.10 **	0.02	0.01	0.01	0.09	0.05
55–64	0.15 *	0.07	-0.12 **	0.01	-0.02 **	0.01	-0.01	0.07
Married	-0.13 **	0.03	-0.04 *	0.02	0.00	0.01	0.17 **	0.03
Dependents								
1	0.03	0.03	-0.03	0.02	0.01	0.01	-0.01	0.04
2–3	0.06	0.04	-0.01	0.02	0.01	0.01	-0.06	0.04
4 & above	0.09	0.06	0.05	0.04	-0.01	0.01	-0.13 *	0.07
Education								
Year 9 or below	0.10 **	0.04	-0.01	0.02	0.00	0.01	-0.09 *	0.04
Year 11	-0.08 **	0.03	-0.01	0.03	0.00	0.01	0.10 *	0.04
Year 12	-0.09 **	0.03	-0.04	0.02	-0.01	0.01	0.14 **	0.04
Certificate	-0.13 **	0.02	-0.02	0.03	-0.01	0.01	0.17 **	0.04
Degree/Diploma	-0.14 **	0.02	-0.04	0.03	-0.02 **	0.01	0.21 **	0.04
Difficulty in English speaking	0.10	0.08	-0.08 **	0.02	0.00	0.01	-0.03	0.09

Base case probability	NILF 0.17			Uemp 0.11			CDEP 0.03			Emp 0.68		
	marginal effects		std. error	marginal effects		std. error	marginal effects		std. error	marginal effects		std. error
Self-assessed health status												
Good	0.06	*	0.03	0.02		0.02	0.00		0.01	−0.08	*	0.04
Fair	0.20	**	0.05	0.05		0.04	−0.01		0.01	−0.25	**	0.05
Poor	0.48	**	0.06	0.06		0.06	0.00		0.01	−0.55	**	0.05
Has disability	0.11	**	0.02	−0.03		0.02	0.00		0.01	−0.08	*	0.03
Live in homelands	0.05		0.03	0.01		0.02	0.01		0.01	−0.07		0.04
Mixed household	−0.03		0.03	−0.05	*	0.02	−0.04	**	0.01	0.11	**	0.03
Attends cultural events	−0.03		0.03	−0.01		0.02	0.01		0.01	0.03		0.03
Indigenous language at home	0.13	*	0.05	0.08		0.04	0.02	*	0.01	−0.23	**	0.06
Removed from natural family	0.09		0.05	0.08	*	0.04	0.00		0.01	−0.17	**	0.06
Queensland only: Torres Strait Islanders	−0.10	*	0.04	−0.05		0.04	−0.01		0.01	0.16	**	0.06
Arrested in last 5 years	0.03		0.03	0.11	**	0.03	0.02		0.01	−0.16	**	0.04

Sample N for regression = 2 722, Psuedo R^2 = 0.27

Note: These marginal effects are computed for a reference person: male, living in a non-remote location, aged 15–24, not married, no dependants, Year 10 education, no English difficulty, non-smoker, excellent self-assessed health status, no disability, does not live on homelands, household composition, all Indigenous, does not attach importance to attending selected cultural events, no Australian Indigenous languages spoken at home, not removed from natural family, not arrested in last 5 years.

* and ** indicate statistical significance at 5% and 1% respectively.

Source: Authors' customised calculations using the 2008 NATSISS (accessed via RADL)

Table 8A.3 Multinomial logit regression estimates on the determinants of labour force status for Indigenous working-age women (marginal effects)

Base case probability	NILF 0.48		Uemp 0.08		CDEP 0.02		Emp 0.42	
	marginal effects	std. error	marginal effects	std. error	marginal effects	std. error	marginal effects	std. error
Remote location	-0.06	0.03	-0.02	0.01	0.06 **	0.01	0.02	0.03
Age								
25–34	-0.12 *	0.04	-0.02	0.02	-0.01	0.00	0.14 **	0.05
35–44	-0.17 **	0.04	-0.04 *	0.01	0.00	0.01	0.21 **	0.05
45–54	-0.18 **	0.05	-0.06 **	0.01	-0.01	0.01	0.25 **	0.05
55–64	0.19 **	0.06	-0.10 **	0.01	-0.01	0.01	-0.08	0.06
Married								
Yes	0.04	0.03	-0.03 *	0.01	0.00	0.00	-0.01	0.03
Dependents								
1	0.16 **	0.04	-0.01	0.02	0.00	0.01	-0.15 **	0.04
2–3	0.23 **	0.04	-0.03 *	0.02	0.00	0.01	-0.20 **	0.04
4 & above	0.37 **	0.03	-0.03	0.02	0.00	0.01	-0.34 **	0.03
Education								
Year 9 or below	0.22 **	0.04	0.00	0.02	0.00	0.00	-0.21 **	0.04
Year 11	0.01	0.04	0.03	0.03	0.00	0.01	-0.04	0.04
Year 12	-0.14 **	0.05	-0.02	0.02	0.00	0.01	0.16 **	0.05
Certificate	-0.28 **	0.04	0.00	0.02	0.00	0.01	0.27 **	0.04
Degree/Diploma	-0.29 **	0.05	-0.03	0.02	-0.02 **	0.01	0.33 **	0.05
Difficulty in English speaking	0.01	0.09	0.06	0.06	0.00	0.01	-0.06	0.09

Base case probability	NILF 0.48		Uemp 0.08		CDEP 0.02		Emp 0.42	
	marginal effects	std. error	marginal effects	std. error	marginal effects	std. error	marginal effects	std. error
Self-assessed health status								
Good	0.08 *	0.03	0.00	0.01	0.00	0.00	-0.09 **	0.03
Fair	0.12 **	0.04	0.01	0.03	0.00	0.01	-0.13 **	0.04
Poor	0.24 **	0.06	0.04	0.03	0.00	0.01	-0.28 **	0.05
Has disability	0.03	0.03	0.03	0.01	0.00	0.00	-0.06	0.03
Live in homelands	0.04	0.03	0.02	0.02	0.01 *	0.01	-0.07 *	0.03
Mixed household	-0.09 *	0.04	-0.04 *	0.01	-0.01	0.01	0.14 **	0.04
Attends cultural events	-0.07 *	0.03	0.00	0.01	0.00	0.00	0.07 *	0.03
Indigenous language at home	0.03	0.05	0.01	0.02	0.01 *	0.01	-0.05	0.05
Removed from natural family	0.03	0.06	0.04	0.03	-0.02 **	0.01	-0.04	0.06
Queensland only: Torres Strait Islanders	-0.01	0.08	-0.02	0.03	0.01	0.01	0.02	0.08
Arrested in the last 5 years	0.17 **	0.05	0.04	0.02	0.02	0.01	-0.22 **	0.05

Sample N for regression = 3 573, Psuedo R^2 = 0.21

Note: These marginal effects are computed for a reference person: female, living in a non-remote location, aged 15–24, not married, no dependants, Year 10 education, no English difficulty, non-smoker, excellent self-assessed health status, no disability, does not live on homelands, household composition, all Indigenous, does not attach importance to attending selected cultural events, no Australian Indigenous languages spoken at home, not removed from natural family, not arrested in last 5 years.

* and ** indicate statistical significance at 5% and 1% respectively.

Source: Authors' customised calculations using the 2008 NATSISS (accessed via RADL)

Table 8A.4 Multinomial logit regression estimates on the determinants of labour force status for Indigenous working-age men, non-remote locations (marginal effects)

Base case probability	NILF 0.45		Uemp 0.08		CDEP 0.00		Emp 0.47	
	marginal effects	std. error	marginal effects	std. error	marginal effects	std. error	marginal effects	std. error
Age								
25–34	-0.02	0.04	-0.04	0.02	0.00 *	0.00	0.06	0.05
35–44	0.06	0.05	-0.09 **	0.02	0.00 *	0.00	0.03	0.05
45–54	0.09	0.06	-0.10 **	0.02	0.00	0.00	0.01	0.06
55–64	0.29 **	0.09	-0.11 **	0.02	0.00	0.00	-0.18 *	0.09
Married	-0.13 **	0.03	-0.04	0.02	0.00	0.00	0.17 **	0.04
Dependents								
1	0.02	0.03	-0.03	0.03	0.00	0.00	0.02	0.04
2–3	0.10	0.05	-0.02	0.03	0.00	0.00	-0.08	0.05
4 & above	0.20 *	0.09	0.03	0.05	0.00	0.00	-0.23 *	0.09
Education								
Year 9 or below	0.12 *	0.05	-0.03	0.03	0.00	0.00	-0.10	0.05
Year 11	-0.05	0.04	-0.04	0.03	0.00	0.00	0.08	0.05
Year 12	-0.05	0.03	-0.05	0.03	0.00	0.00	0.10 *	0.04
Certificate	-0.10 **	0.03	-0.03	0.03	0.00	0.00	0.13 **	0.04
Degree/Diploma	-0.12 **	0.02	-0.03	0.04	0.00	0.00	0.15 **	0.04
Difficulty in English speaking	-0.13 **	0.01	-0.09 *	0.04	0.00	0.00	0.22 **	0.04

Base case probability	NILF 0.45		Uemp 0.08		CDEP 0.00		Emp 0.47	
	marginal effects	std. error	marginal effects	std. error	marginal effects	std. error	marginal effects	std. error
Self-assessed health status								
Good	0.05	0.03	0.02	0.03	0.00	0.00	-0.08	0.04
Fair	0.11 *	0.05	0.07	0.04	0.00	0.00	-0.19 **	0.06
Poor	0.44 **	0.08	0.11	0.07	0.00	0.00	-0.54 **	0.07
Has disability	0.10 **	0.03	-0.02	0.02	0.00	0.00	-0.08 *	0.04
Lives in homelands	0.04	0.03	0.01	0.03	0.00	0.00	-0.05	0.04
Mixed household	-0.03	0.03	-0.05 *	0.02	0.00	0.00	0.08 *	0.04
Attends cultural events	-0.01	0.03	-0.02	0.02	0.00	0.00	0.03	0.03
Indigenous language at home	0.07	0.11	0.20	0.23	0.00	0.00	-0.27	0.20
Removed from natural family	0.14 *	0.06	0.06	0.04	0.00	0.00	-0.20 **	0.07
Queensland only: Torres Strait Islander	-0.06	0.06	-0.07	0.04	0.00	0.00	0.13	0.07
Arrested in last 5 years	0.01	0.03	0.15 **	0.04	0.00	0.00	-0.16 **	0.05

Sample N for regression = 1 752 , Psuedo R^2 = 0.27

Note: These marginal effects are computed for a reference person: male, living in a non-remote location, aged 15–24, not married, no dependants, Year 10 education, no English difficulty, non-smoker, excellent self-assessed health status, no disability, does not live on homelands, household composition, all Indigenous, does not attach importance to attending selected cultural events, no Australian Indigenous languages spoken at home, not removed from natural family, not arrested in last 5 years.

* and ** indicate statistical significance at 5% and 1% respectively.

Source: Author's customised calculations using the 2008 NATSISS (accessed via RADL)

Table 8A.5 Multinomial logit regression estimates on the determinants of labour force status for Indigenous working-age women, non-remote locations (marginal effects)

Base case probability	NILF 0.45 marginal effects	std. error	Uemp 0.08 marginal effects	std. error	CDEP 0.00 marginal effects	std. error	Emp 0.47 marginal effects	std. error
Age								
25–34	−0.12 *	0.06	−0.03 *	0.02	0.00	0.00	0.15 *	0.06
35–44	−0.18 **	0.06	−0.04 *	0.02	0.00	0.00	0.22 **	0.06
45–54	−0.15 *	0.06	−0.06 **	0.02	0.00	0.00	0.22 **	0.06
55–64	0.21 **	0.07	−0.10 **	0.01	0.00	0.00	−0.12	0.07
Married	0.02	0.04	−0.03	0.02	0.00	0.00	0.01	0.05
Dependents								
1	0.21 **	0.05	−0.02	0.02	0.00	0.00	−0.19 **	0.05
2–3	0.27 **	0.05	−0.03	0.02	0.00	0.00	−0.24 **	0.05
4 & above	0.46 **	0.04	−0.04 *	0.02	0.00	0.00	−0.42 **	0.04
Education								
Year 9 or below	0.23 **	0.05	0.00	0.02	0.00	0.00	−0.23 **	0.05
Year 11	0.02	0.06	0.02	0.03	0.00	0.00	−0.04	0.06
Year 12	−0.15 *	0.06	−0.02	0.02	0.00	0.00	0.17 **	0.06
Certificate	−0.27 **	0.04	0.00	0.02	0.00	0.00	0.26 **	0.05
Degree/Diploma	−0.26 **	0.05	−0.03	0.02	0.00	0.00	0.29 **	0.05
Difficulty in English speaking	0.47 **	0.08	−0.08 **	0.01	0.00	0.00	−0.39 **	0.08

Base case probability	NILF 0.45		Uemp 0.08		CDEP 0.00		Emp 0.47	
	marginal effects	std. error	marginal effects	std. error	marginal effects	std. error	marginal effects	std. error
Self-assessed health status								
Good	0.13 **	0.04	-0.01	0.02	0.00	0.00	-0.12 **	0.04
Fair	0.13 *	0.05	0.01	0.03	0.00	0.00	-0.14 **	0.05
Poor	0.29 **	0.07	0.01	0.03	0.00	0.00	-0.30 **	0.06
Has disability	0.05	0.04	0.02	0.02	0.00 *	0.00	-0.08	0.04
Lives in homelands	0.08	0.05	0.03	0.02	0.00	0.00	-0.11 *	0.05
Mixed household	-0.09 *	0.04	-0.04 *	0.02	0.00	0.00	0.13 **	0.05
Attends cultural events	-0.08	0.04	0.00	0.02	0.00	0.00	0.08	0.04
Indigenous language at home	-0.02	0.17	-0.01	0.05	0.00	0.00	0.03	0.18
Removed from natural family	0.04	0.07	0.04	0.03	0.00	0.00	-0.08	0.07
Queensland only: Torres Strait Islanders	0.08	0.11	0.00	0.05	0.00	0.00	-0.08	0.11
Arrested in last 5 years	0.20 **	0.06	0.04	0.03	0.00	0.00	-0.24 **	0.06

Sample N for regression = 2 332, Psuedo R^2 = 0.21

Note: These marginal effects are computed for a reference person: female, living in a non-remote location, aged 15–24, not married, no dependants, Year 10 education, no English difficulty, non-smoker, excellent self-assessed health status, no disability, does not live on homelands, household composition, all Indigenous, does not attach importance to attending selected cultural events, no Australian Indigenous languages spoken at home, not removed from natural family, not arrested in last 5 years.

* and ** indicate statistical significance at 5% and 1% respectively.

Source: Authors' customised calculations using the 2008 NATSISS (accessed via RADL)

8. What are the factors determining Indigenous labour market outcomes?

Table 8A.6 Multinomial logit regression estimates on the determinants of labour force status for Indigenous working-age men, remote locations (marginal effects)

Base case probability	NILF 0.20		Uemp 0.09		CDEP 0.29		Emp 0.42	
	marginal effects	std. error	marginal effects	std. error	marginal effects	std. error	marginal effects	std. error
Age								
25–34	-0.09	0.05	0.02	0.03	-0.01	0.06	0.08	0.07
35–44	-0.16 **	0.04	-0.02	0.03	0.00	0.07	0.18 *	0.08
45–54	-0.15 **	0.04	-0.06 *	0.02	-0.08	0.07	0.29 **	0.08
55–64	-0.06	0.06	-0.10 **	0.02	-0.21 **	0.05	0.38 **	0.08
Married	-0.08 *	0.04	-0.02	0.02	-0.04	0.05	0.15 **	0.05
Dependents								
1	0.02	0.05	0.03	0.04	0.01	0.07	-0.06	0.06
2–3	-0.06	0.04	0.03	0.03	0.05	0.05	-0.03	0.06
4 & above	-0.02	0.06	0.09	0.05	-0.12 *	0.06	0.05	0.08
Education								
Year 9 or below	0.06	0.05	0.04	0.03	-0.03	0.05	-0.06	0.06
Year 11	-0.17 **	0.04	0.06	0.05	0.04	0.09	0.07	0.09
Year 12	-0.14 **	0.04	0.01	0.04	-0.03	0.06	0.16 *	0.08
Certificate	-0.15 **	0.04	0.00	0.03	-0.09	0.05	0.23 **	0.07
Degree/Diploma	-0.13 *	0.06	-0.07 **	0.03	-0.22 **	0.05	0.43 **	0.09
Difficulty in English speaking	0.12	0.07	-0.07 **	0.02	0.01	0.07	-0.06	0.08

Base case probability	NILF 0.20 marginal effects	std. error	Uemp 0.09 marginal effects	std. error	CDEP 0.29 marginal effects	std. error	Emp 0.42 marginal effects	std. error
Self-assessed health status								
Good	0.10 *	0.04	0.01	0.02	−0.06	0.05	−0.05	0.05
Fair	0.46 **	0.08	−0.01	0.03	−0.15 *	0.06	−0.30 **	0.05
Poor	0.57 **	0.08	−0.08 **	0.02	−0.14 *	0.07	−0.36 **	0.05
Has disability	0.11 **	0.04	−0.04	0.02	−0.04	0.04	−0.04	0.05
Lives in homelands	0.05	0.04	−0.01	0.02	0.08 *	0.04	−0.12 **	0.05
Mixed household	0.02	0.07	−0.06 **	0.02	−0.25 **	0.04	0.28 **	0.07
Attends cultural events	−0.11	0.05	0.01	0.03	0.11 *	0.05	−0.02	0.06
Indigenous language at home	0.11 *	0.05	0.00	0.02	0.14 **	0.05	−0.25 **	0.05
Removed from natural family	−0.08	0.05	0.11	0.06	0.00	0.08	−0.03	0.08
Queensland only: Torres Strait Islanders	−0.16 **	0.04	0.03	0.05	−0.03	0.07	0.16 *	0.08
Arrested in last 5 years								
Yes	0.03	0.04	0.02	0.02	0.08	0.05	−0.13 *	0.05

Sample N for regression = 970, Psuedo R² = 0.21

Note: These marginal effects are computed for a reference person: male, living in a remote location, aged 15–24, not married, no dependants, Year 10 education, no English difficulty, non-smoker, excellent self-assessed health status, no disability, does not live on homelands, household composition, all Indigenous, does not attach importance to attending selected cultural events, no Australian Indigenous languages spoken at home, not removed from natural family, not arrested in last 5 years.

* and ** indicate statistical significance at 5% and 1% respectively

Source: Authors' customised calculations using the 2008 NATSISS (accessed via RADL)

Table 8A.7 Multinomial logit regression estimates on the determinants of labour force status for Indigenous working-age women, remote locations (marginal effects)

Base case probability	NILF 0.527		Uemp 0.068		CDEP 0.126		Emp 0.279	
	marginal effects	std. error	marginal effects	std. error	marginal effects	std. error	marginal effects	std. error
Age								
25–34	-0.12 *	0.05	0.03	0.02	-0.04	0.03	0.13 *	0.06
35–44	-0.15 **	0.06	-0.01	0.02	0.01	0.04	0.15 **	0.06
45–54	-0.23 **	0.06	-0.03	0.02	-0.03	0.04	0.28 **	0.07
55–64	0.15 *	0.07	-0.07 **	0.01	-0.05	0.04	-0.04	0.07
Married	0.06	0.04	-0.03	0.02	0.02	0.03	-0.05	0.04
Dependents								
1	0.06	0.06	0.00	0.02	0.00	0.04	-0.06	0.04
2–3	0.15 **	0.05	-0.03	0.02	0.03	0.03	-0.15 **	0.04
4 & above	0.17 **	0.05	-0.01	0.02	0.03	0.04	-0.18 **	0.04
Education								
Year 9 or below	0.18 **	0.05	-0.01	0.02	-0.02	0.03	-0.14 **	0.04
Year 11	0.01	0.06	0.06	0.04	-0.06 *	0.03	-0.01	0.05
Year 12	-0.09	0.06	0.00	0.03	-0.02	0.04	0.11	0.06
Certificate	-0.33 **	0.06	-0.02	0.03	0.01	0.05	0.34 **	0.07
Degree/Diploma	-0.42 **	0.06	-0.05 *	0.02	-0.07 *	0.03	0.54 **	0.06
Difficulty in English speaking	0.01	0.08	0.06	0.05	-0.04	0.03	-0.03	0.08

Base case probability	NILF 0.527		Uemp 0.068		CDEP 0.126		Emp 0.279	
	marginal effects	std. error	marginal effects	std. error	marginal effects	std. error	marginal effects	std. error
Self-assessed health status								
Good	-0.03	0.04	0.04	0.02	0.02	0.03	-0.02	0.04
Fair	0.08	0.06	0.01	0.04	0.01	0.04	-0.10 *	0.04
Poor	0.12	0.09	0.17 *	0.08	-0.08 *	0.03	-0.21 **	0.04
Has disability	-0.02	0.04	0.01	0.02	0.06 *	0.03	-0.04	0.04
Lives in homelands	-0.05	0.04	0.00	0.02	0.07 **	0.02	-0.02	0.04
Mixed household	-0.05	0.06	-0.03	0.03	-0.08 **	0.03	0.16 *	0.06
Attends cultural events	-0.09 *	0.05	0.00	0.02	0.05 *	0.03	0.04	0.04
Indigenous language at home	0.01	0.05	0.00	0.02	0.08 **	0.03	-0.09 *	0.04
Removed from natural family	-0.01	0.09	0.03	0.05	-0.13 **	0.02	0.11	0.08
Queensland only: Torres Strait Islanders	-0.12	0.09	-0.03	0.03	0.00	0.04	0.15	0.08
Arrested in last 5 years	0.09	0.06	0.02	0.03	0.05	0.04	-0.16 **	0.04

Sample N for regression = 1 241, Psuedo R^2 = 0.18

Notes: These marginal effects are computed for a reference person: female, living in a remote location, aged 15–24, not married, no dependants, Year 10 education, no English difficulty, non-smoker, excellent self-assessed health status, no disability, does not live on homelands, household composition, all Indigenous, does not attach importance to attending selected cultural events, no Australian Indigenous languages spoken at home, not removed from natural family, not arrested in last 5 years.

* and ** indicate statistical significance at 5% and 1% respectively.

Source: Authors' customised calculations using the 2008 NATSISS (accessed via RADL)

Acknowledgements

The views expressed in this chapter are the personal views of the authors and should not be attributed to the Australian Government Department of Families, Housing, Community Services and Indigenous Affairs or to the Australian Government. The chapter uses data from the *NATSISS State by Remoteness 2008 Expanded Reissue 1 CURF* (and the corresponding file for the 2002 NATSISS) accessed via the Remote Access Data Laboratory (RADL). We are grateful to the RADL team at the Australian Bureau of Statistics for their help in using RADL and in programming support. Comments provided by Matthew James from FaHCSIA and Matthew Gray (who was Discussant on the earlier draft of this chapter presented at the conference organised by CAEPR on 11–12 April 2011) are also gratefully acknowledged. All errors and omissions, however, are our own.

References

Australian Bureau of Statistics (ABS) 2004. *National Aboriginal and Torres Strait Islander Social Survey 2002*, cat. no. 4714.0, ABS, Canberra.

—— 2006. *Labour Force Characteristics of Aboriginal and Torres Strait Islander Australians: Experimental Estimates from the Labour Force Survey*, cat.no. 6287.0, ABS, Canberra.

—— 2009. *National Aboriginal and Torres Strait Islander Social Survey 2008*, cat. no. 4714.0, ABS, Canberra.

Australian Institute of Health and Welfare (AIHW) 2011. Aboriginal and Torres Strait Islander Health Performance Framework 2010: detailed analyses; 14/9/2011 edition, tier 2 section 17: Indigenous people with access to their traditional lands, cat. no. IHW 53, AIHW, Canberra.

Biddle, N. and Hunter, B. H. 2006. 'Selected Methodological Issues for Analysis of the 2002 NATSISS', in B. H. Hunter (ed.), *Assessing Recent Evidence on Indigenous Socioeconomic Outcomes: A Focus on the 2002 NATSISS*, CAEPR Research Monograph No. 26, ANU E Press, Canberra.

—— and Yap, M. 2010. *Demographic and Socioeconomic Outcomes Across the Indigenous Australian Life Course: Evidence from the 2006 Census*, CAEPR Research Monograph No. 31, ANU E Press, Canberra.

Cai, L. 2010. 'The relationship between health and labour force participation: Evidence from a panel data simultaneous equation model', *Labour Economics*, 17 (1): 77–90.

Daly, A. E. 1995. *Aboriginal and Torres Strait Islander People in the Australian Labour Market*, cat. no. 6253.0, ABS, Canberra.

Gray, M. C. and Chapman, B. 2006. 'Labour market issues' in B. H. Hunter (ed.), *Assessing Recent Evidence on Indigenous Socioeconomic Outcomes: A Focus on the 2002 NATSISS*, CAEPR Research Monograph No. 26, ANU E Press, Canberra.

—— and Hunter, B. H. 2005. 'The labour market dynamics of Indigenous Australians', *Journal of Sociology*, 41: 389–408.

—— and —— 2011. 'Changes in Indigenous labour force status: Establishing employment as a social norm', *CAEPR Topical Issue No. 7/2011*, CAEPR, ANU, Canberra.

Hunter, B. H. 2004. *Indigenous Australians in the Contemporary Labour Market*, cat. no. 2052.0, ABS, Canberra.

—— and Gray, M. 2001. 'Indigenous labour force status re-visited: Factors associated with the discouraged worker phenomenon', *Australian Journal of Labour Economics*, 4 (2): 111–33.

Laplagne, P., Glover, M. and Shomos, A. 2007. 'Effects of health and education on labour force participation', Productivity Commission Staff Working Paper, Melbourne.

Savvas, A., Boulton, C. and Jepsen, E. 2011. 'Influences on Indigenous labour market outcomes', Productivity Commission Staff Working Paper, Melbourne.

Steering Committee for the Review of Government Service Provision (SCRGSP) 2011. *Overcoming Indigenous Disadvantage: Key Indicators 2011*, Productivity Commission, Canberra.

Stephens, B. J. 2010a. 'The determinants of labour force status among Indigenous Australians', *Australian Journal of Labour Economics*, 13 (3): 287–312.

—— 2010b. 'The determinants of labour force status among Indigenous Australians', University of Western Australia Economics Discussion Paper 10.11.

9. The Indigenous hybrid economy: Can the NATSISS adequately recognise difference?

Jon Altman, Nicholas Biddle and Geoff Buchanan

In today's Australia, hunting is an unusual form of productive activity, but for many Indigenous Australians it represents one continuity with the pre-colonial hunter-gatherer mode of production. The settler and state colonisation of Australia has generated a remarkable diversity of available livelihood options and hunting remains one form.

Fig. 9.1 Butchered remains of a feral water buffalo near Mumeka outstation, Arnhem Land

Photo: Jon Altman

We begin with two graphic illustrations of difference because part of the rationale for the NATSISS is to document Indigenous difference as well as diversity. The butchered carcass of a feral water buffalo shown in Fig. 9.1 was located on the side of the main road between Maningrida and Darwin near an outstation called Mumeka, in remote western Arnhem Land at about the time the 2008 NATSISS was in the field. The skilful butchering indicated that the Kuninjku hunters had taken several hundred kilograms of meat for domestic consumption. They had also removed one individual of an introduced species that poses a significant ecological threat to Arnhem Land. The water buffalo (*Bubalis bubalis*) is a feral animal responsible for much damage of wetlands in the surrounding Indigenous Protected Area, which is of high conservation value. Feral buffalo also contribute to global carbon emissions – the removal of this buffalo reduced CO_2 equivalent greenhouse gases by an estimated one tonne per annum (Garnett 2010). So we ask rhetorically, can the National Aboriginal and Torres Strait Islander Social Survey (NATSISS) statistically capture and adequately interpret this hunting event and its productive outcomes? Can NATSISS record distinctive Indigenous activity such as hunting, fishing or gathering of wildlife or cultural production and thus document its economic significance Australia wide?

The map shown in Fig. 9.2 uses information from a number of sources to summarise Indigenous land holdings today and the distribution of what the Australian Bureau of Statistics (ABS) terms discrete Indigenous communities, although most of the larger communities also have non-Indigenous residents. This Indigenous estate covered about 1.7 million square kilometres (in 2010), 99 per cent of which is in very remote Australia. The over 1000 depicted communities have a total population estimated in 2006 of less than 100 000 – about 20 per cent of the estimated national Indigenous resident population. One would not expect people living in these small communities – especially when located on Indigenous-owned land remote from centres of industry and commerce – to live like other Australians. So the question is raised, how do people in such circumstances live and what can the NATSISS tell us about their livelihoods?

In this chapter we begin by defining what we mean by the customary sector and how we see it as part of contemporary Indigenous hybrid economies. We then present a critical discussion of the effectiveness of the NATSISS as a survey instrument to collect information on the customary sector. This includes a brief historical discussion going back nearly 20 years to when a national survey of Indigenous Australians was first mooted; followed by a description and analysis of how data on customary activity were conceptualised, categorised and collected in NATSISS 2008. We especially focus here on why some forms of productive activity are categorised as cultural rather than economic; and why information on the customary has such poor visibility in standard NATSISS 2008 outputs.

Fig. 9.2 Map of the Indigenous estate and discrete Indigenous communities, 2010

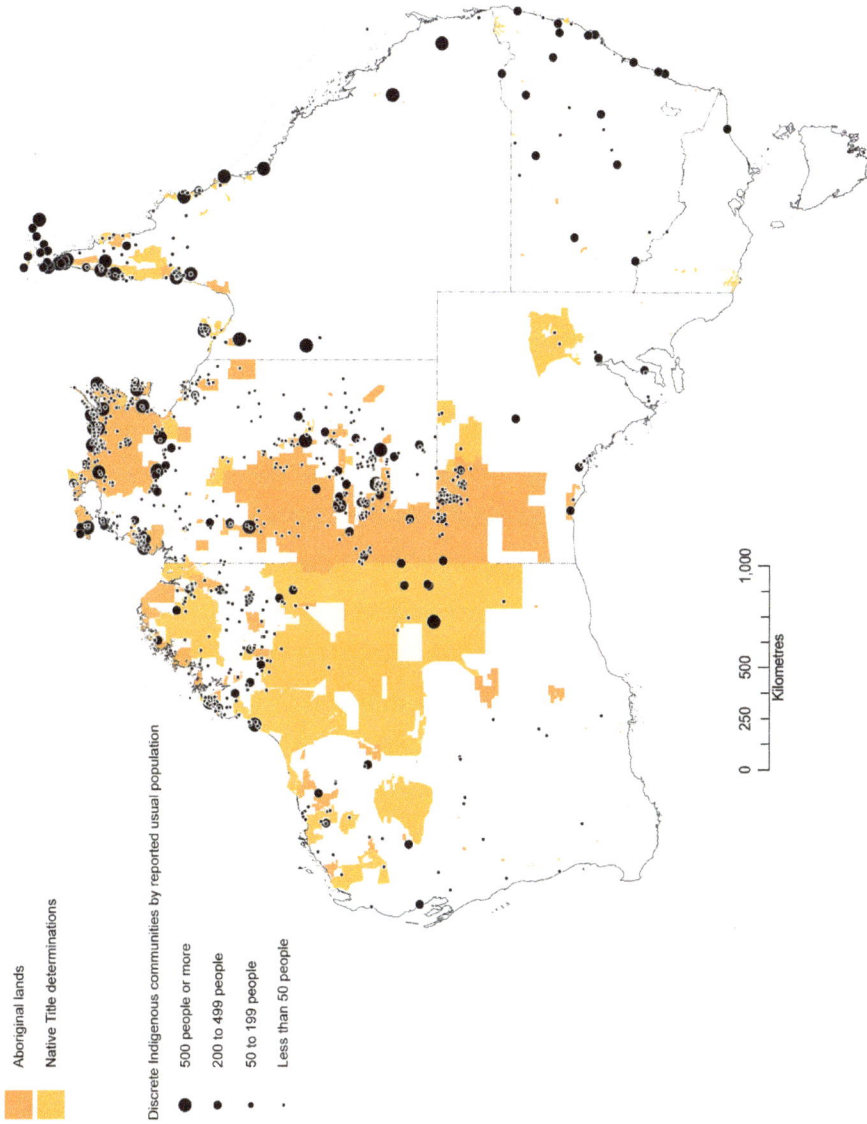

Source: Courtesy of Altman and Hughes, CAEPR

Next we look at the data available in NATSISS 2008 and provide some estimate of the significance of these activities. In accord with a recommendation we made in 2006 (Altman, Buchanan and Biddle 2006: 150) information on wildlife harvesting[1] was collected for all Indigenous Australians in 2008 and not just for those in Community Areas. We are now able to investigate how harvesting and cultural production vary according to place of residence, age, gender, employment status, use of Aboriginal languages, and other variables. We are also able to statistically link available information to some very pertinent policy questions about the factors and motivations that might influence participation in the customary sector.

In the final section we discuss some significant policy and political implications of our findings in two senses: for Indigenous affairs policy making in general and for statistical collection policy making in particular. We ponder the dialectical relationship between the two at a time when policy making is supposedly influenced by evidence and yet the policy community and public discourse largely ignores the evidence. We lament the moral hazard that this presents both to those within the ABS and social scientists who are actually committed to improved data collection and analysis to inform policy making. We conclude by returning to our prefacing vignettes and asking how helpful NATSISS 2008 has been in answering our opening questions.

The customary sector of Indigenous hybrid economies

We are interested in what we term here the 'customary sector' of the Indigenous hybrid economy. By this we mean forms of productive activity, whether for domestic use or for market exchange, that are dependent on Aboriginal custom. In using the term 'customary' we are not suggesting that there are forms of productive activity today that are either pre-colonial or magically divorced from neoliberal globalisation. What we seek to highlight is that there are forms of production that do not fit neatly into the categories of public or private sector or state or market sector because they might be informal or un-marketed. In previous work (see Altman, Buchanan and Biddle 2006) we have depicted the customary sector as a part of hybrid economies, with the customary sector articulating with the state and market sectors. In the example above of the feral buffalo – it was shot with a gun, butchered with a knife, and transported with

---

1   In recent years it has become increasingly common to use the term 'harvesting' as a gloss for hunting, fishing and gathering while overlooking its agricultural connotations. So we would like to emphasise, cognisant of Nadasdy's (2011) critique of such practice, that we are continuing this practice here for comparative purposes only and not to infer anything agricultural in hunting, fishing and gathering practices recorded in NATSISS, Likewise we could include the term 'wildlife' every time we refer to harvesting, but have chosen not to.

a vehicle all of which were bought from the market sector by the hunters using cash income from the state sector and guided primarily by social relations of production, distribution and consumption based on custom and unique to the customary sector (Altman 2005). Arguably, just as there is no 'pure' market or state sector in the hybrid economy, there is no 'pure' customary sector, but rather sectoral overlaps between customary, state and market sectors represented diagrammatically in a three-circle Venn diagram in the hybrid economy model (Altman, Buchanan and Biddle 2006).

Our earlier analysis of the 2002 NATSISS focused on the customary sector in remote Australia. This was not because we did not expect it to occur in non-remote Australia, but rather because wildlife harvesting data then were only collected for Community Areas that replicated by-and-large the discrete Indigenous communities in Fig. 9.2. Intuitively though, one would expect the customary sector to be more significant in remote regions because Aboriginal land ownership and access to natural resources are predominantly in very remote Australia. Indigenous residence on this remote land also reduces opportunity for standard commercial or labour market engagement and so potentially makes the customary more important. We will exploit wider coverage of the customary sector in the 2008 NATSISS to test whether this is empirically the case.

We should emphasise that our focus on the customary is not driven by some academic interest in the esoteric. In our view, a more inclusive and realistic representation of Aboriginal life worlds and wellbeing includes the customary sector of what are unusual hybrid economies in many contexts. It should not be overlooked that activities like harvesting or the production of elements of high or popular culture require effort, might be remunerated, and are often productive in tangible as well as intangible ways.

The national survey and the customary sector

For just on 20 years now scholars from the Centre for Aboriginal Economic Policy Research (CAEPR) have engaged with the ABS and regularly published research findings highlighting the need for the national survey of Indigenous Australians to collect information about difference as well as similarities in Indigenous economic forms. In 1992, before the first National Aboriginal and Torres Strait Islander Survey (NATSIS) 1994, Altman and Allen (1992: 138) highlighted the need for the survey to broaden the notion of employment to include productive activity in what was then termed the informal economy and what we now call the customary sector. This recommendation was responding to the policy imperative of the time to deliver employment and income equality between Aboriginal and other Australians by the year 2000. Altman and

Allen emphasised that work in the informal economy generated employment and income that should not be discounted just because official measures of employment and income status relied on standard social indicators. The ABS responded by positively categorising such work as 'employment and income' but then rather perversely relegated it to the sub-category 'voluntary work'. Researchers were critical of this (see Smith and Roach 1996).

In the 2002 NATSISS, the ABS changed tack and included questions about harvesting, cultural production and the ability to meet cultural obligations while in employment, under the broad category 'Culture'. It is far from clear why this is the case except that some Aboriginal people today do use the term 'cultural economy'. We were critical of this classification but principally for practical reasons: it is likely that responses to economic questions subsumed under the category 'culture' might understate their economic significance (Altman, Buchanan and Biddle 2006). Unfortunately, our views were ignored and in the 2008 NATSISS such materially productive activity continues to be categorised as cultural rather than economic.

Theoretically, we are not averse to the argument made famous by the economic historian Karl Polanyi (1944) that the economy is, as a rule, embedded in social relationships. Carrier (1997: 25) notes that Marx, Weber, Durkheim, Mauss and Polanyi each viewed the economy (in particular the capitalist/market economy) as a social and cultural construction. Along similar theoretical lines, Escobar (1995) analyses economics as culture based on the view that the economy is 'above all a cultural production' (Escobar 1995: 59). But if the ABS shares this view, then all economic questions should be couched as cultural for Indigenous and non-Indigenous Australians. Instead this differential treatment appears to suggest the opposite: that the dominant ideology of the western market mentality – as outlined and critiqued by Polanyi (1944) and Escobar (1995, 2008) (and others, e.g. Block 1990; Carrier 1997; Foucault 1994, 2008; Gibson-Graham 2006a 2006b; Rose 1999; Scott 1998; Throsby 2001) – is acquiesced to by the ABS as if it is unproblematic to those with differing world views. As Waring (1988: 3) notes in relation to the official collection of economic statistics, 'the question of what entails "economic activity" revolves around the question of value'. In its acquiescence to the dominant ideology, the ABS adheres to a value system within which a non-capitalist economic reality such as the customary sector is either ignored or is 'seen as opposite, subordinate, or complementary to capitalism, never as economic practices in their own right or as sources of difference' (Escobar 2008: 74).[2] And so an Indigenous form

---

2   An example of such market-centred ideology is provided by Johns (2011: 206) who states that '[t]he Aboriginal economy is an internal, redistributive economy that creates no value'. For Johns 'the (regulated) market economy is the principal determinant of opportunities' (2011: 41) and 'culture, where it conflicts with adjustment to the market economy, [is] a problem' (2011: 53).

of productive economic activity is reclassified in accord with the dominant discourse of Australian capitalism to marginalise what may be non-mainstream forms of Indigenous comparative advantage, speciality and distinctiveness – not to mention identity.

The problem here is far from just semantic. Part of the project of scholars has been to emphasise to the ABS that the NATSISS currently provides the only official survey instrument that could capture economic reality across Indigenous Australia. That reality includes Indigenous participation not just in the customary non-market sector, but also in productive activities that occur where the customary inter-links with the market and state sectors of local economies. These recommendations for accurate measurement of non-standard forms of Indigenous productive activity have been implemented in a fashion that has reduced the possibilities for time series comparison and/or leaves the logical basis for change unexplained.

Let us demonstrate this with changes that occurred between the 2002 and 2008 NATSISS concretely. We criticised the capacity of the 2002 NATSISS to generate useful data on the customary sector on the following grounds which we summarise here:

- coverage was incomplete, focusing exclusively on Community Areas in remote Australia
- gathering of bush foods was not included as an activity
- land and sea management using Indigenous ecological knowledge was ignored as a customary activity
- the focus was on group activity rather than individual activity, suggesting perhaps that real jobs were viewed as individual and economic and customary work as collective and cultural
- coverage was seasonally limited to activities conducted over the previous three months
- there was lack of comparability with the 1994 NATSIS
- participation in the customary sector was not integrated with other economic activities.

In 2008 a number of questions were asked under 'Cultural Participation.' Importantly, coverage was expanded to include all Indigenous people surveyed regardless of whether they lived in remote or non-remote Australia. Although we don't make use of the data in this paper, the questions were also included in the new child component of the survey (for those over the age of three years at least). The following are summaries of the key 2008 NATSISS questions that we turn to in the next section:

- Q01CULP: 'In the last 12 months have you or your child been involved in any of the following Aboriginal and Torres Strait Islander cultural activities or ceremonies? (from a prompt list)

- Q03CULP: 'Including activities done as part of your job, have you or your child done any of the following activities in the last 12 months? (from a prompt list including gathered wild plants/berries which was missing in 2002)

- Q04CULP: 'In the last 12 months for what reason did you...? (from answers to Q03 from a prompt list).[3]

Other questions asked if activities were undertaken with children; about the source of teaching of activities; the self-assessed importance of participating in such activity; about the frequency of activity; and about respondents' ability to participate and barriers to participation.

Arguably the ABS picked up many of our specific recommendations, but then – as predicted – because of the changes, the possibility for comparison with the 2002 NATSISS was lost. And some questions changed from recording outcomes in 2002 ('Were you paid for cultural production?) to motivation (from a prompt list of possible reasons for participating, with 'Get money as income' as the fourth option).

Our most strident criticism remains though. The ABS in the 2008 NATSISS (as in previous surveys) has consciously or unconsciously ignored the potential economic importance of participating in the customary economy, reducing our national capacity to document what we have previously termed the real 'real' economy in remote Australia (Altman, Buchanan and Biddle 2006) in contrast to the 'real' market economy as depicted by Pearson (2009) and Johns (2011).[4] As noted above, this was identified as problematic nearly 20 years ago and it is even more so now. This is partly because with Commonwealth native title legislation passed in 1993 the Indigenous estate has grown significantly, now covering a much larger part of the Australian continent as shown in Fig. 9.2. This is land held invariably under various forms of limited or restricted common property regimes where one might expect a different form of economy from the individuated leasehold or private property regimes that cover much of the balance of Australia (reserved public lands aside).

In our view there is great potential for a special survey like the NATSISS, to inform the Australian public and policy makers about the diverse forms of the

3 The potential reasons coded by the ABS are: Food; Own enjoyment/fun; Enjoyment/fun with others; Cultural learning or ceremony; Get money as income; Medicinal; School activity; and Other.
4 A key difference between Johns (2011) and Pearson (2000, 2009) is that Pearson explicitly recognises what he calls the 'traditional subsistence economy' as a real economy producing significant value in terms of Aboriginal wellbeing. As footnoted above, Johns (2011) sees no value as being created from what he variously terms a 'mock', 'faux', or 'pretend' Aboriginal economy based on cultural difference.

economy on the Indigenous estate. It is paradoxical that as the Indigenous land base and alternate forms of economy are expanding, the ABS is publishing less and less data about such diversity. Instead the ABS has focused on the dominant policy approach and rhetoric of the day be it 'Employment Equity by the Year 2000', practical reconciliation or Closing the Gap – all approaches that privilege sameness over diversity and difference.

2008 NATSISS results

As social scientists we are disappointed that the national survey of Indigenous Australians conceived and intended to explore Indigenous difference and diversity has design faults. We are interested here in economic difference both between Indigenous Australians and between Indigenous Australians and other Australians, but find little that assists us directly. So we are forced to a second best, and examine the data collected under the rubric of 'Culture'.

Despite our reservations about what is available, we find we can interrogate NATSISS 2008 information on aspects of the customary sector of the hybrid economy in both remote and non-remote Australia. We focus on two areas, wildlife harvesting activities and cultural production. Here we use both description and more sophisticated forms of regression analysis from customised calculations from the 2008 NATSISS to search for relationships between variables in a manner that has never been attempted before. This analysis generates both predictable and surprising findings.

Cross-tabulated information on the proportion of the Indigenous population that participated in harvesting and cultural production activities by demographic, geographic and employment characteristics in 2008 is provided in Table 9.1. Across Australia, it is estimated that 60 per cent of the population aged 15 years and over participated in such activities in the past 12 months. Of the harvesting activities, fishing is more prevalent than hunting which in turn is more prevalent than gathering wild plants/berries. With regards to forms of cultural production, art and craft manufacture seems more prevalent than writing or telling a story which is more prevalent than performing any music, dance or theatre. Note that only an unspecified proportion of this cultural production is marketed commercially.

Table 9.1 Indigenous population (%) who participated in selected activities: By demographic, geographic and employment characteristics, Australia, 2008

Population group	Observations	Any activity	Harvesting activities				Aboriginal and Torres Strait Islander high and popular cultural activities			
			Fished	Hunted	Gathered wild plants/berries	Any activity	Made arts or crafts	Performed any music, dance or theatre	Wrote or told any stories	Any activity
Total population aged 15 plus	8 976	60.1	44.8	22.1	15.8	51.3	17.3	10.8	15.4	28.1
Males	3 992	67.9	55.7	30.2	16.3	62.9	14.1	12.2	14.1	25.7
Females	4 984	52.9*	34.8*	14.8*	15.3	40.7*	20.2*	9.6*	16.6*	30.2*
Aged 15–19	1 086	58.2	41.9*	18.6*	8.8*	48.1*	16.4	11.4	7.7*	23.7
Aged 20–34	2 677	63.2	48.6	24.4	15.3	55.5	16.3	10.5	13.5	27.0
Aged 35–54	2 793	60.7	45.6	23.0	18.8*	51.9	19.8*	11.8*	19.5	31.3*
Aged 55 plus	1 267	52.4*	36.3*	18.6*	19.1*	42.7*	14.8	8.5	20.9*	28.8
Lives in non-remote Australia	5 960	54.7	40.7	12.0	9.8	44.5	15.9	9.0	13.5	24.9
Lives in remote Australia	3 016	76.3*	57.1*	52.7*	33.9*	71.7*	21.7*	16.4*	21.4*	37.6*
Not employed	3 843	54.0	38.9	19.0	14.2	45.2	16.6	9.2	13.3	26.3
Employed	3 980	65.7*	50.3*	25.0*	17.3*	57.0*	18.0	12.4*	17.4*	29.7*
Employed in non-CDEP employment only	3 478	62.8	48.1	20.0	14.4	53.6	16.5	11.3	17.0	27.9
Employed in the CDEP scheme	502	90.3*	69.0*	67.8*	42.3*	85.9*	30.9*	21.6*	20.9*	45.0*

* These values are significantly different from the corresponding category at the 5% level of significance. Base case age group is 20–34 year olds.

Source: Customised calculations from the 2008 NATSISS

Focusing just on results that are significant at the 5% level of significance (marked with a single asterisk (*) in Table 9.1) we make the following observations:

- Indigenous people who live in remote Australia are significantly more likely to take part in wildlife harvesting and cultural production

- the employed (inclusive of those employed through the Commonweatlh Government's Community Development Employment Projects (CDEP) program that had been phased out in urban Australia at the time of the 2008 NATSISS and is being radically reformed in remote Australia) are more likely to participate in all activities than those not employed (except in art and craft manufacture)

- those in CDEP employment, which is often part-time, are more likely to participate in all activities than those in non-CDEP employment

- the age-grade data are somewhat inconclusive but predictable – that is, the old do less harvesting but more story telling than the young

- fewer females participate in harvesting than males, but more females participate in cultural production than males.

Overall, over 76 per cent of those in remote Australia aged 15 years and over do some harvesting or cultural production, 72 per cent participate in harvesting and 38 per cent participate in cultural production. It is hard to compare wildlife harvesting in 2002 with 2008 because in the former the question was only asked in Community Areas where the number (hunted or fished in a group) appears higher but cannot be validly compared. The figures for cultural production which can be compared appear higher in both remote and non-remote areas in 2008. The important question that cannot be answered using NATSISS is how productive were these activities.

Results for the regression analysis using the probability of participating in harvesting activities are presented in Table 9.2. For the analysis presented in Table 9.2 and Table 9.3, the probability of the base case person is given in the second last row of the table and the characteristics in the notes under the table. For example, the predicted probability for those living in remote Australia is compared to an otherwise identical person living in non-remote Australia. Four separate estimates are given in each of the tables. The first two are based on estimations for all of Australia with Model 1 including mainly demographic, geographic and education attainment variables. The second model also includes these variables but, in addition, has variables for education participation, employment and income. The reason for estimating two separate models is that there is a strong possibility that current participation in harvesting activities determines education participation, employment or income, rather than vice versa. It is important to test whether the results for the other variables differ with and without the inclusion of these potentially endogenous variables. Results are presented as marginal effects or the difference in the probability of participating compared to the base case person (whilst holding all else constant). Marginal effects are presented for all variables regardless of their significance; however, variables that were significant at the 1%, 5% and 10% levels of significance are differentiated with asterisks.

Focusing only on statistically significant findings we find that:

- those who live in remote Australia were significantly more likely to participate in harvesting (as in Table 9.1)

- females were significantly less likely to participate in wildlife harvesting, with the difference greatest in non-remote Australia (or alternately, men are more likely to be harvesters)

- those aged 55 years and over were less likely to participate in harvesting activities. However, this was mainly in non-remote as opposed to remote Australia. In remote Australia, those aged 15–19 years were significantly more likely to participate than the base case (i.e. those aged 20–34 years)

- recognising homelands was positively associated with harvesting activities and currently living in a homeland had an extra positive association

- differences in high school education were not associated with participation in harvesting activities. However, those who had completed post-school qualifications had a significantly higher level of participation

- those who spoke an Indigenous language were more likely to harvest than those who did not

- those employed in the CDEP program were significantly and substantially more likely to participate in harvesting activities. It is important to note that this result holds after controlling for remoteness, age and whether or not the person was employed part-time (which by itself, was not significant).

Apart from the findings for education (which were difficult to predict *a priori*) these results are all predictable and to be expected bearing in mind the usual proviso that we are measuring relationships based on theorised not measured causality (see Ziliak and McCloskey 2007). Issues of subjective motivation aside (these will be explored below) we know that people are more likely to harvest because they have access to lands and seas and resources, but they may also harvest because they have to when living in such situations for food security. People are more likely to hunt when they live on homelands, but they may also live on homelands so that they can hunt.

Table 9.2 Factors associated with the probability of participating in harvesting activities in the last 12 months, by remoteness classification, Australia, 2008

	Australia		Non-remote	Remote
Explanatory variables	Model 1	Model 2	Model 2	Model 2
Lives in remote Australia	0.178***	0.158***		
Female	-0.215***	-0.216***	-0.238***	-0.141***
Aged 15–19	0.029	0.032	0.024	0.138*
Aged 35–54	-0.050**	-0.047*	-0.045	-0.039
Aged 55 plus	-0.110***	-0.084*	-0.110**	0.007
Parent or guardian of child aged 0–14 years	0.038	0.063**	0.071*	0.099***
Married	0.040*	0.016	0.023	0.000
Additional person living in the household	0.001	-0.003	-0.016	0.021***
Speaks an Indigenous language	0.224***]	0.229***	0.209***	0.241***
Recognises an area as homelands or traditional country	0.111***	0.102***	0.083**	0.190***
Currently lives in homelands or traditional country	0.101***	0.108***	0.152***	-0.010
Has a profound or severe core-activity limitation	-0.013	0.018	0.023	-0.028
Completed Year 10 or 11	0.008	-0.003	-0.011	0.037
Completed Year 9 or less	-0.026	-0.007	-0.013	0.026
Has a degree or higher	0.096**	0.108**	0.104**	0.187
Has an other non-school qualification	0.061**	0.058**	0.058**	0.072
Cannot access a motor vehicle whenever needed	-0.045*	-0.047	-0.046	-0.065
Is currently a student		0.000	0.027	-0.176**
Is currently a part-time (as opposed to full-time) student		0.013	-0.007	0.147
Not in the labour force		-0.028	-0.034	0.034
Unemployed		0.031	0.025	0.104
Employed in the CDEP scheme		0.169**	0.277**	0.172**
Employed part-time		0.031	0.039	-0.015
Receives a government pension		0.000	0.014	-0.101**
Household equivalised income in the bottom decile		-0.064	-0.057	-0.094
Household equivalised income in the 2nd-3rd decile		-0.028	-0.052	0.044
Household equivalised income in the 7th-10th decile		-0.018	-0.030	0.023
Probability of the base case	0.446	0.466	0.480	0.490
Pseudo R-Squared	0.1320	0.1312	0.0814	0.1366
Number of observations	7 562	6 169	4 159	2 010

Notes: The base case person: lives in non-remote Australia; is aged 20–34; is not a parent or guardian and is not married; lives in a four-person household; does not speak an Indigenous language; does not recognise an area as a homeland or traditional country; does not have a profound or severe core-activity restriction; has completed Year 12 but does not have a post-school qualification; can access a motor vehicle whenever needed; is not a student; is employed full-time but not in the CDEP program; does not receive a government pension; and has a household equivalised income in the 4th to 6th decile (based on the non-Indigenous income distribution).

*** Marginal effect for which the coefficient is statistically significant at the 1% level of significance.

** Marginal effect for which the coefficient is statistically significant at the 5% level of significance.

* Marginal effect for which the coefficient is statistically significant at the 10% level of significance.

Source: Customised calculations using the 2008 NATSISS

Table 9.3 Factors associated with the probability of participating in Aboriginal or Torres Strait Islander cultural activities in the last 12 months, by remoteness classification, Australia, 2008

Explanatory variables	Australia		Non-remote	Remote
	Model 1	Model 2	Model 2	Model 2
Lives in remote Australia	-0.003	-0.006		
Female	0.024***	0.025***	0.024***	0.033**
Aged 15–19	0.030**	0.009	0.008	0.006
Aged 35–54	0.012	0.009	0.006	0.019
Aged 55 plus	0.009	0.022*	0.012	0.066***
Parent or guardian of child aged 0–14 years	0.011	0.012	0.014	-0.003
Married	-0.009	-0.007	-0.006	-0.008
Additional person living in the household	0.004**	0.003	0.003	0.007***
Speaks an Indigenous language	0.121***	0.110***	0.145***	0.098***
Recognises an area as homelands or traditional country	0.156***	0.135***	0.141***	0.087***
Currently lives in homelands or traditional country	0.000	0.000	-0.005	0.024*
Has a profound or severe core-activity limitation	0.029**	0.035**	0.040**	0.012
Completed Year 10 or 11	-0.017**	-0.013*	-0.014*	-0.003
Completed Year 9 or less	-0.010	-0.010	-0.007	-0.014
Has a degree or higher	0.139***	0.125***	0.121***	0.134**
Has an other non-school qualification	0.055***	0.044***	0.042***	0.051***
Cannot access a motor vehicle whenever needed	0.001	0.000	0.006	-0.016
Is currently a student		0.077***	0.085***	0.055
Is currently a part-time (as opposed to full-time) student		-0.017	-0.017	-0.009
Not in the labour force		-0.023***	-0.023**	-0.030
Unemployed		-0.005	-0.009	0.001
Employed in the CDEP scheme		0.034**	0.144***	0.008
Employed part-time		-0.009	-0.015	0.013
Receives a government pension		0.010	0.010	0.010
Household equivalised income in the bottom decile		0.020	0.018	0.030
Household equivalised income in the 2nd–3rd decile		0.014	0.012	0.021
Household equivalised income in the 7th–10th decile		0.002	-0.001	0.023
Probability of the base case	0.061	0.051	0.046	0.077
Pseudo R-Squared	0.1093	0.1140	0.1297	0.0865
Number of observations	7 562	6 169	4 159	2 010

Notes: The base case person: lives in non-remote Australia; is aged 20–34; is not a parent or guardian and is not married; lives in a four-person household; does not speak an Indigenous language; does not recognise an area as a homeland or traditional country; does not have a profound or severe core-activity restriction; has completed Year 12 but does not have a post-school qualification; can access a motor vehicle whenever needed; is not a student; is employed full-time but not in the CDEP program; does not receive a government pension; and has a household equivalised income in the 4th to 6th decile (based on the non-Indigenous income distribution).

*** Marginal effect for which the coefficient is statistically significant at the 1% level of significance.

** Marginal effect for which the coefficient is statistically significant at the 5% level of significance.

* Marginal effect for which the coefficient is statistically significant at the 10% level of significance.

Source: Customised calculations using the 2008 NATSISS

In Table 9.3 we repeat the above analysis using the probability of participating in cultural production in the last 12 months. It is noteworthy that here there was no significant difference in participating in cultural production between those who lived in remote Australia and those who lived in non-remote Australia. It would appear that it is other characteristics of individuals that were driving the significant differences found here. Key findings (again focusing on the statistically significant) include:

- females were more likely to participate in cultural production than males, which makes intuitive sense because males do more harvesting and time is limited

- in remote Australia, those aged 55 years and over were significantly and substantially more likely to participate than the base case

- there was a very large (and significant) difference between those who speak an Indigenous language and those who do not, suggesting that Indigenous language supports a person's capacity to make art, perform a dance, and/or tell a story

- those who recognise an area as a homeland were significantly more likely to participate in cultural production than those who did not. For those who do recognise a homeland, there was no significant difference between those who lived on their homeland compared to those who did not. This suggests that harvesting benefits more from more intimate connection to country than does cultural production

- having a disability or 'severe core-activity limitation' was associated with a higher level of participation

- having a post-school qualification and in particular having a degree or higher degree was associated with participation in cultural activities

- being a student was also associated with participating in cultural activities

- those who were not in the labour force were less likely to participate than those who were employed. There was no significant difference for those who were unemployed

- there was a small (but significant) difference for Australia as a whole for those who participated in the CDEP program compared to the rest of the employed population. However, this relationship only appears to hold in non-remote as opposed to remote Australia.

In Table 9.4 we explore the particular reasons respondents gave for participating in each of the wildlife harvesting or cultural production activities. Respondents were able to list more than one activity and hence the columns sum to more than 100. In order to help understand the results presented in Table 9.4, it is useful to look at a particular column in detail. Focusing on the first ('any activity') column, the first line shows that 57.8 per cent of those who participated in a harvesting or cultural activity did so for food. Reading down, 63.3 per cent reported that they did so for their own enjoyment/fun, 57.3 per cent said they participated in an activity for enjoyment/fun with others and so on.

Key findings from Table 9.4 highlight some significant differences between remote and non-remote Australia:

• people mainly harvest for food, rarely for cash, although harvesting activity is also a source of enjoyment, and social interaction; people are significantly more likely to harvest for food in remote than non-remote Australia

• people in remote regions are significantly more likely to harvest for cultural learning or ceremony, to get money and for medicinal purposes and less likely to harvest for fun

• people engaged in cultural production mainly to learn or engage in ceremony, for their own enjoyment, and for social interaction

• people in remote Australia are significantly more likely to engage in cultural production for cultural learning and to make money and are less likely to do so as a school activity.

Table 9.4 Reasons for participating in selected activities, by remoteness, Australia, 2008

Activity	Any harvesting activity		Any Aboriginal or Torres Strait Islander cultural activity	
	Non-remote	Remote	Non-remote	Remote
Food	60.8	90.9***	0.0	0.0
Own enjoyment/fun	67.8	57.2***	51.5	55.9
Enjoyment/fun with others	52.2	56.0	44.7	49.1
Cultural learning or ceremony	14.8	34.8***	53.9	73.0***
Get money as income	1.1	3.9***	9.4	21.7***
Medicinal	6.0	11.1**	1.2	1.5
School activity	2.9	3.3	25.3	12.1***
Other	2.1	1.0**	6.0	2.1***

*** Differences between remote and non-remote areas significant at the 1% level of significance.

** Differences between remote and non-remote areas significant at the 5% level of significance.

* Differences between remote and non-remote areas significant at the 10% level of significance.

Source: Customised calculations from the 2008 NATSISS

One surprising comparative result here is the apparent decline in people paid for cultural production since 2002 (see Altman, Buchanan and Biddle 2006: 146). Whether this decline is factual or illusory is impossible to tell because different questions were asked in 2002 and 2008: in the former year people were asked what the outcome of their cultural production was (i.e. whether or not they were (or would be) paid), in the latter the motivation for production was sought (i.e. the reason they participated). This illustrates well the problem when questions are changed from survey to survey.

In an exploratory vein we also sought to explore the relationship between participation in the customary sector and self reported measures of health and wellbeing (see Table 9.5). We do not report our results here in detail in part because causality is especially unclear: Was it participation in harvesting or cultural production activities that was influencing self-assessed health and wellbeing, or is causality in the opposite direction? We also found that there were few cells where results were significant, while differentiating remote from non-remote regions would have made the analysis overly complex. Having undertaken the analysis (that we will report in more detail elsewhere) we note the following statistically significant findings:

- those who had fair or poor health were significantly less likely to participate in at least one of the selected activities than those who had good health
- people with a lot of energy a little or none of the time are significantly less likely to fish, hunt or gather
- if people are full of energy they are more likely to hunt, but if they rarely felt full of life they were significantly less likely to fish, hunt or undertake any harvesting activity and are less likely to be a performer, story teller/author, or artist
- hunters are more likely to be happy, but if one is not calm or peaceful one is less likely to fish or hunt
- if one has high psychological distress as measured by a grouped Kessler (K5) score of psychological stress one is more likely to participate in arts and crafts manufacture or perform any music, dance or theatre
- if in fair or poor health one is significantly less likely to fish or participate in harvesting generally.

Table 9.5 Population (%) who participated in selected activities, by health and wellbeing, Australia, 2008

Population group	Observations	Any activity	Harvesting activities				Aboriginal and Torres Strait Islander cultural activities			
			Fished	Hunted	Gathered wild plants/berries	Any activity	Made arts or crafts	Performed any music, dance or theatre	Wrote or told any stories	Any activity
Total population aged 15 plus	8 976	60.1	44.8	22.1	15.8	51.3	10.8	15.4	39.9	28.1
Self assessed health										
Excellent or very good	4 274	60.1	44.2	23.7	16.0	51.9	17.4	12.2	15.0	28.0
Good	2 785	61.9	47.5	21.6	15.0	53.4	17.8	10.2	15.2	28.1
Fair or poor	1 917	57.2*	41.7*	19.9	16.6	46.8*	16.4	9.1	16.8	28.2
Grouped Kessler (K5) score of psychological distress										
Low/moderate	5 205	59.2	44.6	21.9	15.1	50.7	16.2	9.6	14.8	26.3
High/very high	2 497	61.8	45.5	21.9	16.8	52.3	19.7*	13.1*	16.7	31.7*
How often felt calm and peaceful (last 4 weeks)										
All or most of the time	4 547	60.5	45.2	24.4*	15.5	51.7	16.8	10.3	14.8	27.7
Some of the time	1 919	61.3	47.6	20.0	15.3	53.3	17.4	11.4	15.8	28.2
A little or none of the time	1 248	56.3	39.8*	15.3*	16.5	46.1*	19.8	11.5	17.1	29.2
How often felt happy (last 4 weeks)										
All or most of the time	5 568	61.6	46.1	23.7*	16.1	52.7	17.5	11.1	15.5	28.6
Some of the time	1 452	58.3	43.6	18.4	14.0	49.3	17.5	10.1	15.6	27.9

Population group	Observations	Any activity	Harvesting activities				Aboriginal and Torres Strait Islander cultural activities			
			Fished	Hunted	Gathered wild plants/berries	Any activity	Made arts or crafts	Performed any music, dance or theatre	Wrote or told any stories	Any activity
A little or none of the time	697	51.3	38.2	13.8	15.3	43.4	15.5	9.3	14.1	23.3
How often felt full of life (last 4 weeks)										
All or most of the time	4 225	62.6	47.5*	25.0*	16.1	53.9	17.5	11.1	14.8	28.1
Some of the time,	2 052	58.6	44.1	19.5	15.2	50.2	17.6	11.7	16.3	28.6
A little or none of the time	1 434	53.7	37.1*	15.1*	14.7	43.2*	16.5	7.9*	16.2	27.0
How often had a lot of energy (last 4 weeks)										
All or most of the time	3 641	63.0	48.2	26.0	16.4	54.6	17.8	11.9	15.1	28.6
Some of the time	2 358	59.7	44.1	20.4	14.9	50.7	18.0	11.1	16.3	28.8
A little or none of the time	1 715	53.2*	37.9*	13.6*	14.6	43.3*	15.2	7.1*	14.8	25.2

* Significantly different from middle at the 5% level of significance.

Source: Customised calculations from the 2008 NATSISS

Survey, policy and political implications

For this volume we have been asked to consider how the data source utilised and analysis undertaken advance social science and inform Indigenous policy making. Turning to the implications of our analysis during an era that is supposed to have evidence-based policy making, not ideology, as its hallmark, clearly our analysis should make a difference to some of the most hotly-debated current issues in Indigenous affairs.

- What form should economic development take?
- What are the prospects for closing the employment gap, especially in remote regions?
- Does the stated aim of policy to standardise economic norms make sense?
- Will closure of education gaps assist people who harvest and engage in cultural production for a livelihood?
- Should the CDEP program be effectively abolished in all but name through radical reform?
- What evidence is there that the current Australian Government focus on larger 'priority communities' and the Northern Territory Government focus on Territory Growth Towns are rational policy approaches?

Further what is the role of the policy-engaged social scientist in making recommendations to the ABS? – realising of course that in the highly politically-charged environment of Indigenous affairs there will always be diverse and competing statistical interests. Should we, yet again, make constructive recommendations to the ABS and the wider policy community to gather more economic data that will generate a more robust evidence base to answer important questions such as the above, especially given the likely further growth of the Indigenous estate, the likely further strengthening of property rights on Aboriginal-owned land, and the prospects that the Indigenous population in remote Australia will continue to grow rapidly?

In the absence of other compelling official statistics gathered at the national level, our findings highlight first and foremost that there are statistically significant differences in wildlife harvesting and cultural production between remote and non-remote Australia. These of course are broad categories that combine the five-region Accessibility/Remoteness Index of Australia (ARIA) regional geography into just two, a limitation of the publicly available data that has been noted a number of times in this volume. Nevertheless, this finding vindicates our earlier focus on remote Australia and our policy suggestion that the real economy out there includes a robust customary sector. Just how economically significant this sector might be is difficult to say given available statistics.

Arguably, these findings also suggest that a different broad policy approach might be needed in remote Australia. Putting aside for the moment the national level policy obsession with closing statistical gaps, our findings indicate that Indigenous wellbeing and livelihood could be improved through a combination of harvesting and cultural production to supplement available employment. These productive activities in the customary sector are likely to be significantly higher if participants are employed through CDEP and living at homelands/ outstations and speaking an Indigenous language. These findings do not in themselves suggest that participation in harvesting and cultural production will provide a better outcome than formal employment; only that in the absence of enough mainstream opportunity where people live, it might make sense for policy to support such productive activity – to, in a sense, think outside the market square.

These findings fly in the face of the direction that policy has taken since at least 2005 when then Minister for Indigenous Affairs Amanda Vanstone (2005) traduced outstation residence as living in 'cultural museums' and the Minister for Employment Kevin Andrews began to dismantle the CDEP program; as well as more recent Northern Territory Government reform to prioritise Territory Growth Towns over outstations and to eliminate outstation learning and bi-lingual education as a viable schooling option. At a higher policy level, an Australian version of the United Nation's Millennium Development Goals was introduced without consultation in early 2008 by then Prime Minister Kevin Rudd under the policy umbrella of Closing the Gap. This national approach was quickly adopted by the Council of Australian Governments (COAG) that in the economic domain has given priority to the goal to halve the gap in employment outcomes between Indigenous and non-Indigenous Australians within a decade. In July 2009, much of this approach was cemented into the COAG National Indigenous Reform Agreement (NIRA) (COAG 2009). This is not the place to critique NIRA in any detail – this exercise has been undertaken elsewhere (see Altman 2010: 268–9). We just note here that NIRA principles and its policy approach are concerning for those in remote Australia whose livelihoods are strongly supported by or reliant upon the customary sector as it aims to:

- centralise people away from homelands
- focus effort on incorporating remote living people into mainstream employment and the market economy
- alter social norms
- skew available resources away from smaller places, and
- render extremely difficult development problems 'technical' and 'statistical' in an abstract manner that ignores the complexity of lived reality that is partially captured by the data we present here (cf. Ferguson 1990).

In the world of evidence-based policy making is there no information to challenge the hegemonic state approach that promulgates a 21st century version of the modernisation paradigm as the development solution for all Indigenous Australians? Of course there is: there is the NATSISS. But there are ways in which the data are collected and released that has the potential to marginalise findings that may challenge dominant political and bureaucratic perspectives. These forces are evident in many forms, and we provide three illustrative examples.

First, the 2008 NATSISS was clearly designed and locked in before the change of Australian Government in November 2007 and the launch of the Closing the Gap approach. Its design was probably more influenced by the dominant agenda of 'practical reconciliation', a hallmark of the Howard years. But the way that outputs from the 2008 NATSISS have been made available have clearly conformed to the agenda of the government of the day with priority being given to meeting the needs of the Productivity Commission and its biennial Overcoming Indigenous Disadvantage report that by 2009 was already looking to address COAG targets and headline indicators (Steering Committee for the Review of Government Service Provision (SCRGSP) 2009). In assisting the Productivity Commission meet the directives of the government, the ABS was in no position to give high profile to the customary sector in its media releases or visibility in standard outputs.

Second, the Australian Government has invested in a Closing the Gap Clearinghouse to provide access to information about what works to overcome disadvantage (Australian Institute of Health and Welfare (AIHW)/Australian Institute of Family Studies (AIFS) n.d.). This Clearinghouse has search functions but because it is marshalling evidence that 'relate to the COAG building blocks that underpin the Closing the Gap targets' research on the customary sector is not given high priority either in the general or assessed collections. We did manage to find references to our earlier paper on the 2002 NATSISS and the real 'real' economy. It stated:

The real 'real' economy in remote Australia

The informal economy, or customary sector, is often ignored in measures of Indigenous employment and income equality. This paper provides an overview of the customary sector and the hybrid economy model and examines the extent to which the 2002 National Aboriginal and Torres Strait Islander Social Survey documents customary activity in remote areas. It focuses on three issues included in the NATSISS that relate to the customary sector: fishing or hunting as a group activity; participation in and payment for cultural activities; and the ability to meet cultural responsibilities while in employment. The paper then identifies shortcomings in the survey relating to key customary sector activities and makes recommendations for NATSISS 2008.

It is noteworthy that none of our findings on the significance or potential of the customary sector are reported. Nor does the Clearinghouse engage with our political point that the 'real' economy, a term that is bandied around in political and bureaucratic circles with gay abandon, might actually include the customary sector, especially in remote Australia.

Third, aware that information is not available to measure progress in Closing the Gap, the Australian Government is investing $46.4 million over four years from 2009–10 to help build a better evidence base against which to measure progress, without entertaining the possibility that there may not be any progress to measure (Australian Government 2011: 17). There is clearly embarrassment that the annual Closing the Gap Prime Minister's Report is unable to actually tell us whether gaps are closing. Even this is contestable, for two of us have actually found that the ABS publication *Labour Force Characteristics of Aboriginal and Torres Strait Islander Australians, Estimates from the Labour Force Survey, 2009* (ABS 2010) did assist us with annual official information about whether the employment gap was closing. Applying rigorous significance testing to the data at the national level we found that the gap was actually widening (Altman and Biddle 2010). For making this unpopular evidence-based observation we were chided by the Minister for Employment Participation, Senator the Hon. Mark Arbib who erroneously suggested that the ABS survey we used was too unreliable to make assessments of progress at the national level because of 'high margins of error' (Altman and Biddle 2011). Fortunately the ABS publishes standard errors that we had taken into account in our testing for significance.

All this suggests two things to us. First, the Australian Government is keen on measures that show its gaps are closing, but is less than keen on any suggestion that its strategy is misplaced. Second, while ideology can challenge evidence, it can play a very significant role in influencing what evidence is collected. The historical development of links between government, economy, populations, and statistics outlined by Foucault (1994) under his hypotheses on governmentality highlights the political nature of the production of such statistical evidence. For Foucault:

> It was through the development of the science of government that the notion of economy came to be recentered onto that different plane of reality we characterize today as the 'economic', and it was also through this science that it became possible to identify problems specific to

populations ... And, further, that 'statistics' ... now becomes the major technical factor, or one of the major technical factors, of the unfreezing [deblocage] of the art of government (1994: 215).

For Rose (1999: 33), a scholar heavily influenced by Foucault's writings on governmentality, an abstract space such as 'the Indigenous economy' is not brought into existence by ideology or theory alone, but also through the construction of a statistical apparatus through which this space can be 'inscribed, visualised, tabulated, modeled, calculated ... and so forth'. Rose (1999: 212, 213) describes this as 'the fabrication of a "clearing" within which thought and action can occur' and notes that, while abstract, such spaces 'are very material: for they are [inter alia] utilized as a grid to "realize" the real in the form in which it may be thought'. Along these lines we observe that in the context of Closing the Gaps (and its recent predecessors) a massive bureaucratic machinery (including a significant 'statistical apparatus') has been deployed to lend support to the approach being taken by the government of the day – an approach where the economic form of the market is the principle grid of economic intelligibility.[5] As a statistical apparatus of government the NATSISS is being utilised as a grid to realise the real economy of Indigenous Australia, but we maintain our argument (Altman, Buchanan and Biddle 2006) that it fails to realise the real 'real' economy due to its economic neglect and statistical marginalisation of the customary sector.

This leaves the social scientist in a difficult place if the evidence available suggests that either the dominant policy approach is proving unsuccessful or if the somewhat narrow parameters being used to measure economic wellbeing (closing the employment gap) need to be challenged. We realise of course that in the highly politically-charged environment of Indigenous affairs there will always be diverse and competing statistical interests and perspectives, not to mention priorities as outlined above. Nevertheless, yet again we make constructive recommendations to the ABS and wider policy community in relation to gathering economic data that will generate a more robust evidence base to answer such important questions. This is especially important given the likely further growth of the Indigenous estate, the likely further strengthening of property rights on Aboriginal-owned land and the prospects that the Indigenous population in remote Australia will continue to grow.

---

5   The terminology used here is borrowed from Foucault (2008). In his discussion of the nature of American neo-liberalism Foucault (2008: 243) notes that it involves 'the generalization of the economic form of the market' whereby it becomes 'a principle of intelligibility', an 'analytical schema', or a 'grid of intelligibility'.

So what prospects for NATSISS 2014? Will the ABS heed our call by, for example:

- classifying customary activity as economic, not just cultural
- collecting data on people working on country in the provision of environmental services utilising Indigenous ecological knowledge as we suggested in 2006
- collecting better data on work density – how often people engaged in activities – so as to assess their significance,[6] and
- asking some more pertinent questions, not just about motivations but also about outcomes.

What are the prospects of asking some questions in a more open ended manner that might elicit Indigenous responses in accord with Indigenous aspirations and perceptions?

Conclusion

The argument made in this chapter can be summarised as follows. The NATSISS is one survey instrument that just might allow collection of official statistics that capture Indigenous difference – in this instance, economic difference. But this possibility seems to be circumscribed by the ABS working only within the dominant paradigm of normalisation and Closing the Gap. Perhaps this is not surprising, after all the ABS is a mainstream institution and a part of what might be termed 'the bureaucratic field' (cf. Bourdieu, Wacquant and Farage 1994; also Wacquant 2007). We do not question that the collection of statistics is a highly political project, but we do wonder if the ABS may not be sufficiently open to exploring alternatives.

Despite this, some important data were collected in NATSISS 2008 that we are reporting for the first time. These data show that harvesting and cultural production are significant productive activities, especially in remote Australia. These findings are important as they challenge the wisdom of the current Closing the Gap approach and its attenuated policy reforms to abolish CDEP, refocus

---

6 For example, Waring (1988: 254) argues that monetary or market value 'is not the sole criterion for the assessment of work. Work can also be assessed by volume: in terms of the labour power involved in the process (the number of workers) or the work time absorbed (number of hours)'. Alternative conceptions of the economy offer 'us the opportunity for assessing data by way of quality, and quantity, by way of hours and money invested. It invites us to consider interactions. It permits use of all advanced statistical mechanisms' (1988: 254). In this chapter we have touched on the potential of NATSISS to explore correlations and causality between wellbeing (health, happiness, etc.) and Indigenous people's participation in the customary sector. We acknowledge the suggestion by Professor Anne Daly at the NATSISS 2008 CAEPR conference regarding the potential of wellbeing data collected through the NATSISS to provide an outcome measure in the absence of a traditional economic or monetary measure of the contribution of people's participation in the customary sector.

development effort to larger places, and to incorporate Indigenous people into the mainstream. We believe opportunity exists to collect information to test the success or failure of the current policy framework, but there is also a need to collect data that will allow comparison with alternate possibilities like living on, working on, and painting on country. From a statistical sense, the relatively low amount of variation explained in our models highlights the lack of information in the NATSISS around the determinants of participation in harvesting and cultural production. We suspect that the paucity of geographic information in the available version of the NATSISS has contributed to this lack of statistical power. Surely the role of the NATSISS is to collect and disseminate statistics about sameness as well as difference and, surely, an independent ABS should ensure that such information is collected.

We return to where we began: why are data collected – for academic debates or to provide a glimpse into diverse Aboriginal life worlds? We asked at the outset what can the NATSISS tell us about those who pursue livelihood and wellbeing in a fundamentally different way from the mainstream? The answer, in our view, is not enough.

References

Altman, J. C. 2005. 'Development options on Aboriginal land: Sustainable Indigenous hybrid economies in the twenty-first century', in L. Taylor, G. Ward, G. Henderson, R. Davis and L. Wallis (eds), *The Power of Knowledge, the Resonance of Tradition*, Aboriginal Studies Press, Canberra.

—— 2010. 'What future for remote Indigenous Australia?: Economic hybridity and the neoliberal turn', in J. C. Altman and M. Hinkson (eds), *Culture Crisis: Anthropology and Politics in Aboriginal Australia*, UNSW Press, Sydney.

—— and Allen, L. M. 1992. 'Aboriginal and Torres Strait Islander participation in the informal economy: Statistical and policy implications', in J. C. Altman (ed.), *A National Survey of Indigenous Australians: Options and Implications*, CAEPR Research Monograph No. 3, CAEPR, ANU, Canberra.

—— and Biddle, N. 2010. 'Rudd overpromised on indigenous employment', *Crikey*, 4 June 2010, viewed 3 March 2011, available at <http://www.crikey.com.au/2010/06/04/closing-the-gap-rudd-overpromised-on-indigenous-unemployment/>

—— and Biddle, N. 2011. 'The massive indigenous employment gap stagnates', *Crikey*, 1 July 2011, viewed 1 July 2011, available at <http://www.crikey.com.au/2011/01/07/the-massive-indigenous-employment-gap-stagnates/>

——, Buchanan, G. and Biddle, N. 2006. 'The real 'real' economy in remote Australia', in B. Hunter (ed.), *Recent Evidence on Indigenous Socioeconomic Outcomes: A Focus on the 2002 NATSISS*, CAEPR Research Monograph No. 26, ANU E Press, Canberra.

Australian Bureau of Statistics (ABS) 2010. *Labour Force Characteristics of Aboriginal and Torres Strait Islander Australians, Estimates from the Labour Force Survey, 2009*, cat. no. 6287.0, ABS, Canberra.

Australian Government 2011. *Closing the Gap Prime Minister's Report 2011*, viewed 3 March 2011, available at <http://www.fahcsia.gov.au/sa/indigenous/pubs/closing_the_gap/2011_ctg_pm_report/Documents/2011_ctg_pm_report.pdf>

Australian Institute of Health and Welfare (AIHW)/Australian Institute of Family Studies (AIFS) n.d. 'Closing the Gap Clearinghouse', viewed 21 November 2011, available at <http://www.aihw.gov.au/closingthegap/>

Block, F. 1990. *Postindustrial Possibilities: A Critique of Economic Discourse*, University of California Press, Berkley and Los Angeles, California.

Bourdieu, P., Wacquant, L. J. D. and Farage, S. 1994. 'Rethinking the State: genesis and structure of the bureaucratic field', *Sociological Theory*, 12 (1): 1–18.

Carrier, J. G. 1997. 'Introduction', in J. G. Carrier (ed.), *Meanings of the Market: The Free Market in Western Culture*, Berg, Oxford.

Council of Australian Governments (COAG) 2009. *National Indigenous Reform Agreement (Closing the Gap)*, viewed 3 March 2011, available at <http://www.coag.gov.au/coag_meeting_outcomes/2009-07-02/docs/NIRA_closing_the_gap.pdf>

Escobar, A. 1995. *Encountering Development: The Making and Unmaking of the Third World*, Princeton University Press, New Jersey.

—— 2008. *Territories of Difference: Place, Movements, Life, Redes*, Duke University Press, Durham.

Ferguson, J. 1990. *The Anti-Politics Machine: 'Development', Depoliticisation and Bureaucratic Power in Lesotho*, Cambridge University Press, Cambridge.

Foucault, M. 1994. 'Governmentality', in J. D. Faubion (ed.), *Power: Essential Works of Foucault 1954–1984, Volume Three*, Penguin Books, London.

—— 2008. *The Birth of Biopolitics: Lectures at the College de France 1978–1979*, Picador, New York.

Garnett, S. 2010. 'Climate change and invasive species', in M. Jambrecina (ed.), *Kakadu National Park Landscape Symposia Series 2007–2009 Symposium 5: Feral animal management, 3–4 December 2008*, Department of Sustainability, Environment, Water, Population and Communities. Viewed 21 November 2011, available at <http://www.environment.gov.au/ssd/publications/ir/568.html>

Gibson-Graham, J. K. 2006a. *The End of Capitalism (as we knew it): A Feminist Critique of Political Economy*, University of Minnesota Press, Minneapolis.

——2006b. *A Postcapitalist Politics*, University of Minnesota Press, Minneapolis.

Johns, G. 2011. *Aboriginal Self-determination: The Whiteman's Dream*, Connor Court Publishing, Ballan, Victoria.

Nadasdy, P. 2011. '"We don't harvest animals; we kill them": Agricultural metaphors and the politics of wildlife management in the Yukon', in M. J. Goldman, P. Nadasdy and M. D. Turner, *Knowing Nature: Conversations at the Intersection of Political Ecology and Science Studies*, University of Chicago Press, Chicago.

Pearson, N. 2000. *Our Right to Take Responsibility*, Noel Pearson and Associates Pty Ltd, Cairns.

—— 2009. *Up from the Mission: Selected Writings*, Black Inc, Melbourne.

Polanyi, K. 1944 (2001). *The Great Transformation: The Political and Economic Origins of Our Time*, Beacon Press, Boston.

Steering Committee for the Review of Government Service Provision (SCRGSP) 2009. *Overcoming Indigenous Disadvantage: Key Indicators 2009*, Productivity Commission, Melbourne, viewed 3 March 2011, available at <http://www.pc.gov.au/__data/assets/pdf_file/0003/90129/key-indicators-2009.pdf>

Rose, N. 1999. *Powers of Freedom: Reframing Political Thought*, Cambridge University Press, Cambridge.

Scott, J. C. 1998. *Seeing Like A State: How Certain Schemes to Improve the Human Condition Have Failed*, Yale University Press, New Haven.

Smith, D. E. and Roach, L. M. 1996. 'Indigenous voluntary work: NATSIS empirical evidence, policy relevance and future data issues', in J. C. Altman and J. Taylor (eds), *The 1994 National Aboriginal and Torres Strait Islander Survey: Findings and Future Prospects*, CAEPR Research Monograph No. 11, CAEPR, ANU, Canberra.

Throsby, D. 2001. *Economics and Culture*, Cambridge University Press, Cambridge.

Vanstone, A. 2005. 'Beyond conspicuous compassion: Indigenous Australians deserve more than good intentions', Address to the Australian and New Zealand School of Government, The Australian National University, Canberra, viewed 21 November 2011, available at <http://epress.anu.edu.au/anzsog/policy/mobile_devices/ch03.html>

Wacquant, L. 2009. *Punishing the Poor: The Neoliberal Government of Social Insecurity*, Duke University Press, Durham.

Waring, M. 1988. *Counting For Nothing: What Men Value and What Women Are Worth*, Allen and Unwin, Wellington.

Ziliak, S. T. and McCloskey, D. N. 2007. *The Cult of Statistical Significance: How the Standard Error Costs Us Jobs, Justice, and Lives*, University of Michigan Press, Ann Arbor.

10. Is Indigenous poverty different from other poverty?

Boyd Hunter

Closing the gaps and need for reflexivity on Indigenous disadvantage and poverty

The Council of Australian Governments (COAG) adopted six targets in 2008 with the main aim to close the life expectancy gap within a generation. Specific goals are in the areas of mortality, access to early childhood education, reading, writing and numeracy achievements, Year 12 attainment and employment disadvantage. While none of the targets explicitly mention poverty, it would be unreasonable to ignore it and the associated financial stress as both are likely to condition the ability to achieve any of the targets identified. For example, standard measures of income poverty illustrates that many Indigenous people may lack the private resources required to facilitate the behaviour required to substantially improve health, attend educational institutions and even to look for and secure suitable work.

In order to reflect on Indigenous-specific nature of financial and resource needs, this chapter takes a further step back from income poverty that is usually defined using some societal norms of income adequacy. Given that Indigenous society in pre-colonial times was grounded in hunting and gathering activity, it would be appropriate to determine whether contemporaneous Indigenous economic activity includes a substantial non-market component that supplements income and otherwise substitutes for other financial needs.

Not only does this reflexivity allow an analysis of the adequacy of the standard poverty measures for Indigenous Australians, but it is consistent with the need to broaden the notions of poverty to take into account ongoing social relationships. Such considerations sometimes come under the rubric of social exclusion and this chapter briefly touches on such factors in order to provide a more complete reflection of some potential constraints on the ability to achieve various COAG targets that go beyond the lack of household resources.

As the title of this chapter indicates, this research is motivated by the question:

- Is Indigenous poverty different from other poverty?

However, three other research questions are addressed in the research:

- Is there a role of customary Indigenous practices and non-market activities in explaining poverty and financial stress?
- Is income measurement error or household size and composition driving the difference between Indigenous and other Australian poverty?
- What is the relationship between poverty and social exclusion of Indigenous Australians?

The next section of this chapter discusses the existing debate about the difficulties of measuring poverty in the context of Indigenous Australians. After noting the main caveats on Indigenous poverty the incidence of poverty is described for selected household types with a particular focus on the those household categories where a disproportionate number of Indigenous people live. The third section introduces the theoretical and empirical issues for modelling financial stress, especially how social institutions, non-market activities and goods may interact with financial stress for Indigenous people. This discussion uses a paper by Breunig and Cobb-Clark (2006) to reflect on how poverty and equivalence scales might be fundamentally different for Indigenous people and other Australians. The next section discusses how social exclusion or social inclusion might yield additional insights into the nature of Indigenous disadvantage, inter alia, by teasing out how discrimination may weaken the association between income and poverty-related outcomes. The penultimate section provides clear answers to the research question identified above, while the conclusion discusses the implications of the analysis for future data collections.

What is poverty and how might it relate to financial stress and social exclusion for Indigenous Australians?

What is poverty?

Paul Spicker (2007) attempts to grapple with the idea of poverty and hence is a useful starting point for conceptualising what poverty might mean for Indigenous Australians. Spicker's book is even more ambitious than it sounds as it covers more than a narrow notion of deprivation of certain poor individuals as he outlines multiple definitions of underlying concept:

- poverty in terms of being deprived of certain goods and services (i.e. as a specific need)
- poverty as a pattern of deprivation over an extended period of time
- poverty as a low standard of living with low income or consumption
- poverty as a lack of resources (which results in unmet need)
- poverty as an economic distance (or economic inequality where people cannot afford things that others can afford)
- poverty as economic class, which is determined itself by a person's relationship to the means of production
- poverty as social class, which is often defined in terms of low socioeconomic status where poor people lack status power and opportunities available to others
- poverty as a dependency on social assistance or welfare
- poverty as social exclusion where the poor are a marginal group who are excluded from society (either actively or passively). The poor may be unable to participate in society economically, socially or politically, or
- poverty as a lack of entitlement (e.g. Sen 1982).

Spicker classifies these definitions into three main clusters of poverty type categorised as: *material need* (i.e. the first 3 definitions above), *economic circumstances* (the next 3 definitions), and *social relationships* of people (the remaining 4 definitions).

Saunders, Naidoo and Griffiths (2007) conceptualised poverty, deprivation and social exclusion (the second last definition in Spicker's list) as three overlapping spheres that have a small central core that most people think of as social disadvantage. Historically, the concept of poverty has been operationalised in terms of a deficiency in income relative to some norm – however, there is some merit in considering a more expansive notion of social disadvantage. Notwithstanding, it is important to recognise there is a risk that we conflate analytically distinct phenomenon (i.e. the non-overlapping parts of Saunders, Naidoo and Griffiths' (2007) Venn diagram).

It is salutatory to remind ourselves that people mean different things when they refer to poverty, but the majority of this chapter will largely focus on the shortfall in income to meet the needs of Indigenous households – but the discussion will touch on some of the other meanings, notably some reflections on social exclusion in the penultimate section.

Difficulties in defining and measuring Indigenous poverty

In order to contain the discussion to manageable size, the focus here is on several specific difficulties in defining and measuring Indigenous poverty – to highlight some factors that are sometimes go missing in broader poverty analysis (see Altman and Hunter 1998). Indigenous poverty differs from other Australian poverty in that is concentrated in large families where there are large numbers of children and complex demands on the household resources (compared to other Australian poverty where small sole-parent families and the elderly are over-represented). The complexity of current living circumstances combines with historical Indigenous disadvantage to create both an inordinately high level of financial stress and a lack of capacity to deal with personal financial matters and the institutions that provide financial services. Any attempt to evaluate financial stress and develop this capacity to deal with financial institutions needs to take into account, and to some extent be informed by, specific social and cultural circumstances facing Indigenous Australians.

There are many conceptual complexities underlying Indigenous poverty that are not adequately captured in mainstream poverty analysis (Altman and Hunter 1997). A credible analysis must acknowledge both the diversity of Indigenous circumstances and how distinct value systems drive preferences and behaviours that shape the ability of policy to address Indigenous disadvantage. For example, the self determination movement led to many Indigenous people choosing to move to small remote communities (sometimes called outstations or homelands) that are distant from mainstream labour markets and commercial opportunities – thus limiting the number of income earning possibilities and potentially putting the individuals concerned at risk of poverty. The more recent reaction to self-determination is critical of such moves, and the policies that support the decisions to move, as entrenching Indigenous poverty – however such criticisms tend to ignore the issue of Indigenous agency in the choices made.

Subsistence activities, sometimes referred to as 'home production' in the economics literature, also raise issues that complicate the interpretation of Indigenous poverty. Hunting, fishing and gathering play a central role in customary practices. Such activities not only provide direct sustenance which may substitute for goods purchased in the market place, these customary practices also play a crucial role in re-invigorating Indigenous culture and ultimately re-enforcing Indigenous identity – thereby enhancing the welfare of the Indigenous community in less material terms. Despite the intrusion of non-Indigenous settlement, hunting and gathering activities still play an important economic role in many remote and rural communities. Income-based measures used in conventional poverty analysis fail to capture the role of such informal productive, and income substitution activities. Some income-generating activities associated with customary activities may also not be captured if the money is generated in the 'gray' economy that operates outside formal reported income frameworks (especially the tax system).

Altman and Hunter (1997) analysis of the 1994 National and Torres Strait Islander Survey (NATSIS) data concluded that the substitution between non-market subsistence and monetary income was small as there is little difference between the personal income after accounting for hunting, fishing and gathering. Notwithstanding, it is important to revisit this issue in the context of financial stress as respondents may be less inclined to misrepresent their level of financial stress than misrepresent their level of income (survey respondents may (incorrectly) fear that income data may be compared to government tax records).

Daly and Smith (1995) suggests that Indigenous families experience substantial and multiple forms of economic burden arising from the size and structure of families and households. Indigenous households are more likely to have more than one family in residence than other Australian households and are more likely to be multi-generational with older Indigenous people more likely to be living with younger people in extended family households. Hunter, Kennedy and Smith (2003) and Hunter, Kennedy and Biddle (2004) demonstrate that the distinct structure of Indigenous households crucially determines the relative income position and ultimately, the incidence and severity of Indigenous poverty.

The issue of economies of scale in household production also has important implications for the measurement of Indigenous poverty. Equivalence scales used to control for the cost of various household types should accurately reflect the real cost of raising large complex Indigenous families with distinct sharing rules embedded in kinship networks and associated social obligations. Unfortunately, the range of conventional equivalence scales used by poverty researchers becomes significantly wider as the number of children increases (Whiteford 1985: 13, 106–7). This chapter is motivated partially by the need to demonstrate that Indigenous circumstances warrant a specific set of equivalence scales that take into account the distinct costs associated with running their households.

The role of relative prices and expenditure patterns may have a distinct effect on Indigenous people. When there are large differences in the relative price of daily necessities, it is difficult to compare the levels of poverty between groups (Sen 1992: 115). Given that Indigenous people are disproportionately concentrated in high-cost areas that are less accessible to mainstream services, the basic poverty comparisons between Indigenous and non-Indigenous Australians can be problematic.

Ultimately, Indigenous poverty based on standard equivalence scales are misleading because the patterns of Indigenous expenditure on food, housing and transportation is likely to differ substantially from that of other poor people. Low-income Indigenous households appear to spend a higher proportion of their incomes on the basic necessities of life, than the lowest income households in the rest of Australian society. Indigenous expenditure patterns are also characterised by expenditure on poor quality, cheap foodstuffs, second-hand goods, reliance on credit and on subsidised services (Smith 1991). Obviously expenditure patterns like this partially reflect the high price of consumer goods and services in remote and rural areas, but this may also be indicative of cultural differences in the value of such goods.

In a sense, all these issues provide theoretical reasons why Indigenous poverty may be poorly measured. One consequence is that the processes driving financial stress will also be different for Indigenous and other Australians. A following section explores the distinct nature of financial stress among Indigenous people and the theoretical relationship between such stress and poverty. The empirical analysis of financial stress could be used as a rationale for revising equivalence scales to account for Indigenous circumstances and expenditure patterns. Before that, the following examines attempts to measure poverty using the modified Organisation for Economic Co-operation and Development (OECD) equivalence scales, which is the international standard used to control for the effects of household size and composition. It may turn out that these international standards are somewhat flawed in this situation, but they will form a useful benchmark to start our analysis of Indigenous poverty.

Describing Indigenous poverty using OECD equivalence scales

The incidence of poverty for various household types for Indigenous and all Australian households is reported in Fig. 10.1–10.3. The data for Indigenous Australians is drawn from the 2008 National Aboriginal and Torres Strait Islander Social Survey (NATSISS) and is broken down into estimates for remote and non-remote areas. As indicated above, we have good reason to expect that remote Indigenous populations are different to non-remote Indigenous population because accessibility to services in the latter is better by definition. It is also often argued that different colonial histories provide crucial context for understanding settled Australia and consequently remote and non-remote Indigenous peoples should be treated as distinct populations (e.g. Rowley 1970, 1972). Another reason for separating out the remote and non-remote populations is that very few non-Indigenous people live in remote areas – so most surveys of the Australian population concentrate solely on non-remote areas as the cost of surveying in remote areas is much higher.

This analysis uses the 2006 General Social Survey (GSS) to benchmark the analysis for Indigenous Australians from the 2008 NATSISS, but the survey methodology of the GSS means that it is, strictly speaking, only comparable for the non-remote sample of NATSISS. The remote data from the NATSISS can be compared to the results for the non-remote NATSISS data to identify whether the experience of poverty in such areas is significantly different between Indigenous Australians living in remote and non-remote areas.

In this section, the poverty line is set as 50 per cent of the median equivalised income for the Australian households estimated using the 2006 GSS and inflated to 2008 levels, to make it comparable to the results for the 2008 NATSISS. This category of poverty line is not uncontested, but it is the most commonly used form benchmark to identify poor in Australia (Saunders 2005). The 95% confidence intervals of the poverty measures, an indicator of reliability of estimates, are reported as 'whiskers' for respective columns.[1]

The incidence of poverty is not significantly different between various sole-parents categories as shown in Fig. 10.1. About half of sole-parents live in households classified as poor irrespective of Indigenous status or the remoteness category. Being a sole-parent seems to put all Australians at a similar risk of being in poverty, as Indigenous estimates are not significantly different from the GSS estimate using 95% confidence intervals. In contrast, Indigenous couples and other family types are significantly more likely to be in poverty than the analogous average Australian families in non-remote areas (with remote Indigenous couples experiencing even higher poverty rates).

The incidence of poverty is higher for Indigenous households than for other Australian households of all sizes as shown in Fig. 10.2. However, for the largest households (with 7 or more people in them) the difference is not significant largely due to the small number of non-Indigenous households of that size (and the consequent lack of reliability of associated estimates). The largest difference in the incidence of poverty for Indigenous and total Australian households is for households with 3–6 persons in them and the higher overall poverty rate for Indigenous people is driven by the disproportionate concentration of Indigenous households in larger households.

---

1   Confidence intervals are estimated using bootstrapped survey estimates of the standard errors of poverty.

Fig. 10.1 Poverty by family type, Australia, 2008

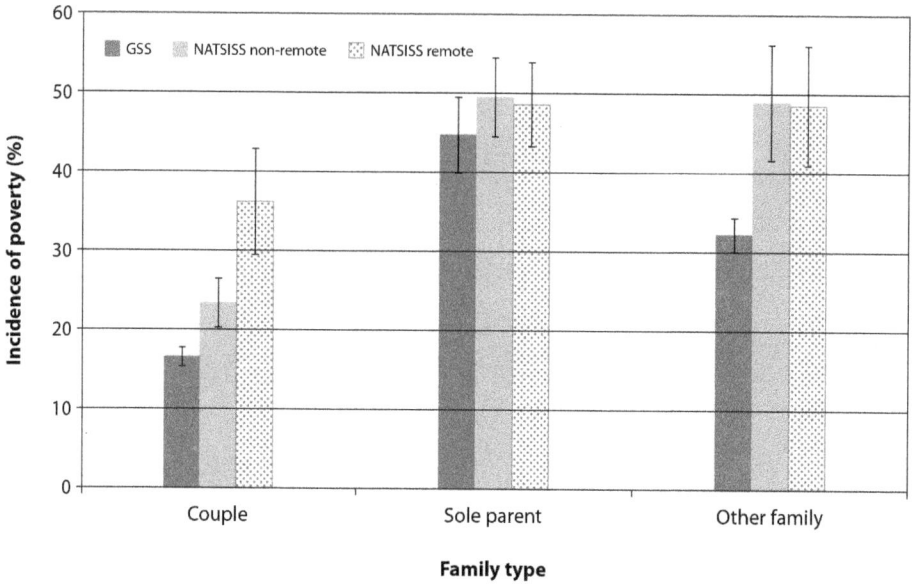

Source: Author's customised calculations using the 2008 NATSISS and 2006 GSS (accessed using the RADL)

Fig. 10.2 Poverty by household size, Australia, 2008

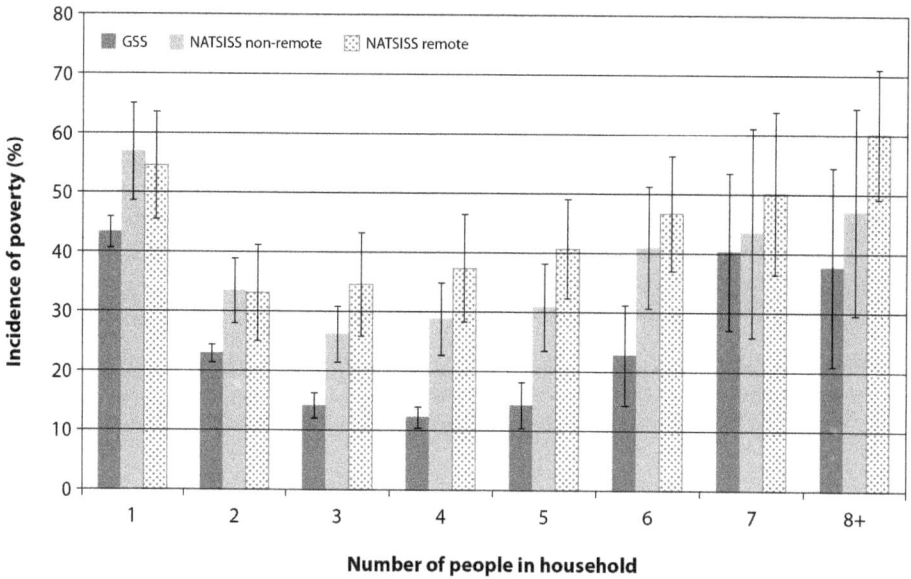

Source: Author's customised calculations using the 2008 NATSISS and 2006 GSS (accessed using the RADL)

Fig. 10.3 Poverty by household type, Australia, 2008

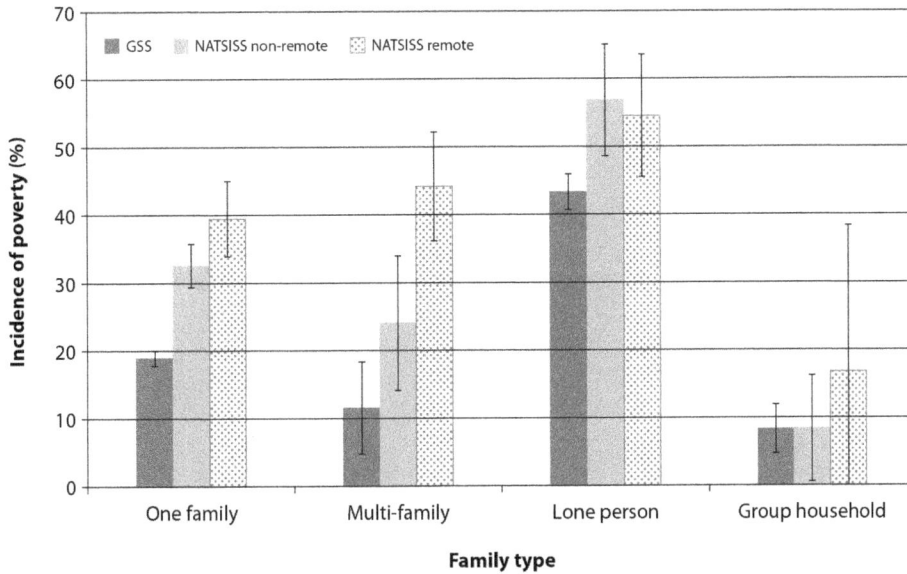

Source: Author's customised calculations using the 2008 NATSIS and 2006 GSS (accessed using the RADL)

The incidence of poverty is significantly higher in Indigenous population in most household types as documented in Fig. 10.3. Furthermore remote Indigenous households are very different to non-remote Indigenous households for both one family and multi-family household categories. Note that the poverty differentials are most pronounced in multi-family households where Indigenous population are between two and four times more likely to be classified as poor (for the non-remote and remote Indigenous populations respectively). As noted above, the incidence of multi-family households is about four times higher for Indigenous compared to other Australian households (see descriptive statistics for the following regression analysis of financial stress reported in Appendix 10A).

There has been some apparent improvement in Indigenous poverty rates since the mid 1970s, but the estimates are not directly comparable with those derived from the earlier NATSIS and related surveys (because of differences in data, methodology and measurement). The following discussion refers to broad trends and relativities to give a sense of the longer run trends in Indigenous poverty. Altman and Hunter (1998) report poverty rates for Indigenous and all Australians measured at the time of the Henderson Report and for the major family types Indigenous people were 2.5–3 times more likely to be in poverty than all Australians. Altman and Hunter (1998) also report estimates by Ross and Mikalauskas (1996) based on 1991 Census data showing that, in broad terms, Indigenous poverty was about 1.3 times that of non-Indigenous poverty for sole-parent families with children and 2.5 times that for non-Indigenous coupled families with children. The long run trends in reducing Indigenous poverty are positive since the 1970s, but it is less clear that they are significantly positive since 1991 as NATSISS based estimates reported above are broadly consistent with those in Ross and Mikalauskas (1996). The new estimates of poverty by remoteness status are one contribution of this chapter and it should be noted that the higher end of the range of measured relative poverty rates is usually associated with living in remote areas. The household types at most variance with the nuclear family archetype common in Western societies, such as multi-family households, are also one of the largest contributors to the apparent poverty rates for Indigenous people. One important research question is whether these observations reflect the circumstances of such families or are simply the product of measurement error caused by the imposition of assumptions that are inappropriate for many Indigenous households. The next section attempts to shed some light on this issue by analysing how the determinants of financial stress vary for Indigenous and other Australians. Given that poverty is an important factor underlying financial stress this allows us to indirectly get an insight into how the processes underlying poverty measurement may differ for groups of Australians.

Financial stress and poverty

Modelling financial stress

In general, financial stress represents the strain in a household associated with either a lack of financial resources or an inability to manage the resources available. After a brief reflection, it should be obvious that financial stress can be associated with people who are not income deficient or materially deprived. Financial stress can be associated with an inability to manage a debt burden effectively or even the lack of access to appropriate financial infrastructure. It must be acknowledged that there is no necessary identity between financial stress and poverty, but there is some scope for overlap. In modelling financial stress, it is important to attempt to control for factors that are associated with debt burden and access to financial infrastructure, so that some inference can be made about the factors that are more likely to be associated with poverty per se.

One background factor likely to be associated with financial stress is the financial skills and capability of individuals concerned. The Nobel Prize winner Amartya Sen has written conceptual contributions on poverty (e.g. the entitlement approach associated with his earlier work on famines) and capability (Sen 2000; see also Robeyns 2000: 5).

Financial stress is one adverse outcome from a prolonged experience of poverty. Before financial hardship manifests itself, the lack of entitlements (or resources) relative to financial and consumption needs must be evident along with behaviours and institutional processes that either reinforce (or fail to address) the underlying deficit in resources, or do not facilitate a suitable line of credit. Like all poverty-related research, it is impossible to get away from the normative nature of the concept. It should be recognised that financial stress can arise from factors other than poverty – for example short-term unsustainable discretionary consumption and temporary circumstances and impediments to access to credit (i.e. where wealth and assets tied up for a short period). The lack of resources not only encompasses a lack of income, but may also include the lack of capacity to manage finances through either poor basic literacy and numeracy (or some more sophisticated notion of financial literacy) or the existence of networks of support and advice.

Identity economics expands upon the idea of preferences and behaviours being, at least in part, socially determined. In particular consumption preferences and other behaviours are shaped to group norms or identities. Such choices, that can easily be characterised as having a cultural dimension, may have positive or negative impacts on outcomes (Akerlof and Kranton 2010). Norms of behaviour and consumption are conditioned by identity and social relations, especially the extent to which an individual associated in social networks with 'like' people who have similar identification and characteristics.

In standard neo-classical economic models, household economic behaviour is based upon a model of households making consumption decisions within a household budget constraint so as to maximise their utility. In such a model, financial stress occurs as a result of an inadequate household budget (i.e. income poverty) or where a household considers that the 'household stress' has a lower disutility than the utility they gain from an alternative pattern of behaviour and consumption. Some outcomes may look like 'hardship', but are really a rational decision by an individual who weighs up anticipated utility and disutility of various consumption options. When examining financial stress of a sub-population like Indigenous population, the fact that some consumption choices may be linked to social or cultural norms should be considered.

Sen (1993) describes a capability framework that provides a critique of the utilitarian approach adopted by neo-classical economists. Central to Sen's approach is that wellbeing should not be simply measured in terms of the actual outcomes that individuals achieve, but is intrinsically linked to the actual range of choices they have, and the extent to which these choices are constrained. 'Capability' refers to all the things people could do with the available resources to which they are entitled. 'Functioning' is another core concept in Sen's lexicon, which refers to what people actually decide to do with the resources that are available to them. 'Choice', or what sociologists refer to as individual agency, is a core feature in Sen's model. Of course, the rhetoric of choice is also essential to many conventional economic debates, but this is largely confined to people choosing what they want to buy or consume. Sen's model allows expansion of the notion of choice so that the capability set of individuals is extended – and so people's freedom to choose and develop is enhanced.[2]

Sen's (1993) model refers to entitlements that might include human capital (e.g. numeracy and literacy), income, non-market goods (hunting, gathering and home production) and social infrastructure. One might also argue that social capital or cultural capital is one form of resource as the experience of social networks may change the choices people make (Bourdieu 1993; Coleman 1988).

Understanding how Indigenous households engage in production, consumption, and savings behaviour is critical to postulating models for capturing aspects of financial stress, along with the failure to achieve wellbeing that is often characterised as poverty.

Breunig and Cobb-Clark (2006) outline a model of financial stress that allows them to make some inferences about how poverty is measured using equivalence scales. Their approach is to parsimoniously model the factors that drive financial stress, and then calculate the level of income that equates the financial stress (or rather underlying welfare) of households of various sizes and compositions after controlling for other relevant factors. Equivalence scales can be thought of as the income for a particular household type that equates the income required to achieve the same welfare in a reference household (say 2 adults and no children). The importance of such an analysis is that it might allow researchers to estimate an Indigenous-specific equivalence scales which could be compared to equivalence scales constructed for the total Australian or other populations using similar methodologies. While there is a theoretical link to the conventional equivalence scales, such as the OECD scale used above, the conventional scales are based on more complete information on consumption and expenditure patterns and a different analytic framework – accordingly, it would be preferable to make any conclusions about Indigenous-specific finding based on an empirical analysis that used the same methodology and as comparable data as is possible. Future research can and should fully operationalise the Breunig and Cobb-Clark methodology, but that is beyond the scope of this chapter. The following research estimates the relationship of equivalised household income (rather than

---

2   Note that choice plays a vital role in Sen's (1993) model and is not taken as given as it is in most economic models (where choice finishes with purchase of the goods and services, or 'resources' might be used to achieve capability and functioning). In a sense, social inclusion is all about enlarging both the capability set and the choices made. The problem for a social inclusion agenda potentially occurs when value judgements are made about people's choices. It is an intrinsically political process of who is judging whom or what (Hunter 2009; Jordan and Hunter 2009).

raw household income used in Breunig and Cobb-Clark) and salient household characteristics to financial stress, and hence it effectively takes existing equivalised scales as given. Notwithstanding, the following empirical strategy is largely symmetrical with that study, and it could be argued that difference between results for Indigenous and all Australians could be associated with differences in the appropriate equivalence scales for the respective populations.

Two specifications of financial stress are considered: a parsimonious specification that allows comparisons between Indigenous and overall Australian estimates and a non-parsimonious specification that controls for a range of factors that are likely to be particularly important in the Indigenous context. While the latter may provide a better description of the data, this non-parsimonious approach will enhance the possibility that reverse causation is affecting any estimated equivalence scales. Notwithstanding, several expanded specifications are used here in an attempt to tease out how the processes underlying poverty in Indigenous and other populations might differ substantially.

In addition to measuring the association between financial stress and income and household size and composition, some measure of Indigenous customary activities (such as living on homelands and hunting and gathering activities) and wealth as proxied by whether the dwelling is owned or being purchased (i.e. there is some equity in the household). Note that household composition also includes information on whether the household has more than one family living in it – however the effect of living in such households may be either positive or negative depending on how integrated are the resident families' finances and living conditions. Households that include both Indigenous and non-Indigenous members are also controlled for, as this will by definition affect the indigeneity of the household. In order to compare for between Indigenous and non-Indigenous populations, who tend to live in very different parts of the country, a highly disaggregated set of geographic indicators were used in the regression (Appendix 10A). Even though we have taken great care in constructing data that is basically comparable between the NATSISS and GSS for most variables, the geography is coded very differently. There is a real analytical problem that will be discussed further in the concluding section.

One approach may be to estimate separate regressions for remote and non-remote areas for NATSISS and control for other geography but this will make the estimate even less reliable than those estimated for the whole population. The following uses the whole sample, and controls for the unobserved geographic factors as best as possible using relatively disaggregated areal controls, to simplify exposition.

Selected data issues

This section attempts to identify the factors associated with financial security/stress for insight into the nature of Indigenous poverty relative to other Australian poverty.

The NATSISS includes several measures of either financial security or financial stress. Those who felt they were more financially secure are captured by whether or not they felt their household could raise $2000 in an emergency. Financial stress over the previous 12 months is captured by whether or not they have run out of money for basic living expenses. There were other measures of financial security and financial stress on both the NATSISS and GSS files, but these were the only two variables where it is reasonably certain the variables were comparable between surveys. Even here there was an issue with the use of a dollar value in the financial security measure as the two surveys were conducted almost two years apart. However, the rate of inflation in Australia between the two surveys was only 4.3 per cent, so $2000 at the time of the 2006 GSS was worth around $2086 by the time the 2008 NATSISS was conducted. That is, it would have been slightly easier for a NATSISS respondent to raise the cash, but the difference was not substantial.

Financial stress is measured at the household level and therefore things that explain it should also be measured at that level. While it would be sensible to assume that a person's household context influences their individual outcomes, the reverse is not necessarily, or even likely to be, the case. Therefore in order to analyse household-level dependent variables using individual data, we should ideally have information on all members of the household so that the characteristics of the household can be fully described. The 2008 NATSISS survey method means that there is, at most, information from two adults in the household. That is, it is not possible to use this information to construct full household level data where there is only individual-level information available on the Remote Access Data Laboratory (RADL) – the method that allows researchers limited and controlled access to ABS confidentialised data). The good news is that the two adult individuals are randomly selected within the household so using individual information should provide an unbiased characterisation of the household – although this characterisation would necessarily be less reliable than if all the individuals in the household were used to estimate the average characteristic for the household.

For the GSS, information on only one respondent per household is provided so the person-level file on the unit record gives a unique correspondence with household level data (although not necessarily entirely accurate information on that level). That is, there is no choice about the individual identified with the household characteristics. The question then becomes: is the individual-level data used to characterise the household likely to have similar information on the GSS and NATSISS? Rather than use all individual-level data on the NATSISS file to construct some sort of household average, it is probably better to use one individual to characterise the household. The person chosen to represent the NATSISS household is the first person listed on the household file – whoever that might be. This has a direct analogy with the GSS respondent who, at the risk of being trite, is in effect the number one respondent.

Despite the logical deficiencies in using individual information to explain household-level phenomenon, I estimate some models with a household-level dependent variable (financial stress) using a mix of household and individual explanatory variables. However, this approach can be justified on the grounds that when separate models are estimated using household-level-only explanatory variables (Models 1 and 2, which are not reported to save space), the coefficients do not vary substantially from those reported (Models 3 and 4).[3] Consequently, despite the flawed logic in the expanded specification that could confound the level of analysis and the effects of various explanatory factors, the coefficients for the household-level-only specifications appear to be robust.

One last data issue is that the financial stress measure is retrospective (over the last 12 months). Arguably, it is methodologically problematic to explain retrospective measures using current characteristics. Ideally one would want to analyse them using information on the household at the start of the period. This is only ever likely to be achieved using longitudinal data sets. Financial security is measured in terms of whether it is possible to raise cash within a week so the use of current values of explanatory variables does not pose any analogous methodological issue for that dependent variable.

Factors associated with financial stress

A logistic regression analysis similar to that done in Breunig and Cobb-Clark (2006) is provided in Tables 10.1 and 10.2. The specification excludes a few explanatory factors that we have theoretical reasons to be related to financial stress and security are omitted from the specification. Biddle (2011) provides a descriptive analysis that includes education and work. One reason to exclude these potential explanatory factors is that one of the aims of this exercise is to gain some indirect insight into equivalence scales which relate household

---

3 Model 1 only includes income and household size, Model 2 includes other household-level information that is coded by the ABS and we can be confident accurately characterises household-level data. Model 3 includes household-level variables derived from the first respondent on the unit record file, while Model 4 includes the broadest specification that also includes some Indigenous specific variables that attempt to capture the role of customary activities. Obviously, Model 4 can only be estimated using NATSISS data.

income (measured in logs) and family composition to financial stress. Inclusion of education and market work will indirectly pick up the influence of market income on financial stress thereby changing the underlying coefficient on equivalised income which is crucial to the derived or implied estimates of equivalence scales.

Overall, the explanatory variables included in the model explain much less of the variation in financial stress than they did for financial security as evidenced by the lower Pseudo R-Squared and the fewer number of variables that were statistically significant. This is probably due in no small measure to the fact that financial stress is a retrospective measure, whereas this measure of financial security is prospective. It is more plausible to predict possible outcomes from the near future in terms of current circumstances rather than retrospectively explaining historical experience of financial stress in terms current information. Analysis which attempts to explain the past in terms of the present could be construed as rationalising the situation *ex post,* and hence can more easily be discounted as resulting in invalid conclusions.

The explanatory variables are the same in Tables 10.1 and 10.2 and given that financial stress is arguably the obverse of financial security, in general it is expected the coefficient for one to be the negative sign of the coefficient in the other regression. This is indeed the case for most coefficients reports in Tables 10.1 and 10.2. For example, the log of household income reduces financial stress and increases financial security. Not surprisingly, they are the coefficients in the respective regressions with the highest significance statistics.

Leaving aside the coefficients for the multi-family household variable for a moment, the second set of variables relate to wealth as embodied in the ownership of a large asset, most likely a house either with or without a mortgage. There is clear evidence that having a large asset improves the respondent's access to the credit market, probably through 're-draw', an increasingly common facility.

A geographic index that captures the local socioeconomic status of an area (Socio-Economic Indexes for Areas (SEIFA), an ABS measure using the Index of Relative Socio-Economic Disadvantage) is included along with the most disaggregated information available on the respective surveys. The lack of direct comparability of much of this geographic information in the GSS and NATSISS, along with the lack of analytical utility of some of that geographic information, is potential problematic for users of both surveys. This point will be discussed in greater detail later in this chapter.

The SEIFA data is coded into deciles which also provide a reasonably refined control for otherwise unobservable geographic factors. Given that it is known to be highly correlated with local amenity, and hence household prices, it will also pick up additional value of local assets, particularly housing prices. Living in higher status areas is associated with a considerably enhanced ability to raise cash quickly, which is consistent with the factor being associated with higher housing prices in such areas. In terms of financial stress, the SEIFA variable is associated with less cash problems for the GSS analysis but was not significantly associated with cash problems in the NATSISS sample. That may be a reflection of it being less important for the Indigenous population because relatively few Indigenous people live in high status areas and even fewer own houses in such areas.

Table 10.1 Factors associated with cash problems in the last 12 months, Australia, 2008[a]

	GSS Model 3	NATSISS Model 3	NATSISS Model 4
Log of equivalised household income (OECD)	−0.4824 (−12.12)	−0.1996 (−3.50)	−0.2069 (−3.62)
Number of people in household	0.1666 (7.05)	0.0985 (4.24)	0.0975 (4.17)
Multi−family household	−0.0247 (−0.13)	−0.3579 (−2.42)	−0.3562 (−2.40)
Owner without a mortgage	−2.0930 (−25.19)	−1.3290 (−7.81)	−1.3267 (−7.76)
Owner with a mortgage	−0.6587 (−10.65)	−0.5309 (−5.33)	−0.5315 (−5.27)
Index of Relative Socio-Economic Disadvantage (SEIFA index)	−0.0649 (−6.17)	0.0193 (1.22)	0.0178 (1.12)
Couple family	−0.3113 (−4.34)	−0.2102 (−1.83)	−0.2089 (−1.67)
One-parent family	0.6124 (6.82)	0.1934 (1.76)	0.1909 (1.71)
Profound or severe disability	0.2851 (2.55)	0.5978 (4.99)	0.5965 (4.95)
Unspecified disability	0.6463 (9.31)	0.3509 (4.81)	0.3528 (4.78)
Household includes Indigenous and non-Indigenous residents	–	–	−0.0037 (−0.04)
Live in homeland	–	–	−0.2113 (−2.35)
Hunting & gathering for medicines	–	–	0.2929 (1.76)
Hunting & gathering for food	–	–	0.0869 (1.09)
Pseudo R^2	0.1646	0.0765	0.0781

a. T-statistics in brackets. The reference household for this analysis is an indigenous-only, lone person household (by definition a 'single family' household) in a dwelling that is not owned by occupants. The individuals in the reference category are those respondents who do not have a disability, live outside their 'homeland', and do not engage in hunting and gathering.

Source: Author's customised calculations using the 2008 NATSISS and 2006 GSS (accessed using the RADL)

Table 10.2 Ability to raise $2000 cash within a week, Australia, 2008[a]

	GSS Model 3	NATSISS Model 3	NATSISS Model 4
Log of Equivalised household Income (OECD)	1.0079 (21.45)	1.0231 (17.20)	0.9973 (16.70)
Number of people in household	−0.1395 (−5.21)	−0.0731 (−3.30)	−0.0658 (−2.93)
Multi-family household	−0.0836 (−0.41)	−0.1553 (−1.15)	−0.1940 (−1.42)
Owner without a mortgage	1.7340 (21.63)	1.8046 (13.36)	1.7300 (12.70)
Owner with a mortgage	0.8953 (12.18)	1.1560 (12.33)	1.0664 (11.25)
Index of Relative Socio-Economic Disadvantage (SEIFA index)	0.1355 (11.55)	0.0960 (6.30)	0.0883 (5.72)
Couple family	0.3911 (4.88)	0.4560 (4.37)	0.1901 (1.68)
One-parent family	−0.4828 (−5.00)	0.0166 (0.16)	−0.0887 (−0.84)
Profound or severe disability	−0.3310 (−2.94)	−0.7440 (−6.00)	−0.7299 (−5.84)
Unspecified disability	−0.6561 (−8.88)	−0.2850 (−4.17)	−0.2453 (−3.54)
Household includes Indigenous and non-Indigenous residents	–	–	−0.5238 (6.40)
Live in homeland	–	–	−0.0840 (−1.02)
Hunting & gathering for medicines	–	–	0.3103 (1.94)
Hunting & gathering for food	–	–	0.1352 (1.80)
Pseudo R^2	0.2382	0.2225	0.2289

a. T-statistics in brackets. The reference household for this analysis is an indigenous-only, lone person household (by definition a 'single family' household) in a dwelling that is not owned by occupants. The individuals in the reference category are those respondents who do not have a disability, live outside their 'homeland', and do not engage in hunting and gathering.

Source: Author's customised calculations using the 2008 NATSISS and 2006 GSS (accessed using the RADL)

Couple families and one-parent families would on balance have an expectation of reverse signs for the coefficients (if they are significant at all). For the whole population, living in a couple is protective against financial stress whereas lone parents are generally associated with such stress. Relationships status, that is either being in a couple relationship or being a lone parent, does not generally have a significant association with financial stress or security for the Indigenous respondents in NATSISS. The only exception to this observation is that living in a couple is associated with financial security if Indigenous-specific factors associated with customary activities are NOT controlled for. This probably indicates that Indigenous financial stress is complicated by the presence of such activities which directly augment household production.

Severe and profound disability and other disability are likely to be associated with substantial costs that place extra demands on the household budgets and increase financial stress. Disability may also curtail ability to raise cash; such effects may occur through loss of income earning potential (i.e. wages foregone). The coefficients for disability are consistent with these expectations.

Living in a household with both Indigenous and non-Indigenous people residents could be an indicator of exposure to non-Indigenous social networks comprising those less likely to be disadvantaged and more likely to be cashed up. Interestingly, living with non-Indigenous people is not significantly associated with financial stress but is significantly associated with financial security. Accordingly, such households appear to affect Indigenous outcomes through an enhanced ability to raise cash quickly.

Customary activities of hunting and gathering for either food or medicines can influence financial stress or security, by augmenting household production and thereby substituting for what would otherwise be purchased. Another potential explanatory variable is a dummy variable that captures whether an individual lives on a remote 'homeland' – broadly defined in the Macquarie Atlas of Indigenous Australia gas 'an Indigenous person's ancestral country' (Arthur and Morphy 2005: 262).[4] The reason why homeland is included in the analysis is because the productivity aspect of hunting and gathering activities is likely to be higher when a person has an intimate knowledge of the local country.

In general, either living on homelands or customary activities is significant when analysing financial security and financial stress models (but both explanations are not significant in any one model). For example, homelands are associated with lower financial stress but are not significantly associated with financial security. Hunting and gathering is significantly associated with financial security at the 10% level, but is not significant for financial stress. This may reflect that there is either some sort interaction between hunting and gathering and homelands or that these explanations are capturing the same underlying factor (say connection with indigenous culture).

The other largely Indigenous-specific factor, which is controlled for in both the GSS and NATSISS regression, is living in a multi-family household. This is associated with lower levels of financial stress, but is not associated with the ability to raise a substantial amount of cash within a week. Multi-family

---

4   The ABS (2007: 111) quite rightly point out that people may not live in their ancestral lands permanently; it is a geographic sense of belonging that relates to an individual rather than an area.

households may act as a form of social insurance for Indigenous families, in terms of an informal line of credit to other household members. Interestingly, there is no significant association between multi-family households and lower levels financial stress for 'all Australian families' which probably indicates the distinct nature of Indigenous intra-household sharing which is more likely to involve kinship and other social obligations (Altman and Hunter 1998).

Social exclusion, social inclusion and Indigenous poverty

Policy makers focus on a number of issues that are often correlated with poverty – including economic disadvantage, social exclusion and social capital – although such issues are clearly not synonymous with poverty. The above analysis illustrates that there is good reason to suspect Indigenous poverty is of a different order to other poverty and may be qualitatively different in nature. The concept of social exclusion may further motivate an understanding of why Indigenous poverty may be fundamentally different to other Australian poverty. This concept arose partially as a response to the perceived inadequacy of the poverty literature which focused excessively on income at a point in time (Spicker 2007). Social exclusion and the related concept of social inclusion emphasise the importance of social relationships with the broader society and are concerned with social processes that are intrinsically dynamic in nature. For a racial minority such as Indigenous Australians, discrimination is a clear example of a problem with social relationships that may lead to social exclusion.

Previous research has highlighted the existence of social exclusion by demonstrating the lack of correlation between income and selected economic, political, health, crime and other social outcomes (Hunter 1999, 2000). While these findings are easily replicated using more recent data, this section focuses on the unique discrimination data provided in the 2008 NATSISS. If discrimination is found to exist for high income groups, this is direct evidence that social exclusion is likely to be evident even when resources are not scarce.

The following analysis measured discrimination for Indigenous households ranked by the overall Australian distribution of equivalised household income. Given the small number of Indigenous households in the fourth and fifth quintiles of Australian incomes, those observations are grouped together so that estimates are reasonably reliable. Note that this top income category represents the top 40 per cent of household incomes in Australia – and such households can in no way be construed as poor.

In the not too distant past, practices that could be considered discriminatory were condoned or even encouraged by the state (Arrow 1998). The rise of anti-discrimination legislation in the 1970s means that any ongoing discriminatory behaviour is more likely to be indirect or covert than overt discrimination (Walker 2001). Covert discrimination is relatively self-explanatory, but indirect discrimination can occur when criteria or practices appear on the surface to be neutral but can lead to exclusions due to other characteristics such as race. Statistical discrimination based on the average characteristics of a group is a well-documented form of racial discrimination which is sometimes justified in terms of the right of firms to maximise their profits. The widespread privilege given to managerial prerogative in the institutions that regulate industrial relations makes it difficult to identify both indirect and covert forms of discrimination – as evidenced by the small number of prosecutions of labour market discrimination under the *Racial Discrimination Act 1975* (De Plevitz 2000; Hunter 2005).

Fig. 10.4 Discrimination by equivalised income quintile, Indigenous Australia, 2008[a]

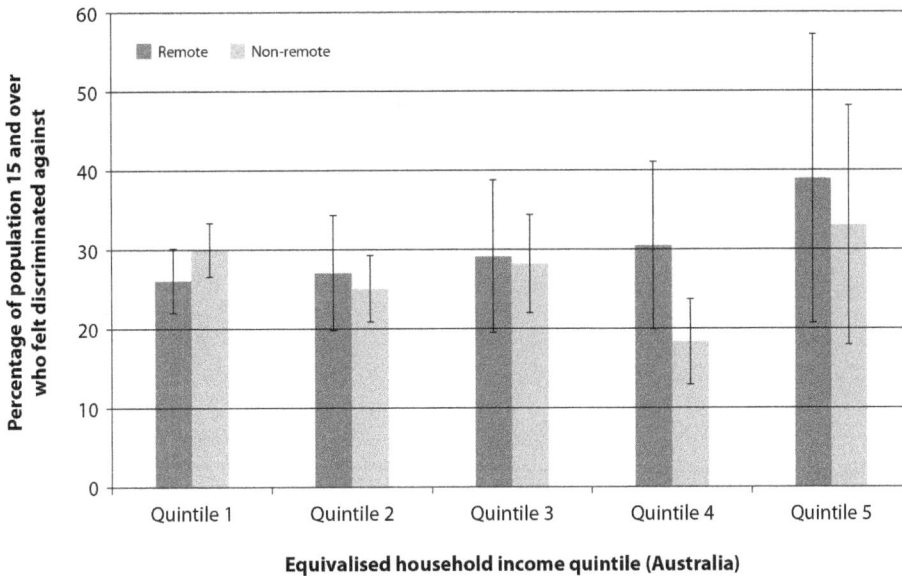

Note: Data on experience of discrimination was not collected in GSS.

Source: Author's customised calculations using the 2008 NATSISS (accessed using the RADL)

While the official level of discrimination reported is often low, the actual experience of discrimination by Indigenous people appears to be quite high. Indeed, Fig. 10.4 shows that around 30 per cent of Indigenous residents in both remote and non-remote areas report experiencing some form of discrimination. Perhaps the most important observation in Fig. 10.4 is that there is no income gradient for the experience of discrimination. Discrimination affects both the rich and poor alike and is one of the fundamental reasons why Indigenous people feel socially excluded from national life. Obviously, it is hard to prove that discrimination exists legally, but the subjective experience or feeling of being discriminated against is potentially important in its own right, in driving the willingness to participate in broader societal processes.

Research questions and answers

By combining information from two datasets – the 2006 GSS, and the 2008 NATSISS – it is possible to answer, more or less completely, the questions raised at the beginning of this chapter.

Research question 1: Is there a role of customary Indigenous practices and non-market activities in explaining poverty and financial stress?

The answer is clearly 'yes', although the precise role of customary practices and activities needs considerable work. Living on homeland, and hunting and gathering activities, do seem to interact but further work is needed to clarify the nature of the interaction. One improvement to the specification is likely to be that the models are separately run for remote and non-remote population. This was not done here to simplify exposition but a disaggregated model is likely to be warranted (see Biddle 2011).

Research question 2: Is income measurement error or differential household size and composition driving the difference between Indigenous and other Australian poverty?

The analysis presented in this chapter indicates that Indigenous equivalence scales are likely to be significantly different from equivalence scales derived for other populations. All poverty studies use culturally specific assumptions for the mainstream population and are likely to embed significant measurement error in existing estimates of Indigenous poverty. This observation includes those estimates of Indigenous poverty reported above, which use the internationally accepted OECD equivalence scales. While equivalence scales were not estimated in this chapter, the empirical analysis points strongly to the possibility that Indigenous equivalence scales are likely to differ from standard equivalence scales.

Research question 3: What is the relationship between poverty and social exclusion of Indigenous Australians?

Many Indigenous people experience multiple disadvantage, which can be construed as social exclusion (Hunter 2009; Steering Committee for the Review of Government Service Provision 2009). This chapter has shown that social relationships are likely to be an important aspect of Indigenous social exclusion, especially the ongoing experience of discrimination. In order to understand Indigenous disadvantage, it is not sufficient to examine income, or even financial stress, as discriminatory processes affect even well-endowed Indigenous households.

Research question 4: Is Indigenous poverty different from other poverty?

The answer to the above three questions means that the answer to this question – which provides the underlying motivation for the chapter – is a resounding 'YES'.

Data gaps and future research directions

Several data issues arose in the analysis. First, the mixing of individual and household-level information in explaining what is arguably a household-level phenomenon: poverty and financial stress. Historically, poverty was seen as a family-level analysis but many analyst have pointed out that it is less culturally biased to focus on the household level (Altman and Hunter 1998; Hunter 2001, 2006; Hunter, Kennedy and Biddle 2004). The main argument is that many cultures do not have social relations that are directly comparable to nuclear families as they have evolved in modern western economies. Rather than ignore these alternative social forms, it is preferable to use households rather than focus on specific types of family. Note that the controls for multi-family households are only one aspect of the different cultural forms in the social life – albeit a quite important aspect in the context of Indigenous Australia – and it is preferable to analyse the household as it is the largest unit available.

The practical difficulty of analysing household-level phenomenon using information that is only collected for individuals is an intractable difficulty. Collecting data from all people in the household, rather than a random or representative individual, would appear to be preferable as this can add considerably to the cost of data collection, exacerbate problems of incomplete data, and considerably complicate analysis.

The adequacy of the nature of the geographic information on GSS and NATSISS, particularly the Indigenous survey, is an issue for this analysis. The statutory requirement for the ABS to ensure confidentiality of respondents combines with a desire to ensure that separate estimates can be constructed for each State and Territory to mean that there is no consistent disaggregated information on local accessibility of an area beyond the remote versus non-remote variable. I argue that it would be preferable to include disaggregated information on accessibility of an area rather than be constrained to reporting uneven categories of accessibility for each State because of historical accidents and different stages of development. For example, less developed jurisdictions like the Northern Territory do not have major metropolitan areas with good accessibility to services. The problem is most pronounced in States and Territories where there is not a sufficient number of respondents to distinguish between, for example, metropolitan, inner regional and outer regional. Given that accessibility to services is likely to be a key factor underlying Indigenous and other development, it would be analytically preferable to ignore the State and Territory information and report the most disaggregated level information available on accessibility. A separate data file for State and Territory level information could be provided on request to administrators and researchers focused on specific jurisdictions; however, it is more important that accessibility to services be consistently available for most research purposes.

This chapter highlights that there is probably some value in pursuing social exclusion based explanations of poverty. Such explanations focus on the social relationships and *processes* underlying disadvantage, especially Indigenous poverty. Income at a particular point in time only captures one aspect of Indigenous disadvantage, and low levels of social capital and discrimination may reinforce Indigenous disadvantage. If one adopts a social exclusion lens to interpret poverty, with its emphasis on processes, this drives the conclusion that cross-sectional data such as that collected in GSS and NATSISS is not adequate. We need to collect longitudinal information that charts people's pathways into and out of poverty with a view to identifying the factors that reinforce Indigenous disadvantage. The Household, Income and Labour Dynamics in Australia (HILDA) Survey is a large sample household-based panel study which permits some of this sort of analysis for the general Australian population.[5] There is no analogous survey for the Indigenous population, although the Longitudinal Study of Indigenous Children (LSIC) does collect information on approximately

---

5   HILDA began in 2001 and collects information annually about economic and subjective wellbeing, labour market dynamics and family dynamics.

1500 children and their families; the study is focused on 11 geographic sites, each with a potentially unique historical context. Some information on the dynamics of household disadvantage may be pervaded by LSIC, but it only collected household information pertaining to child development and will not be an adequate basis for understanding the overall dynamics of Indigenous disadvantage. Indigenous poverty and social exclusion are areas worthy of study in their own right. Failure to properly describe such issues is likely to misrepresent and understate Indigenous disadvantage. More importantly, it will prevent the formulation of effective policy informed by a real understanding of these pressing issues.

Appendix 10A: Tables

Table 10A.1 Descriptive statistics for GSS regressions

Description	Mean	Std. Dev.
Any cash problems in the last 12 months	0.1924	0.3942
Could raise $2000 cash within a week	0.8345	0.3717
Log of equivalised household income (OECD)	6.5016	0.7646
Number of people in household	2.4875	1.3471
Multi-family household	0.0179	0.1325
Owner without a mortgage	0.3300	0.4702
Owner with a mortgage	0.3478	0.4763
Index of Relative Socio-Economic Disadvantage	5.6717	2.8335
Couple family	0.5320	0.4990
One parent family	0.0814	0.2735
Profound or severe disability	0.0564	0.2307
Unspecified disability	0.1430	0.3501
Other regional	0.2115	0.4084
Inner Regional	0.2225	0.4159
Major city	0.5661	0.4956
New South Wales	0.1484	0.3556
Victoria	0.1387	0.3456
Queensland	0.1360	0.3428
South Australia	0.1142	0.3181
Western Australia	0.1190	0.3238
Tasmania	0.1327	0.3393
Northern Territory	0.0964	0.2951
Australian Capital Territory	0.1145	0.3184
Number of observations	11 465	

Source: Author's customised calculations using the 2006 GSS (accessed using the RADL)

Table 10A.2 Descriptive statistics for NATSISS regressions

Description	Mean	Std. Dev.
Any cash problems in the last 12 months	0.2337	0.4232
Could raise $2000 cash within a week	0.4698	0.4991
Log of equivalised household income (OECD)	6.0741	0.6775
Number of people in household	3.5039	2.0708
Multi-family household	0.0902	0.2865
Owner without a mortgage	0.0851	0.2791
Owner with a mortgage	0.1936	0.3952
Index of Relative Socio-Economic Disadvantage	2.9509	2.3801
Couple family	0.5244	0.4995
One parent family	0.2884	0.4530
Profound or severe disability	0.0849	0.2788
Unspecified disability	0.4267	0.4946
NSW Inner Regional	0.0446	0.2063
NSW Outer Regional	0.0281	0.1652
Vic Total	0.1723	0.3776
Qld Major Cities	0.0219	0.1464
Qld Inner Regional	0.0201	0.1404
Qld Outer Regional	0.0239	0.1528
Qld Remote/Very Remote	0.0951	0.2934
WA Non-Remote	0.0561	0.2302
WA Remote/Very Remote	0.0739	0.2616
NT Remote/Very Remote	0.1121	0.3155
Balance of Australia – Non-remote	0.2498	0.4329
Balance of Australia – Remote/Very Remote	0.0473	0.2122
Indigenous and non-Indigenous members in household	0.4186	0.4934
Lives on homeland	0.2371	0.4253
Hunting and gathering for medicines	0.0446	0.2063
Hunting and gathering for food	0.3758	0.4844
Number of observations	5 413	

Source: Author's customised calculations using the 2008 NATSISS (accessed using the RADL)

References

Akerlof, G. A. and Kranton, R. E. 2010. *Identity Economics*, Princeton University Press, Princeton.

Altman, J. C. and Hunter, B. H. 1997. 'Indigenous poverty since the Henderson Report', *CAEPR Discussion Paper No. 127*, CAEPR, ANU, Canberra.

—— and —— 1998. 'Indigenous poverty', in R. Fincher and J. Nieuwenhuysen (eds), *Australian Poverty: Then and Now*, Melbourne University Press, Melbourne.

Arrow, K. J. 1998. 'What has economics to say about racial discrimination', *Journal of Economic Perspectives*, 12 (2): 91–100.

Arthur, W. S. and Morphy, F. (eds) 2005. *Macquarie Atlas of Indigenous Australia*, Macquarie Library Pty Ltd, Sydney.

Australian Bureau of Statistics (ABS) 2007. *Housing and Infrastructure in Aboriginal and Torres Strait Islander Communities: Australia 2006*, cat. no. 4710.0, ABS, Canberra.

Biddle, N. 2011. 'Income, work and Indigenous livelihoods', Lecture 5, *Measures of Indigenous Wellbeing and Their Determinants Across the Lifecourse*, 2011 CAEPR Online Lecture Series, CAEPR, ANU, Canberra.

Bourdieu, P. 1993. *Sociology in Question*, Sage, London.

Breunig, R. and Cobb-Clark, D. 2006. 'Understanding the factors associated with financial stress in Australian households', *Australian Social Policy*, 2005: 13 –64.

Coleman, J. S. 1988. 'Social capital in the creation of human capital', *American Journal of Sociology*, 94 (S): 95–120.

Daly, A. and Smith, D. 1995. 'The economic status of Indigenous Australian families', *CAEPR Discussion Paper No. 93*, CAEPR, ANU, Canberra.

De Plevitz, R. L. 2000. The Failure of Australian Legislation on Indirect Discrimination to Detect the Systemic Racism which Prevents Aboriginal People From Fully Participating in the Workforce, PhD thesis, Centre for Public and Comparative Law Faculty of Law, Queensland University of Technology, Brisbane.

Hunter, B. H. 1999. 'Three nations, not one: Indigenous and other Australian poverty', *CAEPR Working Paper No. 1*, CAEPR, ANU, Canberra.

—— 2000. 'Social exclusion, social capital and Indigenous Australians: measuring the social costs of unemployment', *CAEPR Discussion Paper No. 204*, CAEPR, ANU, Canberra.

—— 2001. 'Tackling poverty among Indigenous Australians', in R. Fincher and P. Saunders (eds), *Creating Unequal Futures*, Allen and Unwin, Sydney.

—— 2005. 'The role of discrimination and the exclusion of Indigenous people from the labour market', in D. Austin-Broos and G. Macdonald (eds), *Culture, Economy and Governance in Aboriginal Australia*, University of Sydney Press, Sydney.

—— 2006. 'Further skirmishes in the Poverty War: Income status and financial stress among Indigenous Australians', *Australian Journal of Labour Economics*, 9 (1): 51–64.

—— 2009. 'Indigenous social exclusion: Insights and challenges for the concept of social inclusion', *Family Matters*, 82: 52–61.

——, Kennedy, S. and Biddle, N. 2004. 'Indigenous and other Australian poverty: Revisiting the importance of equivalence scales', *Economic Record*, 80 (251): 411–22.

——, —— and Smith, D. 2003. 'Household composition, equivalence scales and the reliability of income distributions: Some evidence for Indigenous and other Australians', *Economic Record*, 79 (244): 70–83.

Jordan, K. and Hunter, B. H. 2009. 'Indigenous social exclusion and inclusion: what are people to be included in, and who decides?', *Impact*, Spring: 18–21.

Robeyns, I. 2000. 'An unworkable idea or a promising alternative? Sen's capability approach re-examined', Discussion Paper 00.30, Center for Economic Studies, Katholieke Universiteit, Leuven.

Ross, R. T. and Mikalauskas, A. 1996. 'Income poverty among Indigenous families with children: Estimates from the 1991 Census', *CAEPR Discussion Paper No. 110*, CAEPR, ANU, Canberra.

Rowley, C. D. 1970. *The Remote Aborigines*, ANU Press, Canberra.

—— 1972. *Outcasts in White Australia*, Penguin, Melbourne.

Saunders, P. 2005. *The Poverty Wars: Reconnecting Research with Reality*, UNSW Press, Sydney.

——, Naidoo, Y. and Griffiths, G. 2007. 'Towards new indicators of disadvantage: Deprivation and social exclusion in Australia', SPRC Report 12/07, University of New South Wales, Sydney.

Sen, A. 1982. *Poverty and Famines: An Essay on Entitlements and Deprivation*, Clarendon Press, Oxford.

——1993. 'Capability and well-being', in M. Nussbaum and A. Sen (eds), *The Quality of Life*, Clarendon Press, Oxford.

—— 2000. *Development As Freedom*, Alfred A Knopf, New York.

—— 1992. *Inequality Re-examined*, Oxford University Press, Oxford.

Smith, D. E. 1991. 'Towards an Aboriginal household expenditure survey: Conceptual, methodological and cultural considerations', CAEPR *Discussion Paper No. 10*, CAEPR, ANU, Canberra.

Spicker, P. 2007. *The Idea of Poverty*, The Policy Press, Bristol.

Steering Committee for the Review of Government Service Provision 2009. *Overcoming Indigenous Disadvantage: Key Indicators 2009*, Productivity Commission, Melbourne.

Walker, I. 2001. 'The changing nature of racism: From old to new?', in M. Augoustinos and K.J. Reynolds (eds), *Understanding Prejudice, Racism, and Social Conflict*, Sage, London.

Whiteford, P. 1985. 'A family's needs: Equivalence scales, poverty and social security', Research Paper No. 27, Department of Social Security, Development Division, Canberra.

Woolcock, M. and Narayan, D. 2000. 'Social capital: Implications for development theory, research, and policy', *The World Bank Research Observer*, 15 (2): 225–49.

11. Is there a cultural explanation for Indigenous violence? A second look at the NATSISS

Don Weatherburn and Lucy Snowball

Violence is a chronic problem among Indigenous Australians. The 2002 Australian Bureau of Statistics (ABS) National Aboriginal and Torres Strait Islander Social Survey (NATSISS) found that 22 per cent of Australia's Indigenous population (aged 15 years and over) had been victims of physical or threatened violence in the 12months preceding the survey (ABS 2004). The 2008 NATSISS survey (ABS 2010) showed a very similar result (23%). It is impossible to obtain comparable figures on the prevalence of physical or threatened assault among non-Indigenous people. There is little doubt, however, that serious violence is far more prevalent among Indigenous Australians. In their study of New South Wales hospitalisation data, Clapham, Stevenson and Lo (2006) found that Aboriginal people are five times more likely to be hospitalised for interpersonal violence than non-Aboriginal people. The majority of this violence, of course, is intra- rather than inter-communal (Fitzgerald and Weatherburn 2001; Harding et al. 1995: 29).

At least four different theories have been put forward to explain the high level of violence amongst Australia's Indigenous population. The first, exemplified in the work of Sutton (2001, 2009), Langton (1988) and Martin (1992) asserts that the high level of violence found in Indigenous communities is (at least partly) a vestige of traditional Aboriginal culture. Sutton (2001: 152), for example, points out that archaeological records of pre-historic (Aboriginal) remains reveal a much higher incidence of 'defensive' injuries to the bones of Aboriginal women than to the bones of Aboriginal men, and argues that early versions of what is now called family violence or community violence were widespread under 'traditional' conditions. He contends that recent ethnographies by trained anthropologists leave little doubt that family and community violence were widespread and frequent in Australia prior to white settlement, arguing that '...those with the most recent experience of being drawn into contact with the wider world and with alcohol seem to be facing the greatest problems of interpersonal violence' (Sutton 2009: 101). Langton (1988) and Martin (1992) have also commented on the ritualistic and socially accepted nature of much of the violence in Aboriginal communities. According to Martin (1992), for example, while some contemporary fighting and violence can be attributed to 'intervention by the wider society', violence and fighting are 'also deeply rooted in cultural values' (Martin 1998: 16). Reser (1990: 30) has made a similar point, arguing that Aboriginal people differ markedly from non-Aboriginal people in their willingness to give expression to anger.

The second theory, patterned after social disorganisation theory (Sampson, Raudenbush and Earls 1997) attributes Indigenous violence to breakdown of Indigenous informal social controls following colonisation and dispossession. The Royal Commission into Aboriginal Deaths in Custody took this view, arguing that 'disruption, intervention and institutionalisation' had undermined Aboriginal family and kinship structures, thereby making it difficult for parents and elders to inculcate traditional social norms (Commonwealth of Australia 1991: paras 14.4.39–14.4.43). The third theory, implicit in the work of Devery (1991) and Gale, Bailey-Harris and Wundersitz (1990), sees Indigenous violence as a response to social and economic deprivation. The fourth, patterned after lifestyle/routine activity theory (Cohen and Felson 1979), asserts that the high levels of Indigenous violence are a comparatively recent phenomenon, generated by passive welfare dependence and/or alcohol abuse (Hughes and Warin 2005; Pearson 2001).

Snowball and Weatherburn used data from the 2002 NATSISS (ABS 2004) to conduct a preliminary assessment of these theories (Snowball and Weatherburn 2008). They argued that if the high level of Indigenous violence is a vestige of traditional Aboriginal culture, one might expect to find higher levels of violence among those who:

• lived on traditional homelands

• identified with a clan or spoke an Indigenous language, and

• had difficulties speaking English.

If the social disorganisation theory perspective on Indigenous violence were correct, one would expect higher rates of violent victimisation amongst Indigenous Australians who:

• are not socially involved in their communities[1]

• are sole parents

• have high rates of geographic mobility (as measured by the number of times they moved house)

• are members or have relatives who are members of the stolen generation.

---

1   Social involvement includes: recreational or cultural group activities; community or special interest group activities; church or religious activities; going out to a cafe, restaurant or bar; involvement in sport or physical activities; attendance at sporting event as a spectator; visiting a library, museum or art gallery; attending movies, theatre or concert; visiting a park, botanic gardens, zoo or theme park; attendance at Aboriginal and Torres Strait Islander Commission (ATSIC) or native title meetings; attending a funeral, ceremony or festival; and fishing or hunting in a group.

If Indigenous economic and social deprivation is the key driver of Indigenous violence, one would expect to see higher rates of Indigenous victimisation amongst those who:

- are socially stressed[2]
- are unemployed, or if employed work within a Community Development Employment Projects (CDEP) scheme[3]
- have experienced financial stress[4]
- left school early
- live in a crowded household[5]
- live in a household with more than two dependent children
- have been charged with a criminal offence as a child.

Finally, if lifestyle/routine activity theory is correct then one would expect higher rates of violent victimisation among those who live with or near potential offenders; who cannot readily escape from potential offenders; or who have a lifestyle (e.g. heavy drinking) that exposes them to violence. In terms of NATSISS variables, this would lead one to expect higher rates of violent victimisation amongst those who:

- have a severe or moderate disability and are therefore more vulnerable to attack (Wilson et al. 1996)
- live in an area with neighbourhood problems
- consume alcohol in a high risk manner[6]
- use illicit substances or misuse licit substances[7]
- reside with a person who has been charged with an offence
- do not have access to a motor vehicle (and therefore find it more difficult to escape from or avoid violent situations).

Snowball and Weatherburn (2008) found strong support for lifestyle/routine activity theories, moderate support for social disorganisation and social deprivation theories but little support for cultural theories of Indigenous violence. High-risk alcohol consumption has the highest odds ratio (2.23). Significant effects were also found for most other lifestyle/routine activity

---

2   The stressors included in this variable were: divorce or separation; death of a family member or close friend; serious accident; mental illness; witness to violence; gambling problem; pressure to fulfil cultural responsibilities; and discrimination or racism.

3   This is labour market program in which Indigenous Australians performed work intended to benefit (develop) their community in return for welfare payments.

4   This was measured by whether the household had days without money for basic living expenses in the preceding 12 months.

5   We defined crowded as households where the number of people exceeded twice the number of bedrooms.

6   The ABS classify this using the Australian Alcohol Guidelines.

7   Note that due to data quality concerns in the 2002 NATSISS the ABS only released information on this variable for respondents living in non-remote areas.

variables, including: residing in an area with neighbourhood problems (odds ratio: 1.61), substance abuse (odds ratio: 1.49), having a severe or profound disability (odds ratio: 1.31) and living in a household with someone who has been charged with an offence (odds ratio: 1.15). Other variables with high odds ratios were social stress (odds ratio: 1.94), financial stress (odds ratio: 1.69) and unemployment (odds ratio: 1.21), being a member of the stolen generation (odds ratio: 1.71), being a lone parent (odds ratio: 1.39) and number of dwellings in the previous 12 months (odds ratio: 1.33). In the bi-variate analyses, having difficulties with English, living in traditional homelands, living in a remote rural area and identifying with a clan group or speaking an Indigenous language all showed a higher prevalence of victimisation. None of these variables remained significant in the presence of controls for lifestyle, social deprivation and social disorganisation factors.

The lack of support for cultural theories of violence is surprising given the anthropological evidence on Indigenous violence. However there were three features in the Snowball and Weatherburn (2008) study that might have obscured the effect of Indigenous cultural attachment on risk of violent victimisation. The first is that our measure of cultural attachment relied on simple 'yes' or 'no' answers to questions dealing with whether or not the respondent had difficulties with English, lived in traditional homelands, identified with a clan group or spoke an Indigenous language. We assumed that respondents who answered 'yes' to these questions are more 'attached' to traditional culture than respondents who answered 'no'. While this is not an unreasonable assumption, it could be argued that attachment to traditional Indigenous culture is signalled as much by participation in cultural activities, events, ceremonies and organisations as it is by language, clan membership and residence. Our measure of cultural attachment was insensitive to this participation. The second problem is that the NATSISS data in our 2008 study were analysed without regard to residential location. This is an important limitation because the effects of cultural attachment may be limited to Indigenous Australians living in remote Australia, where most of the anthropological research on Indigenous violence has been conducted. Lumping remote and non-remote respondents together in the one analysis when most (65.2%) NATSISS respondents live in non-remote areas may have obscured the effects of cultural attachment. The final limitation in our study was that the question on violent victimisation in the 2002 NATSISS captured both threats of violence and actual violence. Cultural attachment may have stronger effects on the actual incidence of violence than on threats of violence, which may not have any ritualistic dimension (although see Sutton 2009: 92).

Given the limitations just mentioned and the apparent conflict between our earlier findings and those of anthropologists, it seems appropriate to conduct a further assessment of the relevance of cultural theories of violence. In the present study we attempt to improve on Snowball and Weatherburn (2008) in three ways. First we construct a more sensitive measure of cultural attachment. This measure combines information from questions in the 2008 NATSISS dealing with whether the respondent spoke an Indigenous language; whether the respondent identified with a clan, cultural or language group; whether the respondent identified an area as their homeland or traditional country; whether the respondent presently lives in their homelands or traditional country; whether the respondent participated in selected cultural activities in the preceding 12 months and whether the respondent was involved in cultural events, ceremonies or organisations in the preceding 12 months. Second, rather than define a victim of violence as someone who has experienced either a threat of violence or actual violence, we restrict our definition of a victim of violence to someone has been physically assaulted (not merely threatened) in the preceding 12 months. Thirdly and most importantly, we construct separate models for remote and non-remote respondents. This should give us a better chance of picking up the effects of Indigenous culture if they are confined to remote areas. In the next section we describe the methods used in greater detail.

Methodology

The data from the 2008 NATSISS were collected by the ABS between August 2008 and April 2009 and involved interviews with Indigenous people of all ages. The survey was administered in both community and non-community areas. In non-community areas 89 per cent of households responded to the screening question. The survey response rate in identified households was 83 per cent. In Indigenous communities (where no screening question was required) the survey response rate was 78 per cent. The coverage was 52.6 per cent which is relatively large when comparing with other ABS surveys. In total, 13 307 Indigenous people in 6858 households were surveyed. This study was limited to those aged over 18 at the time of the survey, which constituted 53.8 per cent of the sample (7163 respondents). Five respondents refused to answer the question on victimisation and therefore were removed from the sample, leaving 7158 respondents in the final sample. The victimisation rate in this sample was 14.7 per cent (1,054 respondents) *unweighted*. The weighted rate was 19.8 per cent.

Variable selection

The dependent variable was whether the respondent was a victim of physical violence in the preceding 12 months. As noted earlier, *cultural attachment* was measured using responses to the following questions:

- whether the respondent spoke an Indigenous language

- whether the respondent identified with a clan, cultural or language group
- whether the respondent identified an area as homelands/traditional country
- whether the respondent presently lives in homelands/traditional country
- whether the respondent participated in selected cultural activities in the preceding 12 months
- whether the respondent was involved in cultural events, ceremonies or organisations in the preceding 12 months.

The total number of positive responses to the above questions was determined for each person (with 0 being the minimum possible score and 6 being the maximum). Then each person was classified as low (score of 0, 1 or 2) or high (score of 3+).

Because of the relatively small sample size in the remote grouping we were unable to include a large number of variables in the final model. The variables included as controls in the present analysis were all significant in our previous analysis (Snowball and Weatherburn 2008) and had high parameter values, suggesting they were important factors in victimisation. Three variables that had a high parameter value and were significant in the previous modelling however, were not included. These were 'first charged as a child', 'neighbourhood problems' and 'social involvement'. The variable 'first charged as a child' was excluded because its theoretical significance is uncertain and its inclusion in the present analysis made little difference to the results. The 'neighbourhood problem' variable was not included because of a concern that the response to this question could be influenced by the response to the question of victimisation. That is, if you had been the victim of violence you could be more likely to report that you lived in an unsafe area. The social involvement variable was not included because involvement in activities forms part of the culture variable. The other variables included in the study, therefore, were:

- *Stressors*: Whether or not the respondent personally experienced one or more of a list of stressors in the preceding 12 months. The stressors used in measuring this variable were limited to death of a family member or close friend; not able to get a job; lost a job/sacked/made redundant/retired; treated badly/discrimination. The variable was coded '1' if experienced one or more stressors and '0' otherwise.
- *Financial stress*: Whether or not the respondent experienced financial stress in the previous 12 months (as indexed by responses to the question 'Whether the household members ran out of money for basic living expenses in the preceding 12 months'. The variable was coded '1' if experienced one or more stressors and '0' otherwise.
- *Age*: The age of the respondent, coded '1' if aged under 25, '0' if 25 or over.

- *Gender*: The gender of the respondent, coded '1' if the victim was male; '0' if female.
- *Alcohol use*: Whether the respondent was identified as a *high risk* alcohol consumer in the preceding 12 months, coded '1' if a high risk alcohol consumer and '0' otherwise;
- *Substance use*: Whether the respondent used substances which were non-medically prescribed in the preceding 12 months, coded '1' if the respondent had used substances, '0' otherwise.
- *Lone parent*: Whether the respondent lived in a lone parent household, coded '1' if the respondent lived in a lone parent household, '0' otherwise.
- *Moved*: Whether the respondent had moved in the preceding 12 months, coded '1 if the respondent had moved and '0' otherwise.
- *Stolen Generation*: Whether the respondent or a member of their family were part of the stolen generation, coded '1' if the respondent was a member of the stolen generation and '0' otherwise.
- *Family type*: Whether the household was a lone parent household, coded '1' if a lone parent household and '0' otherwise.

Again as noted earlier, the analysis was carried out separately for remote and non-remote respondents – where remoteness was defined using the Australian Standard Geographical Classification (ASGC). Firstly the bivariate relationship between violent victimisation and the independent variables was the examined. Then the dependent variable was regressed against the independent variables in a logistic model. Where there were missing values for the independent variables a separate and additional variable was created comparing the reference category to 'not stated' (e.g. substance abuse vs no substance abuse and substance abuse vs substance abuse not stated). This variable was then included in the model to avoid losing substantial information. Variables (including the 'not stated' variables) were only retained in the final model if they were significant.

Results

The number of respondents with characteristics used in the model as well as the corresponding weighted percentage are given in Tables 11.1a and 11.1b. The third column gives the number of non stated responses for that variable.

Table 11.1a Frequencies for the non-remote sample, Indigenous Australia, 2008

Variable		Number of respondents	Weighted percentage	Number of missing or not stated
Age	18–24	863	23.61	–
	25 and over	3 829	76.39	–
Gender	Female	2 702	52.95	–
	Male	1 990	47.05	–
Cultural attachment	Low	2 660	56.25	–
	High	2 032	43.75	–
Stressors	Yes	1 759	38.54	–
	No	2 933	61.46	–
Financial stress	Yes	1 315	28.14	25
	No	3 352	71.13	25
Moved location	Moved in preceding 12 months	979	22.42	–
	Has not moved in preceding 12 months	3 713	77.58	–
Stolen generation	Person or family member of stolen generation	2 234	45.09	643
	Not member of stolen generation	1 815	41.76	643
Family type	Lone parent family	1 229	26.98	–
	Other	3 463	73.02	–
Substance abuse	Yes	2 257	45.92	363
	No	2 072	44.91	363
Alcohol use	High risk alcohol use	312	7.29	55
	No high risk alcohol use	4 380	92.47	55

Source: Authors' calculations using the 2008 NATSISS (accessed using the RADL)

Table 11.1b Frequencies for the remote sample, Indigenous Australia, 2008

Variable		Number of respondents	Weighted percentage	Number of missing or not stated
Age	18–24	2 040	21.18	–
	25 and over	431	78.82	–
Gender	Female	1 384	51.93	–
	Male	1 087	48.07	–
Cultural attachment	Low	579	22..17	–
	High	1 892	77.83	–
Stressors	Yes	956	38.76	–
	No	1 515	61.24	–
Financial stress	Yes	682	27.64	21
	No	1 768	71.86	21
Moved location	Moved in preceding 12 months	544	20.87	–
	Has not moved in preceding 12 months	1 927	79.13	–
Stolen generation	Person or family member of stolen generation	885	33.33	235
	Not member of stolen generation	1 351	57.12	235
Family type	Lone parent family	636	74.31	–
	Other	1 835	25.69	–
Substance abuse	Yes	719	28.48	212
	No	1 540	62.31	212
Alcohol use	High risk alcohol use	168	6.00	18
	No high risk alcohol use	2 303	93.33	18

Source: Authors' calculations using the 2008 NATSISS (accessed using the RADL)

Table 11.2 gives the victimisation rates for the variables of interest for non-remote and remote Indigenous Australians. Note that the rates are weighted.

Table 11.2 Victimisation rates by area, Indigenous Australia, 2008

Variable		Non-remote (%)	Remote (%)
Age	18–24	21.1	23.5
	25 or over	12.6	10.7
Gender	Female	14.6	13.0
	Male	14.6	14.2
Cultural attachment	Low	12.5	13.5
	High	17.3	13.8
Stressors	Yes	22.3	18.3
	No	9.7	10.6
Financial stress	Yes	20.7	19.1
	No	12.1	11.3
Moved location	Moved in preceding 12 months	23.9	17.7
	Has not moved in preceding 12 months	11.9	12.5
Stolen generation	Person or family member of stolen generation	19.0	18.9
	Not member of stolen generation	11.1	9.9
Sole parent	Yes	20.4	15.5
	Other	12.4	12.9
Substance abuse	Yes	21.2	23.3
	No	8.4	8.2
Alcohol use	High risk alcohol use	27.4	29.4
	No high risk alcohol use	13.6	12.6
Total		14.6	13.6

Source: Authors' calculations using the 2008 NATSISS (accessed using the RADL)

Table 11.2 suggests the following are related to higher levels of victimisation in both non-remote and remote areas:

- younger ages
- high risk alcohol use
- substance abuse
- family removal
- living in a lone parent household
- stressors

- financial stress
- moved in the previous year
- high cultural attachment (only in non-remote areas).

Males and females have similar levels of victimisation in both areas. Tables 11.3a and 11.3b give the results of the logistic regression modelling for the non-remote and remote sample. Gender was not included in any of the models because of the results of the bivariate analysis. Positive coefficients suggest that the variable is related to higher levels of victimisation. An asterisk denotes a significant variable. Three models were developed for each area. The first contained the age variable and the cultural attachment variables. The second model contained the variables of Model 1 with the addition of the stressors and financial stress variables. The final model contained all the variables that were significant.

Table 11.3a Logistic models for the non-remote sample

	Parameter value (and standard error)	Parameter value (and standard error)	Parameter value (and standard error)
Intercept	−2.0 (0.06)*	−2.5 (0.08)*	−3.23 (0.11)*
Under 25 vs 25 or over	0.60 (0.10)*	0.57 (0.10)*	0.40 (0.10)*
Low cultural attachment vs High cultural attachment	0.33 (0.08)*	0.21 (0.01)*	0.13 (0.15)
Stressors vs No stressors		0.59 (0.08)*	0.48 (0.09)*
Financial stress vs No financial stress		0.87 (0.09)*	0.62 (0.09)*
Family removal vs No family removal			0.36 (0.09)*
High risk alcohol vs No high risk alcohol			0.76 (0.14)*
Substance abuse vs No substance abuse			0.63 (0.09)*
Moved in last 12 months vs Has not moved			0.52 (0.10)*
Lone parent vs Other family type			0.65 (0.09)*

Source: Authors' calculations using the 2008 NATSISS (accessed using the RADL)

Table 11.3b Logistic models for the remote sample

	Parameter value (and standard error)	Parameter value (and standard error)	Parameter value (and standard error)
Intercept	−2.03 (0.13)*	−2.53 (0.10)*	−3.10 (0.13)*
Under 25 vs 25 or over	0.82 (0.13)*	0.84 (0.14)*	0.84 (0.14)*
Low cultural attachment vs High cultural attachment	0.02 (0.14)		
Stressors vs No stressors		0.67 (0.12)*	0.53 (0.12)*
Financial stress vs No financial stress		0.63 (0.12)*	0.54 (0.13)*
Family removal vs No family removal			0.40 (0.13)*
High risk alcohol vs No high risk alcohol			0.91 (0.19)*
Substance abuse vs No substance abuse			0.95 (0.13)*
Substance abuse not stated vs No substance abuse			0.66 (0.21)*

Source: Authors' calculations using the 2008 NATSISS (accessed using the RADL)

In the non-remote models the cultural variable is significant after adjusting for *age, stressors* and *financial stress*. It is no longer significant at a 5% level (p-value = 0.147), however, when the remaining variables are included in the model. Note also that in the first two models low *cultural attachment* is associated with higher levels of victimisation, which is a reverse of the bi-variate results. All other variables that were significant in the bivariate results are significant in the model and in the same direction. In the final model *alcohol use* is the strongest risk factor. Substance use, *family type* and *financial stress*, however, were all significant predictors of victimisation.

Cultural attachment is not significant in any of the remote area models, which confirms the bivariate results. The *sole parent* and *moved* variables are not significant in the final model – even though they were significant in the bivariate analysis. This could be due to the smaller sample size (and associated lower power).

To examine whether the variables behaved differently in each area we built a model with interactions based on the entire sample (so including both remote and non-remote respondents). The interaction between lone parent family and area was significant (p-value = 0.0037). The interaction between moved in previous 12 months and area was not significant although it had a relatively low p-value (0.0682). None of the other interactions were significant.

The marginal effects for selected variables for the two areas are given in Table 11.4. The marginal effects are calculated for a person over the age of 25 with a zero value for all other characteristics. The base value is the probability of victimisation for a person with the base characteristics (over 25 with). The marginal effects are higher in the remote area model however this would be primarily due to the different variables in each model.

Table 11.4 Marginal effects for selected variables for non-remote and remote area models

	Non-remote areas (%)	Remote areas (%)
Base	3.81	4.31
+ Financial stress	6.85	7.73
+ Stressors	6.01	6.79
+ High risk alcohol	7.80	8.79
+ Substance abuse	6.91	7.80

Source: Authors' calculations using the 2008 NATSISS (accessed using the RADL)

In both models high risk alcohol significantly increases the probability of victimisation – by 3.99 per cent in non-remote areas and by 4.48 per cent in remote areas.

Discussion

The present results, like those in Snowball and Weatherburn (2008) provide little support for the hypothesis that Indigenous violence is a vestige of attachment to or involvement in traditional Indigenous cultural life. In fact the findings concerning *cultural attachment* are quite the opposite of what one would expect. Levels of *cultural attachment* and violence were related prior to controlling for other factors but only in non-remote areas. The association remained significant after adjusting significant after adjusting for *age*, *stressors* and *financial stress* but the sign on the coefficient reversed, suggesting that those with low *cultural attachment* actually had a higher risk of experiencing violence. One the full set of controls was introduced, *cultural attachment* ceased to be significant.

Although these findings appear to conflict with cultural explanations for Indigenous violence, the conflict may only be superficial. It is possible that culture played an important role in shaping the frequency, circumstances giving rise to and seriousness of Indigenous violence prior to colonisation but that other factors, such as alcohol abuse, have since come to the fore. In this vein it might also be argued that *cultural attachment* is more likely to affect the severity of Indigenous violence than it is to affect the probability of Indigenous violence. The possibility that there are cultural differences in the severity of Indigenous violence deserves serious consideration, given evidence that the injuries inflicted by Indigenous Australians on each other in central Australia have a ritualistic dimension (Jacob, Boseto and Ollapillil 2007). On the other hand, the 2008 NATISS data show no significant difference in the proportion of victims who were injured among those in the present study who scored high on level of attachment in traditional culture (55.7% injured) compared with those who scored low in terms of attachment in traditional culture (58.7% injured).

A second possibility is that *cultural attachment* affects the incidence of Indigenous violence rather than its prevalence. That is to say, Indigenous Australians who are culturally involved may be just as likely in the course of a year to experience a physical assault but much more likely to experience multiple assaults. This is also possible but it would be surprising to find marked differences in incidence of violence among groups differing in terms of their cultural attachment but and no difference at all in the prevalence of violence. A third possibility is that the effect of cultural attachment on Indigenous violence is hidden by cultural differences in the willingness to disclose an act of physical violence. Those who are more deeply involved in traditional Indigenous culture, in other words, may be more reluctant to disclose an act of violence or less inclined to view an act as violent as such, compared with those who are less deeply involved in traditional Indigenous culture. This is also possible but the ABS went to considerable trouble to ensure that the questions in the NATSISS survey were fully understood by respondents. The measures taken include extensive pre-testing of survey questions in focus groups and, where necessary, the use of Indigenous interpreters. There was a slight difference in willingness to report assaults to police, with 50.5 per cent of respondents in the low *cultural attachment* category having reported the last assault to police, compared with 45.2 per cent of respondents who scored high in terms of attachment in traditional culture. Even if a similar difference existed in willingness to report violence to ABS interviewers, however, the difference the prevalence of violence between those who are strongly attached to traditional culture and those would not be very large. Taken as a whole, the evidence presented here provides little support for cultural theories of violence. As in our earlier study, high risk alcohol consumption, drug use, financial stress and social stress, are the strongest predictors of physical assault.

Some might be tempted to reject the evidence presented here on the grounds that our approach to measuring 'cultural attachment' is misleading and/or simplistic. We recognise that there are other ways of measuring 'cultural attachment' than the one we have chosen here. One might, for example, give more weight to some questions in the NATSISS than others or argue that cultural attachment is a complex construct, some features of which are conducive to violence in some situations and other features of which are conductive to restraint in other situations. We recognise the difficulty in turning an abstract concept like 'cultural attachment' into something that can quantified. It is impossible to test the 'cultural attachment' explanation for Indigenous violence, however, without making some assumptions about how to measure it. Indeed, if the construct 'cultural attachment' cannot be measured in any way, it is hard to make any sense of the claim that Indigenous violence is a vestige of traditional Indigenous culture. It is, of course, entirely open to those who feel our measure of cultural attachment is misleading and/or simplistic to put forward an alternative measure. If the alternative measure of cultural attachment is plausible and yields very different results to those reported here, we shall be among the first to qualify our findings.

Like all observational studies of causal effects, the current study has a number of inherent limitations. The theories we have been testing are theories about violent offending, not violent victimisation. We have measured victim characteristics (e.g. cultural attachment, alcohol consumption, financial stress) on the assumption that they are shared by offenders. This assumption is open to question. Our conclusions would have been stronger and more compelling if we had been able to analyse the correlates of self-reported violent offending rather than the correlates of self-reported violent victimisation. It is to be hoped, for this reason, that the next iteration of the NATSISS includes questions on self-reported involvement in violence (and other offending). A second and related limitation is that it is impossible to be sure in a cross-sectional study such as the NATSISS that the putative causes (e.g. alcohol consumption, financial stress) actually pre-date the effects (violence). While there is little doubt that alcohol use increases the risk of violence, some of what we see as the effect of alcohol use on violence may actually be a reflection of the effect of violence on alcohol use. The only way to properly test claims about causation is through longitudinal research. At present, unfortunately, cross-sectional data is all we have to go on. A third limitation is that the 2008 NATSISS has been heavily criticised for underestimating the prevalence of high risk Indigenous alcohol consumption (Chikritzhs and Brady 2006). The misclassification of high-risk Indigenous drinkers as non-high risk drinkers may have caused us to underestimate the strength of the association between Indigenous high-risk drinking and Indigenous violence.

Acknowledgements

We would like to thank our anonymous reviewers for the careful and constructive feedback they provided on an earlier draft of this chapter.

References

Australian Bureau of Statistics (ABS) 2004. *National Aboriginal and Torres Strait Islander Social Survey, 2002*, cat. no. 4714.0, ABS, Canberra.

—— 2010. *National Aboriginal and Torres Strait Islander Social Survey, 2008*, cat no. 4714.0, ABS, Canberra.

Chikritzhs, T. and Brady, B. 2006. 'Fact or fiction? A critique of the National Aboriginal and Torres Strait Islander Social Survey 2002', *Drug and Alcohol Review*, 25 (3): 277–87.

Clapham, K. F., Stevenson, M. R. and Lo, S. K. 2006. 'Injury profiles of Indigenous and non-Indigenous people in New South Wales', *Medical Journal of Australia*, 184 (5): 217–20.

Cohen, L. E. and Felson, M. 1979. 'Social change and crime rate trends: A routine activity approach', *American Sociological Review*, 44: 588–608.

Commonwealth of Australia 1991. *Royal Commission into Aboriginal Deaths in Custody*, Commonwealth of Australia, Canberra.

Devery, C. 1991. *Disadvantage and Crime in New South Wales*, NSW Bureau of Crime Statistics and Research, Sydney.

Fitzgerald, J. and Weatherburn, D. 2001. 'Aboriginal victimisation and offending: The picture from police records', Bureau Brief December 2001, NSW Bureau of Crime Statistics and Research, Sydney.

Gale, F., Bailey-Harris, R. and Wunderitz, J. 1990. *Aboriginal Youth and the Criminal Justice System*, Cambridge University Press, Cambridge.

Harding, R., Broadhurst, R., Ferrante, A. and Loh, N. 1995. *Aboriginal Contact with the Criminal Justice System and the Impact of the Royal Commission into Aboriginal Deaths in Custody*, The Hawkins Press, Sydney.

Hughes, H. and Warin, J. 2005. 'A new deal for Aborigines and Torres Strait Islanders in remote communities', Issue Analysis No. 54, Centre for Independent Studies, Sydney.

Hunter, E. 1993. *Aboriginal Health and History*, Cambridge University Press, Cambridge.

Jacob, A. O., Boseto, F. and Ollapallil, J. 2007. 'Epidemic of stab injuries: An Alice Springs dilemma', *Australian and New Zealand Journal of Surgery*, 77: 621–25.

Langton, M. 1988. 'Medicine square', in I. Keen (ed.), *Being Black*, Aboriginal Studies Press, Canberra.

Martin, D. F. 1992. 'Aboriginal and non-Aboriginal homicide: Same but different', in H. Strang and S. Gerull (eds), *Homicide: Patterns, Prevention and Control,* Australian Institute of Criminology, Canberra.

Pearson, N. 2001. 'On the human right to misery, mass incarceration and early death', The Charles Perkins Memorial Oration, University of Sydney, 25 October, viewed 5 October 2011, available at <http://sydney.edu.au/koori/news/pearson.pdf>

Reser, J. 1990. 'A perspective on the causes and cultural context of violence in Aboriginal communities in north Queensland', Report to the Royal Commission into Aboriginal Deaths in Custody, James Cook University of North Queensland, Townsville.

Sampson, R. J., Raudenbush, S. W. and Earls, F. 1997. 'Neighbourhoods and violent crime: A multi-level study of collective efficacy', *Science*, 277 (5328): 918–24.

Snowball, L. and Weatherburn, D. 2008. 'Theories of Indigenous violence: A preliminary empirical assessment', *Australian and New Zealand Journal of Criminology*, 41 (2): 216–35.

Sutton, P. 2001. 'The politics of suffering: Indigenous policy in Australia since the 1970s', *Anthropological Forum*, 11 (2): 125–69.

—— 2009. *The Politics of Suffering: Indigenous Australia and the End of the Liberal Consensus*, Melbourne University Press, Melbourne.

Wilson, C., Nettelbeck, T., Potter, R. and Perry, C. 1996. *Intellectual Disability and Criminal Victimisation*, Trends and Issues in Crime and Criminal Justice No. 60, Australian Institute of Criminology, Canberra.

12. NATSISS crowding data: What does it assume and how can we challenge the orthodoxy?

Paul Memmott, Kelly Greenop, Andrew Clarke, Carroll Go-Sam,
Christina Birdsall-Jones, William Harvey-Jones,
Vanessa Corunna and Mark Western

In this paper we consider the sociospatial problem of crowding in Indigenous Australia. Quantitative data are regularly collected in Census and other social surveys by the Australian Bureau of Statistics (ABS) to create quantitative indices of the extent of household utilisation and then 'overcrowding' in Australian society in general, and amongst the Australian Indigenous population in particular. However, in our view, the identification of states of Indigenous crowding requires an understanding of distinct cultural constructs to achieve greater validity of measurement. Our analysis also refers to the interconnected nature of Indigenous crowding and homelessness, a relatedness that has been seldom addressed in the literature,[1] despite its importance to policy development in the Indigenous sector including effects on housing, family violence, education and health.

We draw our central quantitative analysis from statistics derived from the 2002 and 2008 National Aboriginal and Torres Strait Islander Social Surveys (NATSISS), and the 1996, 2001 and 2006 Australian Census of Population and Housing. NATSISS and the census both examine Indigenous housing utilisation and crowding based on calculated occupancy of houses and bedrooms.[2] In the case of NATSISS the percentage of people experiencing 'overcrowding' as a potential 'stressor' in the past twelve months by participants is identified. We use the term crowding in preference to the frequently used 'overcrowding' which is inherently tautological.

There are a number of methodological assumptions in NATSISS and the census examined in detail here. The first is the assumed cultural norms in the way houses are occupied. These norms are embedded in calculable measures of crowding, which are then applied to define what is, or is not, a crowded housing situation. The second assumption is the method of counting the levels of occupancy in houses that does not fully account for the dynamic nature of many Indigenous

---

1   An exception is Birdsall-Jones (2007, 2008, 2010).
2   See Appendix 12A for detail on the methodology used in NATSISS.

households whose central values involve sharing and mobility. This results in what we argue is an undercount of Indigenous people occupying a house at any one time, but also an undercount of who is homeless. A third assumption is that crowding should be defined by number of bedrooms alone, rather than the spatial adequacy of a house and its yard. We argue that crowding is a complex construct whose definition may be affected by a number of other, sometimes culturally specific, factors such as the number of families within one home, climatic and geographic factors such as remoteness, seasonable habitability of outside areas, access to kin, neighbours and other alternative places for entertainment and socialisation.

Our analysis draws on research protocols that were derived in Canada and encompass practices in Australia and New Zealand. We frame these within the cultural, racial and social factors that affect the definitions and policy responses to crowding and homelessness in Australia to critique the applicability of this supposedly culturally 'neutral' model.

This paper is divided into five main parts:

- data from the 2008 NATSISS relating to Indigenous house utilisation and household crowding
- methodological issues in the NATSISS design and execution
- an international social science model on cross-cultural crowding as an alternative
- case studies from Aboriginal Australia illustrating how Aboriginal understandings of crowding are culturally distinct, and
- recommendations.

The NATSISS data

Our entry point to this analysis was originally via two published statistics from the 2002 NATSISS (ABS 2004: 12). In an analysis of 'selected reported stressors in the previous twelve months' which included 'overcrowding at home', the ABS (2004: 5) reported that 42 per cent of Indigenous people in remote areas had experienced 'overcrowding' and that this was the second most frequently cited stressful event, after death of a family member or friend. In contrast approximately 10 per cent of non-remote people experienced 'overcrowding at home' as a stressor in the past 12 months (ABS 2004: Fig. 1). The corresponding figures from the 2008 NATSISS have not been published, but the weighted percentage, Australia-wide, of those reporting 'overcrowding as a stressor' for themselves or their family in the past 12 months was 7.63 per cent (ABS 2008b).

This figure seems low to us, and we discuss possible causes for under-reporting of crowding and the use of 'crowding' as a socially and culturally specific term in our later analysis.

The second set of results that had a bearing on crowding pertained to the nature of dwelling problems and dwelling adequacy as indicated by the need for additional bedrooms. According to NATSISS 2002, 40 per cent of Indigenous people were living in dwellings with structural problems (32% in non-remote areas and 58% in remote areas) and over 60 per cent were living in dwellings which had been repaired or maintained in the last year. In remote areas, 52 per cent of people lived in dwellings that required at least one more bedroom while in non-remote areas 16 per cent of people were in 'crowded' dwellings using this definition (ABS 2004: 12).

We now update these published figures with our own analysis of the 2008 NATSISS data. The 2008 NATSISS uses definitions and follows an enumeration method that is relevant to our analysis in several ways. The term 'usual resident' denotes anyone who usually lives in a given dwelling and who regards that as their primary place of residence (ABS 2009b). This is also the census definition. NATSISS also differentiates between remote and urban or metropolitan Indigenous communities using the 'community sample' and 'non-community sample' terms, each also having a distinct enumeration and analysis method associated with it. We will analyse the impact of these terms and methods as we discuss the underlying assumptions of NATSISS.

Crowding in Indigenous households: The 2008 NATSISS data

To investigate crowding in Indigenous households using 2008 NATSISS we first examine the descriptive relationships between housing utilisation and other characteristics and then carry out a logistic regression analysis to model the likelihood of crowding.

The measure of crowding, used in this part of our analysis is derived from the 2008 NATSISS variable that reports 'household utilisation'. This variable indicates the number of bedrooms a given household requires or has spare, and is derived using the criteria of the Canadian National Occupancy Standard (CNOS); of course a household could also be classed as not requiring any additional bedrooms, nor having any spare. The utilisation variable was best re-coded into a simple dichotomous indicator of crowding, in which those households requiring additional bedrooms were coded as 'crowded' and both those with bedrooms spare and those with none required nor spare, being coded as 'not crowded'.

Significant correlates of crowding were identified by first carrying out statistical chi-squared tests of association between potential explanatory variables and the crowding measure. Of these explanatory variables, the following exhibited significant associations with the crowding variable:

- Household Composition: whether a given household is comprised wholly or partly of Indigenous residents.[3]

- Household Type: whether a household usually accommodated one family, more than one family (includes single family households that had non-family members living with them), a group of unrelated individuals (group household) or a lone resident.

- Remoteness of area: whether a household was located in a remote or non-remote area, as classified by the ABS Accessibility/Remoteness Index of Australia (ARIA).[4]

These variables were subsequently included in a logistic regression model for the dichotomous crowding variable. The analysis estimated the odds of crowding for different levels of the explanatory variables. Each explanatory variable was dichotomised with zero representing the baseline category. In the logistic regression, the coefficients for explanatory variables are reported as odds ratios, which are the relative odds of crowding for the second category of an explanatory variable compared to the baseline category.

Results of 2008 NATSISS analysis: Descriptive analysis

Table 12.1 shows the distribution of different categories of Indigenous housing utilisation by households across remote and non-remote areas. Indigenous households in remote areas are almost three times as likely as those in non-remote areas to require additional bedrooms (i.e. to be crowded), whereas households in non-remote areas are about 1.4 times as likely to have spare bedrooms. About 30 per cent of remote and non-remote households have an appropriate number of bedrooms. This association is highly statistically significant.

---

3 These variables are derived from standard definitions according to ABS, see Appendix 12B.

4 'ARIA measures the remoteness of a point based on the physical road distances to the nearest Urban Centre' (ABS 2009).

Table 12.1 Indigenous housing utilisation by ASGC Remoteness Area, Australia, 2008

Whether has bedrooms needed/ spare		ASCG remote area code		Total
		Non-remote	Remote	
Bedrooms needed	No.	594	325	919
	%	10.52	28.31	13.53
No bedrooms required/ spare	No.	1 664	334	1 998
	%	29.48	29.09	29.41
Bedrooms spare	No.	3 387	489	3 876
	%	60.00	42.60	57.06
Total	No.	5 645	1 148	6 793
	%	100.00	100.00	100.00

Source: Authors' analysis of CURFs from ABS 2008 dataset (via RADL); Pearson chi-squared (2) = 273.81 Pr < 0.001

Table 12.2 presents Indigenous housing utilisation by household composition by Indigenous residents. Similar to the breakdown by remoteness, Indigenous households are twice as likely to require additional bedrooms but less likely to have bedrooms spare than households where not all persons are Indigenous.

Table 12.2 Indigenous housing utilisation by household composition, Australia, 2008

Whether has bedrooms needed/ spare		Household composition		Total
		All Indigenous Persons	Not all Persons Indigenous	
Bedrooms needed	No.	602	316	918
	%	18.02	9.15	13.51
No bedrooms required	No.	1 042	957	1 999
	%	31.19	27.72	29.43
Has bedrooms spare	No.	1 697	2 179	3 876
	%	50.79	63.12	57.06
Total	No.	3 341	3 452	6 793
	%	100.00	100.00	100.00

Source: Authors' analysis of CURFs from ABS 2008 dataset (via RADL); Pearson chi-squared (2) = 150.88 Pr < 0.001

Table 12.3 displays Indigenous household utilisation by household type. Here 'greater than one family' represents both multiple family households as well as households that have at least one family plus non-family members. As can be seen from this analysis, these households exhibit much higher rates of requiring additional bedrooms – around 5.75 more likely than one family households, and

4.7 times more likely than group households. Naturally, lone person households exhibited required no additional bedrooms. Again the chi-squared test indicates that the association between the two variables is statistically significant.

Table 12.3 Indigenous household utilisation by household type, Australia, 2008

Whether has bedrooms needed		Household type				Total
		One family	Greater than one family	Lone person household	Group household	
Bedrooms needed	No.	521	374	0	23	918
	%	10.3	59.27	0	12.57	13.51
No bedrooms required/spare	No.	1 591	150	185	73	1 999
	%	31.45	23.77	20.09	39.89	29.42
Has bedrooms spare	No.	2 947	107	736	87	3 877
	%	58.25	16.96	79.91	47.54	57.06
Total	No.	5 059	631	921	183	6 793
	%	100.00	100.00	100.00	100.00	100.00

Source: Authors' analysis of CURFs from ABS, 2008 dataset (via RADL); Pearson chi-squared (6) = 1,500 Pr < 0.001

As we show later in the paper, although Tables 12.1, 12.2 and 12.3 suggest that 13.5 per cent of Indigenous households nationwide experience crowding, there are good reasons to think this underestimates the prevalence of crowding in both remote and urban or metropolitan settings.

2008 NATSISS analysis results: Logistic regression analysis of crowding

Table 12.4 presents results of a logistic regression model for the odds of crowding, based on whether a household is in a remote area or not, the composition of the household (all Indigenous vs. not all Indigenous) and the household type. The model indicates that, when holding all other factors constant, the odds of crowding in remote households are approximately 2.7 times the odds of crowding in non-remote households. Similarly, in households in which all persons are Indigenous, the odds of crowding are over three times those of household with some non-Indigenous residents. Finally a household with greater than one family has odds of being crowded approximately 11.8 times that of a single-family household (the reference category).[5]

---

5 For this analysis only, single person households were excluded from the model as they predict non-crowding perfectly (that is, by definition, single person households cannot be overcrowded) and group households do not have a statistically significant influence on the odds of crowding over and above the reference category of single family households.

Table 12.4 Logistic regression model of Indigenous crowding (with remoteness, household composition, single family and multiple families)

Variable	Odds ratio	Standard error	P-Value
ARIAC: ASGC Remoteness of Area Code *Reference category: non-remote*	2.69	0.22	<0.001
COMPHOLD_1: Household Composition—all persons Indigenous *Reference category: not all persons Indigenous*	3.04	0.28	<0.001
HHTYPE_1: Household type—greater than one family* *Reference category: one family household*	11.78	1.09	<0.001
HHTYPE_3: Household type—group household *Reference category: one family household*	1.05	0.36	0.895

* This includes both households with two or more families and those with one family plus non-family members.

Model fit: n = 5932 chi-squared (4) = 1760   p-value < 0.001 Pseudo R^2 = 0.27

Source: Authors' analysis of CURFs from ABS, 2008 dataset (via RADL)

Discussion and critique on the NATSISS analysis: Methodological issues

While the NATSISS data provide some useful information about the prevalence and correlates of crowding in Indigenous households, we argue next, that the failure to appropriately contextualise the data collection and survey instrument for aspects of Indigenous culture and circumstances, partially undermines the validity of the NATSISS data. As shown, the analysis of the 2002 NATSISS data, repeated here for the 2008 data, involves a house utilisation measure through the identification of the numbers of bedrooms that a sampled household requires or has spare, by applying the CNOS and then moving to a definition of 'overcrowding'.

The Canadian National Occupancy Standard model

In Australia, the density model of determining crowding using the CNOS, which employs bedroom density to determine the residential capacity of a house, has been used by the ABS for Census and NATSISS calculations and continues to be employed. The basis of the CNOS is that gender and age determine who can share a bedroom (see Table 12.5). Each person occupying a bedroom beyond these rules is deemed to require an extra bedroom, and the house is 'crowded' (or 'overcrowded') (Canadian Mortgage and Housing Corporation 1991). These rules certainly do not have a basis in Indigenous cultures, but appear to be derived from Anglo norms of privacy and individuality.

Table 12.5 Summary of bedroom sharing criteria from the CNOS, 1991

Canadian National Occupancy Standard criteria	Bedroom requirements
General	No more than two people per bedroom
Gender and age	Children aged under five, of the same or different genders can share a bedroom
	Children aged over five and under 18, of the same gender, can share a bedroom
	Children aged over five, of different genders should not share a bedroom
Relationship status and age	Couples and their children should not share a bedroom
	A household of one unattached individual may occupy a bed-sit
	Single household members, aged over 18, should have their own bedroom

Source: Canadian Mortgage and Housing Corporation 1991

The CNOS rules summarised in the above table dictate that children over the age of 5, of different genders, should not share a bedroom. Many authors cite the CNOS as widely used, but it is rarely questioned in terms of validity (although one exception is Jones 1991). However these presumed standards are not reflective of community norms in many cultures including that of the contemporary Anglo-Australia. (Memmott et al. 2011). Rather than the CNOS being an unusual use of density as a measure, crowding has been measured through repeated, blunt density calculations over many decades in Australia as Jones (1991: 7) has pointed out (see Table 12.6):

> The [Canadian National] occupancy standard is…defined by the functional capacity of a bedroom rather than any cultural standard, whether those of Aboriginal and Torres Strait Islander people or those suggested for the wider Australian society.

Yet the CNOS remains as a powerful orthodoxy in Indigenous crowding measurements today. The NATSISS also utilises the CNOS despite known Indigenous issues which compromise its validity: high residential mobility, cultural obligations to accommodate kin and other visitors, avoidance behaviours that determine suitability of particular sleeping and other living arrangements based on complex kin and shame relationships, and preference for outdoor living amongst some groups.

Table 12.6 Models of 'crowding' utilised by various governments

Country of use	Institution and source	Crowding definition
Australia	Australian Bureau of Statistics Family survey 1975 (ABS 1980) Family Survey (ABS 1980) Anderton and Lloyd (1991)	Density derived
Australia	Neutze (1977)	Density derived
Australia	Housing and Locational Choice Survey (National Housing Strategy 1992)	Density derived
Canadian origin; used in Australia by ABS for census and NATSISS	Canadian Mortgage and Housing Corporation (1991)	CNOS; density derived
USA; used as one of several indicators in New Zealand	United States Census Bureau (Statistics New Zealand 2011)	American Crowding Index; density derived
Australia	Australian Institute of Health and Welfare (AIHW 2005)	Proxy Occupancy Standard; density derived
One of several indicators in New Zealand	Statistics New Zealand (2003)	Equivalised Crowding Index; density derived

Source: Adapted from Jones 1991: 7

Policy significance

The effect of this household utilisation standard is to determine in government policy what is required for a house of a decent standard, in terms of bedrooms per person. For example the National Affordable Housing Agreement (NAHA) between the Commonwealth and the States (see Tables 12.7 and 12.8) uses measures of crowding defined by the ABS application of the CNOS to determine baseline levels of crowding against which future performance measures for the provision of housing will be evaluated for Indigenous and non-Indigenous households alike (Steering Committee for the Review of Government Service Provision (SCRGSP) 2009; Council of Australian Governments (COAG) 2009).

Additionally CNOS has been used to determine levels of crowding in Indigenous houses and whether children in particular are being adequately cared for, and whether additional bedrooms, or housing, are required. It appears that these rules on crowding are being used to determine standards of decency in terms of housing use with FaHCSIA staff arguing in the media as recently as March 2011 that crowding causes children to be at greater risk of abuse (ABC 2011).

Table 12.7 Proportion of Indigenous households living in 'overcrowded' conditions, by number of bedrooms, State and Territory, Australia, 2008[a]

	Unit	NSW	VIC	QLD	WA	SA	TAS	ACT	NT	AUST
Number of bedrooms		Numerator – number of overcrowded Indigenous households								
0–2 bedrooms	No.	1 759	244	1 570	593	88	165	34	960	5 412
3 bedrooms	No.	3 624	708	4 663	1 790	889	366	46	3 371	15 458
4 or more bedrooms	No.	1 167	213	1 653	942	235	47	13	799	5 070
Total	No.	6 550	1 166	7 886	3 324	1 212	577	93	5 131	25 940
Number of bedrooms		Denominator – total number of Indigenous households								
0–2 bedrooms	No.	14 348	3 383	12 184	3 513	2 148	2 178	328	3 509	41 590
3 bedrooms	No.	33 111	8 500	25 898	10 968	7 677	4 973	1 010	9 101	101 236
4 or more bedrooms	No.	16 515	3 702	14 676	7281	1 786	2 168	623	2 346	49 096
Total[b]	No.	64 341	15 819	53 179	21 956	11 710	9 323	1 985	15 108	193 421
Number of bedrooms		Proportion of Indigenous households living in overcrowded conditions								
0–2 bedrooms	%	12.3	7.8	12.9	16.9	4.1	7.6	10.4	27.4	13.0
3 bedrooms	%	10.9	8.3	18.0	16.3	11.6	7.4	4.6	37.0	15.3
4 or more bedrooms	%	7.1	5.8	11.3	12.9	13.2	2.2	2.1	34.1	10.3
Total[b]	%	10.2	7.4	14.8	15.1	10.4	6.2	4.7	34.0	13.4

a. Overcrowded conditions are defined using the CNOS for 'needing 1, 2, 3, 4 and >4 bedrooms'.

b. Includes where overcrowded conditions are 'Not Known', which account for approximately 0.8% of all Indigenous private dwellings.

n/a = not available.

Source: Adapted from SCRGSP 2009: 209

Table 12.8 Proportion of Indigenous households living in 'overcrowded' conditions by type of location, State and Territory, Australia, 2008[a]

Location	Unit	NSW	VIC	QLD	WA	SA	TAS	ACT	NT	AUST
			Numerator – number of overcrowded Indigenous households							
Capital city	No.	1 801	626	1 691	862	554	234	93	656	6 517
Balance of State	No.	4 749	539	6 195	2 462	659	344	n/a	4 475	19 423
Total	No.	6 550	1 166	7 886	3 324	1 212	577	93	5 131	25 940
Location				Denominator – total number of Indigenous households						
Capital city[b]	No.	21 339	8 043	16 080	8 539	6 008	3 355	1 985	4 900	70 251
Balance of State[b]	No.	43 002	7 776	37 099	13 416	5701	5 968	n/a	10 208	123 170
Total[b]	No.	64 341	15 819	53 179	21 956	11 710	9 323	1 985	15 108	193 421
Location				Proportion of Indigenous households living in overcrowded conditions						
Capital city[b]	%	8.4	7.8	10.5	10.1	9.2	7.0	4.7	13.4	9.3
Balance of State[b]	%	11.0	6.9	16.7	18.4	11.6	5.8	n/a	43.8	15.8
Total[b]	%	10.2	7.4	14.8	15.1	10.4	6.2	4.7	34.0	13.4

a. Overcrowded conditions are defined using the CNOS for 'needing 1, 2, 3, 4 and >4 bedrooms'.

b. Includes where overcrowded conditions are 'Not Known', which account for approximately 0.8% of all Indigenous private dwellings.

n/a = not available.

Source: Adapted from SCRGSP 2009: 211

Definition of 'community' vs 'non-community' terms in NATSISS

NATSISS categorises settlement units as 'communities' and alternatively 'non-communities'. In our view, the terms 'discrete settlement' and 'dispersed housing settlement' (for a rural town or city) are preferable terms for analysis of Indigenous settlement types (Memmott and Moran 2001). 'Communities' (as bounded systems of social networks) may occur in both types of settlements, but as social units they are not necessarily congruent with settlement units. The term a 'non-community sample' is thus misleading. Most Aboriginal people including those in urban and metropolitan settlements belong to some sort of Aboriginal community, and perhaps several, but some may not (e.g. the 'Stolen Generation'). This suggests there may be an analytic problem in making one set of suggestions about sampling in discrete settlements versus another set in dispersed settlements.

Definition of the 'family' in NATSISS

When asking question(s) that differentiate whether one is part of a resident family or not, how does the interviewer interpret between Aboriginal and non-Aboriginal kinship concepts in responses? The enumeration of 'family' in NATSISS does not include classificatory kin categories, but an Aboriginal interviewee may assume such kin are included as family. In Aboriginal kinship, classificatory relations may be included as family, but such kin may not be close relatives by blood descent or by direct marriage. This suggests there is a potential ambiguity in the responses of Aboriginal interviewees that involve the term 'family' which introduces measurement error into this indicator.

Non-enumeration of visitors and non-'usual residents' in NATSISS

The NATSISS sample of 2008 includes only those who are 'usually resident' in a private dwelling within Australia. 'Usually resident' is defined as anyone who usually lives in a given dwelling or regards it as their primary residence. Note that 'usually resident' excludes visitors. 'Usual place of residence' in NATSISS 'refers to the place where a person lives or intends to live for six months or more' (ABS 2009b).

As visitors are not included among the definition of residents, it is misleading to interpret 'spare' bedrooms as being unoccupied bedrooms. One of the Aboriginal researchers in our team commented in response to the findings in Table 12.1: 'I can't think of any relative of mine who has a spare bedroom' (co-author Corunna, a Nyungar/Palyku woman). The so-called spare bedrooms may well be occupied by visitors. 'Bedrooms needed' is therefore an underestimate in our view. This non-enumeration masks both crowding of those residences, and 'secondary' homeless people (according to the ABS categories of homelessness) who are 'visiting' and not enumerated (see Table 12.9, category 2.2).

Table 12.9 Categories of homelessness employed by ABS

Conceptual category	Operational definition
1. Primary homelessness	Improvised home, tent, sleepers out ('rough sleepers')
2. Secondary homelessness	In temporary shelter:
	Hostels for the homeless, night shelter, refuge
	Visitors to private dwellings with 'no usual address'
3. Tertiary homelessness	Boarding house/private hotel (unserviced room)

Source: Adapted from Chamberlain and Mackenzie 2008: 3, 10

Mobility can be a form of homelessness according to Memmott, Long and Thomson (2006) and moving from house to house can arise from inadequate security of tenure, social problems and violence, inadequate or unsuitable housing and other problems. These movements may contribute to both homelessness, for those fleeing particular social or environmental circumstances, and crowding for those who receive them into their homes.

> If visitors were taken into account in the measure of overcrowding [sic] for Census night 2006, the proportion of people living in overcrowded conditions would increase from 27% to 31% for Indigenous people… It is not possible five years on from the 2006 Census to readily establish the culturally motivated visitors from those people that may have been seeking accommodation because they were experiencing homelessness according to a western context (ABS 2011: 55).

If usual address is defined as being the place at which people will stay or intend to stay for six months, then how is 'no usual address' defined? It should be noted that reporting of 'no usual address' is uncommon in the Aboriginal population (Horspool and Mowle 2011: 6.1; Morphy 2007: 42).

In reality (and based upon both our personal and research experiences), visitors may have several homes in which they are welcome and between which they alternate for accommodation, none of which are their usual address. This situation could be masking one of homelessness, in which a person desires but cannot obtain a permanent home of their own, alternatively visitors may have their own home to which they may, or may not, eventually return.

'Indigenous household' definition in NATSISS

The definition of an 'Indigenous household' used by NATSISS includes any household that has one Indigenous resident (ABS2009b). While this is no doubt intended to capture the variety of living arrangements which Indigenous people use, it does tend to blur the figures relating to crowding, because Indigenous households on this weak criterion are not homogeneous. As demonstrated by the analysis of crowding for all Indigenous households with all Indigenous residents and those that include both Indigenous and non-Indigenous people, exclusively Indigenous houses have three times the odds of being crowded (see Table 12.4). The apparent homogeneity within the term 'Indigenous household' also masks the diversity of families and circumstances within the Indigenous community, and reduces the visibility of crowding in wholly Indigenous households. Given prevalent differences between different types of Indigenous households, relying on this weak definition will understate the extent of crowding.

The challenge of Indigenous enumeration in a remote discrete settlement

If there is a level of inaccuracy in the NATSISS reporting of the number of spare bedrooms, and it is indeed an overestimate, what could account for this? First let us consider that the calculated spare bedrooms are in fact occupied. One reason would be that they were occupied by short-term visitors (staying less than 6 months) as noted above. A second reason would be that interviewees have given false information by under-reporting on the number of actual occupants for fear of eviction by their rental agency due to hosting a greater number of people than allowed by their tenancy agreement.

Now let us assume that a proportion of bedrooms are spare but that this is notwithstanding the potential for crowding to still occur. What hypothetical reasons could there be for this? Firstly, it is possible that people may refuse to utilise a room due to the belief that it contains the spirit or presence of a recently deceased householder who occupied the room, or out of respect for that person even if the spirit is believed to have departed.[6] A second possible reason is that a household (e.g. a nuclear family) may choose to all sleep in one bedroom for preferred closeness and intimacy (see later), thereby leaving one or two other bedrooms empty. A third possible reason is the partial use or non-use of houses with dysfunctional health hardware (showers, toilets, cooking

---

6 Both of the Aboriginal co-authors (Go-Sam and Corunna) of this chapter suggested this as a possible explanation. Interestingly, although we are confident that this belief is widespread there are negligible references in the Aboriginal housing literature to suggest this. We are of the view that the lack of reporting is because it has not been formally studied as a phenomenon. There are nevertheless references to Aboriginal responses to death in houses (e.g. Fantin 2003; Memmott 2003).

facilities, room heaters). The householder of such a dysfunctional house may sleep there but use a neighbour's house for ablutions and cooking, or indeed move in temporarily with their neighbour.

As evidence of this last reason, consider the following statement on household sizes in a remote discrete community taken from the *National Indigenous Housing Guide* and based on six years of data collection from a sample of more than 25 000 Indigenous people:[7]

> In a community with 300 people and 50 houses, it could be assumed that an average of six people live in each house. However only 25 of the 50 houses have functioning bathrooms and toilets, so residents of the non-working houses use the houses in which bathrooms and toilets work, which means the average house population would be 12... If a sports carnival is held in the community, or death occurs or during the annual wet season, the population could double or treble and the demand on working houses could increase to 24–36 people per house (FaHCSIA 2007: 137).

Batten (1999) argues that an orthodoxy of suitable housing has developed in Australia around economic models of efficient use of housing which lead to the perception of under-utilisation of housing amongst some groups. Similarly one could argue, regarding crowding, that an orthodoxy has developed where crowding was defined in a situation removed from Australia decades ago, yet now remains unchallenged as the standard of suitability and continues to be unquestioned. The CNOS, developed in Canada in 1991 by their Government's National Housing Agency, Canada Mortgage and Housing Corporation, state the acceptable levels of occupancy of a house by determining the appropriate use of bedrooms per person, depending on age, gender, relationship status and other factors which are widely agreed to be culturally specific. Yet these standards are applied in Australia, and in Australian Indigenous communities which are very different to the circumstances in Canada. That they have become an orthodoxy is evidenced by their unquestioned use by Australian organisations including the ABS in its NATSISS, the Census and other analysis of data (Horspool and Mowle 2011; NATSISS Glossary in ABS 2009b; SCRGSP 2009). Many academics too have assumed this is a fair and accurate measure of crowding.

---

7   Based on 'Housing for Health' and 'Fixing Houses for Better Health' projects undertaken and drawn from a survey of 3615 houses over a period of 6 years. Houses surveyed include urban, urban fringe, regional, remote and very remote regions, across four states: Western Australia, Queensland South Australia, New South Wales, and the Northern Territory (FaHCSIA 2007: 5, 17).

Current social science models of crowding

Elsewhere, we have recently reviewed the social science literature on crowding (Memmott et al. 2011). We drew liberally on a comprehensive literature review of crowding carried out by environmental psychologist Robert Gifford (2007), which is 40 pages long and cites some 288 references (most written in the post 1990 period, but some as early as 1903), as well as drawing on selected references upon which he bases his analysis. We also utilise an earlier review of the Australian Indigenous crowding literature by Memmott (1991) and a recent audit of the Aboriginal housing literature by Long, Memmott and Seelig (2007).

The social sciences have employed a stress model of 'crowding' for at least 40 years. This model holds that states of crowding involve high-density settings that generate certain stimuli, which induce stress in setting participants according to their values of the environmental acceptability and non-acceptability of these stimuli. However, not all high-density settings are experienced as being crowded for particular groups. Gifford (2007: 191, 192, 194) provides a model of crowding which is experiential, based on stress rather than density:

> Density is a measure of the number of individuals per unit area... Crowding...refers to the person's experience of the number of other people around. Rather than a physical ratio, crowding is a personally defined, subjective feeling that too many others are around...Crowding is a function of many personal, situational, and cultural factors...Crowding and density are not always strongly correlated with one another.

In the case of Aboriginal groups, the stimulus that induces stress is often the presence of inappropriate categories of kin in too close a proximity (Fantin 2003). A second stimulus is often the inappropriate behaviour of such persons as a result of substance abuse (Memmott et al. 2011: 37).

In his comprehensive review of crowding theories, Gifford (2007: 217) attempts to synthesise the various dominant paradigms of crowding into a single integrative theory of crowding which he summarises as follows:

> Certain personal, social, and physical antecedents lead to the experience of crowding. Among these are a variety of individual differences, resource shortages (behavior-setting theory), the number of other people nearby (density-intensity and social physics theories), who those others are, and what they are doing. Sensory overload and a lack of personal control are psychological processes central to the experience of crowding. The consequences of crowding include physiological, behavioural, and cognitive effects, including health problems, learned helplessness, and reactance.

Fig. 12.1 An integrative model of crowding

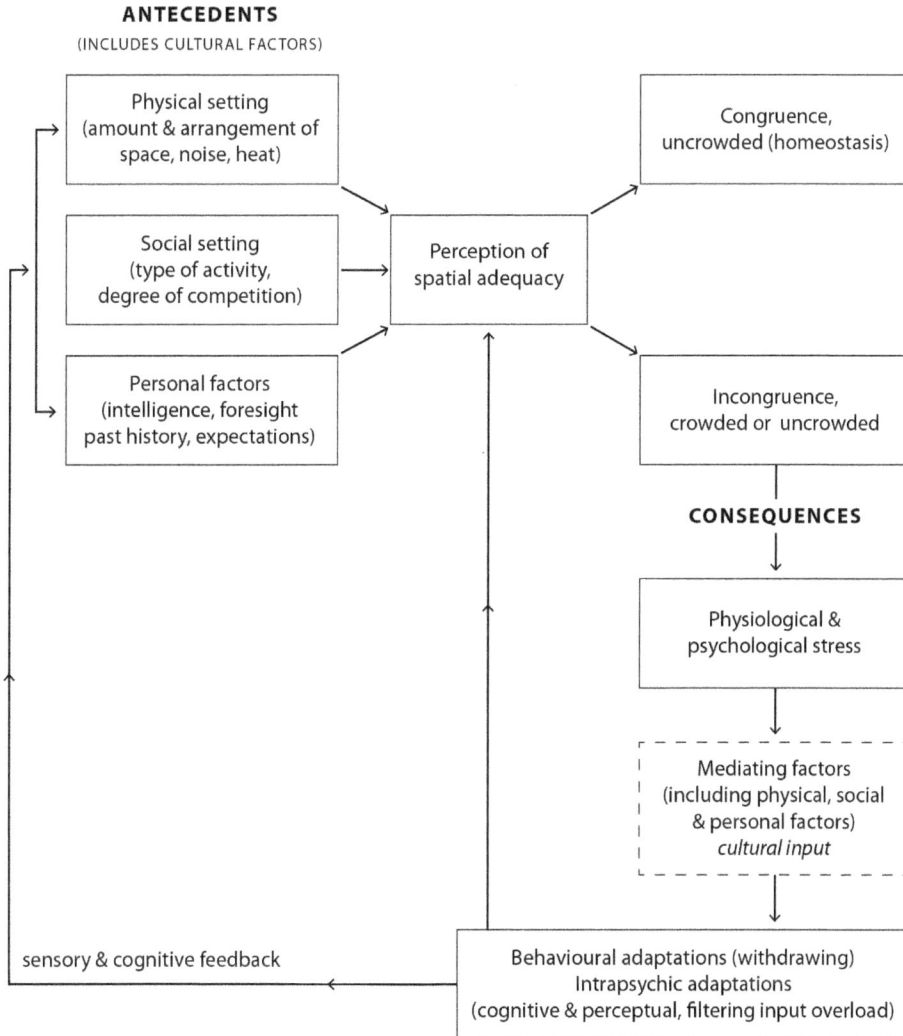

ANTECEDENTS
(INCLUDES CULTURAL FACTORS)

Source: Adapted from Gifford 2007: 195, 214, Fig. 7.12

We have adapted Gifford's diagrammatic theoretical model to crowding (Fig. 12.1), to include the salient cultural factors in his discussion. We note that Gifford incorporates culture into his crowding model in two places: (i) cultural factors are implicit as part of the antecedent factors (e.g. physical and social settings character, past personal and group history); and (ii) cultural factors are also implicit as part of the mediating factors shaping response to stress (Memmott et al. 2011: 17).

With respect to antecedent factors, it is argued that in different cultures, childhood conditioning and socialisation processes equip individuals to adapt to, and to deal with perceived high-density situations in different ways, according to different norms. Thus Rapoport (1976: 18) and others have argued that being with like people will decrease stress frequency in potentially crowded circumstances. Kinship groups (e.g. extended families, multiple family units) and other culturally homogenous groups are most likely to be socially well-structured. Similarly those individuals within the same culture will have common methods to mediate situations that are perceived to be stressful and crowded, and to maintain group sanctions over what is appropriate stress-avoidance behaviour. Of the propensity for cultural factors to act as mediating or moderating influences, Gifford (2007: 21) writes:

> The consequences of crowding and high density depend in part on cultural background. Culture acts as a moderating influence on high density, sometimes providing its members with a shield against the negative effects of high density and sometimes failing to equip them with effective means of coping with high density.

Our literature analysis of crowding (Memmott et al. 2011) thus argues that states of crowding are characterised by the perception of high-density, displaying various stimuli, some of which induce stress in occupants. The determinations of whether these stimuli are stressful, or not, varies according to one's values of the environmental acceptability or non-acceptability of these stimuli. The experience of crowding is also

> ...accentuated by personal factors (personality, expectations, attitudes, gender), social factors (the number, type, and actions of others, the degree of attitude similarity), and physical factors (architectural features and spatial arrangements) (Gifford 2007: 220).

The result may be perceived loss of personal control and/or social and informational overload (comprising a perceptual/cognitive component of the crowding model). Alternatively in response to such a situation, a coping mechanism may be utilised if one is available (a reactive behavioural component to the model). The values that are employed to evaluate the setting state (its stimuli), and to select an appropriate coping or mediating mechanism, and the nature of such mechanisms may vary cross-culturally (Memmott et al. 2011: 20–21).

Three ongoing questions for research arise from the above social science model of crowding with respect to understanding crowding in the context of Indigenous Australia.

• What are relevant Australian Indigenous norms and situational factors of household life?

- How do these norms or situational factors become compromised by density changes, resulting in stress and a perceived state of crowding according to the above model?
- What are Australian Indigenous coping mechanisms for crowding?

Aboriginal case studies of high mobility and household transformation

A cultural driver of Aboriginal crowding is the high rate of circular mobility within regions across the continent that can impact on household transformation. Three short examples have been chosen to illustrate aspects of the nature of Aboriginal mobility as a situational and culturally specific factor that can underlie crowding.

A study of a Warlpiri single women's household in Yuendumu

Yasmine Musharbash's (2003) doctoral study centers upon the occupants of a single women's house (or *jilimi*) in the central Australian desert community of Yuendumu in the Northern Territory over a period of 221 nights, and is a significant contribution to understanding the socially complex nature and composition of this Indigenous household type. Musharbash construed the Warlpiri, or *Yapa*, day-to-day worldview as being founded on three principal behavioural values of mobility, immediacy and intimacy. Musharbash (2008: 4, 7, 62) uses these values to explore and accurately describe everyday life and the finer nuances of inter-relatedness. More specifically, these values become clearly understood as drivers of everyday social practice by Warlpiri people in general and by the residents of the *jilimi* in particular (2008: 8). Her findings on mobility and intimacy have a direct relevance to constructs of crowding.

Mobility is regarded as a valued process rather than an incidental phenomenon that occasionally affects 'household' or 'residential group' composition.[8] Not only do Warlpiri people frequently change and hold multiple residences, but Musharbash found the analysis of this dynamic through cyclical activities such as sleeping arrangements, damper making, meal consumption or demand sharing, renders the static concept of 'household', relatively useless as an analytical tool (Musharbash 2008: 60, 73–76, 115–23, 174–75).

---

8   This approach is specifically employed by Musharbash as a critique of the inadequacy and yet prevalent use of the term 'household', utilised in housing research and in ABS Census data.

Table 12.10 Average numbers of adults and children sleeping in the *jilimi* per night as sampled over 221 nights, 1998–2001

Occupants	Average	Highest[a]	Lowest
Adults	12	19	6
Children	5	11	1
Total[a]	17	30	9[b]

a. This table does not include individuals from *sorry mobs*, in which case these numbers would be substantially higher.

b. This is the lowest number of actual residents present at any one time, not the sum of lowest number of adults and children together.

Source: Adapted from Musharbash 2008: 62, Table 1

The *jilimi* residents thus fell naturally into four categories by such social closeness or distance, (i) core residents, (ii) regular residents, (iii) on-and-off residents and (iv) sporadic residents (see Table 12.11).

Table 12.11 Types of residents in *jilimi* over the 221 nights, 1998–2001

Resident type	Number of individuals	Number of nights
Core residents	11	100 +
Regular residents	12	44–76
On-and-off residents	36	8–36
Sporadic residents	48	1–6

Source: Adapted from Musharbash 2008: 64 Table 2

Musharbash defined these categories partially through their relative frequency of sleeping in the *jilimi*. Core residents were individuals who slept at the *jilimi* between 133 and 221 nights during the study period. The second category, 'regular' residents, stayed at the *jimili* for between 44 and 76 nights. The greater number of individuals belonged to the categories of 'on-and-off' residents totaling 36 individuals staying eight to 36 nights and 48 'sporadic' residents staying one to six nights. The latter two categories of kin were drawn from both actual and classificatory kin. For the recording period of 221 non-consecutive nights, the minimum occupancy was nine people, the maximum 30, and an overall average of 17 individuals. Emphasising the sheer volume of people sleeping in the *jilimi*, it was noted that more than 160 individuals were recorded. However, Musharbash concludes that this was a conservative estimate due to a failure to count nocturnal and early morning residential shifts and 'sorry mobs'[9] (2008: 62–65, 71). It can be argued from Musharbash's model of mobility as valued that much residential mobility is sanctioned, at least within Central Australian Aboriginal communities, and seen as an acceptable and positive phenomenon.

---

9 Group of mourners who travel from other settlements to engage in ritualised mortuary behaviour (Musharbash 2008: 165).

Another of the tripartite values identified by Musharbash (2008: 95–97) is intimacy, knowing closely the bodies of others, generated largely from the fluidity of sleeping arrangements, albeit constrained within the sociospatial categories of married people's camps, single men's camps, and single women's camps. Intimacy was the norm and high density was not usually perceived as a problem. At night, if a woman left the sleeping group for some unexpected reason, the remaining people would close-up the space to be close together. 'Yapa [Aboriginal people] strive for 'gap-free' yunta [sleeping configurations]'... and '[s]leeping alone is an impossibility' (Musharbash 2008: 44).

Fig. 12.2 Example from Musharbash's description of the Aboriginal value of intimacy in Warlpiri single women's households

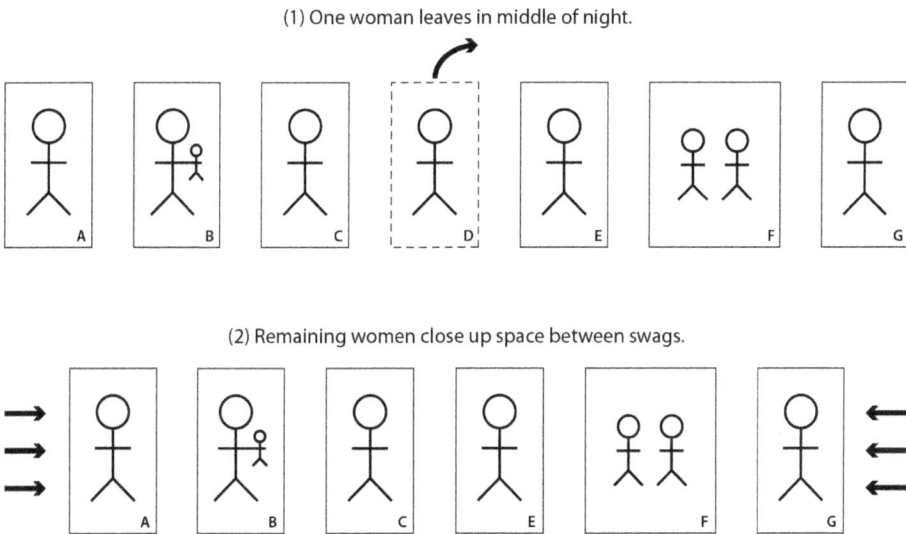

Source: Adapted from description in Musharbash 2008: 43–44

On the direct subject of crowding, little is elaborated upon by Musharbash, other than passing references about frequent tensions arising from 'gambling schools' involving the core residents complaining about the camp becoming 'dirty', or about people who 'just leave their rubbish' and 'use the toilet all the time' as a response to the high volumes of people being hosted. Significantly, the 'gambling schools' that operated day and night on a regular fortnightly basis, became problematic to residents when it interfered with the sleep of core residents. The strategy employed to disperse gambling participants was indirect action by turning off the electricity and declaring the power meter was empty (Musharbash 2008: 127).

Clearly these values and preferences recorded by Musharbash reveal that rather than crowding being a concern, for some people the driver of appropriate levels of intimacy, proper company for individuals so they need not feel alone, is key to many sleeping and household behaviours which determine numbers. Similarly mobility is conceived of as a positive value which allows for the proper behaviours demonstrating kin and place connections. While these preferences for intimacy and mobility can be seen as causes of crowding, the stress caused by inadequate facilities such as bathrooms, cooking facilities and large enough rooms to accommodate desired numbers may be a better way to conceptualise the issue, rather than simple numbers per bedroom. (Memmott et al. 2011: 26–28.)

The following example at Pipalyatjara in South Australia reveals nuances of mobility that in turn affect responses to crowding at both the house and neighbourhood scale.

The Pipalyatjara example

There are few case studies that provide accurate data on residential household dynamics through time. Pholeros, Rainow and Torzillo (1993) use an example from Pipalyatjara that demonstrates mobility within a very remote discrete settlement and can be used to illustrate the variation in household numbers (Fig. 12.3). The relative size of the blackened circles indicates the relative size of households, with the settlement total ranging from 40 to 132 persons.

Mobility can be both a cause of crowding (through new residents arriving) and a coping mechanism in response to crowding (by departing for a perceived non-crowded residence) (Fig. 12.4). While crowding and mobility can be seen as linked, the complexity of the neighbourhood situation is shown through these examples. The desire to be close to particular people at relevant times of celebration, mourning or the result of other factors, means that household sizes swell and shrink according to cultural and social factors which require careful analysis over time.

The following example at Ti Tree (Northern Territory) gives further evidence of these complexities, including the issue of self-constructed housing.

Fig. 12.3 Population distribution within Pipalyatjara on eight survey occasions, 1992

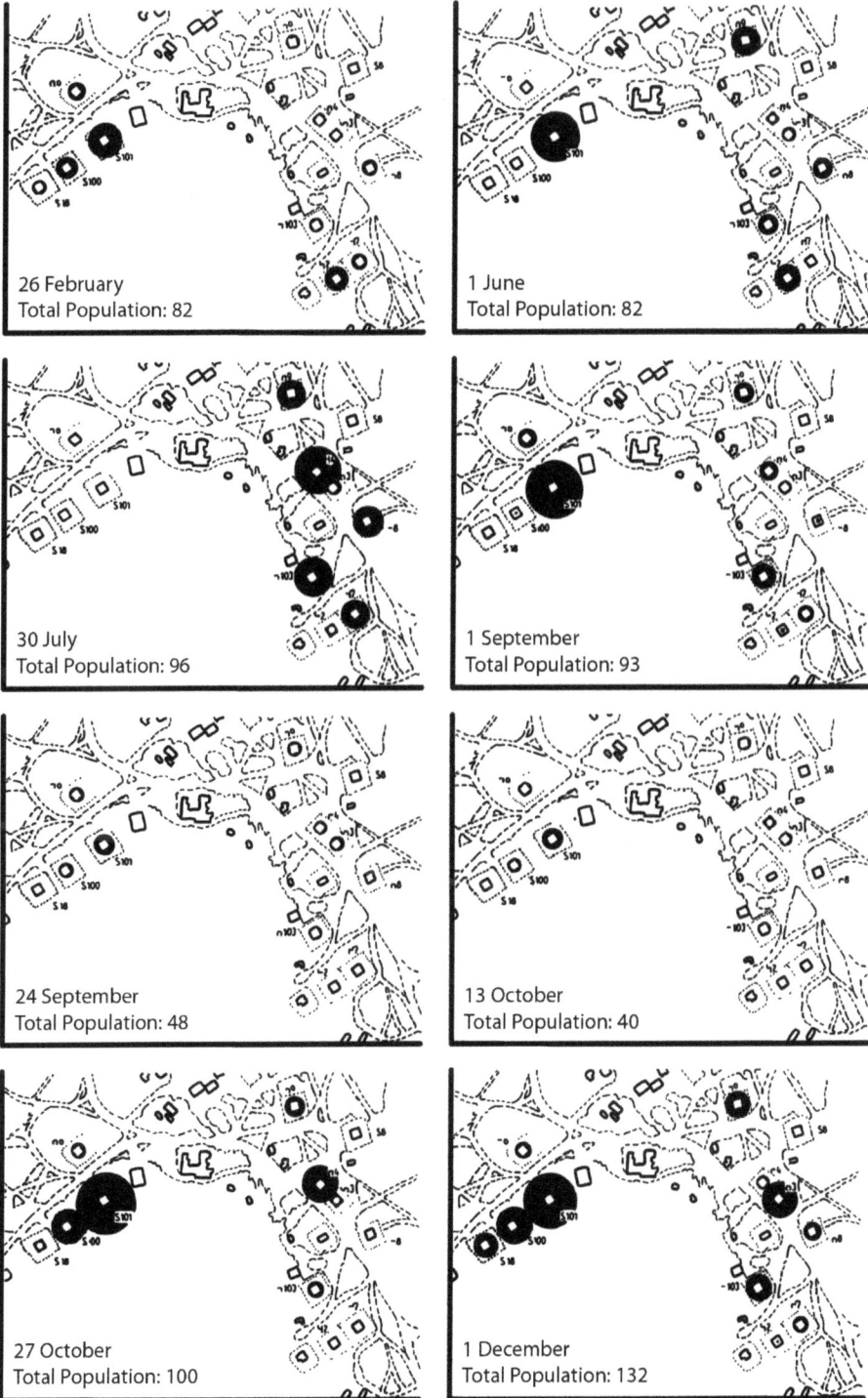

26 February
Total Population: 82

1 June
Total Population: 82

30 July
Total Population: 96

1 September
Total Population: 93

24 September
Total Population: 48

13 October
Total Population: 40

27 October
Total Population: 100

1 December
Total Population: 132

Source: Pholeros, Rainow and Torzillo 1993: 26–27

Fig. 12.4 Family group mobility at Pipalyatjara based on three census times, 1992

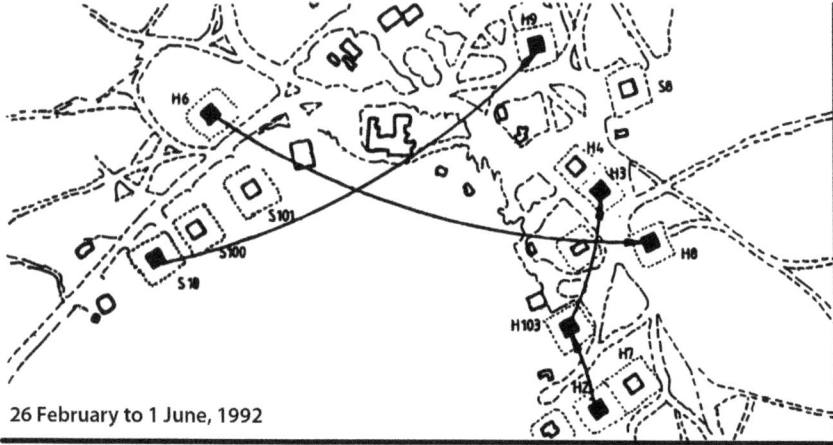

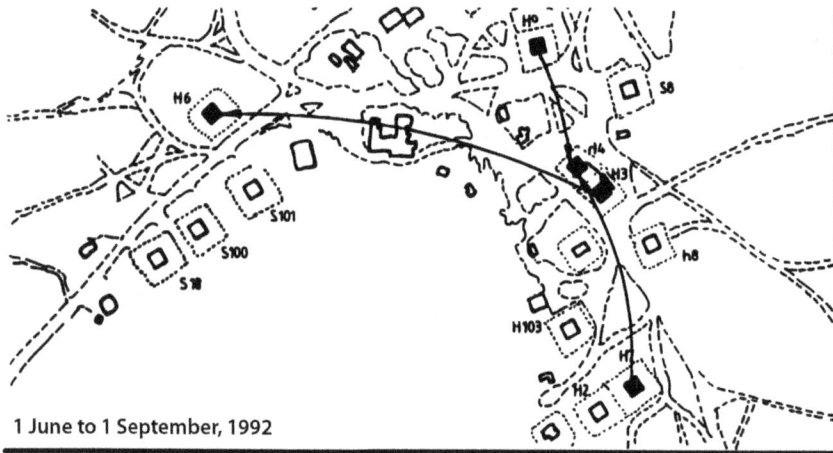

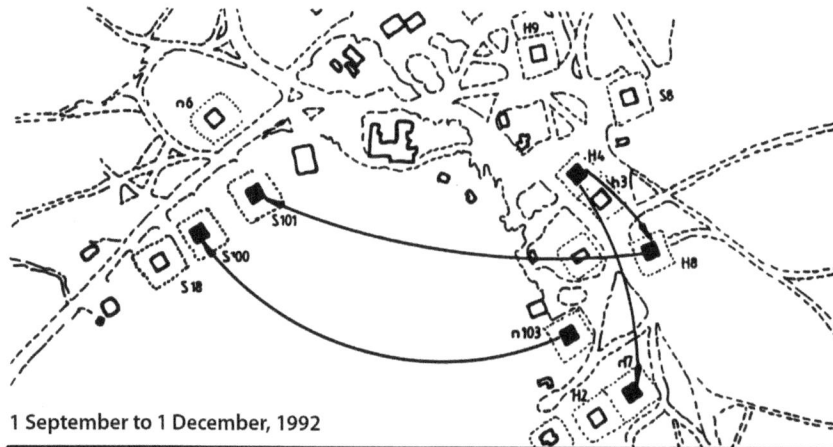

26 February to 1 June, 1992

1 June to 1 September, 1992

1 September to 1 December, 1992

Source: Pholeros, Rainow and Torzillo 1993: 28

The Ti Tree Town Camp example

The changing living patterns of people in a town camp located beside the township of Ti Tree in the Northern Territory over a period of nine months during 2005–06 (see Fig. 12.5 described in Sanders and Holcombe 2006). This area accommodated people in a series of self-constructed camps, which were used by both long-term residents and visitors. The recorded mobility included both intra-settlement movement from camps into nearby houses and back again, and people travelling further afield into the wider region under a variety of motivations. Some camps were abandoned as social groups dispersed in response to the change of seasons or social conditions in the camp and elsewhere, but a number of camps were occupied by people for long periods of time spanning years (Sanders and Holcombe 2006: 3).

Fig. 12.5 Settlement plan of south-west side of Ti Tree Township, Aboriginal campsites occupied and unoccupied, 2005–06[a]

a. Aboriginal campsites occupied indicated by black circles and unoccupied indicated by white circles.

Source: Sanders and Holcombe 2006: 12–15

This study highlights the nature of mobility for some Indigenous people, which can be seasonal, social, employment or health based, and clearly affects the occupation pressures on dwellings (of whatever type), which cannot be captured in a single night snapshot, such as the NATSISS. If one imagines the receiving dwellings at the other end of the outward mobility from Ti Tree, one can infer the occupation of those dwellings swell and shrink also, as visitors arrive or become longer-term residents.

Understanding the Aboriginal rules of allocation of people to household sub-groups

To minimise the stresses arising from high density living in Aboriginal households, a common coping mechanism is the purposefully arranged setting structured by the householders, achieved through rules governing the combinations of people allocated to living and sleeping spaces that establish what are perceived to be ordered and safe behavioural patterns. If for example, a sub-group of unmarried women are allocated a room in a large household, their numbers are unlikely to be a concern and they will sleep within touching distance of one another. The arrangement of people in sleeping spaces thus occurs according to combinations based on age, gender, conjugal status and kin relationships. Despite being a large household it may not be regarded as crowded. If the core members of such a rule-governed household are stable, such households may endure for years.

One sub-group of householders (often including the senior householder) may sleep and live in the 'living room' of the house, irrespective of whether bedrooms are too small or too few. The room is furnished with mattresses on which people will sit or lie engaging in social discourse or sleep as they wish. This differs from the typical Australian living room, which often features a couch and a television, but which is seldom used as a permanent nocturnal sleeping room.

A threshold of stress may arise, even for the rule-governed household, when the density increases to the point whereby there is no means of allocating sleeping space to persons without placing them in situations which compromise the need for respect among kin. Such a situation will induce stress, and emotional responses may include shame, jealousy, anger and violence. The household in this situation is generally crowded. It can be severely exacerbated through substance abuse by particular householders or by their visitors. It will lose stability and may not endure.

The next example demonstrates an architectural response to a particular housing requirement, which accommodates multiple families in a dense, but we argue, not crowded arrangement.

This house was built at Ngukurr (Roper River, Northern Territory) during 1998–99 and designed by the architectural firm Northern Building Consultants, to accommodate a complex Indigenous household. The household genealogy and floor plan show the sleeping locations of the six household sub-units or groups (see Fig. 12.6). The total population of the household was 14 (Memmott et al. 2000).

Fig. 12.6 A house built at Ngukurr, Northern Territory, 1998–99

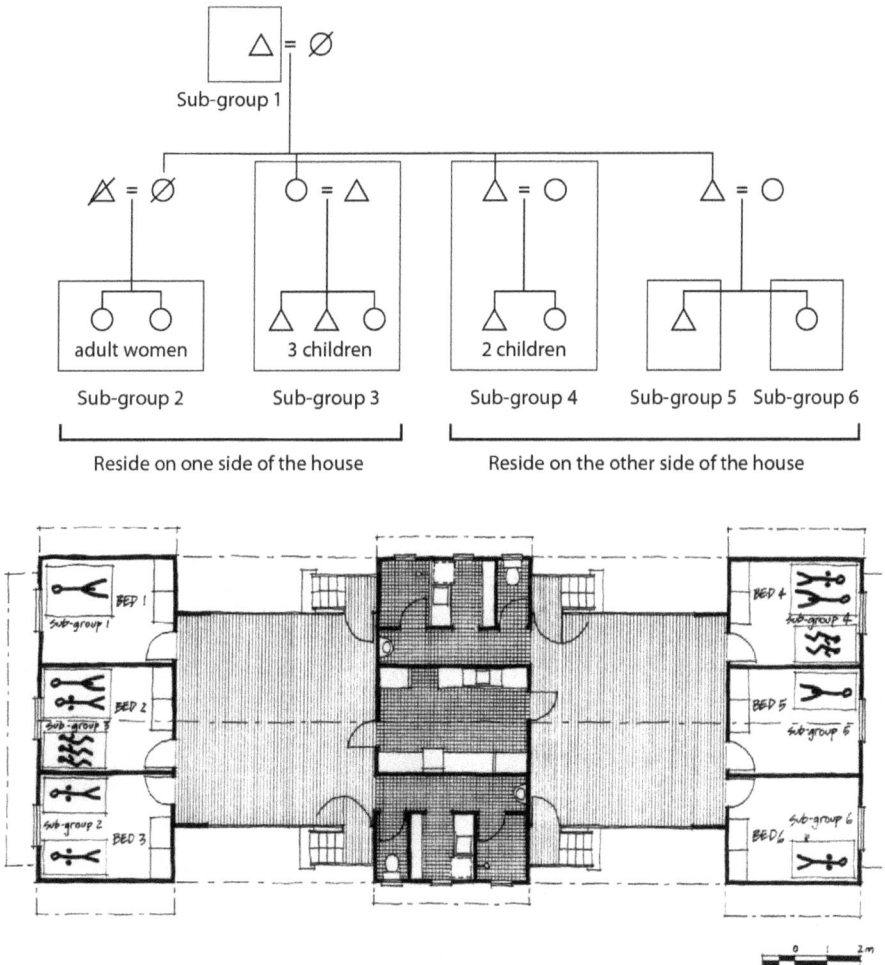

Source: Authors' own research

The design achieved a degree of sociospatial separation from a senior male householder and his adult daughters (in sub-group 3) from his adult son (in sub-group 4), thus conforming to an obligatory avoidance rule between adult siblings of opposite gender. The occupation of a single bedroom by a nuclear family with infants was regarded as acceptable but once the children reached adolescence they occupied separate rooms (sub-groups 3, 5, and 6).

This case study provides an example of the use of sociospatial division and allocation of sleeping spaces combined with avoidance behaviour principles as complementary coping mechanisms to minimise or prevent crowding, in keeping with Gifford's key concept of stress, rather than arguments that all dense situations are stressful, even at a subconscious level. In the case of some Aboriginal groups, as witnessed by Musharbash, such density may be an expression of proper intimacy with kin and others, which in fact reduces stress. This example clearly does not conform to the Canadian National Occupancy Standard. What would cause perceived crowding would be the incorrect juxtaposition of people according to the cultural rules.

Given the high density of many Aboriginal households, the techniques to minimise and avoid crowding include a combination of sociospatial divisions, observance of avoidance and respect rules, the punishment of any rule violation with shaming, adjusting spaces where possible with flexible architectural elements and ultimately, especially under high stress, the deployment of residential mobility within kin networks (Memmott et al. 2011: 56).

Conclusion

Use of the CNOS as a measure of 'crowding' is problematic. It has embedded culturally specific assumptions such as preferable sleeping arrangements of particular genders, relationships etc. which are not necessarily applicable to Indigenous Australians, but few alternatives have been proposed despite critiques of CNOS.

A key problem then, as we have argued here, is that NATSISS, at best, is a snapshot of household sizes and profiles, and probably a blurred one due to the under-reporting of visitors. NATSISS does not readily capture flows in and out of households and other social pressures on Indigenous households. These deficiencies diminish the possibility of an accurate modelling of crowding, even though government departments and other agencies persist in extrapolating findings on crowding from the NATSISS data. The complexity we have demonstrated in the perception, mobility, coping mechanisms and culturally specific drivers of house crowding makes a survey-based density measure as a stand-alone model of crowding unhelpful. Furthermore, scaling up or extrapolating NATSISS survey results may mask local contextual factors. Caution is therefore counselled concerning the use of NATSISS findings to direct government program expenditure in order to redress housing shortages. It may be that more rich or fine-tuned measures are required, despite the potential cost or complexity of gaining such information. In our view NATSISS findings are better used as a first step to decision-making only, to be followed with more in-depth community surveys or consultation prior to expenditure decisions. Just as health diagnoses cannot be made via a simple survey questionnaire separate from medical practitioners, similarly the complexity of house crowding requires a more in-depth and nuanced 'diagnosis'. We do not doubt that crowding exists and that in many cases it is severe, but the cultural and group specific nature of the causes of crowding and possible solutions require more investigations than the NATSISS survey data can currently provide.

The need for terminology and concepts that are meaningful in Aboriginal household contexts

One of our aims in this paper has been to demonstrate that terms whose meanings are briefly defined and taken for granted in the Census and NATSISS surveys do not necessarily make sense when applied in all Aboriginal contexts, which are by no means homogeneous. There is a need to carefully explore and deconstruct the culturally specific semantic meanings of terms such as family, resident, household, community, visitor as well as crowding itself. The use of inappropriate, ambiguous or inaccurate terms in the collection or definition of NATSISS data causes difficulties in being able to make useful interpretations of the data.

Table 12.12 Analysis of current policy terms, household enumeration, Australia

Words currently used by policy formulators	Aspects of semantic deconstruction necessary for Indigenous contexts
community	Community/settlement
family	Agnatic, cognatic and classificatory types of kin as family; all visitors as family
resident (= six months present or 'usual place of residence' or not counted by ABS for census or NATSISS)	Visitors (not enumerated) Sanctioned v. non-sanctioned mobility
household ('common provision' definition)	The residential group present for particular activities (eating, sleeping, nocturnal/diurnal, recreational) but transforming
usual resident	Core resident/long-term/short-term/night visitor/day visitor.
visitor	Classificatory kin/strangers/multiple home bases
crowding	Density/crowding
overcrowding	Crowding/non-crowding/types of crowding

Source: Authors' analysis

Suggestions for improving NATSISS with respect to crowding

Firstly, we suggest that included in NATSISS, should be a count of 'place of enumeration' on the night (or place of residence on the night) as well as 'place of usual residence'. (This was possibly not done because the NATSISS survey may have been carried out over more than one night.)

Secondly we suggest that a statistical algorithm technique be developed to incorporate a 'visitor factor' and/or a 'household mobility factor' into the NATSISS weighting process.

Additional desirable complementary research to NATSISS

In addition to improving the NATSISS survey, we make four suggestions on additional research that should be encouraged to obtain complementary findings for those of the NATSISS survey.

- In general we suggest that there combined quantitative and qualitative methods be developed, to better contextualise and model crowding and spatial needs in Aboriginal households
- More longitudinal case studies should be undertaken so as to understand household dynamics; these ought to be separate studies to NATSISS, but to complement the NATSISS findings
- An effective technique needs to be developed to capture flows of people in and out of households, and
- More research is needed on the nature of the relationships between core and temporary householders. (For example, is 'visitor' an appropriate term? What does it mean to Aboriginal people who are serial or repeated dwellers in a home; do they identify with such a term?)

The need for a new metric of Indigenous crowding

Finally, there is a need for a new metric to assess Indigenous households and whether they are crowded. A key design issue for such a metric would be the level of complexity and the cost (time involved) of using it.

Appendix 12A: Methodological notes

The NATSISS sampled the discrete Indigenous communities, dubbed 'community sample,' of remote Queensland, Western Australia, South Australia and the Northern Territory separately, using a different sampling design from the rest of Australia, the latter urban and metropolitan areas being termed the 'non-community sample' (ABS 2010). For the former, communities were selected at random from the 'Indigenous Community Frame', derived by ABS from the 2006 Census of Population and Housing. From these, a random selection of dwelling and then of Indigenous usual residents within dwellings was derived.

The non-community sample used a multi-stage area sample, which randomly selected a sample of Census Collection Districts (CDs) from each State. From here all 'Mesh Blocks' that contained at least one Indigenous household, according to the 2006 Census, were screened, as well as a random sample of those not recording any Indigenous households. From identified Indigenous households up to two Indigenous adults (aged 15+) and two Indigenous children (aged 0–14) were randomly selected to respond to the survey.

The final sample was of approximately 13 300 Indigenous persons from 6 858 households.

Summary of the NATSISS Sample

Community sample:

Discrete Indigenous communities (remote Queensland, Western Australia, South Australia and the Northern Territory); random selection of:

- communities
- dwellings
- Indigenous usual residents

Non-community sample:

Multi-stage area sample; random selection of:

- CDs
- mesh block
- Indigenous household
- Indigenous usual residents

Weighting of data

The 2008 NATSISS contains weights at both the person and household levels of measurement (ABS 2010). The initial weights 'scale up' the sample data to the in-scope population by multiplying each unit by the inverse of its probability of being selected.[10] These initial weights are then adjusted to population benchmarks in order to compensate for undercoverage, which may have occurred due to sampling bias, non-response, non-identification, etc. Population benchmarks are independent estimates of the population of interest with regards to specific (independent) parameters (usually demographics). The aim of calibrating sampling weights to such benchmarks is to ensure that the distribution of observations is aligned to that of the population, rather than the idiosyncratic distribution of the sample.

Summary of NATSISS Sampling Weights

Probability weights

Scale-up observations by the inverse probability of each person/household being selected.

Adjustment to population benchmarks

Indigenous Household Definition in NATSISS

Calibrated to:

- State
- part of State
- age
- sex
- community/non-community

---

10 For example, if a household was 1 of 4 selected from a particular collection district which comprised 48 households, it would have a probability of 1/12 (4/48) of being selected, and would therefore be assigned an initial weight of 12 (i.e. a weight that multiplied its responses by 12).

Appendix 12B: Selected definitions taken from ABS (2009b)

Private dwelling

The premises occupied by a household. Includes houses, flats, home units, garages, tents and improvised dwellings. Excludes hostels, hospitals and prisons.

Estimated resident population (ERP)

The official ABS estimate of the Australian population, based on the Census count (on a usual residence basis). The estimated resident population is compiled at 30 June each census year, and is updated quarterly between censuses. These intercensal estimates of the resident population are revised each time a population census is taken. For more information, see Australian Demographic Statistics (ABS 2011a). See also 'estimated resident Indigenous population' (ABS 2009b).

Estimated resident Indigenous population

The Indigenous ERP is based on the census count and adjusted for instances in which Indigenous status is unknown and for net undercount. These adjustments are necessary because of the volatility of counts of the Indigenous population between censuses. For more information, see ABS 2009a.

Household

Consists of a person living alone, or two or more related or unrelated persons who live and eat together in private residential accommodation. In this survey, each household contained at least one identified Indigenous resident.

Housing utilisation

This information is based on the CNOS for Housing Appropriateness, a widely used measure that is sensitive to both household size and composition. The following criteria are used to assess bedroom requirements and households requiring at least one additional bedroom are considered to be overcrowded:

- there should be no more than 2 persons per bedroom
- a household of 1 unattached individual may reasonably occupy a bed-sit (ie. have no bedroom)

- couples and parents should have a separate bedroom
- children aged less than 5 years, of different sexes, may reasonably share a room
- children aged 5 years or over, of different sexes, should not share a bedroom
- children aged less than 18 years and of the same sex may reasonably share a bedroom, and
- single household members aged 18 years or over should have a separate bedroom.

Indigenous household

An Indigenous household is a household where one or more of the Usual Residents is Indigenous. See also Indigenous.

Non-remote

Geographical areas within the 'Major cities of Australia', 'Inner regional Australia' and 'Outer regional Australia' categories of the Australian Standard Geographical Classification (ASGC) Remoteness Structure (ABS 2008a). See also 'remoteness area' (ABS 2009b).

Remote

Geographical areas within the 'Remote Australia' and 'Very remote Australia' categories of the ASGC Remoteness Structure (ABS 2008a). This term has been abbreviated to 'Remote' in this publication. See also 'remoteness area' (ABS 2009b).

Respondent

An Indigenous person who was selected to participate in the 2008 NATSISS and who completed an interview. In non-community areas, up to 2 Indigenous adults and 2 Indigenous children per household were randomly selected after all usual residents of the household were listed. In community areas up to 1 Indigenous adult and 1 Indigenous child were randomly selected as respondents. A proxy provided answers on behalf of children aged 0–14 years of age. The collection of information from people aged 15–17 years required parent/guardian permission, if this was not given then an interview was not conducted. See also Proxy.

Usual place of residence

Refers to the place where a person has lived or intends to live for a total of 6 months or more (Compare this definition with the information given about the scope of the survey from the users' guide shown below).

Scope and coverage: Taken from ABS (2010)

The scope of the survey is all Indigenous people who were usual residents of private dwellings in Australia. Private dwellings are:

- houses
- flats
- home units, or
- any other structures used as private places of residence at the time of the survey.

Usual residents are people who usually live in a particular dwelling and regard it as their own or main home. People usually resident in non-private dwellings, such as hotels, motels, hostels, hospitals, nursing homes, or short-stay caravan parks were not in scope.

Acknowledgements

We gratefully acknowledge the assistance of: the Australian Housing and Urban Research Institute (AHURI) for access to concurrent research which the authors were undertaking on Indigenous crowding; ABS for provision of data and access to data for analysis; and the Commonwealth Department of Families, Housing, Community Services and Indigenous Affairs (FaHCSIA) for access to concurrent work on homelessness.

Quantitative analysis conducted by the authors used data from the 2008 National Aboriginal and Torres Strait Islander Social Survey, which was kindly provided by the ABS in the form of Confidentialised Unit Record Files (CURFs). We were granted access to both the 'NATSISS State by Remoteness 2008 Expanded Reissue 1' CURF and the 'NATSISS State/Territory 2008 Expanded Reissue 1' CURF, which were analysed remotely using the ABS Remote Access Data Laboratory (RADL).

References

Anderton, N. and Lloyd, C. 1991. 'Housing Australia: An analysis of the 1986 Census', Report prepared for the Australian Housing Research Council, Canberra.

Australian Broadcasting Corporation (ABC) 2011. ABC online news, 2011, 'Indigenous housing staff on $450k: Senator', 25th February, viewed 1 March 2011, available at <www.abc.net.au/news /stories /2011 /02/25/3148987. htm>

Australian Bureau of Statistics (ABS) 1980. *General Social Survey: Australian Families, May 1975*, cat. no. 4107.0, ABS, Canberra.

——2004. *National Aboriginal and Torres Strait Islander Social Survey 2002*, cat. no. 4714.0, ABS, Canberra.

—— 2008a. *Australian Standard Geographical Classification (ASGC), Jul 2008*, cat. no. 1216.0, ABS, Canberra.

—— 2008b. National Aboriginal and Torres Strait Islander Social Survey 2008, Expanded Confidentialised Unit Record Files (CURF), Remote Access Data Laboratory (RADL), ABS, Canberra.

—— 2009a. *Experimental Estimates and Projections, Aboriginal and Torres Strait Islander Australians, 1991 to 2021*, cat. no. 3238.0, ABS, Canberra.

—— 2009b. 'Glossary', *National Aboriginal and Torres Strait Islander Social Survey, 2008*, cat. no. 4714.0, ABS, Canberra.

—— 2010. *National Aboriginal and Torres Strait Islander Social Survey: Users' Guide, 2008*, cat. no. 4720.0, ABS, Canberra.

—— 2011a. *Australian Demographic Statistics*, cat. no. 3101.0, ABS, Canberra.

—— 2011b. *Methodological Review of Counting the Homeless, 2006*, Discussion Paper, cat. no. 2050.0.55.001, ABS, Canberra.

Australian Institute of Health and Welfare (AIHW) 2005. *Indigenous Housing Needs 2005 A Multi-Measure Needs Model*, cat. no. HOU 129 AIHW, Canberra.

Batten, D. C. 1999. 'The Mismatch Argument: The construction of a housing orthodoxy in Australia', *Urban Studies*, 36 (1): 137–51.

Bell, M. and Taylor, J. 2004. 'Conclusion: Emerging research themes', in J. Taylor and M. Bell (eds), *Population Mobility and Indigenous Peoples in Australasia and North America*, Routledge, London.

Birdsall-Jones, C. 2007. 'Living with your relations: An Australian Aboriginal solution to household overcrowding', Unpublished manuscript.

—— and Corunna, V. 2008. *The Housing Careers of Indigenous Urban Households*, AHURI Final Report No. 112, AHURI, Melbourne.

——, Corunna, V., Turner, N., Smart, G. and Shaw, W. 2010. *Indigenous Homelessness*, Final Report No. 143, AHURI, Melbourne.

Canadian Mortgage and Housing Corporation 1991. *Core Housing Need in Canada*, Canada Mortgage and Housing Corporation, Ottawa.

Chamberlain, C. and MacKenzie, D. 2008. *Counting the Homeless 2006*, cat. no. 2050.0, ABS, Canberra.

Council of Australian Governments (COAG) 2009. National Affordable Housing Factsheet, viewed 27 January 2011, available at <www.coag.gov.au/coag_meeting_outcomes/2008-11-29/docs/20081129_national_affordable_housing_factsheet.pdf>

Department of Families, Housing, Community Services and Indigenous Affairs (FaHCSIA) 2007. *National Indigenous Housing Guide: Improving the Living Environment for Safety, Health and Sustainability*, FaHCSIA, Canberra.

Fantin, S. 2003. 'Yolngu cultural imperatives and housing design: Ramaru, Mirriri and Galka', in P. Memmott (ed.), *Take 2: Housing Design in Indigenous Australia*, Royal Australian Institute of Architects, Red Hill, ACT.

Gifford, R. 2007. *Environmental Psychology: Principles and Practices*, Optimal Books, Canada.

Horspool, N. and Mowle, J. 2011. 'Using the ABS Census of Population and Housing to compile estimates of Australia's homeless', in *Conference Proceedings of the 5th Australasian Housing Researchers Conference*, The University of Auckland, Auckland.

Jones, R. 1991. *The Housing Need of Indigenous Australians, 1991*, CAEPR Research Monograph No. 8, CAEPR, ANU, Canberra.

Long, S., Memmott, P. and Seelig, T. 2007. *An Audit and Review of Australian Indigenous Housing Research*, Final Report No. 102 for AHURI Queensland Research Centre, St Lucia.

Memmott, P. 1991. *Humpy, House and Tin Shed: Aboriginal Settlement History on the Darling River*, Ian Buchan Fell Research Centre, Department of Architecture, University of Sydney, Sydney.

——, Long, S., Fantin, S. and Eckermann, K. 2000. 'Post occupancy evaluation of Aboriginal housing in the N.T. for IHANT: Social response component', in P. Fletcher and D. Bridgman (eds), *Living Spaces: An Evaluation of Housing in Remote Aboriginal Communities*, The Architects Studio Pty Ltd, Darwin.

—— 2003. 'Customary Aboriginal behaviour patterns and housing design' in P. Memmott (ed.), *Take 2: Housing Design in Indigenous Australia*, Royal Australian Institute of Architects, Red Hill, ACT.

——, Birdsall-Jones, C., Go-Sam, C., Greenop, K. and Corunna, V. 2011. 'Modelling crowding in Aboriginal Australia', Positioning Paper for AHURI, Melbourne.

——, Long, S. and Chambers, C. 2003. *A National Analysis of Strategies Used to Respond to Indigenous Itinerants and Public Place Dwellers*, FaHCSIA, Canberra.

——, Long, S. and Thomson, L. 2006. *Indigenous Mobility in Rural and Remote Australia*, Final Report No. 090, AHURI Queensland Research Centre, St Lucia, viewed 11 April 2006, available at <www.ahuri.edu. au/global/docs/doc976.pdf,>

Morphy, F. 2007. 'Mobility and its consequences: The 2006 enumeration in the north-east Arnhem Land region', in F. Morphy (ed.), *Agency, Contingency and Census Process: Observations of the 2006 Indigenous Enumeration Strategy in Remote Aboriginal Australia*, CAEPR Research Monograph No. 28, ANU E Press, Canberra.

Musharbash, Y. 2003. Warlpiri Sociality: An Ethnography of the Spatial and Temporal Dimensions of Everyday Life in a Central Australian Aboriginal Settlement, PhD Thesis, ANU, Canberra.

—— 2008. *Yuendumu Everyday*, Aboriginal Studies Press, Canberra.

National Housing Strategy 1992. *Housing Location and Access to Services*, Issues Paper No. 5, Department of Health, Housing and Community Services, Canberra.

Neutze, M.G. 1977. *Urban Development in Australia: A Descriptive Analysis*, Allen and Unwin, Sydney.

Pholeros, P., Rainow, S. and Torzillo, P. 1993. *Housing for Health: Towards a Healthy Living Environment for Aboriginal Australia*, Healthabitat, Newport Beach, NSW.

Rapoport, A. 1976. 'Toward a redefinition of density', in S. Saegert (ed.), *Crowding in Real Environments*, Sage Publications, California.

Sanders, W. and Holcombe, S. 2006. 'The Ti Tree Creek Camp Study: Reports to Anmatjere Community Government Council', *Case Study Report N.o 1*, Indigenous Community Governance Project, CAEPR, ANU, Canberra, viewed 16 July 2012, available at <http://caepr.anu.edu.au/sites/default/files/cck_misc_documents/2010/06/Reports_toACGCCreekCamp_2006.pdf>

Statistics New Zealand 2003. 'What is the extent of crowding in New Zealand? An analysis of crowding in New Zealand households 1986–2001', *Statistics New Zealand*, Wellington.

—— 2011. Indicator 2c: American Crowding Index: People Per Room, viewed 28 January 2011, available at

Steering Committee for the Review of Government Service Provision (SCRGSP) 2009. *National Agreement Performance Information 2008-09: National Affordable Housing Agreement*, Productivity Commission, Canberra.

13. Do traditional culture and identity promote the wellbeing of Indigenous Australians? Evidence from the 2008 NATSISS

Alfred Michael Dockery

This chapter reports results from one of several ongoing avenues of investigation into the relationship between Indigenous Australians' attachment to traditional culture and their socioeconomic outcomes and wellbeing. In an analysis of the Australian Bureau of Statistics (ABS) 2002 National Aboriginal and Torres Strait Islander Social Survey (NATSISS), Dockery (2010a) presented evidence that Indigenous people with stronger attachment to their culture fare better on a range of outcomes: self-assessed health, substance abuse, incidence of arrest, employment and educational attainment. Motivating this analysis was an attempt to reconsider the enduring debate between the two predominant and opposing schools of thought on how best to address relations between the Indigenous Australian peoples and what has become 'mainstream' society: self-determination versus assimilation. This has been fought out primarily as a normative debate, with different camps offering their views on what should improve the wellbeing of Indigenous Australians. It is also a debate that has been largely premised on the assumption that elements of traditional Indigenous culture are incompatible with the achievement of socioeconomic outcomes valued in mainstream society. Even those who argue for the right of Indigenous people to maintain traditional culture and lifestyles often present this choice as a trade-off with socioeconomic outcomes valued in the mainstream, but as a legitimate choice for Indigenous people to make.

Contrary to this assumption, evidence from the 2002 NATSISS suggests cultural attachment is instead associated with improved socioeconomic outcomes. Stressing that improving wellbeing should be the objective of Indigenous policy, Dockery (2010a) therefore argued that Indigenous culture should be maintained and leveraged as a part of the solution to Indigenous disadvantage, rather than being seen as part of the problem. However, a number of limitations to that analysis need to be acknowledged, and the role of culture in shaping Indigenous socioeconomic outcomes and wellbeing remains a critically under-researched area. Important among those limitations are the following.

First, no explicit channel though which cultural attachment impacts upon outcomes was specified. As the positive effects of culture seemed to extend across a range of life domains, my conjecture is that cultural attachment must impact upon underlying factors intrinsic to wellbeing, such as self-esteem, self-efficacy or self-identity, as possible mechanisms (Dockery 2010a: 330). This lack of a theoretical framework compounds the challenge of 'reverse causality' in the regression results – that it is the achievement of superior socioeconomic outcomes that then leads or empowers people to engage with their culture.

Second, 'culture' or 'cultural attachment' was measured using a single construct derived from factor analysis. In reality, culture is likely to be a multidimensional construct, comprising of a rich tapestry of constituent elements.

Third, there were in fact no direct measures of wellbeing collected in the 2002 NATSISS. The outcome indicators analysed were chosen for their correspondence to widespread media reports of dysfunction in Indigenous communities at the time: poor health, substance abuse, lawlessness, truancy and joblessness. Measuring 'wellbeing' based on mainstream indicators, however, sits uneasily at a conceptual level with the definition of culture adopted, which is based on differences in values and preferences; in much the same way as a tension exists between the spirit of self-determination and the pursuit of statistical equity as implied in the 'Closing the Gap' agenda. What is required is an outcome measure that reflects Indigenous people's own values and preferences. Potentially, measures of 'subjective wellbeing', often based on ratings of life satisfaction or happiness, and in which Indigenous people themselves assess their wellbeing, would meet this criterion. No such measures were collected in the 2002 NATSISS, but a measure of subjective wellbeing and others relating to mental and psychological health are available in the 2008 NATSISS.

In seeking to address these outstanding issues, this paper explores the relationship between culture and subjective wellbeing for Indigenous Australians. The following section provides a brief review of the literature on the links between attachment to traditional indigenous cultures and wellbeing, which comes primarily from other nations in which those cultures are faced with the challenges of persisting alongside a dominant Western economy. The third section then expands on the different elements that appear to capture 'cultural attachment' using a factor analysis of data from the 2008 NATSISS relating to culture. Both the literature review and factor analysis suggest a vital role of self-identity as a mediator between cultural attachment and subjective wellbeing. This is tested and confirmed in the fourth section, in which the relationships between aspects of cultural attachment and indicators of wellbeing are modeled. The concluding section canvasses some policy implications of the findings.

Culture and socioeconomic outcomes

Cultures are, of course, many and varied. At the same time, almost every aspect of human behavior could be deemed to have some cultural dimension to it. At an abstract level, any one definition of culture will never be sufficient for the purposes of all those interested in 'culture'. For an understanding of culture in the context intended here, which relates specifically to indigenous cultures and their persistence within a 'mainstream' culture, a workable definition is that offered by Guiso, Sapienza and Zingales (2006: 2):

> ... we define culture as those customary beliefs and values that ethnic, religious, and social groups transmit fairly unchanged from generation to generation.

with the added qualification that these beliefs, customs and values are likely to be characterised by unique symbols, text and language that in themselves play a role in distinguishing the group's distinctive identity (Throsby 2001).

A small literature exists in economics relating differences in culture at the individual (micro) level, and societal (macro) level, to social and economic outcomes. In this literature, culture has been largely defined on the basis of nation states, ethnicity or religious denomination. A general deficiency, as highlighted by Guiso, Sapienza and Zingales (2006), is that few studies explicitly state the causal mechanisms through which culture is thought to impact upon outcomes. More often, observed differences in outcomes between countries, races or religious denominations are ex poste labeled as 'cultural' differences. Where attempts have been made to construct cultural explanations for differences in outcomes between groups, these have largely followed the spirit of defining culture in terms of differences in beliefs and preferences (or values). For example, Jews being thought to have a relatively strong preference for education and Confucian values promoting growth and entrepreneurship. For empirical work the testing of a priori hypotheses based on a theory of how culture is thought to impact upon outcomes is clearly preferable to ex poste explanations.

A more detailed consideration of the meaning of culture and reviews of the literature relating culture to economic outcomes can be found in Guiso, Sapienza and Zingales (2006) and Dockery (2010a), and a specific discussion of the relationship between Indigenous culture and educational outcomes in Australia in Dockery (2009). This review does not go over that same ground, and focuses only on how cultural attachment may impact upon outcomes in the context of disadvantaged indigenous populations. The pervading theme of that literature is the importance of culture in strengthening one's sense of self-identity as the main mechanism through which cultural attachment enhances life outcomes, or the 'enculturation hypothesis'. According to Wexler (2009: 267), who cites in support a number of studies relating to Indigenous youth in North America, '… studies have consistently found robust correlations between positive affiliation and engagement with their culture and Indigenous young people's wellbeing and resilience'.

Zimmerman et al. (1994) define enculturation as '… the process by which individuals learn about and identify with their traditional ethnic culture' (1994: 199) and '… an affirmation of one's heritage rather than a focus on fitting into the majority culture', which contrasts with acculturation, 'a process by which an ethnic minority assimilates to the majority culture.' (1994: 201). From a factor analysis of a small survey of Native American youth, they identify cultural affinity (pride and interest in traditional culture), family activities and Native American identity as components of enculturation. Some evidence is found that cultural affinity promotes self-esteem; and that cultural identity combined with high self-esteem is a protective factor against alcohol and substance use, while cultural identity combined with low self-esteem is associated with higher risk of alcohol and substance abuse. Whitbeck et al. (2004) also find that enculturation guards against alcoholism among Native American Indians. Enculturation, they argue, provides resilience by preventing individuals from internalising stress associated with historical loss and trauma.

Perhaps the most important evidence on the effect of culture and the critical intermediary role of self-identity comes from the excellent work of developmental psychologist Professor Michael Chandler and colleagues. While Chandler's most relevant work here relates to suicide rates among Canadian youth, the findings suggest a much more general, or intrinsic, role of a sense of persistence of the self in the psychological wellbeing of human kind, indigenous and non-indigenous alike, and has its parallels at the community level (Chandler et al. 2003). A causal mechanism through which cultural attachment is believed to impact upon the outcome is clearly defined, a priori: cultural identification and preservation promotes a strong sense of persistence of self-identity through time, which in turn guards against suicide. This causal link between culture, identity and suicide is well grounded in psychological theory and backed by empirical evidence. In the space available here it is not possible to do justice to this body of research and the philosophy underpinning it. Briefly, it studies the ways in which individuals deal with the paradox of facing inevitable change through time and yet also persisting as the same person through time. Working with Canadian youth, Chandler et al. (2003) classified the strategies young people employ to understand themselves as being the same individual through time. At an individual level, they find a stark inverse relationship between suicide risk and the strength or sophistication of young peoples' understanding of their self-persistence.

When they began working with Canadian Aboriginal youth, for whom suicide rates are far higher, they found the same result, albeit with Aboriginal youth adopting different 'narrative' interpretations of their persistence as the same person through time. They argue that suicide rates are higher among Aboriginal youth because they are at greater risk of losing '… the thread that tethers together their past, present and future …' (Chandler et al. 2003: 2) and of losing a sense of control over their future outcomes. Indigenous cultures in Canada, as elsewhere, have suffered the undermining of their cultural norms and values, face an uncertain future and have lost empowerment over that future. As Chandler et al. (2003: 63) hypothesise '…continuity problems that work to undermine commitments to the future at all of these levels are jointly at work, not just in the lives of individual young persons but at the level of whole cultures.'

This hypothesis is borne out by evidence at the community level. While youth suicide rates are markedly higher for Indigenous youth, there is also considerable variation in youth suicide rates between Aboriginal communities in British Columbia; indeed many communities had very low rates or no youth suicides recorded in the period analysed. Those communities for which there is evidence of greater commitment to cultural continuity – in preserving a shared past and creating a collective future – are found to have significantly lower rates of youth suicide. The clear implication is that cultural continuity at the community level helps the young members of that community to develop a stronger sense of persistence of their self identity through time. Viewed another way, cultural continuity at the community level helps to safeguard against young people losing their own sense of self persistence. In later work, Hallett, Chandler and Lalonde (2007) find that the proportion of people who are fluent in an Indigenous language is a strong marker of cultural persistence within communities and strong predictor of youth suicide rates.

In addition to guarding against suicide, the importance of a strong sense of persistence of self-identity is likely to apply to other activities representing 'investments' in the future, such as education, health, a career, relationships with family and community; and the impact of losing that sense of self continuity is likely to transcend into adulthood. Chandler et al. (2003: 50) speak of the '… expectation that young people who somehow lose the thread of their own and others' personal continuity in time will also behave in ways that show a lack of appropriate care and concern for their own future well-being'. Indeed, they are now collecting data on other indicators that they expect to be sensitive to cultural continuity, nominating school completion rates and academic achievement as two such variables.

Relatively few studies have specifically explored the links between culture and subjective wellbeing. These also generally take the view that attachment to, or identification with, a particular culture can be a source of enhancement of wellbeing for minority and indigenous peoples (see Akerlof and Kranton 2010; as well as Ratzlaff et al. 2000; Suh 2000; and other contributions in Diener and Suh 2000). However, Ratzlaff et al.'s (2000: 55) findings also point to the possibility that identification with minority cultures can lead to 'cultural inconsistencies' in values, and some coping strategies that individuals adopt to deal with these inconsistencies can result in reduced subjective wellbeing.

Defining and measuring culture

As noted, Dockery (2010a) relied on a factor analysis of selected questions relating to culture contained in the 2002 NATSISS. A single measure was generated from the dominant factor, potentially overlooking the fact that culture is a rich concept and likely to be multi-dimensional. To explore the additional dimensions of culture, factor analysis was applied to data from questions contained in the language and culture section of the 2008 NATSISS, with the analysis restricted to persons aged 15 and over. Not all the items relating to culture in the 2008 NATSISS are the same as those contained in the 2002 data. Some significant new questions asked are the frequency with which individuals attend cultural events and the importance they attach to attending cultural events. Appendix 13A Table 13A.1 presents the list of variables included in the factor analysis along with their weighted mean value. As with the 2002 data, there is one dominant factor with a high Eigenvalue. However three other factors returned Eigenvalues of greater than 1 and, following that rule of thumb, these are retained for analysis (see Table 13.1).

The loadings in the rotated coefficient matrix provide four readily interpretable factors, or elements of cultural attachment – henceforth termed participation, identification, language and traditional economic activities (or just 'traditional activities'). Two points to note are that each individual element fits comfortably within our definition of 'culture' as relating to unique values and preferences of Indigenous Australians that may be characterised by unique symbols, text or language. Second, the identity factor – which is most strongly associated with recognising homelands, identifying with a clan, tribal or language group, and how important it is to the individual to attend cultural events – is clearly a close parallel to the concept of self-identity described in the literature as being important to Indigenous wellbeing, and to wellbeing more broadly.

Table 13.1 Rotated factor pattern, cultural variables, Indigenous Australia, 2008[a]

Cultural dimension[b]	Factor 1 Participation	Factor 2 Identity	Factor 3 Language	Factor 4 Traditional activities
Cultural events attended: festival	0.687	0.184	0.035	0.045
Participated in cult. activities: story telling	0.638	0.121	0.139	0.155
Participated in cult. activities: performance	0.629	−0.007	0.209	0.126
Cultural events attended: Aboriginal organisation	0.628	0.284	−0.159	−0.049
Participated in cult. activities: art/craft	0.625	0.104	0.044	0.131
Cultural events attended: ceremonies	0.542	0.147	0.367	0.103
Cultural events attended: NAIDOC week	0.489	0.437	−0.252	−0.078
Recognises homelands or traditional country	0.037	0.784	0.145	0.081
Identifies with clan, tribal or language group	0.159	0.765	0.199	0.026
Importance of attending cult. events	0.363	0.640	0.098	0.221
How often attends cult. events	0.408	0.510	0.094	0.398
Speaks an Indigenous language at home	0.048	0.118	0.884	0.075
Speaks an Indigenous language	0.134	0.197	0.847	0.122
Participated in cult. activities: fish	0.038	0.101	−0.090	0.839
Participated in cult. activities: hunt	0.119	0.117	0.400	0.691
Participated in cult. activities: gathering	0.417	0.058	0.330	0.507
Eigenvalue	5.048	1.896	1.257	1.127

a. Derived using SAS Factor Procedure with the principal components and varimax rotation options. Based on responses from 7 823 Indigenous persons aged 15 and over.

b. Questions on attendance at cultural events and participation in cultural activities relate to the past 12 months.

NAIDOC = National Aborigines and Islanders Day Observance Committee

Source: Author's customised calculations using the 2008 NATSISS, accessed using the Remote Access Data Laboratory (RADL)

To empirically explore the associations between these dimensions of cultural attachment and wellbeing, the standardised scoring coefficients generated from the factor analysis are used to calculate a score for each individual on each of these four dimensions. However, previous research has indicated that the effect of cultural attachment may vary according to context. Specifically, the impact of culture may vary according to whether the individual lives in remote or non-remote areas and, just as significantly, outcome measures may also vary by remoteness. Most obviously, Indigenous Australians living in very remote areas are likely to face lower employment opportunity and have limited access to services in areas such as health and education. Further, the effects of cultural attachment upon outcome variables may not be linear. Dockery (2010a) hypothesised that Indigenous people with low cultural attachment and those with high cultural attachment may experience better outcomes than those with intermediate levels of cultural attachment.

To compare cultural engagement between Indigenous people living in remote and non-remote areas, each factor is standardised to have a mean of zero and standard deviation of 1. Table 13.2 shows that, as expected, cultural attachment varies substantially between the two populations. While there are no significant differences in the remote and non-remote factor scores for participation, those in remote areas have, on average, significantly higher scores in terms of identification, language and engagement in traditional activities. Given this variation, coupled with likely variation in outcomes by remoteness, a major limitation of the 2008 NATSISS confidentialised unit record file (CURF) is that remoteness is categorised into two only levels. In contrast, the initial release of the CURF for the 2002 NATSISS allowed separate identification of those in major cities, inner regional areas, outer regional areas and those in remote/very remote areas. Including Indigenous persons residing in major cities along with those residing in outer regional areas in the one category is most certain to be problematic, though it is possible to further differentiate by geography within some States.

Table 13.2 Standardised cultural factor scores: Mean score for Indigenous people in remote and non-remote areas, Indigenous Australia, 2008[a]

Cultural factor	Mean Non-remote	Mean Remote	T-test (remote v. non-remote)
Participation	−0.03	−0.02	p = 0.71
Identity	−0.15	0.24	p < 0.0001
Language	−0.37	0.80	p < 0.0001
Traditional activities	−0.13	0.39	p < 0.0001
Observations	5 188	2 635	

a. The mean is calculated using ABS-provided person weights.

Source: Author's customised calculations using the 2008 NATSISS (accessed using the RADL)

In relation to each of these factors, individuals were categorised as having strong, moderate, weak or minimal cultural attachment depending upon the quartile of their factor score. The quartiles are specific to their geography so that, for example, an Indigenous person living in a non-remote area would be classified as having 'strong' identity if their factor score is in the top 25 per cent of people living in non-remote areas. Four dummy variables are generated for each factor to allow for non-linear effects in the modeling.

The effect of culture on wellbeing: Empirical estimates

The most straight forward measure of subjective wellbeing available in the 2008 NATSISS comes from a question 'In the last four weeks, how often have you been a happy person?', to which respondents could choose from a set of five options: 'all of the time', 'most of the time', 'some of the time', 'a little of the time' or 'none of the time'. There are however, a range of other indicators of potential interest, including the items making up the Kessler 5-item scale of psychological stress and questions that contribute to the SF-36 measures of mental health and vitality.

To assess the relationship between elements of cultural attachment and wellbeing, multivariate regression models are estimated, with dummy variables representing the quartiles of the cultural factor scores included among the explanatory variables. The number of other explanatory variables is restricted to those that can reasonably be considered 'exogenous' to the relationship being studied between culture and the outcome variable: gender, age, remoteness, marital status, and having experienced removal of, or from, natural families. This is because the main interest is in the 'gross' relationship between culture and the dependent variables, not the residual effect after controlling for potentially mediating variables. As an example, one could include financial prosperity as an explanatory variable, but to the extent that cultural attachment may influence financial prosperity, we want this full effect to be captured in the coefficients on the cultural variables. The analysis of such transmission pathways is left as a matter for future investigation.

Before discussing the results for subjective wellbeing, it is of interest to check if the findings of positive effects of culture on 'mainstream' indicators based on the 2002 NATSISS data (Dockery 2010a) are confirmed by the 2008 data. Results for models estimating the probability of reporting good or very good health, of having completed high school, of being employed, of ever having been formally charged by police and of having consumed a level of alcohol deemed to be risky in the past two weeks are presented in Appendix 13A Table A13.2. For simplicity, these are all specified as binary logit models and the odds ratios reported. Hence, for example, the odds ratio of 1.27 for being married in the model of self-assessed health indicates that married persons are 27 per cent more likely to report being in good health, while the odds ratio of 0.76 in the model for having been charged indicates married persons are 24 per cent less likely to have been charged by police.

The broad picture confirms the previous findings that Indigenous peoples' stronger attachment to, or engagement with, their traditional culture is associated with more favourable socioeconomic outcomes. It is now possible to also look at the different dimensions of cultural attachment and, consistent with the international literature, a significant independent role of cultural identity is apparent in some models. Positive associations are most apparent with participation in cultural events and activities. This is to be expected as this association is most likely to arise due to either reverse causation or omitted variable bias; that is, those with more positive social economic outcomes are already more inclined to engage in their culture. While it could not be claimed that the estimates for the cultural identity factor are completely unaffected by such endogeneity, it can certainly be argued that they are not as susceptible to this challenge. The two main contributing items of recognising homelands or traditional country, and identifying with a clan or language group, can be expected to be relatively permanent traits rather than ones that fluctuate with health status, labour force status or other outcomes. These results suggest that stronger cultural identity is associated with higher educational attainment and a higher probability of being employed. Speaking an Indigenous language is associated with markedly superior health, and a lower likelihood of abusing alcohol or of being charged, but appears to create barriers to employment. The positive association between speaking Indigenous languages and health may relate to the effectiveness of intergenerational communication of traditional knowledge and values associated with health. Participation in traditional economic activities is the one cultural dimension that seems to be associated with inferior outcomes, notably in terms of education and the chances of being arrested or risky consumption of alcohol.

To reiterate, because of the coarse classification of geographical location into only remote and non-remote, these positive associations with traditional culture can confidently be expected to be understated (and the negative associations overstated). Another important, if unsurprising point to take from these results is the legacy of policies of forced removal of Indigenous children from their natural families. The definition for removal from natural family applied is all those who were themselves removed, or who had parents, grandparents/great-grandparents or siblings separated from their natural families. Although no significant impact on educational attainment is observed, those from the Stolen Generation, defined in this way, are around 50 per cent more likely to have been charged by police, 30 per cent less likely to report being in good health, 15 per cent more likely to consume alcohol at risky levels and 10 per cent less likely to be employed.

Table 13.3 Wellbeing indicators: Regression results, Indigenous Australia, 2008

Parameter	Often been happy? (ordered probit)		Mental health (OLS)		Psychological stress (logit model)	
	Coeff.	Sign.	Coeff.	Sign.	Odds ratio	Sign.
Intercept[a]			12.83	***	n.a.	
Remote	0.38	***	1.37	***	0.98	
Male	0.07	***	0.67	***	0.65	***
Married	0.11	***	0.36	***	0.74	***
Age: 15–19 years	0.17	***	0.96	***	0.86	*
20–24 years	0.12	**	0.38	***	1.05	
25–34 years	—		—		—	
35–44 years	-0.05		-0.30	**	1.04	
45–54 years	-0.11	***	-0.64	***	1.09	
55–59 years	-0.05		-0.77	***	1.05	
60–64 years	0.07		-0.52	**	0.83	
65 years and over	0.23	***	-0.17		0.48	***
Removal from natural family	-0.15	***	-0.57	***	1.38	***
Cultural participation: Strong	0.07	**	0.34	***	0.97	
Moderate	0.07	*	0.25	**	0.80	***
Weak	-0.02		0.00		0.92	
Minimal	—		—		—	
Cultural Identity: Strong	0.13	***	0.57	***	1.14	
Moderate	0.06		0.30	**	1.11	
Weak	0.03		0.12		1.24	***
Minimal	—		—		—	
Language Strong	0.12	***	0.41	***	1.14	*
Moderate	0.02		0.18		1.11	
Weak	0.04		0.19		0.95	
Minimal	—		—		—	
Traditional activities: Strong	0.10	***	0.43	***	1.10	
Moderate	0.01		0.10		1.18	**
Weak	0.00		0.04		1.14	*
Minimal	—		—		—	
Observations	7 538		7 524		7 523	
Likelihood ratio					233	***
Adjusted R-sq			0.075			
F-test			26.34	***		

a. Four intercept terms for the probit model not reported.

***, ** and * denote significance at the 1%, 5% and 10% level, respectively.

Source: Author's customised calculations using the 2008 NATSISS (accessed using the RADL)

Turning now to social and emotional wellbeing, three measures are investigated. One of these, the question on happiness, corresponds well to questions typically asked in the subjective wellbeing literature and, importantly, does solicit the individual's assessment of the extent to which they are leading a happy life. The other indicators investigated are the Kessler scale of psychological stress and the SF-36 items relating to mental health and vitality (of which the happiness question is one). These are constructs which can be expected to correlate with subjective wellbeing, but to my knowledge only a modified version of the Kessler scale has been validated among samples of Indigenous Australians (see Dingwall and Cairney 2010: 25). For the single happiness item, an ordered probit model is fitted which estimates the effect of each variable on the likelihood of the individual reporting they were happy more of the time, so a positive coefficient indicates a movement up the scale ranging from 'none of the time' to 'all of the time'. The happiness item is one of four items used from the SF-36: how often in the past four weeks have you felt calm and peaceful and how often you felt happy contribute to the SF-36 measure of mental health; while how often you felt full of life and had a lot of energy contribute to the SF-36 measure of vitality. Here the four measures are incorporated into a single mental health/vitality measure simply by summing the four items, producing a scale ranging from 1 to 20. A simple linear regression model is fitted so that a positive coefficient indicates that increases in the variable are associated with better mental health. The coefficients appear small, but this variable is tightly clustered, with 60 per cent of the sample scoring between 13 and 18, inclusive. Finally, five items from the Kessler 10 instrument have been included, relating to feelings of nervousness, hopelessness, restlessness, that everything is an effort and sadness. Based on these, a binary variable of high/very high psychological stress and low/moderate psychological stress is provided on the NATSISS CURF. A logit model of the probability of exhibiting high/very high psychological stress is estimated, and the odds ratios presented in the final model reported in Table 13.3.

In general the results conform to expectations drawn from the previous literature. Empirical work has consistently found married people to report higher subjective wellbeing than unmarried persons. Here we find Indigenous people who are married report being happier, have better mental health/vitality more generally and are markedly less prone to psychological stress. Indigenous people in remote areas are much happier and report better mental health. While this is consistent with some other evidence of better health among Indigenous people in remote areas, Sibthorpe, Anderson and Cunningham (2001) have noted possible measurement bias in self-assessed health reports for Indigenous Australians whose first language is not English, and this will most often be the case in remote Australia. Males display slightly greater happiness and general mental health, and are around 35 per cent less likely to be classified as having a high level of psychological stress.

There is strong evidence that the socioeconomic disadvantage of persons of the Stolen Generation has its foundations in the impact of those experiences upon psychological wellbeing. Studies of Native American peoples have associated past policies of forced acculturation and 'ethnic cleansing' with intergenerational trauma similar to that observed among descendents of Holocaust survivors and war veterans, with symptoms such as depression and post-traumatic stress disorder attributed to the genocide of American Indians (Whitbeck et al. 2004: 410). Here it is clear that persons who report having experienced removal themselves or of their direct family are less happy, have lower general mental health and vitality and are 38 per cent more likely to display high psychological stress on the Kessler scale. In each case, the magnitude of these effects is larger than the positive effects of being married as opposed to unmarried, a factor known to have a very substantive effect on psychological wellbeing and its maintenance.

So, what of the effects of culture on wellbeing? There is some evidence of greater participation in cultural events and activities being associated with better mental wellbeing, and to a lesser degree greater happiness, though causation could run either way, or both ways. Engaging in traditional economic activities, such as hunting, fishing and gathering, also promotes wellbeing, but those who score in the middle quartiles on this factor appear to experience greater psychological stress.

The most pronounced effects relate to the identity-dimension of cultural attachment, but the initial picture is somewhat unclear. Strong identification with Indigenous culture is associated with greater regularity of feeling happy and better mental health and vitality more generally. However, having 'weak' cultural identity (relative to minimal) is also associated with more psychological stress. Those with moderate and strong cultural identity are also estimated to experience higher psychological stress than those with minimal identification with their culture, although these effects just fail to gain significance at the 10% level. The use of Indigenous languages similarly enhances happiness and mental health while simultaneously incurring psychological stress. These results are reminiscent of Trudgen's (2000) vivid account of the stress, confusion and ambiguity experienced by Indigenous people trying to 'live between two cultures', and clinging to a cultural identity and worldview in the face of a dominant culture. However, it is at odds with much of the international findings that a factor measuring strength of cultural identity and knowledge of Indigenous languages should be associated with higher psychological stress. Recall that Chandler (2000) found that a strong sense of persistence of self-identity was a critical protective factor against youth suicide, and that the maintenance of traditional languages was an effective marker of such persistence. However, a strong sense of self-identity is not the same thing as a strong sense of persistence of that self-identity through time – those who do strongly identify with Indigenous culture may also suffer psychologically from doubts over the survival of that culture, and what their role would be should their connection with that culture be severed.

To explore this finding further, the models reported in Table 13.3 were estimated separately for the remote and non-remote samples. The positive effects of cultural identity, fluency in Indigenous languages and undertaking traditional economic activities upon happiness and mental health are found to accrue primarily in remote areas. The associations between cultural identity and engagement in traditional activities with greater psychological stress, however, appear to apply only in non-remote contexts. Of course, it is in non-remote areas that Indigenous people will most experience the tensions of living between cultures. A further hypothesis warranting investigation is that Indigenous Australians with a stronger sense of cultural identity experience greater psychological stress because they also experience, or perceive themselves to experience, more discrimination. While detailed data were collected in the 2008 NATSISS on feelings of discrimination, providing many possibilities for further investigation in this area, only a simple question on whether or not the respondent felt discriminated against in the past 12 months is used here.

Evidence of the degree of compromise Indigenous people face when trying to maintain their own cultural identity while coexisting with another, dominant culture can be seen in Fig. 13.1. Overall, 27.6 per cent of Indigenous people reported having experienced discrimination, and this figure was virtually identical in remote and non-remote areas. However, Fig. 13.1 shows these proportions across the quartiles of the cultural identity factor scores. In remote areas, a stronger sense of identity with traditional culture does not lead to any greater experiences of discrimination. In contrast, for Indigenous persons living in non-remote areas, it is clear that feelings of discrimination increase directly with the strength of one's cultural identity. In non-remote areas, those scoring in the top quartile of the cultural identity measure are four times more likely to report having experienced discrimination in the past 12 months than those in the bottom quartile.

Table 13.4 reports the results of models which more formally test the role of perceived discrimination in shaping the relationship between cultural attachment and psychological stress. As the association between cultural identity and psychological stress holds only in non-remote areas, the analysis is restricted to persons in these areas. The model for psychological stress from

Table 13.3 is reproduced as Model 1 of Table 13.4, but with the sample now restricted to non-remote areas. In the interests of parsimony, the coefficients on demographic background variables are suppressed, but these variables were included in the estimation. Relative to Indigenous people with the lowest level of cultural identity, individuals with strong and moderate cultural identity are estimated to be around 25 per cent more likely to be in high or very high psychological stress (significant at the 10% level), and those with weak cultural attachment around one-third higher (highly significant).

A simple dummy variable capturing whether or not the respondent felt discriminated against in the past 12 months is then added (Model 2). Experiencing discrimination has a dramatic correlation with psychological stress, with those who experienced feelings of discrimination being twice as likely to be classified as having high or very high levels of psychological stress. It must be stressed that the subjective construction of both these variables means that this relationship must be interpreted with caution – other individual effects are likely to impact upon both measures. This variable accounts for much of the observed higher psychological stress for those with stronger cultural identity. There are now no significant differences in the likelihood of psychological stress between those with high or moderate levels of cultural identity when compared to those with minimal cultural identity. It is those in the second bottom quartile on this measure with the highest level of stress. The higher psychological stress associated with stronger cultural identification therefore appears to be a result of those identifying more strongly with Indigenous culture also being more likely to feel they have been victims of discrimination, as was highlighted in Fig. 13.1. This interpretation is consistent with previous findings by Paradies and Cunningham (2009) based on data from the Darwin Region Urban Indigenous Diabeties study. Using a measure to capture Indigenous experiences of racism, Paradies and Cunningham (2009: 562, 567) find that those who identify more strongly with their culture (as indicated by recognition of homelands/traditional country, identification with a clan, tribal or language group or identifying as a member of the Stolen Generation) are not only more likely to report experiences of racism, but are also more likely to report negative emotional reactions in response to those experiences.

In contrast, Whitbeck et al. (2004) find evidence that 'enculturation' provides resilience by preventing individuals from internalising stresses associated with trauma. To test whether a strong sense of cultural identity has a 'protective' effect that mitigates the negative impacts of perceived discrimination, Model 3 includes interaction terms between the identity measures and the discrimination dummy. However, no evidence of a protective effect is found – the estimated effect of experiencing feelings of discrimination is to roughly double the chance of being in psychological stress irrespective of the strength of one's cultural identity. In a review of studies of personal strategies for coping with racism, Brondolo et al. (2009) nominate 'racial identity development' as one of three major forms of coping. However, as with the results here, they do not find strong evidence from the empirical literature of identity acting as a buffer against race-related stress (Brondolo et al. 2009: 74).

Fig. 13.1 Proportion of Indigenous people reporting experiencing discrimination in past 12 months, by remoteness and strength of cultural identity, Australia, 2008

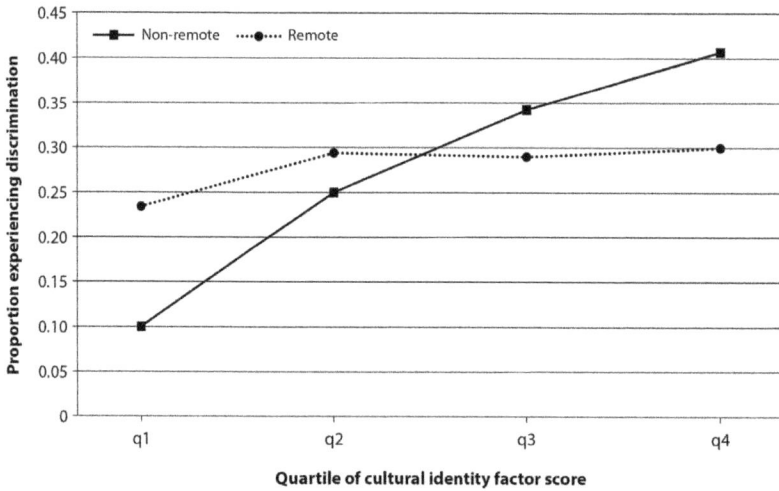

Source: Author's customised calculations using the 2008 NATSISS (accessed using the RADL)

Table 13.4 Psychological stress: Logistic regression results controlling for discrimination, Indigenous people living in non-remote areas (odds ratios), Indigenous Australia, 2008

Parameter[a]	Model 1		Model 2		Model 3	
	Odds Ratio	Sign.	Odds Ratio	Sign.	Odds Ratio	Sign.
Removal from natural family	1.49	***	1.38	***	1.38	***
Cultural participation:						
Strong	0.90		0.76	***	0.75	***
Moderate	0.73	***	0.69	***	0.69	***
Weak	0.87		0.84	*	0.84	*
Minimal	—		—		—	
Cultural identity:						
Strong	1.26	**	1.02		1.01	
Moderate	1.23	**	1.05		1.05	
Weak	1.33	***	1.20	*	1.20	*
Minimal	—		—		—	
Language:						
Strong	1.14		1.07		1.07	
Moderate	1.16		1.14		1.14	
Weak	0.94		0.93		0.93	
Minimal	—		—		—	
Traditional activities:						
Strong	1.19	*	1.11		1.11	
Moderate	1.25	**	1.19	*	1.19	*
Weak	1.13		1.11		1.10	
Minimal	—		—		—	
Felt discrimination in past year			1.98	***		
Interaction terms: Felt discrimination and –						
Strong cult. identity					1.99	***
Moderate cult. identity					2.01	***
Weak cult. identity					1.97	***
Minimal cult. identity					1.95	***
Observations	5 058		5 058		5 058	
Likelihood ratio	207	***	296	***	296	***

a. Intercept and coefficients for gender, marital status and age not reported.

***, ** and * denote that the odds ratio is significantly different from 1 at the 1%, 5% and 10% level, respectively.

Source: Author's customised calculations using the 2008 NATSISS (accessed using the RADL)

Conclusions and implications

In this chapter I have sought to further our understanding of the importance of traditional culture to Indigenous Australians. It provides evidence on the links between cultural attachment and subjective wellbeing, supplementing evidence relating to objective and mainstream indicators of socioeconomic outcomes. I have also sought to cast light on the causal mechanisms through which cultural attachment affects wellbeing and socioeconomic outcomes, by drawing on relevant overseas literature and empirically expanding on the dimensions of cultural attachment included in the multivariate models.

Strong caveats must always be placed on our ability to unearth causal relationships between variables when working with cross-sectional and self-reported data, such as the 2008 NATSISS. That withstanding, the analysis does offer some added rigour over previous work. Culture, and hence cultural attachment, is clearly defined ex ante, and a refutable hypothesis put forward with respect to the causal mechanism through which cultural attachment impacts upon outcomes. The hypothesis is that cultural attachment is important to identity formation for Indigenous peoples, and a sense of self-identity is in turn important for mental health. The results are broadly consistent with this hypothesis. The factor analysis of cultural variables contained in the NATSISS demonstrates that cultural identity is one distinct element to Indigenous Australians' attachment to, or engagement with, traditional culture, along with participation in cultural events/activities, language use and participation in traditional economic activities. Further, cultural identity has robust associations with wellbeing.

So the picture is far from complete, but one more piece has been added, and it has been brought into a somewhat sharper focus through additional empirical evidence. That evidence suggests that cultural identity enhances mainstream outcomes and is associated with greater subjective wellbeing. The finding that the positive effects of cultural attachment and identity extend to subjective wellbeing is important, as subjective wellbeing reflects Indigenous people's own values and preferences. For Indigenous and non-Indigenous Australians alike, achieving outcomes such as higher income, employment status and home ownership inevitably involve trade-offs. Higher income and occupational status, for example, may come at the expense of quality time with family. The advantage of subjective wellbeing as an outcome measure, in theory, is that it encapsulates all these trade-offs. Indigenous people with stronger cultural identification, who speak Indigenous languages and who partake in traditional economic activities are happy more often than others. Presumably, they feel their lives are better.

One inconsistent result with these findings is that strong cultural attachment is associated with greater psychological stress, reminiscent of Ratzlaff et al. (2000) observations on 'cultural inconsistencies' experienced by those of minority cultures and their requisite coping strategies. However, this phenomenon can be readily accounted for empirically by the fact that Indigenous Australians with strong cultural identity are more likely to host feelings of victimisation in the form of discrimination. Indigenous people living in non-remote areas, in particular, appear to pay a high price for maintaining a strong sense of identification with their traditional culture. That price is psychological stress brought about by feelings of discrimination, be that discrimination real or perceived. Their counterparts in remote Australia do not face this trade-off between cultural identity and psychological stress, suggesting that difficulties associated with the coexistence within both a traditional, minority culture and a mainstream culture play an important role in generating this stress.

The results for mainstream socioeconomic outcomes and wellbeing indicators are universal in their condemnation of the most extreme application of the assimilation approach, the forced removal of Indigenous children from their natural families. To some this may seem obvious and unnecessary to reiterate. I disagree. It may now be generally accepted that forced removal was not good policy, but it is not just the extremity with which the policy was executed, the inhumanity of forcibly removing children, that was wrong. The whole approach and the assumptions underlying it were wrong. This point is far from accepted, for many Australians still see assimilation as the only solution to Indigenous disadvantage and traditional Indigenous culture as a barrier to progress. As I have argued elsewhere (Dockery and Milsom 2007), this also seemed to be the 'hidden assumption' underlying much of the Australian Government's evaluations of Indigenous employment programs, since no attempts were made to evaluate programs against the stated objectives of cultural preservation, community capacity building or self-determination.

If the empirical results presented here are to be accepted, then the policy implications that follow would seem clear. The objective of policy should be to maximise wellbeing. Attachment to traditional culture and a strong sense of self-identity not only increase the wellbeing of Indigenous Australians, but are also associated with better 'mainstream' socioeconomic outcomes. Surely, then, Indigenous cultures need to be preserved and strengthened, not slowly left – or helped – to die. Perhaps the reason this is not obvious is that non-Indigenous Australians do not derive wellbeing from Indigenous culture; and therefore do not accept this as a 'legitimate' source of wellbeing. And while attachment to traditional culture enhances the wellbeing of Indigenous Australians, this sort of prejudice (or ignorance?) surely contributes to the psychological stress experienced by those trying to maintain their cultural identity. There seems no solution to this dilemma – unless, of course, Australians all learn to celebrate and respect the cultures of our first peoples. In the current pursuit of equity between Indigenous and non-Indigenous Australians, increasing non-Indigenous Australians' knowledge, understanding and respect of Indigenous cultures may well be the most important gap to close.

Reflections on the 2008 NATSISS

Finally, I conclude with some reflections on the data from the 2008 NATSISS for the purposes of this particular analysis and the wider program of research into culture and wellbeing. Some positives and negatives of the most recent CURF have already been flagged. Undoubtedly, the most significant drawback of the 2008 data is the inadequate controls for remoteness. The remote/non-remote dichotomy permitted in the 2008 CURF compares to the four categories of the Australian Standard Geographical Classification of Remoteness available for the 2002 CURF: major cities; inner regional; outer regional; and remote/very remote. This will not only reduce the statistical certainty of estimates for many purposes but, worse, is likely to lead to biased and even spurious findings. As one example, the measure of cultural attachment used in previous work with the 2002 data (Dockery 2009, 2010a) increases with remoteness, while educational attainment decreases with remoteness. Results from regression models without controls for remoteness suggest that educational attainment is negatively associated with cultural attachment, when exactly the reverse is found upon inclusion of controls for the four classifications of remoteness. As so many variables vary systematically with remoteness, the potential for such misleading findings is pervasive with the 2008 data.

On the positive side, the inclusion in the 2008 survey of measures of subjective wellbeing and mental health is perhaps the most significant enhancement over previous surveys, and provides important new research opportunities. There have also been welcome improvements to the cultural variables, including new questions on the importance individuals place on attending cultural events; and on the frequency of attendance and barriers to attending; and on cultural education. These improvements have been achieved while maintaining enough consistency between surveys to enable comparative analysis: had space permitted in this paper a comparison of rates of cultural engagement and Indigenous language use over time would have been most instructive. Finally, a very basic indicator of experiences of discrimination has proven here to have very strong explanatory power. Further analysis of the much richer information on discrimination (such as frequency and situations) and other variables from the expanded Life Experiences module in the 2008 NATSISS is likely to offer valuable insights into the wellbeing of Indigenous Australians.

Appendix 13A

Table 13A.1 Cultural variables included in exploratory factor analysis and weighted means, Indigenous Australia, 2008

Variable[a]	Mean[b]
Speaks an Indigenous language at home	0.11
Speaks an Indigenous language	0.19
Identifies with clan, tribal or language group	0.62
Recognises homelands or traditional country	0.72
Cultural events attended in past 12 months:	
Ceremonies	0.16
NAIDOC week activities	0.36
Festival or carnival involving arts, craft music or dance	0.23
Involved with ATSI organisation	0.18
Participated in cultural activities:	
Fishing	0.45
Hunting	0.22
Gathering wild plants or berries	0.16
ATSI arts or craft	0.17
Performed ATSI music, dance or theatre	0.11
Wrote or told ATSI stories	0.15
Importance of attending cultural events (1 very important, 2 important, 3 not important, 4 not important at all)	2.90
How often attends cultural events (1 = daily to 7 = less than once per year)	2.47

a. Unless otherwise stated, all variables are binary (1 = yes, 0 = no) dummies.

b. Means are weighted by the person weight provided by ABS.

NAIDOC = National Aborigines and Islanders Day Observance Committee

ATSI = Aboriginal or Torres Strait Islander

Source: Author's customised calculations using the 2008 NATSISS (accessed using the RADL)

Table 13A.2 Logistic regression models for 'mainstream' outcomes (odds ratios), Indigenous Australia, 2008

Variable	Self-assessed Health: P(healthy)		Education: P(completed school)[a]		Employed[a]		Ever charged by police		Risky alcohol consumption in past 2 weeks	
Remote	0.96		0.63	***	1.02		1.12	**	1.07	
Male	1.34	***	1.02		2.42	***	3.71	***	1.57	***
Married	1.27	***	1.33	***	1.78	***	0.76	***	0.71	***
Age: 15–19 years	1.78	***					0.27	***	0.45	***
20–24 years	1.17	*	1.37	***	0.94		0.70	***	1.22	**
25–34 years	—		—		—		—		—	
35–44 years	0.63	***	0.68	***	1.24	***	1.12		0.95	
45–54 years	0.44	***	0.44	***	1.21	**	0.80	***	0.57	***
55–59 years	0.31	***	0.25	***	0.67	***	0.54	***	0.35	***
60–64 years	0.32	***	0.21	***	0.32	***	0.52	***	0.21	***
65 years and over	0.32	***					0.27	***	0.08	***
Removal from natural family	0.70	***	0.92		0.90	*	1.55	***	1.15	**
Cultural participation:										
Strong	1.44	***	2.60	***	2.09	***	0.74	***	0.76	***
Moderate	1.29	***	1.51	***	1.54	***	0.77	***	0.78	***
Weak	1.16	**	1.20	*	1.23	***	0.87	*	0.92	
Minimal	—		—		—		—		—	
Cultural identity:										
Strong	1.07		1.23	**	1.33	***	1.11		0.96	
Moderate	1.09		1.17		1.16	*	1.10		1.04	
Weak	0.93		1.07		1.09		1.16	*	0.99	
Minimal	—		—		—		—		—	
Language:										
Strong	1.24	***	0.87		0.71	***	0.98		0.59	***
Moderate	1.09		0.95		0.85	*	0.81	***	0.68	***
Weak	1.14	*	1.05		0.90		0.93		0.87	*
Minimal	—		—		—		—		—	
Traditional activities:										
Strong	1.08		0.79	**	1.08		1.27	***	1.29	***
Moderate	1.03		0.80	**	1.02		1.29	***	1.31	***
Weak	1.21	***	0.87		1.02		1.08		1.02	
Minimal	—		—		—		—		—	
Observations	7 634		6 088		6 088		7 629		5 656	
Likelihood ratio	631	***	417	***	627	***	1 111	***	624	***

a. Models for having completed school, and being in employment restricted to persons aged 20–64.

***, ** and * denote that the odds ratios is significantly different from 1 at the 1%, 5% and 10% level, respectively.

Source: Author's customised calculations using the 2008 NATSISS (accessed using the RADL)

References

Akerlof, G. and Kranton, R. 2010. *Identity Economics*, Princeton University Press, Princeton, New Jersey.

Australian Bureau of Statistics (ABS) 2010. *National Aboriginal and Torres Strait Islander Social Survey: Users' Guide, 2008*, cat. no. 4720.0, ABS, Canberra.

Brondolo, E., Brady ver Halen, N., Pencille, M., Beatty, D. and Contrada, R. J. 2009. 'Coping with racism: A selective review of the literature and a theoretical and methodological critique', *Journal of Behavioral Medicine*, 32 (1): 64–88.

Chandler, M. J. 2000. 'Surviving time: The persistence of identity in this culture and that', *Culture & Psychology*, 6 (2): 209–31.

—— and Lalonde, C. E. 1998. 'Cultural continuity as a hedge against suicide in Canada's First Nations', *Transcultural Psychiatry*, 35 (2): 191–219.

——, Lalonde, C. E., Sokol, B. W. and Hallett, D. 2003. 'Personal persistence, identity development, and suicide: A study of Native and non-Native North American adolescents', *Monographs of the Society for Research in Child Development*, 68 (2): 1–130.

Diener, E. and Suh, E. M. (eds) 2000. *Culture and Subjective Well-Being*, The MIT Press, Cambridge, Mass.

Dingwall, K. M. and Cairney, S. 2010. 'Psychological and cognitive assessment of Indigenous Australians', *Australian & New Zealand Journal of Psychiatry*, 44 (1): 20–30.

Dockery, A. M. 2009. *Cultural Dimensions of Indigenous Participation in Education and Training*, NCVER Monograph Series 02/2009, National Centre for Vocational Education Research, Adelaide.

—— 2010a. 'Culture and wellbeing: The case of Indigenous Australians', *Social Indicators Research*, 99 (2): 315–32.

—— 2010b. 'The subjective wellbeing of Indigenous Australians', *CLMR Discussion Paper Series 2010/4*, Centre for Labour Market Research, Curtin Business School, March.

—— and Milsom, N. 2007. *A Review of Indigenous Employment Programs*, National Centre for Vocational Education Research, Adelaide.

Guiso, L., Sapienza, P. and Zingales, L. 2006. 'Does culture affect economic outcomes?', *NBER Working Paper No. 11999*, National Bureau of Economic Research, Massachusetts.

Hallett, D., Chandler, M. J. and Lalonde, C. 2007. 'Aboriginal language knowledge and youth suicide', *Cognitive Development*, 22 (3): 392–99.

Paradies, Y. 2005. 'Anti-racism and Indigenous Australians', *Analyses of Social Issues and Public Policy*, 5 (1): 1–28.

Paradies, Y. and Cunningham, J. 2009. 'Experiences of racism among urban indigenous Australians: Findings from the DRUID study', *Ethnic and Racial Studies*, 32 (3): 548–73.

Ratzlaff, C., Matsumoto, D., Kouznetsova, N., Raroque, J. and Ray, R. 2000. 'Individual psychological culture and subjective well-being', in E. Diener and E. M. Suh (eds), *Culture and Subjective Well-being*, MIT Press, Cambridge Mass.

Sibthorpe, B., Anderson, I. and Cunningham, J. 2001. 'Self-assessed health among Indigenous Australians: How valid is a global question?', *American Journal of Public Health*, 91 (10): 1660–63.

Slater, L. 2010. '"Calling our spirits home" Indigenous cultural festivals and the making of a good life', *Cultural Studies Review*, 16 (1): 143–54.

Suh, E. M. 2000. 'Self, the hyphen between culture and subjective wellbeing', in E. Diener and E. M. Suh (eds), *Culture and Subjective Well-Being*, MIT Press, Cambridge Mass.

Throsby, D. 2001. *Economics and Culture*, Cambridge University Press, Cambridge.

Trudgen, R. 2000. *Why Warriors Lay Down and Die*, Aboriginal Resource and Development Services Inc., Adelaide.

Ware, J. E. 2004. SF-36 Health Survey Update, viewed 11 October 2011, available at <www.sf-36.org>

Wexler, L. 2009. 'The importance of identity, history, and culture in the wellbeing of indigenous youth', *Journal of Childhood and Youth*, 2 (2): 267–76.

Whitbeck, L. B., Chen, X., Hoyt, D. R. and Adams, W. 2004. 'Discrimination, historical loss, and enculturation: Culturally specific risk and resiliency factors for alcohol abuse among American Indians', *Journal of Studies on Alcohol*, 65 (July): 409–18.

Zimmerman, M. A., Ramirez, J., Washienko, K. M., Walter, B. and Dyer, S. 1994. 'Enculturation hypothesis: Exploring direct and positive effects among native American youth', in H. L. McCubbin, E. A. Thompson, A. L. Thompson and J. E. Fromer (eds), *Resiliency in Ethnic Minority Families*, Vol I: Native and Immigrant American Families, Centre for Excellence in Family Studies, University of Wisconsin, Maddison, Wisconsin.

14. A mile wide, inch deep: The future for Indigenous social surveys?

Matthew Gray

Shortly after the release of data from the 1994 National Aboriginal and Torres Strait Islander Survey (NATSIS), Jon Altman and John Taylor wrote: 'At some future time, it is likely that the undertaking of the 1994 NATSIS will be regarded as a watershed in the collection of statistics about Indigenous Australians' (Altman and Taylor 1996: 193). Some 15 years later this prediction has proven to be true. The 1994 survey and the subsequent National Aboriginal and Torres Strait Islander Social Surveys (NATSISS) conducted in 2002 and 2008 have become an important source of information on the circumstances of Indigenous Australians. However, now that we have three NATSISS spanning a decade-and-a-half, it is time to consider whether to keep repeating the NATSISS using a similar design and methodological approach, or whether a new approach is required.

The papers in this volume collectively provide an excellent summary of the strengths and limitations of the 2008 NATSISS in relation to particular topics and the types of policy-relevant questions the survey can inform. In this paper I draw together the work in the individual chapters to form an overall assessment of the strengths and limitations of the survey. The chapter also discusses some of the trade-offs that inevitably need to be made when designing a survey such as the NATSISS.

Background to the development of the first national Indigenous social survey

From 1901 until the changes to the Australian Constitution in 1967, the Constitution stated that 'in reckoning the numbers of the people of the Commonwealth, or of a State or other part of the Commonwealth, Aboriginal natives shall not be counted'.[1] For the first Australian Census held in 1911 this section was interpreted to mean that persons of half or less Aboriginal or Torres Strait Islander descent should be included in the count of the Australian

---

1 Section 127 of the Commonwealth of Australia Constitution Act.

population (Australian Bureau of Statistics (ABS) 2011). Following the 1967 Referendum, changes to the Constitution meant that Indigenous people were to be counted in the census. This took effect in the 1971 Census and so we have census data covering all Indigenous people from the 1971 Census onwards.

This has meant that since 1971 there has been relatively comprehensive national data on the number and demographic characteristics of Indigenous Australians and some data on the economic and social circumstances. The censuses do not cover many important issues including physical and mental health, wellbeing or subjective data on experiences. In other areas the censuses provide only limited data (e.g. labour market, housing circumstances). There has been some expansion in the range of areas the census provides data with the 2006 and 2011 Censuses including questions about the need for assistance with daily living, care provided to people with a disability and voluntary work.

Until the 1994 NATSIS the Census remained virtually the only broad based national data on Indigenous Australians. The 1994 NATSIS in fact arose from a recommendation of the Royal Commission into Aboriginal Deaths in Custody that there be 'a special national survey covering a range of social, demographic, health and economic characteristics of the Aboriginal population with full Aboriginal participation' in order to fill an information void on the interrelationships between different aspects of Indigenous disadvantage (Commonwealth of Australia 1991). The Royal Commission also recommended that there be improved indigenous identification on administrative data bases.[2]

Both of these data related recommendations of the Royal Commission have been acted upon. The Australian government provided additional funding to the ABS to undertake a national social survey of the Indigenous population. There has also been a very substantial increase in the amount of administrative data which identifies Indigenous individuals and can therefore be used to provide information on their circumstances and experiences (e.g. ABS 2007).

The extent of the increase in the amount of data available about Indigenous Australians circumstances is illustrated by the Productivity Commission's regular report *Overcoming Indigenous Disadvantage* Report which was first published in 2003 (Steering Committee for the Review of Government Service Provision (SCRGSP) 2003). Between the 2003 and 2011 reports there has been a significant improvement in the data that could be used by the Productivity Commission to measure change in Indigenous outcome across a wide range of wellbeing measures.

While the range and quality of data available has improved, there is a heavy reliance on data from administrative sources. For example, the 2011 *Overcoming*

---

2 Recommendations 49 and 68 (Commonwealth of Australia 1991).

Indigenous Disadvantage Report uses data from around 25 administrative sources,[3] but uses data from only a handful of social or health surveys. In addition to data from the population censuses, there are just two nationally representative surveys used by the Productivity Commission: the NATSISS series of surveys (1994, 2002 and 2008) and the two most recent National Health Surveys that include an augmented sample of Indigenous Australians.[4] The NATSISS remains the main source of survey data on a wide range of aspects of the lives of Indigenous Australians.[5]

In many respects the administrative and survey collections are complementary sources of data with the administrative data often mainly providing information on service use, something that is difficult to collect in surveys. However, the administrative data generally does not include a range of other variables (such as educational attainment) which are central to understanding behaviour and the reasons for differences in outcomes.

Strengths and limitations of the 2008 NATSISS

The overall conclusion which emerges from the chapters in this book is that while the NATSISS provides information on a wide range of topics, for most topics the data collected is high level and that for some topics, the survey provides only superficial information. This limits the utility of the survey for addressing key policy relevant questions. It is a survey that is a mile wide and an inch deep.

In some chapters, the authors conclude that the data is very useful for addressing important policy questions and the authors put the data to good effect in demonstrating how it can be used to help inform such questions. In other chapters in this book the authors conclude that the 2008 NATSISS data has only limited utility. Examples of such areas are alcohol use (Chikritzhs and Liang), the customary economy (Altman, Biddle and Buchanan), demography and particularly fertility (Johnstone and Evans),[6] geographic mobility (Taylor and Bell) and housing (Memmott et al.). Biddle and Cameron find the education

---

3 For the purposes of this calculation, large-scale monitoring surveys such as the Australian Early Development Index and the Australian Government Department of Education, Employment and Workplace Relations post-program monitoring surveys are classified as administrative sources.

4 In addition, two more narrowly focused dental health surveys are used.

5 Longitudinal data has become increasingly important in the social sciences. There is little longitudinal data available on Indigenous Australians, but an important recent development has been the Longitudinal Study of Indigenous Children (LSIC) being run by the Department of Families, Housing, Community Services and Indigenous Affairs.

6 While the ABS publication *Births Australia* provides data on fertility, this data set does not provide the range of variables required to understanding the determinants and outcomes of fertility (ABS 2010).

data so limiting that they in fact base much of their chapter on analysis of data from the Longitudinal Survey of Australian Youth which oversamples Indigenous young people and thus provides a substantial Indigenous sample.

While the breadth is a weakness it also a strength. Omnibus surveys such as the 2008 NATSISS can be used to analyse complex interrelationships between economic, social and cultural factors, something which generally cannot be done using administrative data or more narrowly focused surveys that arguably 'silo' the different aspects of human experience. It is also a framework against which more detailed studies and surveys can be developed in order to provide a great depth of understanding about particular topics. While there is a strong case for breadth in a survey such as the NATSISS, in order to be able to examine complex interrelationships the data on each topic needs to have enough depth to allow a convincing analysis.

The 2008 NATSISS includes a number of new modules. The main ones are: the inclusion of children aged 0–14 years in the sample (information about the children provided by an adult, usually a parent or other relative who has caring responsibility for the child); experience of discrimination; and broadening of the measures of wellbeing to include mental health and subjective wellbeing. While these topics are extremely important and are areas in which there is a real shortage of quantitative information, the space in the questionnaire for their inclusion has been mostly created by reducing the depth of questions in other areas, rather than by dropping entire areas of questions. This has exacerbated the problem of the survey being broad but shallow.

Key policy relevant research questions

There are many policy relevant questions which social survey data could help address, but for which the necessary survey data is not available. Some examples or questions on which the NATSISS 2008 provides data include:

- Does the maintenance of traditional cultural beliefs and practices act as a barrier to achieving outcomes such as subjective wellbeing in health, educational attainment, employment and financial wellbeing or does it contribute to higher levels of wellbeing in such areas.[7]

- Does migration to areas with better educational and employment opportunities result in increased rates of educational participation and employment? Does moving to larger towns or cities have an impact upon a range of other dimensions of wellbeing? Are there some areas of wellbeing where there is a

---

7   This issue has been the subject of considerable debate. See for example, Dockery (2010) and Hughes (2007).

positive effect and others in which this pattern of geographic mobility has a negative effect? The answer to these questions has implications for the extent to which government policies should actively encourage migration to areas with greater educational and economic opportunities and better services.

- What are the impacts of mobility on the demography of the population in different areas and on service delivery needs?

- What are the factors that contribute to some Indigenous children doing well and others not so well? What promotes resilience amongst Indigenous children and what places them at risk?

- To what extent do Indigenous Australians experience discrimination, in what contexts is this most likely to occur and what impact does the experience of discrimination have on different aspects of individual lives?

- To what extent do Indigenous communities benefit from mining activities that occur near their community and in some cases on their land?

- What are the predictors of Indigenous fertility and how is this likely to change in the future?

A number of the chapters in this volume conclude that due to the necessary depth of information not being collected (or in some cases not collected at all), the 2008 NATSISS is of only limited use in answering these questions. This point is illustrated by questions about the impacts of maintaining traditional cultural beliefs and practices. The 2008 NATSISS data is used in chapters in this volume to explore the links between cultural beliefs and practices and other aspects of Indigenous peoples' lives. The chapter by Dockery uses this data to test the relationship between stronger cultural attachment and participation in cultural activities (at least as measured in the 2008 NATSISS) and Weatherburn and Snowball in their chapter use the data to test whether there is support for cultural theories of Indigenous violence. Both of these papers find no evidence that traditional cultural practices and beliefs are associated with worse outcomes in these two dimensions. Ultimately these types of questions can probably only be adequately addressed using mixed methods approach and triangulation of data from different sources.

While the findings of Dockery, and Weatherburn and Snowball are important, there remains a question mark as to whether the 2008 NATSISS items capture cultural practices and beliefs that are sometimes argued to be problematic to operating in a modern market based economy. It is fair to say that the 2008 NATSISS questionnaire only collects data on 'positive' aspects of culture (or the absence of participation in these aspects of culture).

An example of the type of cultural practice that is sometimes considered problematic is traditional demand-sharing practices which it is argued can reduce the incentives of individuals to look for and accept paid employment

(Austin-Broos 2006; Musharbash 2001). This is not an issue on which the NATSISS 2008 provides data and it is arguable as to whether it is possible to meaningful collect this type of information in a large-scale quantitative survey, particularly one conducted by the Australian Government's official statistical agency. The lack of data on the potentially negative aspects of culture means that the conclusions about the links between traditional cultural practices and beliefs need to be treated with caution.

In relation to geographic mobility, Taylor and Bell in their chapter conclude that while the survey is useful for understanding the nature of mobility, it is limited in its ability to inform discussions about the relationship between policy and population movement. For example, the way in which the 2008 NATSISS data have been coded for public release means that it is not possible to get a reliable measure of whether people are moving from smaller to larger places or whether they are moving from larger to smaller places.

The NATSISS data is provided to researchers in a confidentialised form. As part of this process the data is aggregated into broad geographic areas. An almost constant refrain in the chapters in this book is that the geographic classification used by the ABS is too broad and this severely limits the extent to which the data can be used to provide estimates according to geographic remoteness. This is a pity because the relatively large sample size of NATSISS opens up the possibility of using the data to understand the extent to which government policies are likely to have differential impacts in different parts of the country. There are many other questions which the NATSISS data could potentially answer, if more detailed geographic information were to be released. Just one example is the question of whether living near a significant mine has an impact upon the economic and social well being of individuals.

While it is essential that the data be confidentialised in such a way that release of the data is not likely to lead to identification of the persons or organisations to which it relates, this can be achieved in a variety of ways and with differing thresholds of likelihood of identification of individuals. The ABS has taken an approach which results in a greater level of geographic aggregation than is the case for some other government funded surveys such as the Household, Income and Labour Dynamics in Australia (HILDA) survey and the Longitudinal Study of Australian Children (LSAC).

One of the objectives of the NATSISS surveys is to measure change for the Indigenous population. While this is one of the strengths of these surveys, several of the chapters point to changes that have been made to the questionnaire between surveys that mean that this is not possible for certain topics. For example, Altman, Biddle and Buchanan argue that in the area of participation in the customary sector, modifications to the questionnaire mean that change between 2002 and 2008 can't be estimated. Similarly, Taylor and Bell argue that variations to the questionnaire means that changes in mobility between NATSISS collections can't be estimated. In contrast, the chapter on the NATSISS labour force status data (Thapa, Shah and Ahmad) provides a good illustration of how labour force status is changing.

In designing the next wave of NATSISS, emphasis should be placed on maintaining comparability of measures with earlier NATSISS undertaken. As the Productivity Commission's 2011 *Overcoming Indigenous Disadvantage* Report finds, despite the increases in the amount of data available about Indigenous Australians, it is hard to know how things are changing for Indigenous Australians and to assess whether current policy approaches are working and what changes in approach may be needed (SCRGSP 2011). This emphasises the importance of future social surveys of Indigenous Australians maintaining a high degree of comparability with the 2008 survey.

Objective versus subjective measures of wellbeing

The inclusion of both objective and subjective measures of wellbeing in the 2008 NATSISS highlights a very important issue. According to virtually any objective measure of wellbeing (at least those identified in the Closing the Gap policy agenda), Indigenous Australians have poorer outcomes than are found in the Australian population as a whole. Yet, on many of the subjective assessments of wellbeing Indigenous Australians rate their wellbeing quite highly.

Some examples of this are provided by the chapters in this volume. According to parents, rating of the overall health status of their child, only 1 in 25 children had fair or poor health with the majority in excellent or very good health. Furthermore, according to parental assessment, the health of children in remote and non-remote areas was similar (Shepherd and Zubrick). This assessment of child health differs to more objective measures of health. For example, Indigenous women are twice as likely as non-Indigenous women to have a low birth weight baby and Indigenous children are more likely to have been hospitalised than are non-Indigenous children (SCRGSP 2011).

While the data on children is a valuable addition to the survey, the question of the reliability of the child's carer (often a parent) to assess children's developmental outcome needs further examination. Shepherd and Zubrick find that the majority of Indigenous children are in excellent or very good overall health, although there are some developmental danger signs for a significant number of children. Other evidence suggests that Indigenous children are more likely than other children to have significant health problems (e.g. Zubrick et al. 2004). Further research is required on how parental assessment of the health of Indigenous and non-Indigenous children compare, and how the assessments by the parents of Indigenous children compare to the picture that would emerge if clinical assessment rather than parental self-report was used. An important question is whether the higher rates of health problems and poorer developmental outcomes found amongst Indigenous children in some communities means that parental perceptions of what it means for a child to be healthy or to have normal developmental outcomes is lowered by the poor outcomes in their community.

Another example relates to children's happiness at school. Indigenous Australians are on average happier at school at the age of 15 than non-Indigenous Australians (data from the Longitudinal Survey of Australian Youth).[8] The objective outcome is that Indigenous children are less likely to be at school at the age of 15 than other Australian children and have far poorer academic outcomes (SCRGSP 2011).

Self-reported health status provides a slightly different example of this general issue. While Indigenous Australians self-reported health status is lower overall than that of other Australians, Indigenous Australians in remote areas report having better health than those in non-remote areas. This finding is surprising given that most clinical data suggests the reverse.[9] In contrast, the more objective measures of wellbeing (or at least socioeconomic outcomes) such as income, experience of financial hardships, paid employment, and education collected in the NATSISS 2008 are much lower for the Indigenous population that is found for the Australian population as a whole.

It is hard to know how to interpret these data, although there are a range of possible explanations. One is that subjective assessments of wellbeing are usually based on a social comparison and are thus relative. The social norms against which many Indigenous people assess their circumstances may differ to that used by the overall Australian population and therefore Indigenous people may give a higher assessment of their subjective wellbeing than a non-Indigenous person in the same objective circumstances. There may be adaptation and habituation to continuing conditions of disadvantage and poor health. Third, the answers to the survey questions may be affected by the respondent's desire to not look bad to the interviewer; to not 'be shamed' (social desirability bias). Another possible explanation is that doing well in areas such as paid

---

8   Further information on the Longitudinal Survey of Australian Youth is available from the study website <http://www.lsay.edu.au>
9   This issue was discussed in Cunningham, Sibthorpe and Anderson (1997) based on their analysis of the 1994 NATSIS.

employment, income, education and housing circumstances are less important for the subjective wellbeing of Indigenous people than is the case for non-Indigenous Australians.[10]

Clearly, there are at least some differences between Indigenous and non-Indigenous people in what is important in determining their wellbeing (e.g. Dodson 2012). As Taylor (2008: 123) writes 'Indigenous peoples' perceptions and understandings of well-being extend beyond, and sometimes conflict with, many of the indicators currently adopted by global reporting frameworks.' and could include factors such as ability to access ritual or religious knowledge and reciprocity in social and economic relations.

It is not possible using the 2008 NATSISS data to assess the extent to which the disparity between subjective and objective measures of wellbeing for Indigenous Australians is explained by difference in social norms, a process of habituation or adaptation, or qualitatively distinct determinants of wellbeing between Indigenous and non-Indigenous. However, resolving this question does have important implications for both assessing the current circumstances of Indigenous Australians and policies specifically aimed at improving the wellbeing of this group. The answer to this question has implications for the extent to which closing the gap in outcomes between Indigenous and non-Indigenous Australians should be a measure of policy success, and whether it is sensible to use closing gaps in some – but not all – of the outcome measures which currently are the target of policy.

What should the future be for national social surveys of Indigenous Australians?

This question needs to be considered in the context of other data developments, particularly in relation to the recent improvements in administrative data. While such data is very useful, its main limitation is that the range of data collected is generally restricted to that required to administer a program. This means that it generally provides information on only a limited range of factors and cannot be used to examine inter-relationships between outcomes and more complex causal pathways.[11]

---

10 An overview of the research on subjective wellbeing is provided by Deiner et al. (1999).

11 While, in principal, this limitation can be at least partially overcome by linking different sources of data, in practice linking administrative data sets is very difficult, not always technically possible, and can be subject to privacy related-concerns. Nonetheless there are a range of data linkages currently in existence or in the development phase including the ABS Indigenous Identification Mortality Data Linkage Project.

The other major limitation of administrative data is that it does not provide information on Indigenous people's own assessments of their circumstances and relationships (subjective wellbeing measures) and what is important to them. There are ongoing concerns in relation to accurate identification of Indigenous people in administrative datasets although this has been much improved recently. Of course administrative data have strengths as well, including that they do not increase the burden on respondents; that they usually provide accurate information on individual's interactions with government or government funded services; that they often provide objective measures of people's circumstances (e.g. health services used); and the collection often provides longitudinal data (although this can be limited by privacy concerns).

Indigenous involvement in and control over social surveys of Indigenous Australians

The difficulty of collecting data on Indigenous cultural practices and beliefs partly arises from data collection by Australia's national statistics office. The opening paper at the *Social Science Perspectives on the 2008 National and Aboriginal Torres Strait Islander Social Survey* conference by Peter Yu (delivered by his Yawuru countryman, Professor Mick Dodson) was about the power of data in Aboriginal hands. Yu (2011: 1–2) writes:

… I want to talk about the critical role that data can play in development scenarios, when Aboriginal people are in control of collecting, managing and interpreting data… The view I have about data is a long way from the current paradigm where data is collected on Indigenous society by governments for their purposes; rather than to support the objectives that Indigenous people want to determine.

… However, one has to look only as far as the National Aboriginal Torres Strait Islander Social Survey conducted by the ABS to appreciate how far this reform agenda has to travel. That ABS survey is designed to assist governments, commentators or academics who want to construct policies that shape our lives or encourage a one sided public discourse about us and our position in the Australian nation.

The view presented by Yu is a fundamental challenge to the ABS and the largely non-Indigenous users of the NATSISS data. On the one hand it is important that data is collected which allows the circumstance of Indigenous Australians to be understood through the lens of non-Indigenous Australian culture. On the other it is vital that Indigenous people are increasingly involved in collecting, managing and interpreting the data collected pertaining to them and their communities.

Looking ahead

All surveys involve trade-offs, and any resulting survey design has tensions within. Trade-offs are required for a range of reasons including budget and respondent burden. The NATSISS is no different and, perhaps because of its position as THE national social and economic survey of Indigenous Australians, it faces more constraints than many other surveys.

This chapter has argued that the 2008 NATSISS has erred on the side of being too broad and lacking depth. This outcome is perhaps not surprising given that the NATSISS is the only large-scale nationally representative social survey of Indigenous Australians.[12]

In considering the future design of social surveys of Indigenous Australians, it is timely to review the objectives of the 1994 NATSISS and their relevance to twenty-first century needs. The objectives of the 1994 NATSISS were to 'provide the most needed statistics in a range of social, demographic, health and economic areas, thereby providing a stronger information base for planning for the empowerment of Australia's Indigenous people and for measuring progress in meeting their objectives, aspirations and needs' (Sarossy 1996: 190). While these objectives are laudable and remain relevant, it is worth reconsidering what and who should be the primary purpose and the primary users of the survey.

The range of potential objectives for social surveys of Indigenous Australians, such as the NATSISS, include:

- monitoring progress in closing gaps in outcomes between Indigenous and non-Indigenous Australians and in changes in the circumstances of Indigenous peoples over time

- providing information on the distinctive nature of the lives of Indigenous Australians, their aspirations and their experiences, and

- empowering Indigenous communities by providing information which they can use to plan and advocate on behalf of members of their communities, in order to improve their lives.

In my view, it is not possible for a social survey of Indigenous Australians to simultaneously meet all three purposes. The future approach depends upon which of these objectives is given priority. If it is monitoring progress in closing gaps between Indigenous and non-Indigenous Australians, then there needs to be a high priority placed on maximising the comparability between the questions in the Indigenous-specific social survey and question in other surveys of the general Australian population. If this is the key objective of the survey

---

12 The Indigenous health surveys run by the ABS are focused on health, and therefore provide limited information on other areas of individual lives.

then it may be worth considering supplementing other survey samples (such as the Labour Force Survey) with a sample of Indigenous Australians, rather than using an Indigenous-specific social survey. A further implication is that there needs to be no or minimal change in the variables analysed. This position is becoming more defensible as the range of administrative sources of data that identify Indigenous Australians increases and the prospects for carefully considered data linkage across administrative sources improve.

If the main aim is to provide information on the distinctive nature of the lives of Indigenous Australians, then the survey will have less overlap with other existing surveys and there clearly needs to be a separate Indigenous specific social survey. This approach would mean that the content of NATSISS would have much less overlap with those of other surveys of the general Australian population run by the ABS. The greater the focus is on the distinctive nature of the lives of Indigenous Australians the more important becomes Indigenous involvement in the design and conduct of the survey.

If priority is given to the third objective, then this would require a total rethink of the NATSISS. Meeting such an objective would probably require community-level surveys, and the control over the content and nature of data collection would be quite different. Surveys designed to meet such an objective would be driven by Indigenous communities and likely result in surveys quite different to anything undertaken up to the present. Under these conditions, a national survey such as the NATSISS would remain essential in order to gain an understanding of the circumstances of Indigenous people in different communities and to allow a national picture to be painted. There are some initial steps being taken in this area with some communities undertaking such surveys, including in Broome (Taylor et al. 2012; Yu 2011).

A social survey such as the NATSISS can ultimately never tell those responsible for developing public policy what to do, but it can provide useful information to inform policy decisions. The chapters in this monograph cover a wide range of topics and illustrate ways in which NATSISS 2008 data can be used, and the strengths and weaknesses of the data. Taken as whole, they demonstrate that NATSISS 2008 can contribute to our understanding of the diversity of circumstances in which Indigenous Australians live. They also demonstrate that for many areas the NATSISS has become too broad and too shallow to be useful in informing policy making. It is time to rethink the real purpose of social surveys of the Indigenous population and to focus the design of the survey on this purpose.

Acknowledgements

The author is grateful to Kim Farley-Larmour, Boyd Hunter, David Stanton, John Taylor and two anonymous referees for comments on an earlier version of this chapter.

References

Altman, J. and Taylor, J. 1996. 'Statistical needs in Indigenous affairs: future options and implications', in J. Altman and J. Taylor (eds), *The 1994 National Aboriginal and Torres Strait Islander Survey: Findings and Future Prospects*, CAEPR Research Monograph No. 11, CAEPR, ANU, Canberra.

Austin-Broos, D. 2006. '"Working for" and "working: among Western Arrernte in Central Australia', *Oceania*, 76 (1): 1–15.

Australian Bureau of Statistics (ABS) 2007. *Directions in Aboriginal and Torres Strait Islander Statistics, June 2007*, cat. no. 4700.0, ABS, Canberra.

—— 2010. *Births Australia 2009*, cat. no. 3301.0, ABS, Canberra.

—— 2011. *Reflecting a Nation: Stories from the 2011 Census*, cat. no. 2071.0, ABS, Canberra.

Carson, B., Dunbar, T., Chenhall, R. and Bailie, R. (eds) 2007. *Social Determinants of Indigenous Health*, Allen & Unwin, Crows Nest.

Cunningham, J., Sibthorpe, B. and Anderson, I. 1997. *Occasional Paper: Self-Assessed Health Status, Indigenous Australians*, cat. no. 4707.0, ABS, Canberra.

Diener, E., Eunkook, M., Suh, R. and Smith, H. 1999' 'Subjective well-being: Three decades of progress', *Pyschological Bulletin*, 125 (2): 276–302.

Dodson, P. 2012. Mahatma Gandhi Inaugural Oration, 30 January 2012, University of New South Wales, Sydney.

Dockery, A. M. 2010. 'Culture and wellbeing: The case of Indigenous Australians', *Social Indicators Research*, 99 (2), 315–32, DOI: 10.1007/s11205-010-9582-y.

Hughes, H. 2007. *Lands of Shame: Aboriginal and Torres Strait Islander 'Homelands' in Transition*, Centre for Independent Studies, Sydney.

Musharbash, Y. 2001. 'Yuendumu CDEP: The Warlpiri work ethic and Kardiya staff turnover', in F. Morphy and W. Sanders (eds), *The Indigenous Welfare Economy and the CDEP Scheme*, CAEPR Research Monograph No. 20, ANU E Press, Canberra.

Commonwealth of Australia 1991. *Royal Commission into Aboriginal Deaths in Custody, National Report,* Vol. 5, AGPS, Canberra.

Steering Committee for the Review of Government Service Provision (SCRGSP) 2003. *Overcoming Indigenous Disadvantage: Key Indicators 2003*, Productivity Commission, Canberra.

—— 2011. *Overcoming Indigenous Disadvantage: Key Indicators 2011*, Productivity Commission, Canberra.

Sarossy, G. '1996. 'Findings from the NATSIS evaluation', in J. Altman and J. Taylor (eds), *The 1994 National Aboriginal and Torres Strait Islander Survey: Findings and Future Prospects*, CAEPR Research Monograph No. 11, CAEPR, ANU, Canberra.

Taylor, J. 2008. 'Indigenous people and indicators of well-being: Australian perspectives on United Nations global frameworks', *Social Indicators Research*, 87: 111–26.

——, Doran, B., Parriman, M. and Yu, E. 2012. 'Statistics for community governance: The Yawuru Indigenous population survey of Broome', *CAEPR Working Paper No. 82*, CAEPR, ANU, Canberra.

Yu, P. 2011. 'The power of data in Aboriginal hands', Paper read by Professor M. Dodson, *Social Science Perspectives on the 2008 National and Aboriginal Torres Strait Islander Social Survey* Conference, 11–12 April, CAEPR, ANU, Canberra, available at <http://caepr.anu.edu.au/seminars/conferences/natsis2011>

Zubrick, S., Lawrence, D., Silburn, S., Blair, E., Milroy, H., Wilkes, T., Eades, S., D'Antoine, H., Read, A., Ishiguchi, P. and Doyle, S. 2004. *The Western Australian Aboriginal Child Health Survey: The Health of Aboriginal Children and Young People*, Telethon Institute for Child Health Research, Perth.

CAEPR Research Monograph Series

19. *Aboriginal Nutrition and the Nyirranggulung Health Strategy in Jawoyn Country*, J. Taylor and N. Westbury, 2000.

20. *The Indigenous Welfare Economy and the CDEP Scheme*, F. Morphy and W. Sanders (eds), 2001.

21. *Health Expenditure, Income and Health Status among Indigenous and Other Australians*, M. C. Gray, B. H. Hunter, and J. Taylor, 2002.

22. *Making Sense of the Census: Observations of the 2001 Enumeration in Remote Aboriginal Australia*, D. F. Martin, F. Morphy, W. G. Sanders and J. Taylor, 2002.

23. *Aboriginal Population Profiles for Development Planning in the Northern East Kimberley*, J. Taylor, 2003.

24. *Social Indicators for Aboriginal Governance: Insights from the Thamarrurr Region, Northern Territory*, J. Taylor, 2004.

25. *Indigenous People and the Pilbara Mining Boom: A Baseline for Regional Participation*, J. Taylor and B. Scambary, 2005.

26. *Assessing the Evidence on Indigenous Socioeconomic Outcomes: A Focus on the 2002 NATSISS*, B. H. Hunter (ed.), 2006.

27. *The Social Effects of Native Title: Recognition, Translation, Coexistence*, B. R. Smith and F. Morphy (eds), 2007.

28. *Agency, Contingency and Census Process: Observations of the 2006 Indigenous Enumeration Strategy in remote Aboriginal Australia*, F. Morphy (ed.), 2008.

29. *Contested Governance: Culture, Power and Institutions in Indigenous Australia*, Janet Hunt, Diane Smith, Stephanie Garling and Will Sanders (eds), 2008.

30. *Power, Culture, Economy: Indigenous Australians and Mining*, Jon Altman and David Martin (eds), 2009.

31. *Demographic and Socioeconomic Outcomes Across the Indigenous Australian Lifecourse*, Nicholas Biddle and Mandy Yap, 2010.

For information on CAEPR Discussion Papers, Working Papers and Research Monographs (Nos 1-19) please contact:

Publication Sales, Centre for Aboriginal Economic Policy Research, College of Arts and Social Sciences, The Australian National University, Canberra, ACT, 0200

Telephone: 02–6125 3875
Facsimile: 02–6125 9730

Information on CAEPR abstracts and summaries of all CAEPR print publications and those published electronically can be found at the following WWW address: http://caepr.anu.edu.au